Ernest Thayer's "Casey at the Bat"

Ernest Thayer's "Casey at the Bat"

Background and Characters of Baseball's Most Famous Poem

JIM MOORE *and*
NATALIE VERMILYEA

McFarland & Company, Inc., Publishers
Jefferson, North Carolina, and London

The present work is a reprint of the library bound edition of Ernest Thayer's "Casey at the Bat": Background and Characters of Baseball's Most Famous Poem, *first published in 1994 by McFarland.*

Title page illustration: Ernest Thayer in 1885
(courtesy of the San Diego Public Library)

LIBRARY OF CONGRESS CATALOGUING-IN-PUBLICATION DATA

Moore, Jim, 1940–
Ernest Thayer's "Casey at the bat" : background and characters of baseball's most famous poem / Jim Moore and Natalie Vermilyea.
p. cm.
Includes bibliographical references and index.

ISBN 978-0-7864-6711-2
softcover : acid free paper ♾

1. Thayer, Ernest Lawrence, 1863–1940. 2. Thayer, Ernest Lawrence, 1863–1940. Casey at the bat. 3. Poets, American—19th century—Biography. 4. Sportswriters—United States—Biography. 5. Baseball in Literature. I. Vermilyea, Natalie, 1941– II. Thayer, Ernest Lawrence, 1863–1940. Casey at the bat. III. Title.
PS3014.T3Z77 2012
811'.52—dc20 944-18911

BRITISH LIBRARY CATALOGUING DATA ARE AVAILABLE

Manufactured in the United States of America

McFarland & Company, Inc., Publishers
Box 611, Jefferson, North Carolina 28640
www.mcfarlandpub.com

This book is dedicated to the memory of
VEBLEN PLATTE VERMILYEA
April 5, 1908–June 9, 1993

Acknowledgments

We wish to thank the following people for their valuable help:

Anita Schiller, Bob Westerman, Edith Fisher, Phil Smith, Steve Staninger, Paul Zarins, Brad Altman, Ruth Anthony, Larry Cruse, Betty Jean McClintock, Fran Newman, John Omega, Dennis Sun, John Workman and Nellie Wright, University of California, San Diego, Library, without whom this book would not have been possible.

Jane Bradley, the niece of Ernest Thayer, who is a big part of this book. We are deeply grateful to her for her warm hospitality, friendly encouragement, and invaluable assistance. In 1988, Casey's centennial year, Jane and two of her cousins, Benjamin and Lawrence Hammett, collected their uncle's letters and papers, and presented them to the Santa Barbara Historical Society where they are now available to the public. Above and beyond this public service, Jane was more than happy to share her delightful recollections of her Uncle Ernest with us, and her family photographs, and we feel very fortunate to be able to include some of them in our book. Thanks also to Viola Buel, who introduced us to Jane.

Michael Redmon, librarian of the Santa Barbara Historical Society, for his professional assistance in guiding us through the Thayer family papers, providing us with copies of letters, and granting us permission to publish them.

Mike Raines, James McCarthy, Virginia L. Smyers and the rest of the cheerful, efficient staff at the Harvard University Archives, where we spent a number of memorable days chuckling over the first few volumes of the *Harvard Lampoon,* and also investigated other, more serious documents of vital historic importance.

Harley P. Holden, curator of the Harvard University Archives, for permission to publish a selection of materials pertaining to Harvard athletics, Thayer, and "Casey at the Bat."

Nancy Gaudette, librarian of the Worcester Room in the Worcester Public Library, for introducing us to "The Heart of the Commonwealth" and its remarkable history.

Vincent Powers, author of an important book on the early history of Worcester, for providing us with a copy of his book, telling us many things about the city's baseball history that are not to be found in print, and for sharing the results of his researches on the neighborhood where the Thayers lived.

Thomas Knoles, curator of manuscripts at the American Antiquarian Society, for his fine hospitality, and for guiding us to documents relating to the early history of baseball and sports in the Worcester area. Joanne Chaison, Dennis O'Leary, and Virginia Tracy were also most helpful in providing access to rare books and newspapers in the society's collections. Other librarians and their staff members in Worcester also contributed a great deal to the book: Dorothy E. Mosakowski, Clark University Library Archives; Joan Bedard, Polly Cutler and Beverly Osborne, Worcester Historical Museum Library; and Lora T. Brueck, Worcester Polytechnic Institute Archives.

Gladys Hansen, who welcomed us to the San Francisco Room in the San Francisco Public Library the week before the Seismic World Series of 1989, and showed us the extraordinary collection of California Baseball League scorebooks which her father had carefully preserved and given to the library.

Hugh MacDougall, a leading authority on James Fenimore Cooper and the history of Cooperstown, who gave us the benefit of his valuable discoveries regarding Cooper's novel *Home as Found,* and its relation to the early history of Cooperstown.

The many librarians, staff members and researchers who so generously gave us their assistance and encouragement during the seven years we spent collecting materials for this book: Tom Heitz, Dan Bennett, Bill Deane, Pat Kelly, Ginny Reinholdt, Helen Stiles, and Gary Van Allen, National Baseball Library; Adele Johnson, Deborah McCaffery, Eileen O'Brien, Dawn Wilcox and Wayne Wright, New York State Historical Association Library; Joan Tripp, Deborah Dalton, and Hess Engelking, Village Library, Cooperstown; Daria D'Arienzo, Amherst College Archives; Mary Gilmore, Seymour Library, Auburn, New York; Kim Tenney, Boston Public Library; Dianne M. Gutscher, Leanne N. Pander, and Susan Ravdin, Bowdoin College Library and Archives; Ann E. Cohen, Broome County Public Library; Marjory B. Hinman, Broome County Historical Society Library; Martha L. Mitchell, Brown University Archives; John R. Gonzalez and Lorraine M. Lineer, California State Library; J. Richard Abell, Cincinnati Public Library; Joan L. Clark, Cleveland Public Library; Barbara Clune and Peter Koonz, College of St. Rose Library; Kenneth C. Cramer and Barbara Krieger, Dartmouth College Archives; James H. Marksbury, Deerfield Academy Archives; David Proper, Deerfield Memorial Libraries; Mary Fabiszewski, Essex Institute Library; Elise Bernier-Feeley, Forbes Library, Northampton, Massachusetts; Winifred M. Grotevant, Hingham Public Library; Betty Ashley, Holliston Public Library; Virginia H. Smith, Massachusetts Historical Society Library; Gerard F. Laflash and Rosemary Waltos, Millbury Public Library; Paul Cyr, New Bedford Free Public Library; John Rathe and Sam Register, New York Public Library; Joan Hoose, Ed McGuire, and Paul Mercer, New York State Library; William W. Sturm, Oakland Public Library; Edouard L. Desrochers, Phillips Exeter Academy Archives; Diana Gin, Sacramento Public Library; Alice V.N. Johnson, Salem Public Library; Tod Ruhstaller, Haggin Museum, Stockton; Dominic George, Stockton Athletic Hall of Fame; Dan Chapman, Stockton Ports Baseball Club; Sandra Pelose, Karen Ramos, Maggie Schaus and Bill Walker, Stockton Public Library; Daryl Morrison, Holt-Atherton Center for Western

Studies, University of the Pacific; Jill Ausel, University of Massachusetts at Amherst Library; Nancy MacKechnie, Vassar College Archives; Sylvia B. Kennick, Williams College Archives; Diane E. Kaplan and Judith Ann Schiff, Yale University Archives.

Table of Contents

"Casey at the Bat"

(A Ballad of the Republic, Sung in the Year 1888)

The outlook wasn't brilliant for the
Mudville nine that day;
The score stood four to two with but
one inning more to play.
And then when Cooney died at first,
and Barrows did the same,
A sickly silence fell upon the patrons
of the game.

A straggling few got up to go in deep
despair. The rest
Clung to that hope which springs
eternal in the human breast;
They thought if only Casey could but
get a whack at that—
We'd put up even money now, with
Casey at the bat.

But Flynn preceded Casey, as did
also Jimmy Blake,
And the former was a lulu, and the
latter was a cake;
So upon that stricken multitude grim
melancholy sat,
For there seemed but little chance of
Casey's getting to the bat.

But Flynn let drive a single, to the
wonderment of all,
And Blake, the much despis-ed, tore
the cover off the ball;
And when the dust had lifted, and
the men saw what had occurred,
There was Johnnie safe at second
and Flynn a-hugging third.

Then from 5,000 throats and more
there rose a lusty yell;
It rumbled through the valley, it
rattled in the dell;
It knocked upon the mountain and
recoiled upon the flat,
For Casey, mighty Casey, was ad-
vancing to the bat.

There was ease in Casey's manner as
he stepped into his place;
There was pride in Casey's bearing
and a smile on Casey's face.
And when, responding to the cheers,
he lightly doffed his cap,
No stranger in the crowd could doubt
'twas Casey at the bat.

Ten thousand eyes were on him as he
rubbed his hands with dirt;
Five thousand tongues applauded
when he wiped them on his shirt.
Then while the writhing pitcher
ground the ball into his hip,
Defiance gleamed in Casey's eye, a
sneer curled Casey's lip.

And now the leather-covered sphere
came hurtling through the air,
And Casey stood a-watching it in
haughty grandeur there.
Close by the sturdy batsman the ball
unheeded sped—
"That ain't my style," said Casey.
"Strike one," the umpire said.

From the benches, black with people,
there went up a muffled roar,
Like the beating of the storm-waves
on a stern and distant shore.
"Kill him! Kill the umpire!" shouted
someone on the stand;
And it's likely they'd have killed him
had not Casey raised his hand.

With a smile of Christian charity
great Casey's visage shown;
He stilled the rising tumult; he bade
the game go on;
He signaled to the pitcher, and once
more the spheroid flew;
But Casey still ignored it, and the
umpire said, "Strike two."

"Fraud!" cried the maddened
thousands, and echo answered
fraud;
But one scornful look from Casey and
the audience was awed.
They saw his face grow stern and
cold, they saw his muscles strain,
And they knew that Casey wouldn't
let that ball go by again.

The sneer is gone from Casey's lip,
his teeth are clinched in hate;
He pounds with cruel violence his bat
upon the plate.
And now the pitcher holds the ball,
and now he lets it go,
And now the air is shattered by the
force of Casey's blow.

Oh, somewhere in this favored land
the sun is shining bright;
A band is playing somewhere, and
somewhere hearts are light.
And somewhere men are laughing,
and somewhere children shout;
But there is no joy in Mudville–
mighty Casey has struck out.

–PHIN

(*San Francisco Daily Examiner,* June 3, 1888)

Note: This is the way the poem was originally printed in the *Examiner*. Notice that Blake's first name changes from Jimmy to Johnnie.

The Humorous Editor

moves in an unflattering obscurity. Occasionally one of his good things is quoted, (with, however, a strange and inexplicable lack of information as regards the author)

Harvard Lampoon, April 6, 1883

Introduction

"Casey at the Bat" has been a big hit with readers of all ages for more than 100 years. Ernest Lawrence Thayer's remarkable combination of baseball, balladry, and humor captured the spirit of the game and its hold on the public so perfectly that it is just as gripping today as it was when it was first written. This miniature masterpiece of American literature continues to fascinate baseball fans and nonfans alike, despite having been written in a baseball era that has been all but forgotten. "The outlook wasn't brilliant" and "There is no joy in Mudville" are phrases heard and read over and over again every season. Thayer's verses have been memorized and recited by three generations of schoolchildren as well as grown men and women, made into movies, and fittingly expressed in the fine arts of music, painting, and sculpture. And yet, though much has been written about "Casey," surprisingly little has been written about the author himself. This book is about him, the places where he lived, worked, and went to school, and the extraordinary times that produced his "Ballad of the Republic."

Thayer was only 24 years old when he wrote "Casey." Born in Lawrence, Massachusetts, on August 14, 1863, and raised in nearby Worcester, he graduated from Harvard in 1885 and spent a year traveling in Europe before going to work for his old college friend William Randolph Hearst on the *San Francisco Daily Examiner*. After a year and a half on the coast writing news, editorials, and ballads, he returned to his home in Worcester in February 1888 and went into the family business manufacturing wool. But the muse was not done with him yet. Thayer wrote "Casey" in May, and sent it to the *Examiner* with a subtitle that proved to be prophetic: "A Ballad of the Republic." Hearst, who had taken charge of the morning paper the year before and beefed up the baseball coverage considerably, ran "Casey" on the editorial page, next to the startling announcement that the *Examiner*'s circulation had skyrocketed to 52,628 readers, making it the most popular paper in the Pacific metropolis. And so, amidst much fanfare, a legend was created (Vermilyea and Moore, 43).

Writing for a California newspaper, Thayer naturally drew some of his materials from his experiences on the Pacific slope. Most of the people who picked up the *Examiner* that day would have had no trouble recognizing the names of three well-known California League ballplayers – Blake, Cooney, and Flynn – and two major landmarks that needed no names, Mount Diablo and the San Joaquin Valley, which provided a spectacular setting for the poem. Most California readers would also have connected Thayer's "Mudville Nine" with Stockton's vaunted California League club, better known to *Examiner* readers as the "Slough City Nine" which, after a big preseason buildup in the press, got off to a pitifully slow start on the field. They still won the league title that year, but on June 3 – the day "Casey" appeared – the San Joaquin Valley boys slid to the bottom of the league standings. There was "no joy in Mudville" *that* day.

If Thayer did, in fact, have Stockton in mind as the model for Mudville – and there is little doubt that he did – this is the picture that unfolds in the opening lines of the poem: Flynn let drive a single, Blake tore the cover off the ball, Casey advanced to the bat, and a crowd of about 5,000 spectators filled the whole great valley with their hurrahs! So much for those Eastern myths of laid-back West Coast baseball fans.

After that sensational debut in the West, Casey's fame soon spread to the East. Jim Kennedy, editor of the *New York Sporting Times,* read the poem in the California paper and noticed a remarkable similarity between the Mudville slugger and Boston star Mike "King" Kelly, who had just returned from the winter season in San Francisco and was at the peak of his popularity. Kennedy substituted "Kelly" for Casey and "Boston" for Mudville, cut the first five stanzas, and published "Kelly at the Bat" in the July 28, 1888, issue of his paper, acknowledging that it was "adapted from the *San Francisco Examiner.*" These editorial shenanigans must have annoyed Thayer a good deal, but they were nothing compared to the claim made by the *New York Sun* in 1895 that "Kelly at the Bat" was the original poem, that it had first appeared in the *Sun,* and that the name "Kelly" was changed to "Casey" in later variations to give the poem a universal flavor. A prompt rebuttal from Hearst apparently had little effect, for as late as 1935, according to anthologist Burton Stevenson, "many old-time devotees of the diamond still treasure it in its adapted form, believing it to be the original one." At about the same time, commenting on the substitution of "Kelly" for "Casey," one of Thayer's classmates observed that this was "easily understood by those who are old enough to remember that 45 years or so ago 'Mike' Kelly was by far the most conspicuous baseball player in the country. It may fairly be said, also, that, in spite of the reputation of 'Babe' Ruth and other notables, no player in all the subsequent history of the game has quite attained the heights on which Kelly stood" (*HUC,* 7 [1910]: 219; Burton Stevenson, 118–19; "Casey," 533; Gardner, 7; Murdock, 19; and NBL, Casey folder).

The connection with Kelly did much to popularize "Casey." But the man who really made the ballad a national epic was a rising young comedian and bass singer by the name of De Wolf Hopper. A rabid Giants baseball fan, Hopper recited Thayer's original verses at Wallack's Theater in New York on

August 14, 1888, for an audience that included the Chicago White Stockings and his beloved Giants. Kelly had played for both clubs: seven years with Chicago (1880–86), and the past winter with New York, and his unseen presence no doubt had something to do with the tremendous reception "Casey" was given that night. Hopper brought the house down, and repeated the performance all over the country, onstage and over the radio, more than 10,000 times during the next 40 years. To his everlasting credit, Hopper at once recognized the universal qualities of Casey's story. As he said in his memoirs: "It is as perfect an epitome of our national game today as it was when every player drank his coffee from a mustache cup. There are one or more Caseys in every league, bush or big, and there is no day in the playing season that this same supreme tragedy, as stark as Aristophanes for the moment, does not befall on some field" (Gardner, 5, 177; and Vermilyea and Moore, 46–47).

Hopper was introduced to Thayer at the Worcester Theater in 1892, when the distinguished manufacturer identified himself as the author of "Casey." Asked what had inspired him to write the poem, Thayer chuckled and said "Sam Winslow," a childhood friend and captain of the 1885 Harvard nine. But the author, for whatever reason, was reluctant to explain in any detail how he came to write "Casey." This encouraged other would-be poets to claim the authorship for themselves or their friends once the ballad became famous. These claimants bit off more than they could chew, for Thayer had the whole Harvard class of 1885 and their associates up in arms, ready to track down every detail behind any bogus claims and expose them for what they were. Fortunately, the controversy over the authorship was pretty much settled by the time Albert G. Spalding published his monumental history of baseball, *America's National Game,* in 1911. Spalding gave Thayer credit for "Casey," included a portrait of the author, and threw in an interesting story about Sam Winslow, though he did not connect the Harvard athlete with the ballad. Despite Thayer's backing from Spalding, the wrangling over the authorship continued. And there was still the question of inspiration. Thayer was exasperated, and told Burton Stevenson in 1923 that he wasn't sure if the poem had given him more pleasure than annoyance. In the next few years, however, his changed his tune. Attending the fiftieth reunion of Harvard's class of 1885, Thayer was gratified to see a classmate carrying a large banner that read: "An '85 Man Wrote *Casey*!" (Southwick, 78; *HUC,* 7 [1910]: 218–19; "Casey," 532–35; Albert Spalding, 448–54; Burton Stevenson, 126; and Gardner, 10).

Earlier in 1935, as plans were being made for establishing the Hall of Fame in Cooperstown, New York, former Phillies star Dan Casey revived a claim he had first made in 1900 that he was, in fact, the original Casey. Newspapers and radio shows gave his story plenty of publicity, and a whole new generation of baseball fans began clamoring to know "the truth about Casey." A poet to the end, Thayer did nothing to dispel the clouds of obscurity that had gathered about the legendary slugger over the years. His last statement on the subject was made in 1930. Writing to the editor of the *Syracuse Post-Standard* with regard to a claim made on behalf of O. Robinson Casey of that city, he said, "the verses owe their existence to my enthusiasm for college baseball, not as a player but as a fan, and to my association while in college with Will Hearst, who engaged me to come to the *Examiner* in San Francisco after I graduated." As for Casey, he added: "The poem has no basis in fact. The only Casey actually involved, and I am not sure about him, was not a ball player." And that was the way he left it (Vlasich, 60; *HUC,* 10 [1935]: 373–74; and *SP-S,* 9/3/1935 [note that Thayer said he was "not sure" about Casey]).

This book will attempt to follow up on Thayer's remarks, and show how his experiences in the East as well as the West helped to prepare him for the writing of "the great American epic." The first part is about the author's childhood home in Worcester, "the Heart of the Commonwealth," which was the scene of some of the most important developments in the history of American athletics. George Bancroft was born there at the dawn of the nineteenth century, and Thomas Wentworth Higginson lived and worked in the city 50 years later. Their work in the field of physical education and intercollegiate athletics was a major influence at the time, helped to shape the nineteenth-century concept of the athletic hero, and was a vital part of Thayer's heritage. Higginson was largely responsible for bringing the first college regattas and the first Harvard-Yale baseball games to Worcester in the late 1850s and 1860s.

From Worcester Thayer went to Harvard, the nation's oldest university and the leader in the field of intercollegiate athletics. From his official post as president of the *Harvard Lampoon* he surveyed the college baseball scene, opposed the faculty's crusade against "professionalism" in college athletics, and heralded the exploits of Sam Winslow and Harvard's 1885 nine. Harry Thurston Peck, a Columbia classics professor, read much of Thayer's work at the turn of the century and concluded: "The writings of Mr. Thayer both in the *Harvard Lampoon* and the San Francisco *Examiner* show humor, facility of expression, and literary skill, such as one might expect from the author of 'Casey at the Bat'." We believe that Thayer's work also has something important to tell us about the author, as well as the origins, meaning, and durability of his popular ballad (Peck, 954).

Thayer lived and wrote about baseball during one of the most exciting eras in the game's long and colorful history. For all of its flaws, this was an age marked by the emergence of two major professional baseball leagues (the National League and the American Association), the first World Series, the first college baseball association, and the expansion of the so-called "minor" leagues, a misnomer if there ever was one, from the Atlantic to the Pacific. The game's phenomenal growth fueled a veritable explosion of baseball literature, as three national sporting weeklies sprang into existence in the

1880s and competed with dailies like Joseph Pulitzer's *New York World* and Hearst's *Examiner* to bring readers what was probably the best press coverage the game has ever had. There was no doubt about it: baseball was America's national game. All that was needed was a national epic. Thayer supplied it with "Casey at the Bat."

PART I

The Heart of the Commonwealth

CHAPTER 1

A City on the Rise

Ernest Thayer had the best of both worlds. Growing up in Worcester during the second half of the nineteenth century, he was living in a city which, as Senator George Frisbee Hoar said in his autobiography, combined the "youth and vigor and ambition of a western city with the refinement and conveniences, and the pride in a noble history, of an old American community." From 1848 to 1900 Worcester grew from a city of 15,000 to a city of 130,000 people, and demonstrated in many ways that it was, in fact, what the local Board of Trade claimed it was, "A City on the Rise" (Hoar, 1:158).

In 1859 Worcester hosted the first intercollegiate regatta in the country on Lake Quinsigamond, two miles east of the city, continued the event through the 1860s, and combined baseball with boating beginning in 1864, when Harvard and Williams raised some eyebrows by playing under the "New York" rules, which had been adopted by the National Association of Base Ball Players, instead of the more familiar rules of the "Massachusetts Game." The next year Harvard returned to Worcester to row against Yale and play the Charter Oak nine of Hartford for the championship of New England. The year after that, in 1866, two freshmen clubs from Harvard and Yale crossed bats for the first time, the New Haven boys being a little slower in fielding a ball club than they were in putting a first-class crew on the water. The same clubs played again in 1867, this time as sophomores, and finally Yale sent her varsity nine to meet Harvard in 1868. These fiercely contested ball games all took place at the old Agricultural Grounds on Highland Street, just a few blocks from Thayer's home, and must have made a deep impression on the youngster's mind (Harvard, 59–68).

City seal of Worcester (courtesy of the Worcester Room, Worcester Public Library).

Professional baseball came to Worcester about ten years later. Mayor Charles B. Pratt was elected president of the club, which brought baseball back to the hallowed Agricultural Grounds when Thayer was a teenager. For three brief but glorious years (Worcester finished ahead of archrival Boston in the 1880 pennant race), the club was one of the first in the country to belong to the National League of Professional Base Ball Clubs. Worcester's location close to Boston was an important factor in the city's baseball history, particularly as part of the background for "Casey at the Bat," which was written the year after Chicago sold Mike Kelly to Boston for the fabulous sum of $10,000. Kel was crowned "King of the Diamond" by Boston fans, sparked one of the biggest baseball booms that ever hit the Hub, and supplied sportswriters with plenty of material to work with for the next several years (Goslow, 133–54; and below, Chapter 25).

There were also some long-range factors at work in Worcester's sports history. Ultimately, perhaps, they were more important than any geographical advantages the city enjoyed, since they provided a framework for the development of sports in America, and helped to shape the modern concept of the athletic hero. George Bancroft, Worcester's most well-known native son, and Joseph Cogswell founded the Round Hill School at Northampton, Massachusetts, in 1823. This was the first school in the country to promote the physical as well as the mental and moral education of the students. Bancroft and Cogswell, both Harvard graduates, created a new ideology of sports and games by linking them with the mental and moral growth of the students. Their teaching and writing inspired educators, physicians, statesmen, writers, and a whole new generation of students to think and write about sports and exercise, and their importance for the future of the rapidly expanding nation.

Dr. Abel Peirson, another Harvard man, summed up the new attitude toward physical education in an address he delivered at Salem in 1831. "Physical education," he declared, "is a science of vast importance," a subject that directly concerns "the destiny and glory of a nation, as on it depends, in a great measure, the manners, energies, and morals of the people." By this time, Harvard students had been playing baseball for at least 100 years. In the late 1820s and 1830s the game was also played informally at colleges and prep schools such as Round Hill, Amherst, Bowdoin, Brown, Dartmouth, Deerfield Academy, Exeter, Williams, and Yale. *The Book of Sports,* by Robin Carver, published in Boston in 1834, was the first to include printed rules for "Base Ball," although the game had undoubtedly been played by these or very similar rules for many years. The author's object was to "serve the cause of physical education" by directing the attention of the young to "sports of a healthful and invigorating tendency." Though somewhat of an old man, Carver said that he had not forgotten the games and pastimes of his boyhood, and decided to write them down for the rising generation. One of the chief features of this book is an illustration of a group of boys playing baseball on the Boston Common, with the dome of the State House rising prominently in the background. The illustration also appeared in a book of sports published at New Haven in 1835, with a caption below, "A GAME AT BASE BALL." Obviously, an increasing importance was being attached to the game at this time, not only in the Boston area but also in Connecticut. Josiah Dwight Whitney, a Yale student, wrote to his sister Elizabeth in March of 1837: "It is about time now for playing ball, and the whole green is covered with students engaged in that fine game: for my part, I could never make a ball player. I can't see where the ball is coming soon enough to put the ball-club in its way" (Peirson, 145; Ronald A. Smith, 8; Seymour [1990], 131–2 and [1960], 5, 8; Moore [1993], 8; Boys, 10–12; Brewster, 20).

James Fenimore Cooper, another Yale man, began one of his most important novels at this time. *Home as Found,* published in 1838, contains a spirited account of "a game of ball" which not too surprisingly, perhaps, appears to be an early form of our national pastime. Cooper leaves no doubt about the game's tremendous popularity with the young working men of the village, who try to get in a good ball game on their lunch hour, but get no cooperation whatever from the irate property owners or the village authorities, who have banned playing ball in the streets. More importantly, Cooper was the first writer to connect the game with the national character, and to recognize its vital place in American life. Considering his enormous influence on the age, Cooper's accomplishment must be regarded as a major turning point in the evolution of our national game (Moore [1993], 1–2, 13–20).

Home as Found provided Abner Doubleday and Alexander Cartwright with a powerful motive for organizing baseball clubs in New York State in the late 1830s and 40s. Doubleday, as everybody knows, organized some games in Cooperstown in 1839 or 1840, and probably returned to the village in 1841 to see how his improved version of the game was going. A few years later, in 1845, Cartwright organized the Knickerbocker Base Ball Club of New York, which is generally considered the first "permanent" club in the game's history. But the man who was responsible for the club's survival and eventual success was Dr. Daniel L. Adams, a graduate of the Harvard Medical School, and the first product of the physical education movement to take a major role in the development of our national pastime (Moore [1993], 11–12; Voigt, I, 8; below, 57).

The pastor of the Worcester Free Church, the Rev. Thomas Higginson, wrote an influential argument for sports and exercise which appeared in the March 1858 issue of a new magazine called the *Atlantic Monthly.* His comments on our national game are of great interest, for he welcomed the growth of "our indigenous American game of base-ball," and followed Cooper's lead by connecting the game with the national character. Within six months after the publication of his article the first baseball clubs were organized in Worcester, at Harvard, and in Chicago and San Francisco, and a convention of baseball clubs meeting in New York City voted to call their organization the National Association of Base Ball Clubs. As George Kirsch has noted, a wave of political and cultural nationalism was sweeping the country at this time. Baseball was beginning to be viewed as a unifying force, a simple but effective way of transcending cultural, sectional, and ethnic differences, and forging a bond between North and South, East and West, natives and immigrants, and, eventually – after a long and sometimes painful process – between black and white, and all the different races and nationalities that make up the great melting pot of the United States (Higginson [1858], 593; Lucas and Smith, 112–15; George Kirsch, 91–108; and Jim Moore [1993]).

The 1859 regatta on Lake Quinsigamond was one of the first manifestations of "Higginson's Revival," as the locals called the athletic crusade, or "Muscular Christianity," as the national press sometimes referred to it. At the same time Harvard, Yale, and Brown were racing on the lake outside of Worcester, Amherst and Williams met at Pittsfield, Massachusetts, to play the first college baseball game. The next year, on July 27, 1860, after the second regatta in Worcester, the *New York Tribune* saw a "splendid significance" in these events, for they drew together some of the finest young men of the country, who showed, by their strength, activity, and endurance, their protuberant muscle and clean shape, that "the soundest man is that whose mind and body are fairly exercised." Reuben Guild, the Brown librarian, added his own thoughts to the subject on June 27, 1863, when Harvard and Brown played their first intercollegiate baseball game on the Providence grounds. Writing up the game for the *Providence Journal*, Guild remarked that baseball, more than any other sport, required the "*sana mens in sano corpore.*" Granted, Bancroft might have preferred gymnastics, but he would hardly have objected to the spirit of the occasion (Guy Lewis, 222–29; Bronson, 345; and Brown University Archives).

Thayer was born in the right place and at the right time. He must have had many fond memories of his boyhood days in Worcester, playing baseball and billiards with his brothers, Sam Winslow, and the rest of the boys, and boating on the lake; but, like most people, he never wrote much about them. He did, however, tell his Harvard classmates in his 1885 Ivy Oration: "I was once a boy myself, and joyful recollections of that delightful period come over me with a rush. I call to mind the boyish sports and the boyish trials which you know so well." And one of the gems recently found in the family papers at the Santa Barbara Historical Society is a newspaper report about a professional women's baseball club, written while he was a student at the Worcester Classical and English High School. This curious item appeared in the first issue of *The Courier*, a paper published and edited by Thayer himself, and is dated March 10, 1880. A few weeks before this, the local papers had announced that Worcester was going to have a club in the National League for the first time, and this, of course, was the talk of the town. Thayer, oddly enough, has nothing to say about the prospects for the new National League club, and appears to be much more concerned about the possibility of forming a professional women's baseball club in Worcester. Although women did not have "A League of Their Own" until the 1940s, the first "femi-nines" were tossing and batting the ball around when Thayer was still a babe. Vassar was first in the field with the Laurel and Abenakis baseball clubs in the spring of 1866, the year the college opened its doors, and the school had seven or eight clubs by the 1870s. Two clubs were organized at Smith College in 1878, and in the summer of 1879 three Boston women played the game well enough to join a professional women's club from New York that was barnstorming the country with a Philadelphia club. The women ball-tossers drew large crowds everywhere they went, and created quite a sensation when they played in Boston and Worcester. In a related development, as Thayer was writing his article for *The Courier,* a group of women athletes were busy drumming up publicity for a pedestrian race at Mechanics Hall, which would be a fundraiser for Worcester's new National League club. Thayer writes: "Contributions for the new nine come in slowly. I think a little interest might be had in such a cause. Only 1,000 shares have been sold, 49,000 still remain. The reputation of Miss Phetterplace as a pitcher is well known. Miss Wood is unsurpassed as 1st base woman. While the catcher Miss Gates, has a world wide reputation" (*SBHS*, Thayer papers; BG, 7/31/1879; and *WG*, 7/30, 8/6/1879; Seymour [1990], 443–65; Berlage, 12–16. Already, by the tender age of 16, Thayer had begun to develop a humorous way of looking at things, and was taking a serious interest in writing and in the newspaper business. He was also waking up to the importance of women's athletics. Another indication of his early views on the subject may be found in an editorial on co-ed athletics which appeared in the Harvard *Lampoon* on May 22, 1885, just before his graduation:

> This week's double-page shows what a zest co-education would lend to Athletics. There would be no indifference any longer. Every man in College would try for a place on some one of the teams. And what animated scences would Holmes and Jarvis present! Rosy-cheeked, radiantly clad damsels would fly hither and thither, playing tennis, lacrosse, base ball and what not, to the intense delight of themselves and every one who saw them. On the River, too, what changes we should see. The coxswains would no longer make the air blue with profanity, but would "speak gently to the erring ones." Decidedly, co-education must come.

In this respect, of course, Thayer was far ahead of his time. But his enthusiastic support for women's athletics is easily understandable when viewed in the context of the enlightened and progressive thinking that characterized his native city. Which tells us little about "Casey," perhaps, but a lot about Thayer – and The Heart of the Commonwealth.

CHAPTER 2

The Thayer Family

Ernest Lawrence Thayer was born on August 14, 1863, in Lawrence, Massachusetts. He was the fourth and last child of Edward Davis and Ellen Darling Thayer, and the sixth generation of the Thayer line to be born in America. Thomas and Richard Thayer, brothers and shoemakers, came to this country from Thornbury, England, before 1639. They are the ancestors of all Thayers in New England. Thomas, progenitor of Ernest and most of the Thayer families in Worcester, came first, with his wife and four children, and settled in Braintree, Massachusetts, where he obtained a grant of 76 acres of land in 1639. Ferdinando Thayer, second child of Thomas, was a teenager when he came to America with his father. He moved to Mendon, on the Blackstone River, after his father's death in 1665, and became one of the largest landholders in the new township. Ferdinando provided all of his sons with farms, many of which were still owned by Thayer descendants into the twentieth century (Crane, IV, 153–54; and Nutt, III, 130–31).

Thomas Thayer, sixth child of Ferdinando, was born in Mendon in 1664 or 1665. He married Mary Adams of the Braintree Adams family, and they kept the line going with ten children. John, their seventh child, was born in 1706. He married Ruhamah Smith and settled on land inherited from his father near the present town of Blackstone, Massachusetts, near the Rhode Island border. Their first child, Pelatiah, born in 1739, married Hannah Thayer, daughter of Aaron and Jemima Thayer. They had eight children, all sons. Henry, the seventh son, was born in Mendon in 1777. He married Urbana Thompson in 1800 and lived for several years on a portion of his ancestor's farm at Mendon, then moved to Five Corners, where he kept a hotel and store. They had ten children, one of whom died in early childhood.

Edward Davis Thayer, father of Ernest, was the tenth and last child of Henry and Urbana. Born in Mendon, now a part of Blackstone, on July 22, 1822, he became one of the most prominent wool manufacturers in New England. His father died in 1824 when he was only two years old, leaving his mother with nine children to care for, seven of whom were teenagers or younger. In two or three years the family moved to Millville, where small mills were the chief industry, and in these mills his older sisters soon secured employment. After receiving some early quality education at Uxbridge and the Dudley Academy, Edward was sent to work in one of the mills when he was 12 years old, and in a few years' time learned the trade of a wool sorter. In 1849 he went into business for himself in Burrillville, Rhode Island, where he ran a small wool mill for about two years. Then he formed a partnership with Moses Buffum, and together they ran a mill in Oxford manufacturing fine black wool cloth.

On October 14, 1851, Edward married Ellen Maria Darling, born in Connecticut on June 21, 1829, in Millville. Their first child, Albert Smith, was born in Oxford on January 6, 1854. The next year Edward sold his interest in the business to Buffum, and the Thayers moved to Worcester, where their second child, Edward Davis Thayer, Jr. was born on June 24, 1856. In 1860 Mr. Thayer became an agent of the Washington Mills in Lawrence, which later became a plant of the American Woolen Company. He was very successful there. The company had never paid any dividends up to this time, had failed once, and had just been reorganized. Thayer ran the mills during the Civil War and made large profits for the owners. The family lived in Roxbury for a while, where Ellen Olive Thayer was born on April 10, 1861. Shortly after this they moved to Lawrence, where Ernest was born.

At the end of the war Mr. Thayer saw great opportunities in the growing city of Worcester, "The Heart of the Commonwealth," and moved the family there in 1865. The children were educated in Worcester, while Edward, Sr., and Ellen lived in the city for the rest of their lives, most of that time in the family home at 67 Chatham Street. Edward was an attendant and pew holder at the Church of the Unity, on Elm Street, a few blocks north. For the next 20 years he was actively engaged in the woolen industry. His first factory was the Fox Mill in Worcester, near the Green Street Station. He also ran the Upham Mill in Spencer before taking over the Bottomley Mill in Cherry Valley, which was the largest plant he operated. He was located there until 1886 or 1887, when he retired, and turned the business over to his son Edward.

In 1865, their first year back in Worcester, the Thayers rented half of a two-family house at 29 Crown Street, around the corner from the Samuel Winslow family. After living there for a year, they rented a larger place at 29 Chatham Street that the Winslows had just left to move into their own home at 6 Linden Street, just a couple of blocks away. So Ernest Thayer, the future author of "Casey at the Bat," and Sam Winslow, one of the greatest intercollegiate athletes of his time, apparently began their lifelong friendship at an early age.

In 1868 Mr. Thayer bought a house at 67 Chatham Street, on the southwest corner of Crown and a little farther up the hill from Main Street. This was to be the family home for the next 35 years. It was a good place to live, work, and raise a family, conveniently located within walking distance of Mr. Thayer's business at 421 Main Street, the Oxford Street grammar school, the Classical and English High School on Walnut Street, the Agricultural Grounds, where Harvard and Yale played their first baseball games in the 1860s, and Mechanics Hall, which was the cultural center of the city as well as a meeting place for the mechanics. Lake Quinsigamond, the site of the first intercollegiate regattas in the country, was a popular place for the kids in the summer, and only three miles away. The house itself was a substantial but not extravagant residence, probably built in the 1840s or 1850s, in the Greek Revival style, like most of the houses in the neighborhood, many of which are still standing. When Edward Thayer, Ernest's father, died in 1903, the house was sold to Charles Padula. After he died his widow lived there for many years. In 1967, when the home at last gave way to the forces of "progress," Louise Carruth wrote a sketch of it for the Worcester Public Library, describing it as a "fine home," "truly representative of an elegant era." The house had parquet floors and an Adam fireplace in the library, which were probably there from the time it was built. Other features were obviously more modern, probably added by the Padulas. In the drawing room, music room, and library, for example, were panels of pink marble extending from floor to ceiling, framing Venetian mirrors. At the base were pink marble seats. There was also a handsome, black marble bathroom with a built-in electric steam bath. Oddly enough, Carruth does not mention the much-used billiard table that occupied one of the rooms when the Thayers lived there, and no doubt inspired one of the articles Ernest later wrote for the *Harvard Lampoon.* Perhaps the Padulas were not billiard players and so had the table removed? (Louise Carruth.)

Crown Hill, where the Thayers lived, is an old residential neighborhood west of Main Street, Worcester's central business district. It was originally the Gardiner Chandler farm, but with the growth of Worcester in the 1830s it was subdivided into lots for real estate development. Vincent Edward Powers has studied the neighborhood and found it to be a heterogeneous one, both by social class and even by ethnicity. On reflection, he writes, this was to be expected, for Worcester had only begun its internal transportation system in the 1860s, and the town still remained mainly a densely settled and heterogeneous pedestrian community. How mixed was Chatham Street? Powers found that one of Thayer's nearby neighbors was John S. Baldwin, publisher and editor of the area's biggest, oldest, and most important newspaper, the *Massachusetts Spy*. But factory laborers also were neighbors.

Powers also discovered that the Thayers had a domestic servant named Cora Woods, who was 40 years old and born in Ireland. She is listed in the 1870 U.S. Census. At her age, he believes, there is a very good chance that Cora may have been a longtime servant. She was beyond the usual marrying age that affected the employment of much younger girls. The older the servant, the less likely they would leave employment to enter a marriage, and the higher the odds the same servant could be found with a family over many years. Was Cora the nurse Thayer fondly recalled during his Harvard days, and spoke of so movingly in his Ivy Oration? Addressing his classmates on Class Day, June 19, 1885, he called to mind the "gentle ministrations" of his nurse, "who filled my young soul with indignation at the wrongs of Ireland; who, when by some unaccountable accident my most valuable pieces of *bric-a-brac* were shattered to bits, never failed to sooth me with soft, pleading words of comfort" (Taylor, 16–22; and personal correspondence from Powers).

Albert, who was 11 years old when the Thayers settled in Worcester in 1865, graduated from Worcester High School in 1871. He was elected Ivy Orator of his class at Harvard, where he graduated in 1875. Following that he attended Harvard Law School, graduating in 1878, and then took up the practice of law in New York City, with an emphasis on real estate law. He lived in Flushing, Long Island, most of his adult life.

Edward, Jr., also attended Worcester High School, and then entered the Lawrence Scientific School at Harvard at the age of 16, before his class graduated from the high school. He was a fine amateur ballplayer, the youngest and strongest member of the 1876 Harvard crew, and an outstanding all-around athlete. The records are not clear, but he may have helped to organize a series of ball games played in 1875 between Worcester Polytechnic Institute and graduates of the high school. In his studies Edward excelled in mathematics, and graduated from Harvard summa cum laude in 1876 with a degree in civil engineering. After touring Europe, he learned the textile business at the Slater Mill in Webster and at his father's mill. In 1879 he struck out on his own, manufacturing satinets at Hunt Mill. Later he bought Ashworth and Jones Mill, the first of many mills he would own and operate. He was extremely successful and was well respected by his employees.

Ellen (Nellie) graduated from Worcester High School in 1879. She and Ernest were very close since their brothers were away at college when Nellie and Ernest were still young. They were left behind with only each other for company; luckily, they apparently got along well together.

If a humorous outlook is inherited or learned, Ernest most likely inherited or learned his from his mother. Her letters show a wry sense of humor. She was not shy about giving her opinions on current events and readily applied her own slant to various subjects. She was strongly in favor of the temperance movement, a fact that is exposed time and time again in her letters to Ernest, as when she kept an eagle eye on her new cook, Bridget, who was satisfactory in every way but had a reputation for getting drunk. Mrs. Thayer saw the irony when Bridget burned a pudding one Sunday and said she was never so ashamed of anything in her life. "I hear she has been drunk but that was nothing to a burnt pudding," she wrote to Ernest.

The Thayers were Unitarians, members of the Church of the Unity on Elm Street, whose first pastor was Edward Everett Hale. They were regular churchgoers, but Mrs. Thayer was not averse to sending Mr. Thayer and Nellie on their own at times. When the Unity was closed for three weeks during the

Edward Thayer and the 1876 Harvard Crew (standing, from left) Irving, Cheney (Cox), LeMoyne; (sitting, back row) Jacobs, Bolan, Bancroft, Thayer; (front) Morgan (capt.), James (courtesy of the Harvard University Archives).

summer, she chose not to join them on the longer walk to the First Unitarian church. On another occasion Mr. Thayer went to Unity alone while she stayed home and read a biography of Charlotte Brontë.

Ernest's father, on the other hand, seemed to take life pretty seriously; perhaps having to work hard from the age of 12 had cost him the opportunity to develop a sense of fun. The few times he wrote a note to Ernest it was about a specific matter and was written matter-of-factly, not affectionately and certainly not humorously. He was affectionate, almost doting, with pets and his grandchildren, though. Mrs. Thayer once wrote to Ernest: "Nellie has left a small kitten in my charge, which gets all its petting from your father, while I keep its saucer filled with milk." When Josie, Albert's wife, returned home with her baby daughter from a visit to the Thayer home in Worcester, she wrote to Ernest, "Ellen was a great hit especially with her grandfather who carried her about all the time. It was very pretty to see them together."

Albert enjoyed his life and often made fun of himself. He got to be quite the country gentleman in Flushing. He was very proud of his yard and garden. When he had to spend the night in New York City after getting used to the quiet of the country, he told Ernest the city noises kept him from getting much sleep. He collected humorous anecdotes that he shared with Ernest concerning his activities, such as starting up his law practice with his partner Starbuck, and how smoking had injured his digestion. He told Ernest a short story that described how hard it was to get household help way out in Flushing, and how hard it was to keep it: "About the time I wrote you last our servant left us and we had a little trouble to get another. I went servant hunting one day myself and found a girl who, I thought, was just the thing, but she went back on me and did not come to Flushing at all. I hunted her up the next day to learn the reason why, but she only said she had changed her mind. Now we have just the girl we want, and she and the nurse make a very sharp team. She is about as tall as I am and about twice as big."

Ed, Jr., was a caring brother, from the tone of his letters. He addressed himself almost totally to his brother's activities, although he had plenty to crow about in his own career. Now and then he gave Ernest some advice. He seemed too busy to show much humor, but he might have shown some subtle wit when he addressed letters to "Dear Earnest."

Nellie had an impish sense of humor. She often teased Ernest in her letters to him, and asked impertinent questions. He had left a girl, Gracie, behind in Worcester as he gallivanted around the world and across the country, and Nellie kept him up to date on how it affected the young lady. Once she wrote, "I see almost nothing of Gracie C. I think she must have given you up or she would be more diligent in her attention to your sister." Another time she wrote, "Of Grace I hear and see very little. When I did see her I thought she was looking a bit old and care-worn. No knowing how much suffering your neglect is causing her."

This was Ernest's family, and he was a very family oriented person. Although he rebelled, at least temporarily, from joining the family business, when he came back from San Francisco he worked in the mill and lived in the family home for years. When he was in San Francisco he looked for a family to room with, even though he liked his rooms at 215 Post Street, with his pal Fatty Briggs right across the hall. He just wanted to live in a family environment. He considered the *Lampoon* staff a sort of family, and enjoyed having dinner every night with the "Harvard Brigade" after workdays at the *Examiner*. He didn't get married until his nieces and nephews were grown up, and then he married into a readymade family.

About That Billiard Table

No respectable family could afford to be without a billiard table in Ernest Thayer's day. It was truly a sign of the times. Billiards was recommended as an excellent indoor pastime, especially in the winter, when the season for outdoor sports was over. On December 19, 1857, the *New York Clipper,* a popular sporting paper, advised all of its readers, whether male or female, to learn the game, as it would minister to their health, amusement, and instruction. Here was a game where the physical as well as mental faculties are simultaneously brought into operation; the intellectual powers are not exhausted in undue proportion to those of the body, but that being occupied at once, both are proportionately strengthened; hence its adoption as a favorite winter amusement. The game taught a correct judgment of distance and calculation of forces, as well as the most exact execution, by the body, of diagrams formed and matured in the mind, thus offering a ready appreciation of mathematical precision and geometric truth, while at the same time it promoted an expansion of the chest and an easy and graceful motion of the limbs. Its adaptability as an exercise for both sexes was another great point in its favor, said the *Clipper*, noting that a number of ladies, many in the highest walks of life, had taken delight in this favorite pastime.

The increasing popularity of the game may be inferred from other articles which appeared in the *Clipper* during the 1860s. On January 21, 1860, the paper reported that "this eminently scientific and beautiful parlor pastime is becoming more and more popular in every civilized country, but in none more so than in America." Among the "upper ten" a billiard table is to the gentlemen what a piano forte is to the ladies, and many a pleasant evening hour is passed in "describing curves and angles with the little ivory balls on the green clad board." Many people, to whom "proper and sufficient exercise" is as "necessary as their food," are resorting to billiards as one of the few pastimes that are available in the way of winter exercise. What's more, claimed the *Clipper*, the game is "scientific and exciting, furnishing at all times occupation for the mind as well as the body."

On December 1, 1866, the *Clipper* published a letter from a Dr. Marcy recommending that billiard tables be introduced into private houses and presented to the entire family – men, women and children – as a means of daily exercise and recreation. Nothing, said Dr. Marcy, contributed more to the physical, moral, and intellectual development and health of a community than suitable modes of recreation. Billiards was one of the best, both from a moral as well as a sanitary point of view. Young America was naturally "frisky," naturally enthusiastic, exuberant, and fond of excitement and fun. These natural instincts for diversion could be directed into wholesome channels by providing the home with a few of the attractions which beckoned them elsewhere. With a billiard table in the home, "the most indolent and stupid will, by practice, soon acquire a fondness for the game"; and the improvement in the sanitary and moral condition of those who habitually indulge in it, "will commend it in the strongest manner to the heads of families."

This was a far cry from the 1820s, when there was a terrific uproar over a billiard table President John Quincy Adams bought for about $100, allegedly at the public expense, and installed in the White House. This was outrageous, thought Representative Samuel Carson of North Carolina, a Jacksonian, and he stood up and said that putting a billiard table in the White House was enough to "shock and alarm the religious, the moral, and reflecting part of the community." Adams bought it in 1825, shortly after his inauguration, as "a resource both for exercise and amusement," as well as for his family and guests. Much was written about it in the papers. In 1826 Charles Hammond, editor of the *Cincinnati Gazette*, speculated that the table had been left in the White House by the previous administration. When an inventory of President Monroe's furniture taken when he left the White House disproved that contention, Hammond wrote that if Adams was going to be condemned for his billiard table, what about Jackson, who was "adept at billiards, cards, dice, horse-racing, cock-fighting, and tavern brawls!" (Miles, 31–43).

But the issue was not about to go away. In 1827 a Jacksonian assembly in Wayne Township, Ohio, protested vehemently against "the erection of *Billiard Tables,* and costly and extravagant furniture in the President's House." One Western congressman reportedly attributed his defeat to "the d______d billiard table," and Representative Francis Johnson of Kentucky, who also lost his bid for reelection in 1827, said he would never play the game again: "I used to play, when a young man, but I'm sick of it *now.*" When Jackson won the election of 1828, a "Respectful Epistle to John Quincy Adams" appeared in the *Oneida Observer:*

> John Adams Q. my Joe John
>   Now don't you think 'twas rash
> For billiard balls and cues, John
>   To spend the people's cash?
> For billiard tables too, John
>   Alas, by doing so,
> You've "holed" yourself – you're on the shelf,
>   John Adams Q. my Joe.

The athletic revival of the 1850s and 1860s brought with it a whole new attitude toward health and recreation. There was nothing rash about spending some cash on billiard balls, cues, and a table for the home: it was plain common sense. The table at the Thayers' home must have been pretty popular with all the boys in the neighborhood, judging from a letter Ernest's mother wrote to him in the summer of 1880, just before his seventeenth birthday, when he and Nellie were staying with some friends or family in Jefferson. "I suppose the boys are all away," she writes, "at least I have seen none of them since I came home, and the billiard table is having a long rest" (EMT to ELT, 8/10/1880). Ernest was undoubtedly an expert at the game by the time he wrote the following sketch, which appeared in the *Lampoon* on March 14, 1884:

The Billiardist

> All men eat, but there are few epicures; all men reason, but there are few philosophers; all men play billiards, but there are few *billiardists.* It is one of my pleasures, which as it costs me nothing I frequently indulge, to go where I may watch a billiardist – a real billiardist – at

work. If after admiring his graceful, haughty bearing, I turn for a moment to the contemplation of a mere chance billiard-player, I am dreadfully annoyed and disgusted. Mark the contrast!

The chance billiard-player actually plays with his coat on, and ha, ha! I have seen one who wore his overcoat through a game of one hundred points. When he chalks his cue, he makes a labor of it, looks cross-eyed at the tip which he holds close to his face; and likely as not he will end by dropping the chalk on the floor, and, what is still more offensive, he will pick it up again. The chance billiard-player ever hesitates before he plays, is slow to see the most promising shot, finally selects the most difficult one, and withal handles his cue in a very awkward and bungling fashion. If he commits one of those misdemeanors which in billiard parlance are called scratches, he always commits himself by a shame-faced smile. When he marks his points on the string, he takes both hands to his cue, and with his head thrown back till his mouth opens perforce, he engages in a long and disgraceful struggle to get his cue between the proper buttons. Then he never knows what to do with himself till his partner is done playing.

But the *billiardist*! Dash! spirit! grace! perfect ease! The billiardist is revealed by his shirt sleeves, and sometimes by his embroidered silk suspenders. He chalks his cue with the least perceptible effort, almost, it seems, unconsciously; and if he drops his chalk, it is precisely as if he had intended to do so, for he neither notices its fall nor stoops to pick it up. When he plays, one may remark a half-defined sneer on his face, the reason whereof must be contempt for the inability of the balls to prevent him from running out the game. First he flourishes his cue like a fencing master testing a foil; then drags its tip through beautiful and unexpected curves on the cloth. Now he sinks his chin meditatively on his chest; anon supports his right ear on the corresponding shoulder, and sucks air through his teeth while glancing with the most profound gravity and intensity around the banks. Then follows a period when his striped trousers are tastefully grouped in the most intricate and bewildering patterns all over the table.

The balls answer to his touch like magic. Accidents, however, will happen, and perchance, he makes a most abominable scratch; the spectators essay a smile in order to draw him into their confidence, but their overtures are met with a stolid immobility of feature, that oppresses them with a sense of disgrace at having ridiculed a very remarkable shot.

Finally the billiardist fails to count; he smiles languidly as if he had stopped on purpose, but would rather not say anything about it. He shows no haste to mark what he has made, but picks his cigar from the rail, and stands for a few moments puffing meditatively with his cue slung gracefully over his shoulder. Suddenly as if the thought had but that moment occurred to him, with a mere glance at the string and a lazy elliptical sweep of his cue, his run is swung away into the space between what he has made before and what he hasn't made at all. Then he folds his arms about his cue, and watches the play of his opponent with a smile on his face, a kind well-meaning smile, such as a father bestows when he sees his son gravely strutting about in his first full-length trousers. The billiardist in his proper sphere is so lofty, so unapproachable, so coldly courteous, that I am quite convinced that the class to which he belongs is the nearest approach to a nobility in this broad but democratic land.

CHAPTER 3

The Heart of the Commonwealth

Worcester's transformation from an isolated agricultural town into a modern industrial city and inland transportation center began in the 1820s and 1830s, and was soon followed by a rapid increase in the number of the inhabitants. On January 5, 1848, the *Worcester Spy* reported that the town's population had grown from about 7,500 to more than 15,000 since 1840, and declared that "such a fact as the doubling, in seven years, of a town of the size of Worcester, in an old and long-settled section of the country, and without any one great leading branch of business to build it up, is, so far as our knowledge extends, without a parallel." This helped to generate public support for a bill that was brought up in the legislature the next month to establish Worcester as a city. The bill was passed and signed into law by the governor on February 29, 1848. Levi Lincoln, a former governor and congressman, was elected the first mayor of Worcester on April 8, 1848 (Chasan, 11–25).

One of Lincoln's first official acts was to appoint a committee of the new city council headed by Alderman Stephen Salisbury to choose a seal. They reported back on January 23, 1849, that the seal of the city "shall be circular in form, having in its center the figure of a heart encircled with a wreath," and in the margin, beginning at the center of the left side, the words "Worcester a Town June 14, 1722; a City February 29, 1848." The city council passed an ordinance adopting the seal by a unanimous vote on March 30, 1849, and Worcester has since been officially known as "The Heart of the Commonwealth." The first recorded reference to Worcester's motto had been made by Lincoln himself on October 4, 1831, during a speech commemorating the one hundredth anniversary of the incorporation of Worcester County. John Warner Barber seconded the motion in 1844, and added that the central situation of the town both in regard to the county and the state, the fertility of its soil and that of the surrounding country, and the industry, intelligence and wealth of the inhabitants, justly entitled it to the honor of being called "The Heart of the Commonwealth" (Ordinances, 75; Sandrof; and Barber, 618).

A fine picture of Worcester and its people at the time of the town's centennial in 1822 is afforded by the indefatigable traveler and writer, Timothy Dwight. President of Yale from 1795 to 1817, Dwight was a great believer in exercise and the great outdoors, and rode thousands of miles on horseback during the time between terms. Galloping through Massachusetts on one of his annual jaunts, heading toward Boston, he was impressed by the land, the lakes, and the people of Worcester County, and by the superb views available to the traveler from a number of vantage points. In his well-known account of his ramblings he remarked upon the "universally undulating" surface of the land, the gently rolling hills, "rarely lofty, or steep," hence easy to climb, and the valleys, "not uncommonly of considerable breadth." Both the hills and the valleys, green to the tops of the hills, "are in many instances beautiful," and "the prospects from the heights are in several instances extensive and noble" (Timothy Dwight [1969], 1:261–75; Chasan, 11; and Brooke, 1–3).

Our guide was anything but gullible. The highest mountain in the region, he noted, was Mount Wachusett, near Princeton, 15 miles north of Worcester, and 52 miles west of Boston. John Winthrop, the honorable professor of mathematics and natural philosophy at Harvard, had estimated this mountain to be 3,012 feet above sea level, but Dwight had his doubts. "This estimate is, I suspect, at least five hundred feet higher than the truth." And he was absolutely correct, for as Margaret Erskine has said in her recent, highly readable, and beautifully illustrated history of Worcester: the true height of the mountain to the north is exactly 2,108 feet. Not quite high enough, perhaps, to supply all of the inspiration for the mountain that dominates the landscape of "Casey at the Bat," but a mountain, nevertheless (Erskine [1981], 14).

By Dwight's count, the land contained about 40 small lakes, "many of them very beautiful, and adding a fine brilliancy to the surface," and was "abundantly watered with springs, brooks, and mill-streams," full of pike, trout, and other fish common to the fresh waters of New England. On the eastern edge of the town of Worcester, at the entrance to Shrewsbury, was the largest and finest of these lakes:

> At the entrance of this township from Worcester lies a beautiful lake, called Quinsigamond; about one acre of which is comprised within the bounds of Worcester, and the rest in those of Shrewsbury. This lake is about four miles long, and from one hundred rods to a mile broad, and is the largest and handsomest piece of water seen from the great road in this county. Its form is a crescent. From the high ground in Shrewsbury it furnishes a fine feature of the landscape, and exhibits to the eye the appearance of a noble section of a majestic river.

Dwight observed that the hills of the county are moist to their summits, perfectly suited to the production of grass, and, like the hills of New England in general, admirably adapted for grazing. "Excellent neat cattle abound in the county of Worcester," he said, "and beef is perhaps nowhere better fattened upon grass." Horses and pigs were also found in great numbers, and the quantity of cloth manufactured throughout the county (7,000 yards of cloth dressed annually by a single typical clothier) is "a sufficient proof that the number of sheep is considerable."

Among the public buildings were a courthouse, a schoolhouse, two churches, and a bank. The courthouse was built of brick, with two stories, and, in Dwight's estimation, "in a very pretty style." The lower story contained the county offices; the upper contained the courtroom and its accommodation. "This building cost twenty thousand dollars, and is an honour to the county, at whose expense it was erected." The bank was even bigger, "a beautiful structure of three stories, exhibiting an union of simplicity and elegance, not often seen in this country." The schoolhouse was also "a good building."

Above all, Dwight was impressed by the people. "In no part of this country, ... is there a more industrious or thrifty collection of farmers." The barns were universally large and good, the enclosures of stone well formed, effectual, strong, and durable. The township of Worcester was divided into farms, "which were a cheerful and prosperous aspect," and contained about 120 houses, generally well built. Few towns in New England, he thought, "exhibit so uniform an appearance of neatness and taste, or contain so great a proportion of good buildings, and so small a proportion of those which are indifferent, as Worcester." The number of public officers, professional men, merchants, and mechanics, was proportionally great, and produced "a very lively appearance of activity and business." Worcester had three printing offices, four gristmills, four sawmills, a large paper mill, and two fulling mills, the proprietors of which carried on the clothiers' business "to a great extent, and with skill, supposed not to be excelled in the state."

Isaiah Thomas, the proprietor of one of the printing offices, "has probably done as much printing business as any other man in New England within the same period of time." He had published a considerable number of large and expensive works, together with a great multitude of smaller ones; and for many years had been the head of a well-furnished bookstore in Boston, as well as in Worcester. Born in Boston in 1749, Thomas had founded the *Massachusetts Spy* there in 1770. Three nights before the Battle of Lexington and Concord, he smuggled his printing press out of Boston and set it up in Worcester. Thomas became the leading printer, editor, publisher, and bookseller in the United States after the war. At one time his printing establishment employed 150 people and included 7 presses, the paper mill, and a bindery, with branches in Portsmouth, Newburyport, and Albany. Among the more than 400 titles he published were a large number of religious and educational books, including a handsome folio Bible, the first printed in English in the United States. Recognizing the need to preserve and study the materials of American history, Thomas founded the American Antiquarian Society in

Worcester in 1812, and became its first president. The AAS is the third oldest historical society in the country, and the first to be national rather than regional in its purpose and in the scope of its collections (Timothy Dwight [1969], 1: 265–66; Vail, 435–36).

Thomas was also famous for his children's books. He published tens of thousands of copies of more than 100 such books, including the first American edition of *Mother Goose's Melody* in 1786. Although Dwight for some reason did not mention the fact, Thomas also published the first known baseball verses in America. The lines appeared in *A Little Pretty Pocket Book*, published in Worcester in 1787, almost exactly 100 years before "Casey at the Bat" made its debut in the pages of the *San Francisco Daily Examiner*. Most of the text and the woodcuts are taken from the English edition of John Newbery, published in 1770. The author was much influenced by the educational theories of John Locke, who had advanced the principle of "a sound mind in a sound body" in *Some Thoughts Concerning Education* (1693). The baseball verses appear on page 43, accompanied by a woodcut which shows three boys playing the game with three bases and a ball, but without a bat: (Newbery [1787], 43; Rosenbach, 54; Robert Henderson [1937], 288; and Newbery [1967], 44, 90).

Base-Ball.

The Ball once struck off,
Away flies the Boy
To the next destin'd Post
And then Home with Joy.

Moral.

Thus Seamen for Lucre
Fly over the Main,
But, with Pleasure transported
Return back again.

Speaking of the inhabitants of New England in general, Dwight observes that their "principal amusements" are visiting, dancing, music, conversation, walking, riding, sailing, traveling for pleasure, shooting at a mark, draughts, chess, "and unhappily, in some of the larger towns, cards, and dramatic exhibitions." They also fish and hunt. Riding in a sleigh, or sledge, is also very popular. "Boys and young men," he notes, "play at foot-ball, cricket, quoits, and at many other sports of an athletic cast, and in the winter are peculiarly fond of skating" (Timothy Dwight [1969], 4:250–51).

Ball games of all kinds were so popular in some places that they became a nuisance. In Worcester, for example, the voters discussed the following article at the town meeting of May 20, 1816, after selecting Abraham Lincoln as moderator: "To see if the said Inhabitants will adopt any mode, or make such regulations as will in future prevent the playing Ball and Hoops in the public Streets in said Town, a practice so frequent and dangerous, that has occasioned many great and repeated complaints." No action was apparently taken at this time. About 20 years later, however, at the town meeting of June 11, 1838, the voters made this the first of the 23 bylaws of Worcester: "If any person shall play at any game of Ball, or strike at any Ball, with a Bat-stick, or his foot, or shall throw any Ball into, in, about, across or along any of the Streets or Roads in the Town of Worcester, he shall, for each offence, forfeit and pay the sum of Two Dollars" (Rice [1891], 337; Holliman, 64; Rice [1895], 143; and Chasan, 31).

There were never any laws against bowling, it ought to be noted, possibly because the people who did the bowling also made the laws. Christopher Columbus Baldwin, a native of Templeton, Massachusetts, who practiced law in Worcester in the 1820s and 1830s, and served as the librarian of the American Antiquarian Society, wrote in his diary for June 19, 1829: "Attend court, which rises at nine A.M. According to immemorial use the members of the Bar in Worcester devote the afternoon to *rolling nine pins*; it is usual for court to rise on Saturday but it fell this time on Friday; have a very pleasant time, and don't lose any money; I bet only one fourpence per game" (Baldwin, 25; Tymeson, 11).

In the concluding remarks of his work Dwight saw a great future for the United States. He characterized the people as "well made, robust, and hardy," and "fitted for every enterprise which demands energy of body or strength of mind." They are possessed of vigorous constitutions, able defenders of their country, well prepared to meet those difficulties which demand firmness of body as well as resolution. "The inhabitants of no country," he said, "unite more strength with more agility." They were destined to fill almost the whole continent of North America, and "station themselves, within half a century, on the shores of the Pacific Ocean." And when they did, they brought with them a new game they had perfected, a game that seemed to fit the national character perfectly. A game they called "Base Ball" (Timothy Dwight [1969], 4:235–51, 361–73).

CHAPTER 4

Thayer's Worcester

A traveler visiting Worcester in 1865, the year the Thayers settled down there, would have found a bustling city of 30,000 people, a very different place from the quiet little country town where Dwight had stopped half a century earlier. In 1815 the village's sole contact with the outside world was a weekly stagecoach from Boston to the west. Ten years later, when the Erie Canal was completed, the Blackstone Canal Company imported a crew of Irish construction workers who had worked on the Erie to build a canal from Worcester to Providence. This waterway, according to the *Massachusetts Spy,* "would be the most exciting development in the history of the town." Building a canal was no simple matter, but challenged the combined talents of engineers, artisans, masons, carpenters, and laborers, and brought a new labor force of 1,000 men to Worcester and the Blackstone Valley. The canal was completed in 1828, and turned Worcester into a booming canal port almost overnight (Howland, 46; and Powers, 94–100, 125–31).

Some of the Irish stayed to work on the Boston and Worcester Railroad, which began in the state capital in 1831. As Powers has said, the papers were alive with the excitement of a continued transformation of the town. The *Spy* predicted that the iron tracks would make Worcester an important industrial center, while the *National Aegis* said that the town would soon become a city, and the *Worcester County Republican* speculated that the railway, once completed to Albany, would bring the wealth of the great west and great profits to all (Powers, 205–9).

The first locomotive from Boston pulled into Worcester on July 4, 1835, "a wonderful and awesome sight." The route to Albany presented more difficult terrain, but it seemed that nothing was impossible for Yankee ingenuity. The railroad reached the New York State capital in 1839, and by 1865 there were 15 trains a day passing through Worcester on this railroad alone, 8 bound for Boston, 7 for Albany and the West. Four other railroads connected Worcester with Nashua, Norwich, Providence, and Fitchburg, making Worcester the center of a transportation network that stretched in all directions (Erskine [1981], 58; and Howland, 47).

In 1865 the completion of a transcontinental railroad was only 4 years away, although rumors that a Yankee inventor had already ridden a train to

California had been circulating for 25 years. In 1839 the *Knickerbocker* magazine had reported that Jabez Doolittle, a Connecticut man, had been seen riding his locomotive in several different parts of the country, always at full speed. A correspondent wrote from St. Louis:

> You must know that I was one among the first band of trappers that crossed the Rocky Mountains. We had encamped one night on a ridge of the Black Hills, and were wrapped up in our blankets, in the midst of our first sleep, when we were roused by the man who stood sentinel, who cried out, "Wild fire, by–!" We started on our feet, and beheld a streak of fire coming across the prairies, for all the world like lightning, or a shooting star. We had hardly time to guess what it might be, when it came up, whizzing, and clanking, and making a tremendous racket, and we saw something huge and black, with wheels and traps of all kinds; and an odd-looking being on top of it, busy as they say the devil is in a gale of wind. In fact, some of our people thought it was the old gentleman himself, taking an airing in one of his infernal carriages; others thought it was the opening of one of the seals in the Revelations. Some of the stoutest fellows fell on their knees, and began to pray; a Kentuckian plucked up courage enough to hail the infernal coachman as he passed, and ask whither he was driving; but the speed with which he whirled by, and the rattling of his machine, prevented our catching more than the last words: "Slam bang to eternal smash!" In five mintues more, he was across the prairies, beyond the Black Hill, and we saw him shooting, like a jack-o'-lantern, over the Rocky Mountains [Crackenthorpe, 445–46].

There was no doubt that the driver was Doolittle, on his way to Astoria, and that he was now scouring California, perhaps, or whizzing away to the North Pole. "He is the first person that ever crossed the Rocky Mountains on wheels," said the Missourian; "his transit shows that those mountains are traversable with carriages, and that it is perfectly easy to have a rail-road to the Pacific." Such was the spirit of the times.

The impact of the canal and the railroads on the growth of Worcester is reflected in the census figures for 1830 and 1850. In 1830 the town had a population of just over 4,000, and was only the eighteenth largest town in the region. But in the next 20 years the population more than quadrupled to over 17,000, making Worcester the sixth largest city in the region. Only Lowell, with its rapidly expanding cotton mills, grew at a faster rate as its population increased fivefold, from 6,500 in 1830 to 33,000 in 1850, when it replaced Salem as the second largest city in the region. Boston remained the largest city in the region but moved at a snail's pace by comparison, as the population increased from 60,000 in 1830 to 140,000 in 1850, about doubling in size (Blouin, 137).

Mechanics Association

In 1841 Anthony Chase, the Worcester County treasurer and former shoemaker, called a meeting at the town hall for the purpose of forming a mechanics association, with membership open to "operative and master mechanics and manufacturers." Ichabod Washburn, a wire manufacturer who had invented machinery for drawing wire, was elected chairman of a committee which organized the Worcester County Mechanics Association on February 5, 1842, with 115 charter members. William Wheeler, an iron founder, was elected president, and Washburn vice president. Within the next ten years the loom, the sewing machine, the cotton gin, and the lathe were all invented, and all of them within 20 miles of Worcester (Erskine [1977], 4–5; and Chasan, 163–66).

In 1848 the association held its first fair, and proclaimed: "From an almost purely agricultural community, the County of Worcester had become distinguished also for the number of its Mechanical and Manufacturing establishments; for the amount of industry employed and capital invested therein; and for the extensive variety and superior excellence of the products of genius and art." With the rise of the mechanics Worcester began to take on a creative, progressive spirit which drew men like George Hoar to the Worcester bar in 1849, and Thomas Higginson to the pulpit of the Worcester Free Church three years later. In his autobiography Hoar paid high tribute to the "unsurpassed ingenuity" of Worcester's mechanics, and described the city and county as "the spot on the face of the earth where labor got the largest proportion of the joint production of labor and capital." Higginson called Worcester "a new cradle of liberty," and characterized the members of his congregation as "intelligent mechanics, a special breed . . . with keen eyes for machinery and reform." In general, he found Worcester "a very thriving and active place materially, intellectually and morally; there is as much radicalism here as at Lynn, but more varied, more cultivated, and more balanced by an opposing force; a very attractive place, and this free church movement a very strong one." When his article appeared in the *Atlantic Montlhly* in 1858 the mechanics were the first in the city to respond, organizing the Mechanics Base Ball Club (Chasan, 168; Brooke, 372–83; Hoar, 1:159; Mooney, 192).

Mechanics Hall

In 1854 the association had grown to almost 500 members, and began making plans to build a hall. Ichabod Washburn started the ball rolling with a gift of $10,000, and other members pledged to contribute an additional $65,000. Ground was broken in July 1855, and the cornerstone was laid on September 3, with Mr. and Mrs. Thayer, perhaps, looking on. Margaret Erskine has captured the significance of the events that followed:

> As the building rose, it dominated the skyline of the city, larger and more impressive than any other structure. . . . From the opening day on, the history of the hall would be a central part of the history of the

> city. Speeches, rallies, memorials, concerts, and important events of every kind would take place there. It became the center of the artistic, political, and intellectual life of a thriving city filled with young and energetic people who were building a new world based on the arts of the mechanic [Erskine (1977), 12–22].

The hall was to have a front of 100 feet with high arching windows, and be 145 feet long; the main floor to contain, besides the four stores in front, a back hall 50 feet wide and 80 feet long, 17 feet high, seating 600 people; the upper floor to contain a great hall 80 feet wide, 145 feet long, and 88 feet high, seating 2,000 people, with galleries in front and on the sides, covering an area of some 11,000 square feet on the floor. In the course of construction the great hall remained 80 feet wide, but was raised 2 feet and shortened by 14. At the dedication ceremony on March 19, 1857, Alexander Bullock predicted: "It will rise above the temporary embarrassments, – it will buffet the storms of evanescent adversity, – it will burst the restraints of timid counsels, – it will plant new hopes and establish new foundations over the ashes of failure, – and above the buttresses of brick and mortal and iron, – it will fling out its colors to catch the radiance of the sun which never sets – *but to rise again.*"

From the beginning, Mechanics Hall was meant to provide a focal point for the cultural life of the city and county of Worcester. The great hall has always been noted for its acoustics, which are considered among the best in the world today. Henry Ward Beecher, James Russell Lowell, Charles Dickens, Henry Thoreau, Ralph Waldo Emerson, Susan B. Anthony, Elizabeth Cady Stanton, Mark Twain, Charles Sumner, Richard Henry Dana, Jr., Edward Everett Hale, Thomas Higginson, Horace Greeley, Ignacy Paderewski, Antonin Dvorak, Enrico Caruso, Artur Rubinstein, and presidents McKinley, Teddy Roosevelt, Taft, and Wilson have come to Mechanics Hall to speak or sing or play.

One of the early performers turned out to be a great favorite with Thayer. This was Charles Farrar Browne, whose alter ego, Artemus Ward, had made him quite well known on both sides of the Atlantic by the time he appeared in Mechanics Hall in 1865. Worcester had its own Artemas Ward – slightly different spelling – from an earlier era. He was a Revolutionary War general and chief justice of the Worcester County Court, which perhaps helps to explain the humorist's standing with Thayer. In any event, in January 1865 the public was respectfully informed that Ward would be in town *for two nights only,* and that "this Friday Evening, January 20th, 1865, and ensuing evening, will most positively be the only appearance of ARTEMUS WARD, in Worcester, this season," although a notice in small print added that there would be a "Grand Matinee, for Ladies and Children, on Saturday Afternoon, at 2 o'clock. Admission to all parts of the house, 25 Cents." The program started off with "Music on the Grand Piano," an ingenious medley, introducing the touching ballad, "Mother, You Are One of My Parents" (Program in WHM).

Ward was the foremost American humorist in the Civil War era. Born in Waterford, Maine, on April 26, 1834, he started as a teenaged printer for several New England periodicals and, while still in his teens, began to write filler and small items. His first important writing was for *The Carpet-Bag,* a Boston weekly. In 1853 he went west to Ohio, where he wrote for small papers in Tiflin and Toledo, then moved to Cleveland in 1857 where he became local editor of the *Plain Dealer*. In Cleveland he made the acquaintance of an eccentric old gentleman whose actual name was Artemus Ward, a P.T. Barnum–like circus showman with a few "wax figgers," birds, "snaix," a kangaroo, and a "menajery of livin wild beests." Browne had a popular humor column, "Facts and Fancies," and began signing his sketches "Artemus Ward." Among these were letters he "received," full of Ward's phonetic spelling of dialect speech, with "goaks" and "poeckry," "2 B sure." Artemus Ward and Charles Browne became indistinguishable in the public eye. Browne took Ward to *Vanity Fair* in November 1860, and in six months they became joint managing editors of that leading American humor magazine. From there, in 1861, Browne began giving comic lectures around the country. His down east humor, with its unique speech pattern, was combined with southwestern humor, which relied more on "tall tales"—sensational stories told with great embellishment. When he was touring in the west he met Sam Clemens and encouraged the young journalist to send him a story, and he would publish it in one of his books. Clemens did so, but his tale about a "Jumping Frog" arrived too late for the book, and appeared separately. In 1866 Ward traveled to London, wrote Artemus Ward letters for *Punch,* and, despite becoming weaker and weaker from tuberculosis, gave a series of lectures at Egyptian Hall to enthusiastic audiences. His last performance was January 23, 1867, and on March 6, one month before his thirty-third birthday and at the height of his career, Browne died. In addition to influencing Mark Twain and others with his deadpan delivery of outlandish stories, Browne's humor played a role in moving popular literature from romanticism toward realism. He ridiculed the sentimental romance by setting a romantic scene with flowery prose, then dousing the mood with a dose of cold reality (Abrams, 60–68).

In 1865, a generation after the first train reached Worcester, the city still retained some of its old rural flavor with a diversified collection of 1,331 horses, 1,184 cows, 306 heifers, 349 pigs, 258 sheep, 224 oxen, and 100 steers, not to mention all the cats and dogs. But there were unmistakable signs that Worcester was now a city. Just 500 of the city's 30,000 people, 1 in 60, were still working on the farms, yet this small percentage of the population managed to produce an astonishing 36,000 bushels of potatoes, 22,000 bushels of corn, 12,000 bushels of oats, 6,000 bushels of turnips, 3,000 bushels of carrots, 20,000 pounds of butter, and 250,000 gallons of milk (mostly for the 6,000 children of school age, between 5 and 15). This small but dedicated band of farmers somehow found the time to cultivate more than 40,000 apple trees, almost 20,000 pear trees, and an assortment of more than 6,000 other fruit trees (Howland, 46).

The Agricultural Society and Horticultural Society helped to preserve and perpetuate this aspect of Worcester's life. According to the directory, the annual exhibition of flowers and fruits in the hall of the Horticultural Society, held in September, "has attracted much attention, and given a great impulse to the cultivation of good fruit in this vicinity." During the previous few years weekly exhibitions of fruits and flowers, and conversations in relation to them, had been held in the library room on Thursday afternoons, "which have proved interesting to those who have been present." The Agricultural Society owned nearly 20 acres of land on Highland Street for its annual exhibition, had built a spacious hall on the grounds, and had also laid out one-half mile trotting park. The attendance was large on the days of the agricultural exhibition, as well as on racing days, while "the *quality* of the attendance on each, well illustrates the comparative value of the two shows to the industry of the community." The Agricultural Grounds were also the scene of many exciting college baseball games in the 1860s, notably the 1864 Harvard-Williams contest, the first college game played in New England under the New York rules, and the fiercely contested Harvard-Yale games of the later 1860s, when the schools crossed bats for the first time (*ibid.*, 41).

By this time, most of Worcester's working people were working in the city. And judging from Howland's *City Directory* for 1866, they had a great variety of occupations to choose from. More than 9,000 people (6,600 men and 2,500 women) were employed in about 500 shops which produced more than 100 different types of goods and services, ranging from apple parers (7 men in one shop produced 25,000 parers) to wheels (15 men in one shop shipped out 2,500 sets). The business that employed the most people was the manufacture and sales of men's and women's clothing and woolen goods, as about 2,100 people (1,650 women and 450 men, including Mr. Thayer) worked at 66 of these shops. In a related business, 8 cotton and woolen machinery shops employed 600 men. Footwear was the next biggest business, with 1,900 people (1,500 men and 400 women) working in 27 shops producing 650,000 pairs of shoes and 510,000 pairs of boots. In railroad-related businesses, 7 car and carriage shops manufactured 170 railway cars, while 2 rolling mills for iron employed 500 men, and 6 iron casting shops put another 300 to work. Agricultural machinery was made in 4 shops which employed 300 men in the production of 5,000 mowers and 14,000 plows, while 7 gun shops employed 350 men to make 12,000 rifles and 15,000 revolvers. Wire manufacturing became a big business with the spread of the telegraph, as 675 people (635 men, 40 women) were employed at 3 shops in spinning out 5,000 tons of wire. For those who were not in that much of a hurry to get their message across, Worcester also produced 38 million envelopes, and, not too surprisingly, perhaps, for "The Heart of the Commonwealth," 2 shops employing 23 women and 2 men specialized in making valentine cards (*ibid.*, 44–46).

The card shops were begun by Esther Howland, New England's first career woman, who made valentines for America for more than 30 years. Born in Worcester on August 17, 1828, she graduated from Mount Holyoke College in 1847. Emily Dickinson was also a student at the college about that time, and if a letter she wrote to her brother Austin is any indication, valentines were all the rage. On February 14, 1848, she wrote: "Monday afternoon Mistress Lyon arose in the hall and forbade our sending any of those foolish notes called valentines."

Esther began making valentines in 1848. Her father was the leading stationer and bookseller in Worcester, and with his help she imported from England the materials needed to create the lacy, flower-bedecked cards. Her brother Allen traveled by horse and buggy each fall through northern Massachusetts, Vermont, and New Hampshire, peddling the company's wares, and he took along some samples. When he returned with orders for $5,000 worth of cards, she was astonished! Esther asked her friends for help, and set up an assembly line in a room in the family home at 16 Summer street. By 1865 she was doing $100,000 per year in business; Howland valentines were sold across the country. In 1879 she published *The New England Valentine Co.'s Valentine Verse Book for 1879,* which contained 31 pages of 131 verses made in 3 different sizes, and explained: "It is frequently the case that a valentine is found to suit, but the verse or sentiment is not right. In a case like this, the book is given them, and one is selected, cut out, and pasted over, making it satisfactory." This was not satisfactory to Thayer, however, if we can believe an editorial he wrote for the *Harvard Lampoon.* He claimed that a man should compose a valentine and write it himself, "or he is no true lover" (Emerson, 5–16; and Ruth Lee, 51–65).

Libraries

Howland's directory also noted that Worcester had a new public library building. "This splendid edifice, situated on the south side of Elm Street, a few rods from Main, was erected in 1861–2, for the safe keeping and distribution of the Free Public Library of the city; and it now affords room for that purpose, besides accommodating the Worcester District Medical Library, the Library of the Farmers Club, the Cabinets of the Natural History Society, and a Grammar School for girls." The library contained about 18,000 volumes, which embraced a "very wide range of topics of interest to all classes of the community." When the catalogue was completed, which it nearly was, so that people could "know something about the variety and value of this branch of the Public Library, a new interest will doubtless be excited, and the number of visitors largely increased." Hours were 9:00 A.M. to 8:00 P.M., the reading room till 9:30 P.M. Z. Baker was the librarian; and Mrs. Z. Baker and Miss C. Barnes were the assistants.

In addition, the American Antiquarian Society had by this time acquired a collection of over 40,000 bound volumes, besides many pamphlets, antiquities, and works of art. The Mechanics Association also provided "a choice library of more than 1,400 volumes," and a "very pleasant, nicely fitted-up and well-supplied reading room, open from 9:00 A.M. till 9:30 P.M. daily except Sundays, at room No. 4 Mechanics Hall building, besides other valuable privileges," to its members (Howland, 39).

Schools

Worcester has long been known for the quality of her public and private schools. The Latin Grammar School was founded in 1752 to prepare students for college. John Adams taught there after graduating from Harvard in 1755 and remained until 1758. The school continued until 1845, when it was merged with the Girls' High School into the Classical and English High School, which Ernest Thayer attended in the 1870s (Erskine, [1981], 25; Workman, 161–62; Roe [1901], 563; and Nutt, 2:713).

The letters and diaries of Adams are full of wit, humor, and philosophy, and tell us a great deal about the school, the town, and the people of Worcester. In a letter of September 2, 1755 – one of the first surviving productions of his pen – he told his friend Richard Cranch that the situation of the town is "quite pleasant," and that the inhabitants, so far as he had an opportunity to know their character, are "a sociable, generous, and hospitable people." But the school itself was "indeed a school of affliction," attended by "a large number of little runtlings, just capable of lisping A B C, and troubling the master." To subdue them, and keep his subjects in order, took all of the means at his disposal: "Sometimes paper, sometimes his penknife, now birch, now arithmetic, now a ferule, then A B C, then scolding, then flattering, then thwacking, calls for the pedagogue's attention. At length, his spirits all exhausted, down comes pedagogue from his throne, and walks out in awful solemnity, through a cringing multitude." Dr. Savil had told him that "by cultivating and pruning these tender plants in the garden of Worcester, I shall make some of them plants of renown and cedars of Lebanon." Adams, however, was certain that keeping the school any length of time "would make a base weed and ignoble shrub of me" (John Adams [1851], 1:27–28; and John Adams [1961], 3:263).

In time, of course, as he got to know his students a little better, Adams began to see some possibilities in them. Indeed, he began to revel in his role as a teacher, and sometimes, in his more sprightly moments, imagined himself as a dictator at the head of a commonwealth, a little state which held "all the great Genius's, all the surprizing actions and revolutions of the great World in miniature." His thoughts on the subject are developed at some length in his diary entry for March 15, 1756 – over 100 years before Thayer's time, perhaps, but the observations appear to be timeless:

> I have severall [*sic*] renowned Generalls [*sic*] but 3 feet high, and several deep-projecting Politicians in petticoats. I have others catching and dissecting Flies, accumulating remarkable pebbles, cockle shells &c., with as ardent Curiosity as any Virtuoso in the rcyal society. Some rattle and Thunder out A, B, C, with as much Fire and impetuosity, as Alexander fought, and very often sit down and cry as heartily, upon being out spelt [*sic*], as Cesar did, when at Alexanders sepulchre he recollected that the Macedonian Hero had conquered the World before his Age. At one Table sits Mr. Insipid foppling and fluttering, spinning his whirligig, or playing with his fingers as gaily and wittily as any frenchified coxcomb brandishes his Cane or rattles his snuff box. At another sitts [*sic*] the polemical Divine, plodding and wrangling in his mind about Adam's fall in which we sinned all as his primmer has it. In short my little school like the great World, is made up of Kings, Politicians, Divines, L.D., Fops, Buffoons, Fidlers, Sychophants, Fools, Coxcombs, chimney sweepers, and every other Character drawn in History or seen in the World. Is it not then the highest Pleasure my Friend to preside in this little World, to bestow the proper applause upon virtuous and generous Actions, to blame and punish every vicious and contracted Trick, to wear out of the tender mind every thing that is mean and little, and fire the new born soul with a noble ardor and Emulation. The World affords no greater Pleasure [John Adams (1851), 2:9–10; and John Adams (1961), 1:13–14].

In 1845, when Worcester's Classical and English High School was founded, visitors came from all over the state to see the new building on Walnut Street, examine its facilities, and observe the school in operation. Soon the local newspapers began bragging about the school's reputation, claiming that "A gentleman familiarly acquainted with the Boston Schools, said to us that this was unquestionably the best school in the State." The fact that a claim like this could even be made, whether it was an exaggeration or not, did nothing to hurt the town's case for becoming a city. And there is no doubt about one thing. Worcester's leaders always recognized the central importance of a good school system. In his inaugural address to the city council on April 17, 1848, Mayor Lincoln proclaimed: "There is no better, and I might well say, there is no *other* assurance for the enjoyment of the blessings of good government, of civil and religious liberty, of personal and national independence, than in the cultivated intelligence of the people." According to the new city's first mayor, the city of Worcester had inherited an excellent school system. "It is cause for unreserved congratulation this day," said Lincoln, "that little remains to be done, in reference to the Public Schools, but to continue and carry out the excellent arrangements, which are already in a course of successful and satisfactory operation." Mayor Lincoln's basic views on education were expressed again by Mayor James B. Blake on January 3, 1870: "The character, the intelligence, and the moral and social standing of our people of to-day, draw its strength and power and permanence from the schools of twenty years ago; the welfare of this community and the perpetuity of our institutions in the distant future, depend chiefly upon the vitalizing power and the intellectual status of the schools which are now placed in our hands for care and support." Blake, a native of Boston, was a member of the Church of the Unity with the Thayers (Chasan, 103–25).

James Fitzgerald Chaflin was the principal of the high school in 1865, and probably encouraged the development of baseball at the school. Back in his student days at Amherst, in 1859, after Higginson's article had appeared in the *Atlantic Monthly,* Chaflin had captained the baseball team and organized the first college baseball game with Williams. Besides the high school, there were 75 public schools in the city, instructed and managed by 85 women and 7 men. Forty years after the founding of the Round Hill School, Bancroft's influence was at work as physical education was becoming a permanent part of the curriculum: "Gymnastic exercises have been introduced into some of the public schools," according to Howland's directory, "and will doubtless prove useful and healthful" (Amherst College Archives; and Howland, 36).

There were also many private schools. "The College of the Holy Cross," founded in 1842 and the first institution of higher learning in the city, "is situated on the beautiful eminence formerly known as Pakachoag Hill, now as Mt. St. James, and is designed exclusively for the education of young persons of the Catholic faith. It has recently received a charter from the Legislature of Massachusetts, and consequently enjoys equal rights with the other colleges of the State" (Howland, 36–37).

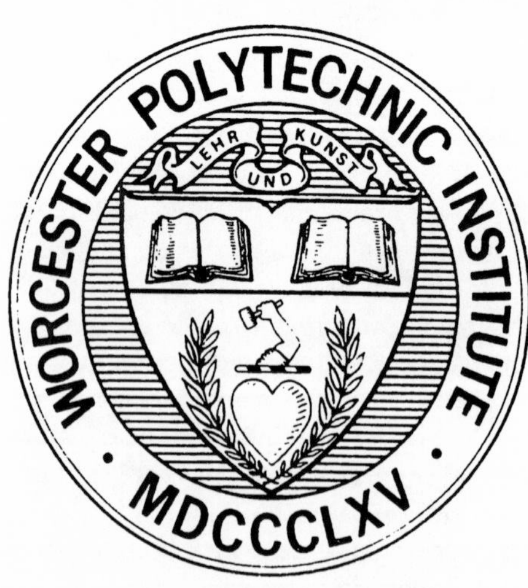

Worcester Polytechnic Institute seal (courtesy of the Worcester Polytechnic Institute Archives).

Worcester Polytechnic Institute, (WPI), founded in 1865, may well have been one of the main reasons why the Thayers moved their family back to Worcester. In the spring of 1865 John Boynton of Templeton placed in the hands of David Whitcomb of Worcester the sum of $100,000, to be used for the endowment of a school of industrial science, which should be located in Worcester, but open to citizens of the whole county of Worcester, on the condition that the people of Worcester should furnish a suitable location and buildings for the proposed school, ready for occupancy before May 1,

1867. A word or two on this remarkable man. Boynton was born on May 31, 1791, in Mason, New Hampshire. He worked with his father as a farmer until his thirtieth year in 1821, and then moved to New Ipswich, Massachusetts, and began to manufacture tinware. Soon afterward he moved to Templeton, Massachusetts. In a public letter of May 1, 1865, Boynton provided that "The aim of this School shall ever be the instruction of youth in those branches of education not usually taught in the public schools, which are essential and best adapted to train the young for personal life; and especially that such as are intending to be Mechanics, or Manufacturers, or Farmers." The students were to be residents of the county, without restriction of sex or color, between the ages of 14 and 21. The people of Worcester responded to this generous gift by immediately subscribing $50,000. Ichabod Washburn also subscribed $10,000 to erect a suitable machine shop, and Stephen Salisbury gave the institute a splendid lot of over five acres of ground, bounded on Salisbury and Waldo streets, known as Salisbury's Woods, worth at least $10,000 more. While Boynton lived, the trustees of the institute respected his desire to avoid personal distinction in his new foundation, but after his death in 1867 they named the principal building for instruction Boynton Hall, to perpetuate the name of the founder of the institute, and to enlarge the good influences of his wise and liberal benefaction (Howland, 37–39; and WPI Archives).

The seal of the institute was designed by Professor Alonzo S. Kimball, popular head of physics and electrical engineering, and adopted by the board of trustees in 1888. Kimball's seal included two open books, an arm and a hammer, a heart, and a banner with the German moto *Lehr Und Kunst* (School and Skill). Herbert F. Taylor described the symbolism of these items in *Seventy Years of the Worcester Polytechnic Institute*: "The heart is from the seal of the City of Worcester, the Heart of the Commonwealth. The German motto was selected to indicate the combination of academic learning, also symbolized by the books, and practical arts, symbolized by the arm and hammer. The latter device was adopted at the opening of the Institute in 1868" (Roger Perry 47). In a way then, the WPI seal was a natural extension of the seal of the city of Worcester, a visible representation of what Worcester has always stood for: a sound mind in a sound body.

CHAPTER 5

The Irish Factor

The first Irish construction crews arrived in Worcester in the late 1820s to build the Blackstone Canal. More came to work on the railroads, and in 1832, when construction began on the Boston and Worcester Railroad, they built the first Catholic church in the state outside of Boston, which happened to be the largest church in town. When it was dedicated, the *Massachusetts Spy* took note of the occasion with a few lines about the town's newest and largest house of worship, and added that sheer size was not the most important measure of religious matters. From the Irish point of view, however, it was a simple expression of their faith, and a sign that they were going to play an important role in the town's future (Powers, 241–48).

Bishop Benedict Fenwick of the diocese of New England assigned Father James Fitton, a 27-year-old native of Boston, to be the pastor. In 1835 Tobias Boland, an Irish contractor acting as the agent for the diocese, purchased 80 acres of land on Bogachoag Hill some two miles south of the village. The next year Boland's crew built a combination classroom and residence hall on the property and a small cottage for Father Fitton. That September St. James Seminary opened to Catholic children as a grammar and secondary school. More property was purchased on the hill, and in 1842 Father Fitton presented Bishop Fenwick with the deed to 60 acres of land. Irish workers built two classroom structures and a dormitory on this land, and in 1843 the College of the Holy Cross opened its doors, the first institution of higher learning in Worcester and the first Catholic college in New England (*ibid.*, 278–80).

While the town's most influential leaders were hospitable and friendly to the Irish, some of the natives regarded the newcomers with suspicion—and for good reason. Powers retells the typical story of John Nazro, a native, who found himself living next door to Michael Healy, a newly arrived Irishman, in 1832. After Healy's arrival Nazro's garden was subjected to daily raids by hens. He assumed the unruly fowls belonged to his new neighbor and when exasperated went over to Healy's house. "Mr. Healy," he said, "if you don't keep your hens out of my garden I will shoot them." "Do as you must, Mr. Nazro," Healy replied; "only send their bodies home to me after you have shot them." Nazro carried out his threat and weeks later found out that his Irish neighbor kept no hens (*ibid.*, 240).

Irish-American leaders became important figures in Worcester's Democratic Party activities during the 1830s. Thomas Magennis and John Russell were elected to the School Committee in 1849, and became the first Catholic Irish to win public office. Henry Murray was the first to win a Common Council position in 1852. Magennis held office for ten years and was the first successful Irish politician in the city. A native of County Mayo, Ireland, he had come to Worcester from the Boston railroad in 1835, operated a railway supply concern, became a storekeeper, and was popular with both Yankees and Irish. In 1852 he sponsored legislation that led to the establishment of a summer teacher-training program that would prepare young girls to be teachers. One of the first graduates of this program was Mary J. Mack, the 17-year-old niece of Magennis, and he appointed her to a vacancy in a Ward Three school. Born on a ship sailing to America in 1835, she had been orphaned in a fire in 1838 and was raised by the Magennis family. In 1852 Miss Mack became the first Irish Catholic public schoolteacher in Worcester and began a remarkable 67-year career in the classroom (*ibid.,* 255–59, 394–98).

These political and educational changes were brought about by the action of Worcester's growing Irish community. In 1845, when the population of the town reached 12,000, there were only 600 Irish Americans. Five years later, after the Great Famine forced waves of Irish men and women to leave the Emerald Isle, this ratio of 1 in 20 changed to 1 in 5 as the Irish increased to 3,300, while the city's population grew to 17,000. By 1850, according to Powers, Sullivan, not Smith or Jones, was the most popular surname in Worcester. The Catholic Irish could be found in every neighborhood in the city, whereas before they were concentrated on the east side which was set off from the remainder of the residential areas of the town by canal, railroad yards, and commercial and manufacturing businesses. Also, by 1850 Worcester's Irish had become factory workers, a change from the earlier occupations in building, heavy construction, and transportation, and they were also entering the medical profession. Four of the seven doctors in Worcester in 1850 were of Irish heritage (*ibid.,* 331–35, 367, 379).

By the time the Thayers settled in Worcester in 1865 the Catholic Irish were the single most numerous group in the city. In 1888, the year Ernest Thayer returned to his hometown and wrote "Casey," the Irish made up almost half of Worcester's population of 70,000 which made it one of the nation's 25 largest cities. Irishmen held 9 of 16 seats on the Common Council, 9 of 24 positions on the school board, and 2 of 8 aldermanic posts. Andrew A. Athy, a native of Galway City who had immigrated to America in 1847 and went from Boston to Worcester in 1848, won a seat on the Common Council in 1865, served for 13 terms, and was also an alderman 6 times. In 1887 he became the first Irishman to run for mayor, challenging the incumbent Mayor Samuel Winslow, father of the well-known ballplayer, and lost his job as well as the race. Winslow, a skate manufacturer, was Athy's employer and fired the upstart Irishman for having the audacity to run against his boss (*ibid.,* 433–40).

Over 15,000 Catholic Irish men and women belonged to the Ancient Order of Hibernians, which held high-spirited picnics and sporting events throughout the 1880s. On June 29, 1880, the *Worcester Gazette* announced that a number of gentlemen interested in the field sports of "Old Ireland" would bid all who might come *Caed Mille Falthe* to a field day at the ball park on July 5. Some temperance advocates objected that such an event would only encourage "riot and drunkenness." But the idea won the support of the Knights of Father Mathew, a temperance organization, and the affair turned out to be a "brilliant success," affording amusement and entertainment to fully 5,000 people. A dancing platform was set up in front of the grandstand, the Father Mathew Band played during much of the day, and bagpipe music abounded. Michael and Mary McGillicuddy probably made the short trip to the park that day from East Brookfield with their seven children, including a 17-year-old son by the name of Cornelius, the Connie Mack of baseball fame. In any event, said the *Gazette,* "Good order was preserved throughout the day, and the sports were honored by the presence of a number of the clergy, and Bishop O'Reilly visited the Park for a few moments during the morning. . . . With so many sports in progress, no one failed of plenty to see, and the entire affair is unanimously complimented" (*ibid.,* 430, 435, 461; Rosenzweig, 76–79; and *WG*, 7/6/1880).

Edward Everett Hale, pastor of Worcester's Church of the Unity, which the Thayers belonged to, was one of the few American writers of the age who raised his voice on behalf of the Irish. He described them as "fugitives from slavery," driven from Ireland by the invasion of modern systems of agriculture, manufacture, and commerce. It was the duty of Americans, he wrote, to "receive the scattered fugitives, give them welcome, absorb them into our own society, and make of them what we can." Instead, the immigrants were being received with a colossal indifference. Hale contrasted this appalling lack of concern for the Irish with the efforts that were made on behalf of the fugitives from Southern slavery:

> Here in Massachusetts we writhe and struggle, really with one heart, lest we return one fugitive who can possibly be saved to Southern slavery; but when there come these fugitives from "Irish Bastilles," as they call them, we tax them first and neglect them afterwards, and provide by statute, and take care, in fact, to send back to Ireland at the public expense, poor creatures who are as entirely fugitives from a grinding slavery as if their flight had been north instead of west;–fugitives, indeed, who come in obedience to an unchanging law of human movement, which we can no more sweep back than could Mrs. Partington sweep back the sea [Hale (1852), 51].

Hale was not just welcoming the Irish out of the kindness of his heart. He had a good practical reason for making the immigrants feel at home, for "when they come in among us, they come to lift us up." There was a divine plan at work in the "Celtic Exodus," as it was called, which would not be denied. "You thought," he tells his readers, "these men were ignorant ditchers and delvers. To your eye they were. But God, when he supplied them, was freeing other laborers for your higher and wider uses, to be your men of ingenuity and of trade, and of letters" (*ibid.*, 51–56; and Merwin, 292).

The problem with the Irish, in Hale's view, was that they were hard to assimilate. Their "clannish spirit," he claimed, "has ruined them in one country, and does a great deal to ruin them in another," and "attracts them to persons who may have the slightest tie of community or neighborhood." Citing an example within his own experience, he says that in the winter of 1850–51 "fourteen persons, fresh from Ireland, came in on the cabin-hospitality of a woman in Worcester, because she was the cousin of one of the party – all of whom had sailed together." To the Irish, of course, it was a simple matter of hospitality. As Hasia R. Diner has remarked, "Paddy is never known to show a cold shoulder to a former friend, or to disown a compatriot, however poor and destitute" (Hale [1852], 33; and Diner, 41).

Thomas Nichols was another writer who was quick to recognize the contributions which the Irish were making to life in America. This native of New Hampshire studied at Dartmouth for a while, did a great deal of traveling, and published his bestseller, *Forty Years of American Life,* in 1864. According to Nichols, the great majority of the Irish people that immigrated to America had lived in Ireland chiefly on potatoes, oatmeal, and buttermilk – on a simple, almost entirely vegetable diet. They did not have the means, even if they had the inclination, to drink much whiskey, or use much tobacco.

"They land in America," Nichols said, "with clear, rosy complexions, bright eyes, good teeth, and good health generally. They are as strong as horses." While the men dug the canals, built the railways, and did the rough work of the cities of the North and West, vast numbers of Irish women found employment as servants in families. And they had their virtues: "They are reasonably honest, and almost invariably chaste. Their kindness and generosity to their relations also appeal to our best sympathies. Thousands – hundreds of thousands of poor Irish girls, working in American kitchens, have sent home the money to maintain their families, or enable them also to emigrate. Millions of dollars have been sent by poor servant girls in America to the land of their birth" (Nichols, 1:70–74).

From all accounts, Irish women were very much in demand. A contributor to *All the Year Round,* a popular magazine edited by Charles Dickens, claimed in 1869 that most of the maids in the hotels of New York, Philadelphia, and Chicago were "buxom Irish girls," and at least nine-tenths of the servants in the private homes in the North and East were from the same nation. They had many fine qualities, and if they were sometimes found "wanting in taste" and a little too generous with the family provisions, this could easily be remedied by the mistress of the house:

> The healthy Irish girl who leaves her own country to seek her fortune beyond the ocean, has in her excellent stuff for the fulfilling of household duties. She is strong, she is quick to learn, she is willing to work, and wherever she is wanting in taste, tutelage by the mistress goes far to mend it. Many family matrons prefer to take a raw emigrant rather than a girl who has been long in America. She is more honest, she is not troubled with too many beaux and acquaintances, she blunders yet is willing to learn, she does her best, and she has not yet acquired those *grand notions* of dress and independence which the Irish girl long resident is apt to have picked up. She is capable of making a really good plain cook, and if she be taken straight from shipboard, may be educated to her mistress's peculiar style of cookery—every mistress, be it said, having a style and dishes of her own [Dickens (1869), 513].

The main trouble with the Irish servant, in this writer's opinion, is that "she is prone to be too social in character, readily makes acquaintances, and holds high carnival in the kitchen with the family provisions." Still, with all her shortcomings, "she is nothing less than invaluable to American households" (*ibid.*).

One of the most remarkable tributes ever paid to the thrift and industry of the Irish came from unexpected quarters when Mark Twain penned "The Widow's Protest" in 1870. Written for *The Galaxy*, a monthly magazine published in New York City, this purported to be the true story of a Mrs. Dan Murphy of Corning, New York, as told to Twain by a banker's clerk who believed it to be one of the saddest things that had ever come to his notice. Dan Murphy, her husband, enlisted as a private in the Civil War, and fought very bravely. What money he made, he never failed to send it home to his wife to bank for him. She was a washer and an ironer, and knew enough by hard experience to keep money when she got it. She didn't waste a penny. On the contrary, she grieved to part with a cent, poor creature, for twice in her hard-working life she had known what it was to be hungry, cold, friendless, sick, and without a dollar in the world, and she had a haunting dread of suffering so again. Well, Dan died from a wound he received in battle, and the boys liked him so much that instead of burying him on the spot, as was the custom, they telegraphed to Mrs. Murphy to see if she would like to have him embalmed and sent home. Mrs. Murphy jumped to the conclusion that it would only cost two or three dollars to embalm her dead husband, so she telegraphed back at once, "Yes." It was at the "wake" that the bill for embalming arrived, and was presented to the widow. As Twain described it, "She uttered a wild, sad wail, that pierced every heart, and said: "Sivinty-foive dollars for stoofin' Dan, blister their sowls! Did thim divils suppose I was goin' to stairt a Museim, that I'd be dalin' in such expinsive curiassities!" The clerk said there was not a dry eye in the house (Arthur Robert Williams, 227).

The Irish have always been noted for their humor. As several writers have observed, it seems to be an essential characteristic in the sons and daughters of the Emerald Isle, wherever they may be found. From what he had read and heard, and particularly from his own observations made during his travels in New York State, Timothy Dwight was persuaded that they were unsurpassed in "native activity of mind, sprightliness, wit, good nature, generosity, affection, and gratitude." William Carleton, the father of modern Irish literature, elaborated on this Irish characteristic in the introduction to his *Traits and Stories of the Irish Peasantry*: "It has been said that the Irish, notwithstanding a deep susceptibility of sorrow are a light-hearted people; and this is strictly true. . . . Fun, or the love of it, to be sure, is an essential principle in the Irish character; and nothing that can happen, no matter how solemn or how sorrowful it may be, is allowed to proceed without it." In 1864 Thomas Nichols admitted that the Irish waiters he had met on the Mississippi "blunder a little, but they are invincibly good-natured, and have the merit of good intentions, plenty of mother wit, and an ever-amusing faculty of blarney" (Timothy Dwight [1969], 3:375; Carleton, xxiii–xxiv; and Nichols, 2:10).

At its best, Irish humor has a touch of deep feeling mixed with the merriment. "In essence," as Alfred M. Williams said in 1883, "it is an attempt to encounter or to relieve misfortune by gayety, and the deep feeling is always struggling through the jest." To a certain extent, of course, this form of humor is common to all races and nationalities, though the Irish have perhaps been blessed with a little more than their share. Brought to America, and combined with baseball, it set the right tone for the strangely moving ballad of "Casey at the Bat" (Alfred M. Williams, 61).

CHAPTER 6

George Bancroft and the Round Hill Legacy

On October 3, 1890, George Bancroft celebrated his ninetieth birthday. One of the letters he received on that memorable occasion was from Robert C. Winthrop, a former senator and president of the Massachusetts Historical Society, who summed up Brancroft's life work in one line: "You have both written the History of your Country, and made yourself a part of it." As his first biographer, Mark A. De Wolfe Howe said long ago, no one fit that description better than Bancroft (Howe, 1:1).

The man chiefly remembered as the "Father of American History" was a man of action as well as a man of letters. Whether he was teaching, preaching, founding the Round Hill School, writing and delivering speeches, socializing in Boston, New York, and Washington, founding the Naval Academy, directing the Pacific Fleet during the Mexican War, or representing the United States at the courts of Great Britain and Germany, Bancroft was as much at home in the world as he was in his own private study. His vitality and longevity were astonishing, as his lifetime spanned almost the whole of the nineteenth century. And he was a central figure in the development of physical education, history, politics, and sports in America during that century.

This unique and multitalented man has naturally presented some problems for his biographers. What Bancroft said late in life of his old friend Oliver Wendell Holmes could easily be turned around and applied to Bancroft himself: "He is like a man who has three or four estates of land lying out of sight of each other, and none but his friends take cognizance of the vastness of his possessions." Or, better yet, "his merits are as stars in different constellations, which no telescope can bring into one field of vision" (*ibid.*, 2:301).

Fortunately, there is only one field we need to get a focus on for this book: the baseball field. "The Game of Base Ball," as Henry Chadwick said in 1860, owed much of "the high position which it now occupies, as the leading game of out-door sports," to the claim that it was "important and necessary as a branch of physical education." As a teacher, writer, and cofounder of the physical education movement in America, Bancroft was a major influence on public opinion regarding sports in general, and helped to create the conditions in which baseball grew and prospered and finally gained recognition as our national game (Chadwick, 31).

Born in Worcester on October 3, 1800, George Bancroft was the fourth son and the eighth of 13 children of the Rev. Aaron Bancroft and his wife, Lucretia Chandler. Aaron Bancroft was the author of the popular *Life of Washington* (1807), one of the founders of the American Antiquarian Society (1812), and the first president of the American Unitarian Association (1825). As George recalled him in 1865, his father was "a bright and cheerful man; fulfilling the duties of life with courage and hearty goodwill; naturally given to hospitality, and delighting in the society of intelligent friends, who were attracted by the ready sympathy of his nature, his lively and varied conversation, and the quickness and clearness of his perceptions." Writing to Holmes 20 years later, Bancroft credited his long life partly to his constitution, and partly to the treatment he had received as a child. "My father," he said, "suffered me to go out in all weather; to play in the snow; to meet the extremest cold with scanty preparation for it; to play abroad in the summer's pouring rain as well as in sunshine; and in the late summer and autumn to devour all the fruit I could honestly come by." In the same letter to Holmes, Bancroft said that his father taught all of his children never to believe anything on authority, not even to accept his own religious opinions without first searching to learn the grounds for accepting them as right. He taught "that intelligence is better than wealth, that the great end was *vitam impendere vero*, to search for the truth with a mind wholly free from bias" (Howe, 1:6; 2:303).

Lucretia Bancroft, as George remembered her in one of his letters, was "remarkable for benevolence, very uncommon gifts of mind, and playful cheerfulness." In another letter he describes her as "a woman who excelled for largeness of heart; if she saw want it was a necessity to her to relieve it; a woman of feeling not of metaphysics, she had an inimitable power of narration, and a quick sprightliness of manner and mind to the last day of her life." His only regret was that, "full as she was of vivacity, and loving me with an intensity of affection, she could, from the excessive burden of her household affairs, give little of her time to me the eighth of her thirteen children. I left home for Exeter in my eleventh year, and as it were never to return to my father's house except in vacations, having been a rover all my life" (*ibid.*, 1:7; 2:304).

Besides the fact that Lucretia Bancroft had 12 other children to look after, another reason why George may not have seen that much of her was that he was hardly ever at home. In the summertime he used to go rafting down a river near Worcester with one of his friends, Stephen Salisbury, whose mother took a dim view of their activities. Mrs. Salisbury was a lady of great dignity, very precise in her manners and ways of life, and apparently did not approve of Bancroft's unconventional upbringing. Bancroft told one of Stephen Salisbury's cousins in 1889,

> I was a wild boy . . . and your aunt did not like me. She was always fearful that I would get her son into bad ways, and still more alarmed lest I should some day be the cause of his being brought home dead. There was a river, or piece of water, near Worcester, where I used to beguile young Salisbury, and having constructed a rough sort of raft he and I would pass a good deal of our playtime in aquatic amusements, not by any means unattended with danger. Madam's remonstrances were all in vain, and she was more and more confirmed in the opinion that I was a "wild, bad boy." However, nothing serious beyond an occasional wetting ever occurred, yet I never rose in her estimation, and a "wild boy" I continued to be up to manhood [Tuckerman, 230].

After some schooling in Worcester, in 1811 George was sent to the Exeter Academy in New Hampshire to prepare for college. After two years at Exeter, where the principal was Dr. Benjamin Abbot, one of the truly great teachers of the time, he entered Harvard, and graduated with the class of 1817. Encouraged by Edward Everett, his Latin tutor at Harvard, Bancroft then went to Germany to continue his studies in theology and philology, receving a Ph.D. and M.A. from the University of Göttingen in 1820. Returning to America in 1822, he became a tutor in Greek at Harvard. After a year of teaching there he left the college and, with Joseph Cogswell another Harvard instructor, founded the Round Hill School at Northampton, Massachusetts, where they taught modern languages along with the classics, and pioneered the physical education movement in America (Gerber, 245–51; and Handlin, 92–96).

Bancroft's work at Round Hill was quite an accomplishment in itself, but it was only one of his many projects. In 1823, the year the school opened, he published a book of poems, most of which he had written in Europe. In the next few years he edited and translated several textbooks for use at Round Hill and other American schools, reviewed the works of Goethe and Schiller for the *North American Review,* and wrote several other articles for that magazine and the *American Quarterly Review.* Politics also interested him. On June 4, 1826, the fiftieth anniversary of the Declaration of Independence, Bancroft gave a speech in Northampton calling for "a democracy, a determined, uncompromising democracy," and hailing Thomas Jefferson as America's great statesman, "whose principles are identified with the character of our government, and whose influence with the progress of civil liberty throughout the world." In this early speech he expressed the faith in democratic equality and divine guidance which characterized him through his long life: "The popular voice is all powerful with us; this is our oracle; this, we acknowledge, is the voice of God" (Nye, 87–98; Canary, 134–35; and Schlesinger, 159).

In 1830 Bancroft left the Round Hill School and began working on his monumental *History of the United States,* which appeared between 1834 and 1875, in ten volumes, and established the author as "The Father of American

History." Within a year the first volume had found its way into nearly one-third of the homes of New England, and the author's name was well on its way to becoming a household word. In the preface Bancroft stated his belief that "the fortunes of a nation are not under the control of a blind destiny," and declared that his object would be to "follow the steps by which a favoring Providence, calling our institutions into being, has conducted the country to its present happiness and glory." As Dwight had done in his *Travels*, Bancroft attached great significance to Berkeley's famous prophecy, and had this line engraved on the cover of volume one: "Westward the star of empire takes its way." As Russel B. Nye has observed, Bancroft's *History of America* is the history of "a divinely-inspired state destined to bring safely into the world as an example to mankind a government founded in freedom and grounded in liberty, a nation built on a belief in the worth and dignity of the common man" (Nye, 102–3).

Bancroft's political writings and speeches brought him to the attention of President Van Buren, who appointed him as collector of the port of Boston in 1837. As a delegate from Massachusetts he attended the National Democratic Convention of 1844, and played an active part in the nomination of James K. Polk for the presidency. His historical teachings provided the background and much of the rationale for the doctrine of "Manifest Destiny," a term coined by his friend John L. O'Sullivan for the *Democratic Review* in 1845. Appointed secretary of the navy by President Polk, Bancroft founded the Naval Academy at Annapolis in 1845. When the Mexican War began, Bancroft acted swiftly to carry out Polk's policy in the Pacific, directing Commander Sloat to occupy San Francisco and other important California ports, and at the same time urging him to maintain the friendly relations which had long existed between the Mexicans and Americans in the province, encouraging the former to adopt a position of neutrality. This enlightened course of action helped to bring the war to a civilized conclusion, and paved the way for California's admission to the Union in 1850 (Sloane, 480–82; Howe, 1:275–94; and Handlin, 214–19).

Preferring a foreign post to a seat in the cabinet, Bancroft was appointed as U.S. minister to Great Britain in September 1846, and served in that position for 3 years. Returning to America, he settled in New York and lived there for the next 18 years, working primarily on his *History*. He also published his *Literary and Historical Miscellanies* in 1855. In the middle of a turbulent decade, on the eve of the Civil War, Bancroft took for one of the main themes of his book the unity of the human race. It may be found in one form in "The Office of the People in Art, Government, and Religion," a speech he had delivered at Williams College in 1835. "There is a *spirit in man*," he said, not in the privileged few, but in each member of the human family. This spirit is the guide to truth, that places us in connection with the world of intelligence and the decrees of God. In this respect there is no difference between the man of refinement and the savage.

> "I am a man," said Black Hawk nobly to the chief of the first republic in the world; "I am a man," said the barbarous chieftain, "and you are another." . . . You cannot discover a tribe of men, but you also find the charities of life, and the proofs of spiritual existence. Behold the ignorant Algonquin deposit a bow and quiver by the side of the departed warrior; and recognise his faith in immortality. See the Comanche chieftain, in the heart of our continent, inflict on himself severest penance; and reverence his confession of the needed atonement for sin. . . . And shall we reverence the dark-skinned Caffre? Shall we respect the brutal Hottentot? You may read the right answer written on every heart. It bids me not despise the sable hunter, that gathers a livelihood in the forests of Southern Africa. All are men. When we know the Hottentot better, we shall despise him less [Bancroft, 408–15].

The theme is further developed in "The Necessity, the Reality and the Promise of the Progress of the Human Race," a speech he delivered to the New York Historical Society in 1854, the fiftieth anniversary of its founding. On this occasion Bancroft asserted the essential goodness and equality of man: "He alone," of all other classes of animal life, "has the faculty so to combine thought with affection, that he can lift up his heart and feel not for himself only, but for his brethren and his kind. Every man is in substance equal to his fellow man." The essay is notable for a clear statement of Bancroft's belief in the progress of the human race:

> The love for others and for the race is as much a part of human nature as the love of self; it is a common instinct that man is responsible for man. . . . The good time is coming, when humanity will recognise all members of its family as alike entitled to its care; when the heartless jargon of over-production in the midst of want will end in a better science of distribution; when man will dwell with man as with his brother; when political institutions will rest on the basis of equality and freedom [*ibid.*, 481–83, 514].

As the Civil War approached, Bancroft's opposition to slavery and to any dissolution of the Union made him a strong supporter of President Lincoln and his policies. On February 12, 1866, he delivered his "Memorial Address on the Life and Character of Abraham Lincoln" in the House of Representatives. The next year, when President Andrew Johnson offered him the post of U.S. minister to Berlin, he accepted the opportunity to return to the country which had extended a warm hospitality to him as a young student half a century before. In 1874 he returned to America, settling this time in Washington, and began work on a centenary edition of his *History*. This appeared in 1876–79, and was followed by his *History of the Formation of the Constitution of the United States* in 1882; "The Author's Last Revision" of his *History*, including the new material on the Constitution, in 1885; and a biography of Martin Van Buren in 1889. Working practically up to the last day of his life, Bancroft died in Washington on January 17, 1891, and was laid to rest four days later in Worcester's Rural Cemetery. On the western side of the granite monument marking the spot are the following words: "Historian of America, he made it the high purpose of a life which nearly spanned a century to show her part in the advancement of man, and from the rare resources of his genius, his learning and his labor to ennoble the story of her birth" (Roe [1900], 180).

The Round Hill School

Founded by George Bancroft and Joseph Cogswell at Northampton, Massachusetts, in 1823, the Round Hill School was the first in the country to recognize physical education as a regular part of the course of instruction. Although it lasted only 11 years (1823–34), its influence was enormous. At one time there were nearly 150 boys attending the school, sons of some of the most cultivated and wealthy parents in the country, and they came from almost every state in the Union. Fifty years after its founding the school was still being spoken of with enthusiasm by men who had "played under the chestnut trees there, and looked up with respect and affection to the scholarly masters who governed them." In 1923, the centennial of its founding, George Cheever Shattuck called Round Hill a great school far ahead of its time, an institution that had left seed which, after many years, "took deep root and bore fruit abundantly" (Scudder [1877], 704–5; Shattuck, 205–9; and Mabel Lee, 36–38).

In their *Prospectus of a School to Be Established at Round Hill, Northampton, Massachusetts,* which was signed June 20, 1823, Bancroft and Cogswell announced that they were going to open the school in the fall. The site had been chosen for its salubrity, beauty, and its convenient location, as stages passed from Boston, Hartford, and Albany in less than a day, and transportation to New York was direct and constant. The teachers promised parents of prospective pupils that their purpose was "to preserve the health and improve the morals and the mental powers of their sons." A liberal education would be offered with much attention to the classics. The curriculum emphasized languages, both ancient and modern, as French, German, Italian, and Spanish were to be taught along with Greek and Latin. Students would also study reading, writing, mathematics, geography, history, moral philosophy, composing, elocution, rhetoric, and practical subjects like bookkeeping and surveying. In addition to the regular course of instruction, the directors assured the public that sports and gymnastics would be a regular and important part of the program: "We would also encourage activity of body, as the means of promoting firmness of constitution and vigour of mind, and shall appropriate regularly a portion of each day to healthful sports and gymnastic exercises" (Bancroft and Cogswell [1823], 3–17).

On October 1, 1823, the Round Hill School opened its doors with 15 boarders and 10 day students. The grounds originally covered about 50 acres, with three buildings on the site. In 1825, to accommodate the increasing number of students, the directors purchased an additional 35 acres, built another building, and constructed an outdoor gymnasium under the supervision of Charles Beck, an immigrant from Germany, who became an instructor of Latin and gymnastics that year. The enrollment jumped to 40 by the summer of 1825, went over 100 by the next summer, and peaked at almost 150 in 1827, but after that the number of students was limited to 100. In 1826 the *American Journal of Education* reported that there were ten instructors besides the 112 boys and two directors. The instructor of mathematics at this time was Cornelius C. Felton, who later became president of Harvard, and served as the first president of the Normal Institute of Physical Education, founded in Boston in 1861 (Round, 437; Gerber, 246–47; and Leonard, 233–34, 256).

A contemporary report in the *United States Literary Gazette* of February 15, 1825, provides an interesting record of the progress Bancroft and Cogswell were making in the early days of their Round Hill experiment, and describes a typical day in the life of a student. Noting that the establishment of "this novel institution" had awakened considerable interest in Northampton and elsewhere, the *Gazette* said that it seemed "worthy of notice and attention." Bancroft and Cogswell, the founders, had traveled and studied extensively in Great Britain and on the continent, and borrowed some ideas from the most diverse sources: one principle from the schools at Berlin, another from Hofwyl, a third from Edinburgh, and so forth. They were aware that a mere imitation of a foreign model would never succeed, and were attempting to adapt all things to the United States. Two circumstances were very much in their favor. First, they were responsible only to the public, not to any tribunal or board; they "gladly acknowledge[d] the value of the public opinion, and in general the justice of the public voice." Second, they were favored by their situation; they lived "in the midst of a healthy, moral, and thriving population, and are surrounded by scenery of great beauty, and of a cheerful character. All this has a favourable influence on the forming mind." A full schedule of work and play kept the students busy and out of trouble. They rose in winter at 6:00 A.M., began the day with devotional exercises, and were busy with teaching and study until 8:00 A.M., at which time came breakfast. "They then engage in some vigorous exercise till nine," when the season for intellectual labor again commenced, and continued till noon. "Two hours are allowed for exercise, dining, and for rest," when, at 2:00 P.M., studies were resumed, and continued till 4:00 P.M. An hour and a half was then employed in "the sports and exercises suited to the season." The evening meal was over by 6:00 P.M., when some time was passed attending to declamations, and then about an hour and a half was given to study and the exercises of devotion. The instructors and pupils spent a few moments around the fire, and the boys were sent to bed at 8:30 P.M. "As for health," the story concluded, "they have as yet had no sickness; and now, out of forty boys, there is not one who does not enjoy firm health, though many were received in a weak state of body" (School, 332).

Bancroft and Cogswell elaborated on the physical education theme in *Some Account of the School for the Liberal Education of Boys,* a circular published in 1826 and reprinted the following year in the *American Journal of Education.* They recalled the educational ideals of ancient Greece, admitted the difficulty of introducing them into a modern school, and discussed the methods and objects of the Round Hill program in some detail:

> It may be impossible to engraft [*sic*] on any modern nation a system of physical education, corresponding to that which prevailed in ancient Greece. But something must be done. Food, sleep, and exercise must be regulated, purity protected, life guarantied [*sic*] against casualties, and temperance and exercise be set, even in the dawn of existence, to keep watch over health. Games and healthful sports, promoting hilarity and securing a just degree of exercise are to be encouraged. Various means of motion are to be devised and applied; and, where these are regularly used, every thing is done to assist nature in strengthening the youthful constitution. If in addition to regularity in the use of exercise, the kinds of it are so arranged, that the several powers of the body may successively be brought into action and gradually led to greater exertions, it will not be long before the physical being assumes a new appearance, and in addition to the acquisition of a control of the body, beneficial results will be visible in general industry, deportment, and morals. The attempt, therefore, to provide the various means for gymnastic exercises, merits to be encouraged; and whether the methods are by turns strange or common, complicated or simple, the best that are known should be employed.

Commenting on the physical education program at Round Hill, the editor of the *American Journal of Education* said in 1827: "The success of this department is well known to those parents whose sons have spent even a few months at the school, and particularly in the case of some pupils whose health has been in a short time restored from a state of weakness" (Bancroft and Cogswell [1827], 462; and Hyde, 44).

In the summer of 1825 Duke Bernard of Saxe-Weimar-Eisenach visited the United States to meet with John Adams, inspect the new gym at the Round Hill School, and travel on the newly completed Erie Canal. Landing at Boston, he proceeded to Northampton where he met Bancroft, Cogswell, and Beck, and was given a tour of the grounds. The duke was very impressed by the attention being given to gymnastic exercises in the New World. As he remarked in his *Travels,* "The gymnastic exercises, for which a place is provided in the woods, with the necessary apparatus, form a principle part of the instruction of this seminary" (Bernard, 55).

Although Bancroft and Cogswell put more of an emphasis on the gymnastics program, their students were more likely to remember baseball and the other "healthful sports" popular at Round Hill. According to John Murray Forbes, who entered the school with the first class of students in 1823: "The boys were taught to ride, had skating and swimming in their seasons, and wrestling, baseball, and football; and, during the summer, excursions on the 'ride and tie' plan, of sometimes over a hundred miles and back, were undertaken, accompanied by Mr. Cogswell, who was himself a great walker." Another Round Hiller, Dr. George Cheyne Shattuck, who attended the school from 1825 to 1827, recalled that "Base-ball, hockey, and foot-ball" were the main sports played in his day, and added that "developing the bodily powers and strengthening the constitution were there first recognized as of great importance in the education of boys." Shattuck later founded St. Paul's Academy in Concord, New Hampshire, taking the Round Hill School for his model. As things turned out, a St. Paul product played an important part in the first publication of "Casey at the Bat": a young man from California by the name of William Randolph Hearst (Hughes, 43–46; Hartwell, 22; Bradlee, 277–78; and Hyde, 44–47).

The Round Hill School was not the first school where baseball was played, but it was the first to officially recognize the importance of sports and gymnastics for the education of the young and to incorporate them into a regular program of physical education. As Ronald Smith has recently discovered, Harvard students were playing the game at least as early as the 1730s. John Adams, who remembered playing a game called "Bat and Ball" during his boyhood days in Braintree, Massachusetts, near Boston, was probably one of the best old-time ballplayers at Harvard, judging from the amount of time he spent practicing the game. As he wrote in his autobiography, "My enthusiasm for Sports and Inattention to Books, alarmed my Father, and he frequently entered into conversation with me upon the subject." One of these father-son talks has been re-created for us by Catherine Drinker Bowen in her fictionalized biography of Adams: "Mr. Adams knew all at once that if his son would put one half the effort into his Latin that he put into his ball practice, he would be in Harvard in no time. . . . Suddenly, John hit the ball a tremendous crack; it sailed across the field in a straight, low, beautiful line. John, his face radiant, turned to his father. Just in time, Mr. Adams checked the words *Well done.* 'John,' he said, 'put down your bat'." (Ronald Smith, 12; Old, 332; John Adams [1961], 3:261–62; Bowen, 50, 619; and Cleaver 16.)

Daniel Webster played ball during his student days at Dartmouth in the late 1790s. According to one of his classmates, he never required as much time for his studies as most other students, and put his free time to good use: "He took time for exercise and recreation, and joined in the sports and amusements common to students at that time," which included "the game of ball and other athletic exercises." Also in the 1790s Parson Peabody, principal of the Atkinson Academy in Atkinson, New Hampshire, recorded spending ninepence for a ball for John Adams Smith, grandson of President John

Adams. The game was also popular at the Deerfield Academy in Deerfield, Massachusetts, which in 1810 passed a rule against playing ball too close to the buildings: "No Pupil shall be permitted to play at Ball, or any other sport or diversion, in or near the Academy, by which it may be exposed to injury, on penalty of being fined, not less than six cents, for the first offense, and suspended or expelled if the offense is often repeated." By comparison, the people of Cooperstown, New York, could be fined *one dollar* for playing ball in the main streets of the village. Hugh MacDougall, a local historian and Cooper scholar, has recently discovered this notice in the *Otsego Herald* of June 6, 1816: "*Be it ordained,* That no person shall play at Ball in Second or West street, in this village, under a penalty of one dollar, for each and every offence." As MacDougall pointed out, this law is part of the background for Cooper's *Home as Found.* The full significance of his discovery may be gathered from the fact that the intersection of Second and West streets (now named Main and Pioneer) is right next to Doubleday Field, where Abner Doubleday began his baseball crusade right after the publication of Cooper's novel (Webster, 1:66; Holliman, 65; Marr, 160; Deerfield Academy Archives; MacDougall, 38; and Jim Moore [1993], 15–19).

"Bat-ball," a primitive form of baseball, was popular at the Phillips Exeter Academy during Bancroft's student days (1911–13). Alpheus S. Packard, one of his classmates, recalled that the outdoor amusements at Exeter, besides walks in the village and its environs, were "football in autumn, skating on 'Little River' in its season, and bat-ball in the spring." From Exeter Packard went to Bowdoin College in 1812, graduated in 1816, became a tutor there in 1819, was made an officer of the college in February of 1824, and taught there for more than 60 years. Bancroft had a high regard for him, and said in 1883: "Strong and healthy, sober-minded and industrious, and in his studies very successful, he bore a high character every way; he was at home on the play-ground as well as at his books." Packard may have been responsible for the Bowdoin policy of encouraging baseball when Longfellow was a student at the Maine school. On April 11, 1824, the poet wrote to his father,

> ...within the last week, the Government, seeing that something must be done to induce the students to exercise, recommended a game of ball now and then, which communicated such an impulse to our limbs and joints, that there is nothing now heard of, in our leisure hours, but ball – ball – ball. I cannot prophecy with any degree of accuracy concerning the continuance of this rage for play, but the effect is good, since there has been a thorough-going reformation from inactivity and torpitude [Cunningham, 166, 232; Crosbie, 233; Marr, 160; Longfellow, 1:87; Seymour (1990), 131–32; Exeter Archives; and Bowdoin Archives].

A description of the simple equipment used in the game of bat and ball has been found in the diary of William Bentley (1759–1813). Born in Boston on June 22, 1759, he entered Harvard in 1773, graduated in 1777, and from that year to his death in 1813 served as pastor of the Second Congregational Church in Salem. Under the date of April 28, 1791, he writes that now is the time for "Bat & Ball. The Ball is made of rags covered with leather in quarters & covered with double twine, sewed in Knots over the whole, while the Bat is from 2 to 3 feet long, round on the back side but flatted considerably on the face, & round at the end, for a better stroke." Writing in the 1850s, Dr. Alfred L. Elwyn describes the game of "bat and ball" in some detail, and says that it was probably "a game of Yankee invention." From his account, it was an early form of baseball:

> Sides were chosen, not limited to any particular number, though seldom more than six or eight; the toss up of a cent decided who should have the first innings. The individual who was first chosen, of the side that was in, took the bat and his position at a certain assigned spot. One of his adversaries stood at a given distance in front of him to throw the ball, and another behind him to throw back the ball if it were not struck, or in any way to assist in getting the advantage of his opponents. After the ball was struck, the striker was to run; stones were placed some thirty or forty feet apart, in a circle, and he was to touch each one of them, till he got back to the front from which he started. If the ball was caught by any of the opposite party who were in the field, or, if not caught, was thrown at and hit the boy who was trying to get back to his starting place, their party was in; and the boy who caught the ball, or hit his opponent, took his bat. A good deal of the fun and excitement consisted in the ball not having been struck to a sufficient distance to admit of the striker running round before the ball was in the hands of his adversaries. If his successor struck it, he must run, and take his chance, evading the ball as well as he could by falling down or dodging it. While at the goals he could not be touched; only in the intervals between them [Bentley, 1: 253–55; Dulles, 33; and Elwyn, 18–19].

The Round Hill School was a major influence not just on the development of baseball but on the physical education movement in general. In 1825, a few months after the Round Hill gymnasium was built, Dr. John Collins Warren, Daniel Webster's family physician and a professor of anatomy and surgery at the Harvard Medical School, began a drive to establish gymnasiums for Harvard students and the Boston public. Webster lent his name to the Boston project and gave it his wholehearted support. Writing to Warren on November 17, 1825, the senator told the doctor he was "highly pleased with the idea of a gymnasium." The subject had often occupied his thoughts, and he believed that the fashion of the times needed to be changed. The ones in charge of education "seem sometimes to forget that the body is a part of the man," and that if the intellect should be cultivated it was equally important, as far as this world is concerned, that there should also be a sound body to hold it in. Webster concluded with a promise to back "any measure calculated to enforce on the rising generation a sense of the invaluable advantages to temperance and exercise" (Webster, 1:397; and Betts (1968), 794).

The movement soon spread from Boston and Harvard, and small gymnasiums were established in connection with many of the schools, academies, and colleges in the country, both male and female. Aside from the immediate results of improved constitutions, there were long-term benefits of the movement. As Warren said, "the educated part of the community [has] become perfectly well informed of the importance of developing the physical as well as the moral and the intellectual qualities of their sons and daughters." In his 1830 address "On the Importance of Physical Education," he expressed his confidence that if "the spirit of improvement, so happily awakened, continue[s] to animate those concerned in the formation of the young members of society, we shall soon be able, I doubt not, to exhibit an active, beautiful, and wise generation, of which the age may be proud." A few years later that prediction was realized. Dr. Daniel L. Adams, one of Warren's students, was born in Mount Vernon, New Hampshire, on November 14, 1814. He attended Amherst and Yale, graduating from Yale in 1835, and from there went on to the Harvard Medical School, receiving his M.D. in 1838. Adams then moved to New York, joined the Knickerbockers in 1846, and was elected club president in 1847. He guided the club through some difficult times in the next ten years, issued the call for the first baseball convention in 1856, presided over the convention, held in January of 1857, and set the bases at 90 feet. In 1896, at the age of 81, still hale and hearty, Adams was hailed by *The Sporting News* as "The Father of Base Ball." But baseball was just a sideline for him. Like Archie Graham in the classic movie, *Field of Dreams,* Doc's real calling was medicine (Edward Warren, 225–26; John Collins Warren, 51; Voigt, I:8; and Harvard University Archives).

CHAPTER 7

America's First Baseball Heroes

"Mighty Casey has struck out!" The shock and disbelief felt by Mudville fans the day Casey went down swinging is something that any baseball fan can relate to. Thayer's ability to strike the common chord is, of course, one of the main reasons for his ballad's astonishing durability. Commenting on the final words of "Casey" in 1910, Yale athletic director Walter Camp noted that from every little village band who "choose up" on the back lots, to every local town nine and "bush" league, and all the way up to the American and National league teams, there is always some "mighty Casey," the hero of the crowd. Thousands upon thousands of Americans from Maine to California, from Canada to the Gulf of Mexico, were discussing the relative merits of rival players like Wagner and Cobb, until over 20 million people recognized a baseball favorite. All this, according to Camp, had come about within a little more than 50 years. In that time, he wrote, "America has made a game that is typical and characteristic of its people–rapid, exciting, with no long-drawn-out delays, and settled one way or the other with promptness and despatch. It is truly a national game" (Camp [1910], 936).

From the beginning, the people have always demanded that a ballplayer had to have something more than courage and physical ability to become a true hero. The writings of cultural and educational leaders like Bancroft, Everett, Hale, Higginson, Porter, and pioneer baseball writer Henry Chadwick reinforced this belief, and played a major role in shaping the popular attitude toward the game and the players, as well as toward athletes in general. In 1855, for example, Bancroft emphasized that the main object of forming "a healthful body" was to be "the dwelling and the instrument of a healthful mind." Later that year the Rev. A.A. Livermore, pastor of the Unitarian Church in Cincinnati, who, like Bancroft, was a graduate of Exeter and Harvard, wrote an influential article on physical education for the *North American Review.* The "spirit of the age," he said, required schools and colleges to develop the physical and moral as well as the intellectual powers of the students, "since only as all the capacities are harmoniously unfolded can any one of them attain its maximum of strength, usefulness, and happiness." The mission of the schools was clear: "Strength, health, and beauty are to be quarried out of the rich materials stored away in human nature by a bountiful Creator." All that was required was the application of "a normal natural education" to create "new wonders of physical grace and vigor, equal to those of the Grecian time, adorned and sanctified by a coronet of Christian virtues never known to the Porch or the Academy" (Bancroft, 42; and Livermore, 67–69).

William T. Porter also made the connection between moral and physical health in his *Spirit of the Times.* When the first baseball convention was held in January 1857, he predicted that the game "will be more popular than ever, and renewed health, both physically and morally, must accrue to those who practise this healthful out-door exercise." A few months later he reported the amazing growth of the game in Brooklyn, where new clubs were being organized at the rate of almost one per day. "As numerous as are its church spires, pointing the way to heaven," said Porter, "the present prospect indicates that they may be soon outnumbered by the rapidly increasing ball clubs," with the result that Brooklyn, which was already the "City of Churches," was fast becoming the "City of Base Ball Clubs." Observing that baseball clubs "may be considered as important and valuable adjuncts to the church," he concluded: "God speed the churches and ball clubs of our sister city" (*PST* 3/7/, 6/20/1857; Seymour [1960], 24; and Adelman, 278).

Higginson's 1858 article in the *Atlantic Monthly,* together with the English novels of Thomas Hughes and Charles Kingsley, helped to popularize the movement that soon came to be called "Muscular Christianity." The term was coined in an 1857 review of one of Kingsley's novels, but it was Hughes who gave the term currency. His Tom Brown novels were enormously popular: *Tom Brown's School Days* (1857) followed by *Tom Brown at Oxford* (1859–61). The Oxford novel included a fine exposition of "Muscular Christianity," which in the author's view was based on "the old chivalrous and Christian belief, that a man's body is given him to be trained and brought into subjection, and then used for the protection of the weak, the advancement of all righteous causes, and the subduing of the earth which God has given to the children of men" (Worth, 148–53; and Oriard, 10–12).

Chadwick began covering baseball for the *New York Clipper* in 1858 and continued writing about the game in papers, books, and journals for the next 50 years. His lifetime of dedicated work in the field earned him the distinction of being the only professional sportswriter to be elected to the Hall of Fame. Early in his career "Father Chadwick" originated some definite ideas as to what a ballplayer should be, presented them to the public, and, except for the part about playing for money, kept right on preaching these ideals for the rest of his long life. In his sketch of "The Model Base Ball Player," first published in the *Clipper* in 1861, and then in *The Base Ball Player's Book of Reference* in 1866, he gives the "Moral Attributes" of the model player first and then the "Physical Qualifications." Admitting that the model player "is somewhat of a novelty," since "this is an individual not often seen on a ball ground," Chadwick maintains that he nevertheless exists, and gives a "pen photograph" of him in the hope that his admirable example will find many followers (*NYC*, 11/9/1861; Appel and Goldblatt, 66–67; and Adelman, 174).

The principal rule of action of the model baseball player, says Chadwick, is "to comport himself like a gentleman on all occasions," especially on match days. In so doing he abstains from profanity, always has his temper under control, and takes matters good humoredly; or, if angered at all, keeps silent. He never censures errors of play, whether made by a member of his club or by an opponent. He never disputes the decision of an umpire, either by his words or actions; but, when a judgment has been rendered, he silently accepts the decision. He never takes an ungenerous advantage of his opponents, but acts toward them as he would wish them to act toward himself. Regarding the game as a healthful exercise, and a manly and exciting recreation, he plays it solely for the pleasure it affords him, and if victory crowns his efforts in a contest, well and good; but should defeat ensue he is equally ready to applaud the success obtained by his opponents. He never takes a pecuniary interest in a game, for he values its welfare too much to make money an object in playing ball. He abides by every rule of the game, as long as it is legally in force; if it does not meet with his approval he awaits the proper time to have it removed from the statute books. He is prompt and punctual in his attendance; readily obeys the commands of the captain; plays the game throughout, whether winning or losing, to the best of his ability, and retires from the field perfectly content with the result, whatever it may be.

The physical qualifications of the model player are no less demanding: to bat a fast- or slow-pitched ball, hit it near the ground or above the shoulder with equal facility; to command the bat so as to hit the ball either to the right, left, or center field, on the ground, or in the air, as best fits the occasion; and to run swiftly and stop suddenly while making the bases, and run from home to home without becoming distressed. He must be fearless in facing and stopping a strongly batted or thrown ball. He must be able to catch a ball either on the "fly," or bound, either within an inch or two of the ground, or eight or ten feet from it, with either the right or left hand, or both. He must have the ability to run swiftly, to check himself suddenly, and pick up a ball while running; to throw a ball with accuracy of aim a dozen or 100 yards; to occupy any position on the field creditably, but to excel in one position only; and to be familiar, practically and theoretically, with every rule of the game and "point" of play. In conclusion, said Chadwick, the conduct of a model baseball player "is as much marked by courtesy of demeanor and liberality of action as it is by excellence in a practical exemplification of the beauties of the game," since his highest aim is to make every contest in which he is engaged as much "a trial as to which party excels in the moral attributes of the game, as it is one that decides any question of physical superiority."

George Flagg, Harvard's first catcher and captain, is a good example of the type of ballplayer Chadwick was talking about. Born in Millbury, Massachusetts, a couple of miles outside Worcester, on May 2, 1845, Flagg was educated at Phillips Exeter Academy and entered Harvard in 1862. In December of that year he and another freshman, Frank Wright of Auburn, New York, organized the '66 Base Ball Club to play the New York game. As Harvard historian John Blanchard has said, this "laid the corner stone of one of our present major sports," and hastened the ascendancy of the New York over the Massachusetts game among the various clubs of New England (Blanchard, 150).

On October 12, 1864, Flagg and Wright organized Harvard's first varsity baseball club. The first season of play was a memorable one as Harvard won the championship of New England by victories over Williams College at Williamstown, the Lowells of Boston at Boston Common, and the Charter Oaks of Hartford, champions of Connecticut, at Worcester. A home and home series was then arranged with the Brooklyn Atlantics, champions of the United States, with the first game scheduled to be played on Boston Common on September 27, 1865. The Atlantics, led by the famous O'Brien brothers, were the baseball celebrities of the age. They had recently returned from a trip to Washington where they were received by President Johnson at the White House, and were greeted by a crowd of over 10,000 spectators, including Mayor Lincoln, at the Common. The game was close for a while, but the Atlantics won going away, 58–22. A few days later, still smarting from their first defeat, Harvard bounced back to beat the Lowells, 73–37. Flagg scored 11 runs in this game without being put out once, a record that still stands today. But his accomplishments on the field during the road trip to New York the next spring were even more impressive (Blanchard, 152–56; Gipe, 81; and *NYC*, 9/9, 10/7/1865).

Harvard went to Brooklyn to play the return game with the Atlantics on Wednesday, May 30, and followed that up with three games against other clubs in the vicinity. "The object of the Nine," said the *Harvard Advocate*, "is not to win balls and a great reputation; but simply to get practice, and to let it be known that there is such a club as the Harvard in existence." Although the collegians lost all four games on the trip, they won the respect of their opponents and the New York press with their pluck and endurance. Flagg astonished the crowd in the game against the Atlantics by standing up close to the plate despite a series of injuries, and catching three fly-tips from the edge of the bat. "We cannot close our remarks," said one New York daily, "without commending in the highest terms the ability, spirit, and endurance of Flagg. With both hands used up, a battered face, and a half-blinded eye, he stood up to his post as unflinchingly as if he had been Casabianca on the traditional burning deck" (*Harvard Advocate*, 5/25/66; and Blanchard, 156).

The next day, playing against the Eureka Base Ball Club, champions of New Jersey, Flagg was back at his post again, "notwithstanding his hands, which are bandaged in three or four places." On Friday his hands were in "horrible condition," but he caught his third game in three days against the Brooklyn Excelsiors. And on Saturday he was once again behind the plate for the final game of the trip against the New York Actives, taking another fly-tip hot off the bat. Chadwick was greatly impressed. He wrote in the *Clipper*,

> In the late series of matches in which the Harvard College club were engaged, ... no close observer of things could have failed in noticing the many manly characteristics these games developed, and which are requisites to success in every first class game of base ball. The courage shown in boldly facing swiftly pitched, batted or thrown balls; the indomitable pluck manifested by players sustaining severe injuries and yet manfully continuing at their posts of duty despite the pain they suffer; the presence of mind so necessary to take advantage of every weak point in the opposing nine's play, and the judgment and nerve required on exceedingly difficult plays at critical periods of a contest, are all marked features of a first class base ball match.

In the same issue was an ad for "the celebrated Harvey Ross Balls" which proudly announced that "these balls, on account of the careful manner in which they are made and their wonderful elasticity," have been adopted by the Atlantics, the Excelsiors, the Athletics of Philadelphia, the Lowells of Boston, Harvard, "and first class clubs generally." The college boys were in good company (*NYC*, 6/16/1866).

Flagg was one of the first players featured in a series of illustrations of "baseball notabilities" that appeared in the popular New York weekly, *Frank Leslie's Illustrated Newspaper,* in the summer of 1866. The series began on July 21 with cover portraits of John Wildey, president of the National Association of Base Ball Players, and four other officers. Introducing the series, the paper said that "the National Game of Base Ball has unquestionably become an institution of the country," and added that all classes of people were participating in the game, "from the school-boy of twelve to the literateur and divine." Flagg's portrait appeared four weeks later on August 18, accompanied by a write-up that emphasized his "moral attributes" and "gentlemanly style of play," and put him in the same class with men like Franklin and President Grant. A compliment was also paid to the entire Harvard club. During their recent trip to the metropolis, "they most favorably impressed the fraternity here with their skillful exhibitions on the field, and by their quiet, gentlemanly deportment, and manly play generally, they won hosts of admirers, and most creditably sustained the excellent reputation of the fraternity of New England."

According to the *Illustrated News,* had the selection of Harvard's best player been left to a committee of the clubs they played on their recent trip to the metropolis, there is no doubt that Flagg would have received the palm of superiority. His "unassuming manner," "thorough Yankee pluck," "excellent play in his position," and "the fact that he led the averages of his club in the series of games, and made the most difficult fly catches" alone would have led to him being regarded as the outstanding player. But, in addition, if there was one attribute of a first-class ballplayer that merited approbation more than another, it was "that quiet, gentlemanly style of play which characterizes such players as Flagg." Next to those "thoroughly good-humored chaps" like Woods, of the Ekfords, the editor preferred the

> quiet and modest, but plucky and enduring players like Flagg, who, even under the most exciting circumstances, never forget themselves, and who are always to be relied on in critical positions in a closely contested game. Skill in the physical excellencies of the game is worthy of admiration, but to excel in these moral attributes is to achieve a reputation any man might be proud to attain, for it ranks with the highest honor that society can confer on him. It has marked a Grant and a Farragut, and characterized a Franklin, and we are happy to say has been made a feature of the American character, especially of those of eminence hailing from New England.

Among the other players featured in the *Illustrated News* that summer were representatives of baseball clubs from Boston to St. Louis: Adam North, Empires of St. Louis; W.F. Williams, Nationals of Washington; Archie Bush, Knickerbockers of Albany; Frank Pigeon, Eckfords of Brooklyn; C.C. Cummerford, Waterburys of Connecticut; and James D'Wolf Lovett, Lowells of Boston.

Of all the baseball celebrities included in this historic series, Bush is perhaps the best known today. After an outstanding career with the Knickerbockers of Albany, he enrolled at Harvard in the fall of 1867 and took Flagg's place behind the plate. During the four years he was in Cambridge, Harvard played 104 games, and lost only one of them to an amateur nine. In the summer of 1870 Bush led the club on a 43-day tour of the country. In all they played 26 games, winning 18 and losing 8, all but one to professional teams. A notable game was played on July 13, when they defeated the strong Niagara club of Buffalo by the score of 28–14. "The Harvards are a fine gentlemanly lot of men," said a local paper, "and their modest demeanor shows off their admirable playing to the best of advantage." Said another: "Of the individual play of the Harvards we shall not attempt to particularize, as all members of the Nine played so well. We must be pardoned however for making special mention of Mr. A. McC. Bush, captain of the Nine, and the present worthy president of the National Base Ball Association. He is certainly one of the best general ball players that we have ever seen." The next day, after Harvard defeated the Niagaras of Lockport, New York, by the score of 62–4, a local paper reported: "it is needless to say that this result was anticipated on the part of the Niagaras, for their opponents were members of a club whose reputation is comparatively world wide" (*Illustrated News*, 8/11/1866; and Blanchard, 172–76).

On July 18 Harvard arrived at the Union Grounds in Cincinnati to play the professional Red Stockings, billed as "the virtual champions of the world." This was the biggest game of the trip. Cincinnati led 9–3 after three innings, but in the top of the fourth Bush hit a line drive off the head of Asa Brainard, the Red Stockings pitcher, which "rattled" him a bit, as the visitors rallied for 4 runs. Harry Wright came in to pitch the next two innings, but Harvard pounded the crafty reliever for 10 more runs and led 17–11 after six innings. Both teams were "whitewashed" in the seventh, Cincinnati scored one run in the eighth, and trailed 17–12 going into the bottom of the ninth. With two out, one run in, and Brainard on first, "Sweasy drove a terrific ball at [Harvard pitcher] Goodwin's leg, almost breaking it," which bounded beyond third base, giving the Red Stockings runners on first and second. Goodwin has "stretched out for a while, but finally resumed pitching, though with less speed and effect." McVey, the next batter, "struck the ball down near the home plate and it bounded on past Goodwin," who "had but the use of one leg and did not handle the ball for victory." Then, with the bases loaded, and two outs, George Wright went to the bat and cleared the bases with a two-bagger, bringing Cincinnati to within one run of Harvard, 17–16. Wright took third on a wild pitch, and came home with the tying run on a clean base hit. The Harvard hurler, still hobbling around on one leg, gave up four more runs before the final out could be made. Thus ended, in the words of a Cincinnati paper,

> one of the most remarkable games on record; remarkable in the first place for the absolute and thorough beating at bat and in the field of a club of professionals who, on their record, ought to have defeated their amateur opponents easily; and in the second place, as another instance of the star of destiny which has so often brought the Red Stocking Nine out of desperate situations. Nothing but sheer luck in this instance saved them from a defeat, which would have been honorable because administered by the Harvards [*NYC*, 7/30/1870; and Blanchard, 176–78].

Harvard's great game against the famous Red Stockings was the talk of the country for a while, and gave amateur clubs in the cities on the rest of the tour something to think about. After a game in Indianapolis on July 30, won by the Cambridge club, 45–9, the local paper said: "Our boys seemed to regard the Collegians as nine anacondas, who were threatening to devour them whole, and in the field, as well as at the bat, their nerve forsook them and they played like men with fever and ague." On August 13 they defeated the Stars of Brooklyn on their own grounds, 12–6, and this was a club which up to that time was regarded "the amateur champions of the country" (*NYC*, 8/13, 8/20/1870).

Bush was one of the last of the great old-time catchers who played the game close to the bat without a mask, glove, helmet, chest protector, shin guards, or any of the protective equipment considered essential for a catcher today. Cheever Goodwin, his old battery-mate at Harvard, recalled him many years later in these words:

> You know I pitched for Harvard from '69 to '72, and Archie was my catcher for nearly all that time, and when I think of how he held my swift delivery with no gloves, no mask, no protector, and only a small piece of hard rubber in his mouth to protect his teeth, sending the ball back to me often be-smeared with blood from the splits in his hands, with no indication in his play that he knew what a hurt was, my admiration for him is almost idolatry [Seymour (1956), 116].

An article published in the Harvard *Magenta* in 1874, written over the initials "J.F.K.," gives us some indication of how the students in general might have felt about Bush and some of the school's other early baseball heroes. Reporting that the clubhouse and seats on Jarvis Field were about to be torn down, and new ones built, J.F.K. asked: "'How can we bear to leave you,' O boxes, whence we issued forth on those eventful afternoons feeling ourselves able to win victory from whatsoever club might combat us, on whose doors are inscribed the beloved names of Bush, Wells, Eustis, Perrin, White, and others over whose memories we linger with feelings nearly akin to reverence?" His sadness departed when he remembered that the old doors would be carefully preserved and inlaid on the frescoed walls of the future Jarvis Hall (*Magenta,* 11/20/1874).

A number of magazine articles and newspaper reports testified to the widespread popularity of college athletics in the 1870s, and to the influence of the "Muscular Christianity" movement. In 1873, for example, Higginson wrote in *Scribner's Monthly* that the individuals who had introduced physical as well as mental training into the educational system had done their work well, perhaps even too well. "Who is, at present," he asked, "the most popular man in any American college?" Who is followed, boasted of, pointed out in the streets? Whose photograph is sold? "By confession of all, the stroke-oar of the crew, or the captain of the baseball nine." Their names and the names of their colleges were sent flashing over the wires, while the eminent scholar of the university, the brilliant writer, and the able debater had but a local reputation. As a remedy, Higginson proposed that academic scholarships be established, and that students compete for them just as they did in sports. Horace Scudder, writing about Harvard for the same magazine a few years later, said: "The story of this victory or that defeat is told in college with more ardor than attends the recital of intellectual exploits, and the heroes of the class are the athletes." Since 1852, when Harvard and Yale raced on Lake Winnipesaukee, the interest in college athletics had been steadily increasing, helped by "the doctrine of muscular Christianity." B.D. Dwight noted in the *New Englander* that the times were conspicuous for the great and increasing zeal for physical development and prowess among the candidates for professional life, and agreed that "nothing, next to a true and noble character, deserves to be more earnestly sought, during the academic and collegiate courses of study, than permanent bodily vigor." In addition, he believed that "the religious inspiration, when strong and true, is the highest inspiration of the human heart," and that "its exalting influence upon the elements of physical elasticity and vigor is no less positive and beneficial, than in every other part of our compound nature" (Higginson [1873], 366; Scudder [1876], 343; and B.W. Dwight, 251–53).

But Dwight also cautioned against an overemphasis on physical development. He was particularly alarmed by the demonstrations that followed the intercollegiate regatta held July 14, 1875, on Saratoga Lake. The crew of 13 colleges, long and carefully trained for the approaching struggle, had wrestled together there and then, as if for life or death, for the recognized mastery of the oar. The race was two miles long, and the finishing order was Cornell, Columbia, Harvard, Dartmouth, Wesleyan, Yale, Amherst, Brown, Williams, Hamilton, Union, and Princeton. On the day of "the great victory," as it was deemed, President White of Cornell had telegraphed to Saratoga: "The University chimes are ringing, flags flying and cannons firing. Present hearty congratulations to both the victorious crews" (Cornell also won the Freshman race). Governor Hoffman of New York awarded prizes to the victors, who were also honored with formal addresses full of praise, and with balls and festive entertainments on an expensive scale. When they left for their home in Ithaca, a special drawing-room car was provided for them by a New York State senator, and another car for their boats was supplied by Commodore Vanderbilt of the New York Central Railroad. Their passage homeward was a continuous show of triumph. Guns were fired, church-bells were rung, bands of music greeted them, festive dinners were offered, and flags were displayed, as on a national holiday, in various towns and cities along the way. As B.W. Dwight said, "Not the President of the nation or any guest from abroad, however distinguished, could expect greater demonstrations of honor." On the arrival of the already overpraised crew at Ithaca in the early evening, bonfires, torchlights, fireworks, processions, and speeches awaited them; the bells of churches, factories, and fire-engine houses were rung; and pealing above all of them sounded forth the great bell of the university. "The press of New England," said one leading journal, "unites with that of New York in praise of the admirable manner in which the sturdy crew of Cornell won the greatest college boat-race in history." Dwight, on the other hand, strongly objected to the introduction of athletic contests into college life on the grounds that they were diverting students from higher pursuits. Students, he agreed, should maintain regular habits of eating, exercise, studying, and sleeping, but he thought that their physical exercise should be "moderate in its type, instead of violent, social, instead of solitary, full of gleeful cheerfulness, instead of being sober and dull." If muscle and nerve be regarded as great and indispensable treasures to society, the world was full of people who aspired to nothing higher than the sphere of material things; "but let not the choicest specimens of American life and hope be borne, with spontaneous satisfaction or forced consent, to the altar of sacrifice" (B.W. Dwight, 254–56, 276–77).

A different view of intercollegiate athletics can be found in the fictional works of the age. The regattas at Worcester figure prominently in the background of William T. Washburn's novel, *Fair Harvard: A Story of American College Life* (1869), the first of its kind, and Mark S. Severance's *Hammersmith: His Harvard Days* (1879), which signified Harvard's continuing dominance of the intercollegiate athletic scene. Three years after Hammersmith's debut, W.W. Mumford introduced the first fictional college baseball hero in "Bracemore on the Nine," which appeared in the Harvard *Crimson* on May 5, 1882, during the spring of Thayer's freshman year. There is always the possibility that subconsciously, at least, Thayer drew some of the elements of "Casey" from Mumford's tale of the haughty Harvard batsman who struck out against Yale, sending a shudder through the assembled wits and beauties of Boston, and later atoned for his terrible misdeed:

Bracemore on the Nine

> It was a clear, cloudless day. In the vault of the empyrean soared the bald eagle, ever and anon stopping to swoop on his timid prey. O happy eagle! for thou lookest on a scene such as princes and emperors would gladly cast the crown from their brows could they but once have beheld it. Happy eagle! for thou seest the aristocracy of Boston and vicinity hurrying all towards a common centre. And what is that common centre? The Harvard Nine. And what is the centre of that centre, the cynosure of that cynosure? Bracemore.
>
> Bracemore stood a little apart from the rest. His was not a soul that could delight in the vain babbling of the common herd. A scornful smile illuminated his handsome but haughty features.
>
> "They come," said he,—"the enemy"; and his mocking laugh could be heard far over the field, as he pointed at the blue uniforms, every muscle in his countenance quivering with majestic rage. Again he was silent, and quiet as a statue, but his fierce eye told the fire within.
>
> All the beauty and wit of Boston and vicinity crowded about, endeavoring to win one look or one smile from him, but it was impossible. For he was Bracemore. There was vengeance working out an expiation concealed in his haughty breast, and until that was satisfied none might win Bracemore's smile for herself. For the remorse of the man was terrible and immortal.
>
> The game was called. Bracemore stepped up to the bat, but a shudder ran around the beauty and fashion there assembled. Bracemore had struck out. For the first time in many years Bracemore had struck out.

A cold sneer illuminated his features, and there appeared in his eye a thirst for vengeance which nothing but blood could quench. Blood he had in the next innings, for he drove the ball with terrific force against the pitcher who had wounded his honor. The pitcher was borne senseless from the field.

Again Bracemore smiled, a smile like that of the vulture, who has glutted itself on the flesh of his victim. But Bracemore's vengeance was to be complete. One man could not satisfy it; it would devour the whole universe in its immensity.

Bracemore was at the bat in the ninth innings. The score was seventeen to nothing in favor of Yale.

"Ho, fellow," said Bracemore, addressing the Captain of the Harvard Nine, "bring me a goblet of my 1847 Johannisberger Cabernet." It was brought at once with ready acquiescence. Bracemore swallowed it at a draught. Again he seized the bat. The first two balls pitched he struck at carelessly, scarcely seeming to notice them. The third time he hit it, and made the ball go as the ball always went when struck by Bracemore's bat. The Yale Nine was demoralized; the Harvard victorious. Eighteen runs followed in quick succession, Bracemore finding time to put in carelessly two other home runs.

The game was saved by one man. The man was Bracemore.

The Professionals

Many of the same beliefs and values that inspired the rise of amateur baseball clubs were also important factors in the development of professional baseball. In 1869 the Cincinnati Red Stockings, the first professional baseball club, was widely regarded as "the model Club, not only in skill, but morals." First organized as an amateur club in 1866, with Harry Wright as the manager, it was made up mostly of young attorneys, men like Nicholas Longworth, one of Flagg's classmates at Harvard, and a number of other Harvard and Yale graduates of the late 1850s and early 1860s, whose enthusiasm for college baseball naturally carried over into the professional arena (*CDE*, 7/2/1869; Ellard, 39–40; and Harvard University Archives).

Aaron B. Champion was elected president of the Cincinnati club in 1868. Born in Columbus, Ohio, on February 9, 1842, he studied at Antioch, where Horace Mann was president, from 1856 to 1860, moved to Cincinnati in 1864, practiced law, and was active in the Unitarian church. At a meeting held in his office in 1868 the club's uniforms and nickname were discussed, and the Red Stockings were adopted. The idea was a revolutionary one, since all baseball clubs up to that time had worn long pants, but the pioneers of professional baseball may have been trying to connect their club with a famous fictional pioneer, the hero of James Fenimore Cooper's popular *Leatherstocking Tales*. The Red Stockings, like the Leatherstocking, derived their nickname from their clothes. But the resemblance goes far beyond that. Cooper's frontiersman was a champion of sports and fair play, among other things, and represented all that was best in the national character. In his recent study of sports and literature in American culture, Michael Oriard portrayed the Leatherstocking as "the archetypal sportsman of Western myth" (Ellard, 83; Goldstein, 108–11; Oriard, 18; and the public library of Cincinnati and Hamilton County).

In the summer of 1869 the Red Stockings completed a triumphant tour of the East and were hailed as conquering heroes. Portraits of the club appeared in *Frank Leslie's* and *Harper's Weekly,* while the *Spirit of the Times* said the Red Stockings "are the only true exponents of the game today. Full of courage, free from intemperance, they have conducted themselves in every city they visited in a manner to challenge admiration, and their exhibitions of skill in the art of handling both ball and bat call for unexampled praise. Their present tour has done more to elevate the game than any trip of the kind ever before known." In Washington, President Grant watched the Red Stockings play the Nationals, treated them cordially, and complimented them on their play. When the club returned to Cincinnati, men, women, and children lined the streets along the route of the march, "all eager to give a hearty welcome to the men who had by their unrivaled skill and gentlemanly conduct spread Cincinnati's good name throughout the length and breadth of the land." After a banquet at the Gibson House, Champion was toasted as the man who had suggested the tour, "and to whom, more than any other member of the Club, is due the credit of organizing our Nine, and of bringing it to its present status of discipline." Responding to the toast, Champion said that he had been asked the night before whether he would prefer to be President Grant or president of the Cincinnati Base Ball Club, and replied that he would rather be the latter. Some people might think he had no high ambition, but he believed that the game could accomplish much good, if carried on properly. He remembered how, as a student, he had read Tom Hughes's books, and said that it was his desire "to see our people, or at least the Western people, muscular Christians." And, he thought, "Our game aids to accomplish that purpose." Some Easterners had said that the Red Stockings were fed on bread and milk, put to bed early, and sung to sleep with nursery songs, but his only response was to point to the scores, and advise them to do likewise (Albert Spalding, 135–37; Voigt I:28–29; Goldstein, 115; and *CDE*, 7/2/1869).

The 1869 Cincinnati Red Stockings traveled from the Atlantic to the Pacific playing the best baseball clubs in the country, and did not lose a single game. They covered 11,877 miles by rail and by boat, including the trip to California on the new Union Pacific Railroad, played before more than 200,000 people, and won 56 of 57 games played, a tie game with the Haymakers of Troy, New York, at Cincinnati, being the only indication that the Red Stockings might be human just like everybody else. George Wright, Harry's brother, led the club in the field, at the bat, and on the bases, making incredible plays at shortstop, hitting 59 home runs, and scoring 339 runs, or about what an entire professional *team* would score today in a 60-game season (Spalding, 138–39).

Cincinnati's spectacular record provided the incentive for sports-minded people in other cities to organize their own professional baseball clubs, and soon led to the formation of the first professional league. After the 1870 season, when the directors of the Cincinnati Club announced that they were no longer willing to pay the "enormous salaries" demanded by the professionals, the Wright brothers signed with Boston's new club. According to a report in the *New York Times,* the directors of the club were "wealthy Boston merchants, whose ambition it is, as admirers of the national game, to put a thoroughly first-class nine on the field, as exemplars of the fielding beauties of the game, and as a model professional organization." The *New York Times* congratulated the Bostonians for "selecting the ablest Captain of the day, with the model shortstop of the country to assist him," and predicted that "with such a basis, the other positions can be readily filled, so as to make up a very powerful team." Harry Wright arrived in the Hub on January 14, 1871, and at once went to work to organize the new club. At the same time he helped to create the National Association of Professional Base Ball Players, the first professional league. Organized on March 17, 1871, a cold St. Patrick's Day in New York City, the association prospered for five seasons before giving way to the National League of Professional Base Ball Clubs in 1876 (*ibid.,* 139; Seymour [1960], 56; Goldstein, 117–19; and *NYT*, 1/16/1871).

The Boston Red Stockings dominated the first decade of professional baseball, winning four straight pennants in the National Association (1872–75) and two of the first three National League flags (1877–78) for an all-time record total of six league championships in one decade. They perfected the hit-and-run, the epitome of offensive teamwork, and averaged 11 runs per game over five seasons in the National Association. Four future Hall of Famers played for those Boston teams: the Wright brothers, pitcher Albert G. Spalding, and first baseman "Orator" Jim O'Rourke. In addition, "Deacon" Jim White caught for four of Boston's first five pennant-winning clubs (1873–75 and 1877). White, one of the great nineteenth-century players who for some reason has been overlooked by the Hall of Fame, also caught for Chicago's 1876 National League champions, which gives him the honor of catching for the nationwide champions for five consecutive seasons – a record matched only by the immortal Yogi Berra (1949–53) (Hardy, 9; *TSN*, 10/9/1897; Appel and Goldblatt, 34–37, 305–6, 350–51, 396–99 and *NYC*, 6/14/1879).

Chadwick regarded White as the best catcher in the country as early as 1870, when he caught for the Forest Citys of Cleveland. "This nine," he wrote in the *Clipper*, "made a very favorable impression in the metropolis by their excellent deportment both on and off the field." On the field Chadwick said he had never seen "a catcher so quick and expert in his movements behind the bat," and as for pluck, "he is fearless of the hottest balls, and stands

J. Lee Richmond (courtesy of John Richmond Husman).

dangerously close to the bat at times." In the early days of the game the catcher usually stood far behind the bat so as not to get hit by a foul tip or the bat, but by the 1870s catchers were playing so close to the plate that Chadwick thought they were interfering with the batters. At the end of the 1871 season he proposed a rule that the catcher had to stand at least six feet behind the plate. "The position taken by some catchers," he argued, "who are apparently reckless of injuries in their strenuous efforts to take sharp fly tips close to the bat, has been such as to really amount to an obstruction to the batsman." In fact, a batter could hardly swing at a ball without running the risk of "knocking the catcher senseless or breaking his arm." It was all right for the catcher to say, "you go ahead and strike, and I'll take care of myself," but the batter's attention was divided between an effort to hit the ball squarely and at the same time avoid hitting the catcher. "This," said Chadwick, "amounts to a positive obstruction" (*NYC*, 1/21, 11/25/1871).

Chadwick's proposal never gained much support, but he was far from discouraged. "Catchers, as a general thing," he wrote in a review of the 1874 season, "too often wasted their time and labor in unnecessary and dangerous work in playing too close up behind the bat." Pluck in a catcher was a quality to be admired, he admitted, but wear and tear on the catcher should be taken into consideration. In addition, Chadwick thought that the main incentive for "playing up close" was generally "because it is plucky, and the spectators applaud it" (*ibid.*, 12/26/1874).

With runners on base, of course, catchers had to play close to the plate, which Chadwick did not deny. White, however, believed that even with no runners on base, a pitcher would be more effective if the catcher stood close to the plate and provided a target. Harvard captain Fred Thayer settled the issue in the spring of 1877 by inventing the catcher's mask, though it met with some resistance at first. The new device was made of spring wire and padded with camel hair filling, and sold for $3 at Peck and Snyder's sporting goods firm in New York. "It works fairly well," said Chadwick, "but needs a powerful thrower to use it, as it is apt to jar the head, thereby upsetting the aim of the thrower." White gave it a try when Harvard and Boston played that spring. Spalding tossed him a few pitches, but the catcher had trouble seeing the ball, missed a few, and finally "tore off the mask and, hurling it toward the bench, went on without it." Judging from Chadwick's report halfway through the season, other professional catchers thought there was something unheroic about the mask, and refused to even give it a try:

> **Injuries to Catchers.**—It is really surprising, in view of the serious injuries catchers, facing swift pitching close behind the bat, are subjected to, that the wire-mask—a perfect protection against such injuries—is not in more general use among professional catchers. The idea seems to prevail among a prejudiced few of the fraternity that it is not plucky or manly to wear the mask. It is nonsensical to run the risk of such severe injuries simply because a pack of foolish boys may ridicule you. Look at Clapp of the St. Louis nine, who now lies ill and disabled with a broken cheek-bone, due entirely to the fact of his not wearing a protective mask. We regard the Harvard collegian's invention as one of the best things out for saving a catcher from dangerous injuries [*NYC*, 4/14, 6/2, 8/25/1877; Albert Spalding, 476–77; and Voigt, I: 85–88].

A year and a half later some professionals were still catching without a mask. Two fatal accidents marked the 1878 season, one involving a catcher who was struck in the chest by the knee of a player who was running home, and the other from "a very swiftly-pitched ball, which struck the catcher in the stomach." Although these were "exceptional occurrences," said Chadwick, "under the swift pitching now in vogue serious injuries must undoubtedly occur unless catchers resort to the use of the protective catcher's mask, introduced by Mr. Thayer of the Harvard College Club." A few catchers "possessed more reckless pluck than moral courage," and were responsible for the "absurd prejudice" against the use of the masks; "but it is disappearing as fast as the public perceive the value and importance of them as protectors from severe blows in the face." Soon even the pluckiest catchers were wearing Thayer's mask, or "bird-cage," and were prepared to follow Harvard catcher Herbert T. Allen when he donned the first chest protector for a game with Yale at New Haven on May 17, 1884—won by Harvard, 8–7 (*NYC,* 1/11/1879; and Blanchard, 200).

As professional baseball's first dynasty, the Boston Red Stockings were lionized by the press and became the heroes of the day. In 1874 Chadwick wrote brief sketches of each player for the *New York Clipper,* highlighting their characters as well as their baseball abilities. White, the subject of the first sketch, was described as "a young man of excellent moral character, and quite religiously inclined." Repeating the claim made in 1870 that White was the best catcher in the business, Chadwick said that his "great activity," "thorough American pluck," "keen sight," and "powers of endurance" made him "eminently the catcher to face swift pitching," while at the bat he was "keen-sighted, and hits hard from the shoulder." He was, in short, a model catcher: "Quiet and unobtrusive in demeanor, honorable in all his actions, as agile in his movements as a cat, and as plucky withal as a bulldog, he presents in himself the qualities of a model catcher." Spalding, the pitcher, had no superior in "judgment, command of the ball, pluck, endurance and nerve." His eduation and "gentlemanly qualities" placed him well above the average. "Orator" Jim O'Rourke, the first baseman, "is a quiet, gentlemanly, Connecticut youth, with Irish blood in his veins, and, therefore, full of pluck and courage." He is "a fine general player," who "especially excels at first base, a position in which a man has to catch the swiftest of thrown balls, either almost out of reach above his head or on a sharp rebound from his feet, while standing with one foot on his base" (*NYC,* 7/25, 12/19/1874).

Chadwick's highest praise was reserved for the Wright brothers, who were in fact half brothers. Samuel Wright, their father, was a professional cricket player in England who moved the family to New York City in 1836. Harry's mother was Ann Tone Wright; George's mother was Mary Love Wright. The boys were born a dozen years apart, Harry in England on January 10, 1835; and George in Harlem on January 28, 1847. George, according to Chadwick, "is generally regarded as a model baseball player, especially in his responsible position of shortstop." He is "a jolly, good-natured youth, full of life and spirit, up to all the dodges of the game," who was particularly noted for his "sure catching of high balls in the infield, and for his swift and accurate throwing." An injury had slowed him down, but Chadwick could still say, "At the bat, too, he excels." George established the standard for all-around play that has rarely been matched. When he played, fielding gloves were not worn by infielders or outfielders. Since he was ambidextrous, he would have been hampered by wearing a glove, for he would scoop the ball up with either hand and make a strong throw to first in one motion. He was known to kick the ball, soccer style, to the second baseman for a force out when a hard-hit ball bowled him over and popped out of his hands. Cap Anson once said that George "could pull down a ball that would have gone over the head of almost any other man in the business, bounding into the air for it like a rubber ball." He was a clever player, always thinking, and up to all the "dodges" of the game. He was the first to drop an infield fly to set up a double play, a trick that was still popular in the 1890s when the infield fly rule was passed. And he once started a triple play by catching the ball in his cap! In 1937 George became the first baseball pioneer elected to the Hall of Fame, beating his brother Harry by 16 years (*NYC,* 7/25/1874; Voigt, I:88; Appel and Goldblatt, 396–97; and NBL, George Wright folder).

Captain Harry Wright was rightly given most of the credit for Boston's success, and was also recognized for his fine work with Harvard's championship club. Chadwick said in 1874: "As a trainer and captain of a baseball nine, he stands alone; his high character, honesty of purpose, and aptitude in governing his men with kindness, making him very successful. He is highly and deservedly esteemed in Boston and throughout all the baseball cities of America. He is the 'coacher' of the Harvard College baseball nine, the champions of the American colleges for years." The following year, when Boston clinched a fourth straight pennant in the National Association, Chadwick observed that Wright trained his players to "play for the side," to work together as a whole, to study and practice all the points of the game, as batting, fielding, and base-running, and always to play earnestly and persistently to win "for the credit of the club, *and for nothing else*!" Harry demanded that his players act like gentlemen on and off the field, and they complied. Many years later, summing up Wright's managerial career, Chadwick said that "His high integrity of character, his unassuming manner and his perfect knowledge of the game commanded the respect of every player who ever played under him" (*NYC,* 7/25/1874, 8/7/1875, and NBL, Harry Wright folder).

Unlike George, who was outgoing and confident in his manner, Harry was modest, quiet, and unassuming. His baseball career began in 1858 when he joined the Knickerbockers of New York as a catcher and shortstop. He caught for the New York all-stars against the Brooklyn all-stars that year. In 1867 he became playing manager of the Cincinnati Club at a salary of $1,200. Harry was an effective "change" pitcher, changing positions with the pitcher at strategic points in the game, and relying on a drop ball and various off-speed pitches to keep batters off balance. When he was not pitching he usually played in center field, where he "keeps his eyes on all parts of the field, and carefully notes down the least symptom of carelessness on the part of any player," or second base, where "he is very good, facing the hottest species in a plucky, self confident manner very refreshing to look upon; he is also a good thrower." As a batter, Harry once hit seven home runs in one game. But he is best remembered as "The Father of Professional Baseball." He was "a base-ball Edison," said the *Cincinnati Enquirer*. "He eats base-ball, breathes base-ball, thinks base-ball, dreams base-ball, and incorporates base-ball in his prayers." In 1953 he was elected to the Hall of Fame, joining his brother George (*NYC*, 1/1, 3/26/1870, 2/11/1871; Seymour, [1960] 66–72; and Voigt, I:35–59).

The National Association of Professional Base Ball Players was a democratic organization open to any club that could afford the $10 admission fee. The problem was, no matter how many clubs joined the race, Boston was the only one that ever seemed to win. In 1875, for example, no less than 13 clubs – a record for any league – paid the $10 fee to enter the great race for the championship pennant, and fought furiously for the right to fly that pennant, emblem of supremacy in the American National Game, during the grand centennial celebrations. Boston, Hartford, New Haven, Brooklyn, New York, Chicago, Keokuk, and Washington fielded one club each; St. Louis, making her professional debut, experimented with two clubs, one stocked with local talent and the other with "imported" players; while Philadelphia, designated the "Centennial City," threw three clubs into the race in a desperate attempt to seize the pennant from Boston, where it had flown for the past three years, and bring it back to Philadelphia, which had won the first flag in 1871. All of this was to no avail. The Red Stockings did not lose a game at home during the entire 1875 season and breezed to their fourth straight pennant, precipitating a movement to break up the club and start a new league (Goldstein, 134–49).

This led to the founding of the National League of Professional Base Ball Clubs on February 2, 1876, with charter members in Boston, Hartford, New York, Philadelphia, Cincinnati, Louisville, Chicago, and St. Louis. Since membership in the National League was limited to the larger cities, other leagues were soon formed to accommodate smaller cities and towns: the International Association and New England League in 1877, California League in 1878, and Northwestern League in 1879. By the end of the 1870s, the first full decade of professional play, it was obvious even to the most skeptical observers that professional baseball was here to stay. The American public was completely sold on the idea of paying a dime, a quarter, or as much as half a dollar to witness a good ball game. The press played an important role in promoting the game, supplying the public with news about their favorite players, and shaping the popular image of America's newest profession (Seymour [1960], 99–103; and Vermilyea, 36).

An editorial appeared in the *Albany Argus*, for example, on April 15, 1879, announcing that two professional baseball clubs were organizing in the Empire State capital to compete in the National (formerly the International)

Association, and urging the public to give both clubs their wholehearted support. "The national game," said the paper, "is something that is and that has come to stay, something that is the pastime of millions and the direct pursuit of hundreds of persons, who are called 'professionals,' and whose support is gained by their skill and diligence in batting, pitching, throwing and catching a ball, or in running bases." Every year thousands of young men were giving law, journalism, divinity, medicine, teaching, politics, dentistry, saloon-keeping, and baseball some thought when they decided upon a career, and every one of them, given the chance, would pass the humble callings by and "proudly prefer the cerebral and competitive profession of base ball to all the others." Players were often injured, but "the sufferings, sacrifices and heroism demanded by the game are at once the concern and the crown of those who play it," and they cheerfully faced any amount of pain, injury, and even "martyrdom" in the "noble cause" (Seymour [1956], 585–86).

One of the young men who joined the professional ranks that year was John Lee Richmond, a Brown University ballplayer who became Worcester's first big-league star. Richmond led his college club to the 1879 championship, signed with Worcester's National Association team, and hurled a no-hitter in his first appearance on the mound in a Worcester uniform, an exhibition contest against Chicago's National League leaders on June 2. "His forte," said the *New York Clipper,* in a biographical sketch which accompanied a portrait of the celebrated pitcher on August 2, "is a happy combination of speed and strategy." Richmond was also "a very good batsman, ranking in that respect far above the average." With the arrival of Richmond and Arthur Irwin, a good young shortstop recruited from a Boston semipro team, Worcester began a steady climb from last place to fourth in the association, and defeated all of the best National League clubs in exhibition contests, paving the way for Worcester's admittance to the National League in 1880. On June 12, 1880, playing at the old Agricultural Grounds, Richmond pitched the first perfect game on record against a heavy-hitting Cleveland club, and characteristically gave most of the credit to his teammates (*NYC,* 8/2, 12/13/1879; Barry, 27–29; and Husman, 65–70).

Born in Sheffield, Ohio, on May 5, 1857, Richmond was one of twelve children in "a large and highly respected family," according to the *Worcester Gazette.* His father, the Rev. Cyrus R. Richmond, and one of his brothers were Baptist ministers. He attended the preparatory department of Oberlin College from 1873 to 1876, pitched for his class nine, then enrolled at Brown. One of his roommates, W.H.P. Faunce, who later became president of Brown, recalled him as "a striking and engaging personality, a fun-loving and quick-witted classmate, and a superb athlete, supple and erect of form, clear of eye, and steady of nerve." After graduating from Brown in 1880, Richmond became a medical student at the University of the City of New York, continued his pitching career, and received his medical degree from the College of Physicians and Surgeons there in 1883, the same year that Brown awarded him an M.A. He retired from the game, practiced medicine in Ohio for the next ten years, and then taught in the Toledo public schools and the University of Toledo. As a ballplayer, doctor, and teacher, Richmond was living proof of the soundness of the old adage that George Bancroft had been teaching for over 50 years, "*mens sana in corpore sano*" (a sound mind in a sound body) (*WG*, 7/3/1880).

On January 17, 1880, the *Clipper* noted that the national game had given rise to "many poetic effusions," and published the first in a series of "Bad Ballads; or Lyrics of the Field of Baseball." A few weeks later, a Providence, Rhode Island, poet composed a ballad about Richmond and his famous curve ball, or "twister," which appeared in the *Providence Press* and was reprinted in the *Worcester Gazette*. The gentleman reportedly singing the ballad is not George, but Frank Bancroft, the Worcester manager:

> *Scene, Worcester, Mass.: time—May first, 1880.*
> *Enter Bancroft, who renders the solo whilst the directors of his nine take up the refrain.*
>
> When our enterprising Richmond gets to twistin'—
> gets to twistin',
> And the sphere begins to zig-zag down the line—
> down the line,
> Then the batters of the League will get to wishin'—
> get to wishin',
> That Bancroft hadn't got this man to sign—
> man to sign [*WG*, 3/6/1880].

Mayor Charles B. Pratt, president of the Worcester Base Ball Club, and the directors were determined to put a first-class club on the field to represent Worcester in the National League. Their attempts to sign the veteran George Wright created quite a stir in baseball circles. Wright had left Boston in 1879 to manage and play for Providence, and led the Rhode Island club to the pennant, five games ahead of brother Harry's second-place Boston club. The large salary George would command was no deterrent to the Worcester club backers, who had high hopes for a pennant with Wright and Richmond on the club. "Should the excitement grow," said the *Gazette*, "it seems possible that there may be no financial bar to the consummation of such a scheme, in which case, with two such drawing cards as Wright and Richmond, it is considered certain by the more sanguine that the increase of the salary list would be fully made good by the increased patronage of the club's games both at home and abroad." Unfortunately for Worcester, the National League directors had met after the 1879 season and instituted the "reserve rule," which gave each club the right to reserve five players from the past year's club as a nucleus for the next year's club, with the guarantee that no other club in the league could sign these players. Providence reserved Wright for 1880, and as the season approached would not agree to pay him what he was paid in 1879. As a result, Wright "said emphatically that he will not play in Providence." Providence said just as emphatically that he would not play anywhere else. Manager Bancroft had a lengthy interview with President Root of the Providence club, but the latter would not "let up" on Wright. The *Gazette* did not like the new rule, and complained that "Worcester, as a member of the league, must quietly submit to be the victim of this dog-in-the-manger policy" (*ibid.,* 3/6, 3/9, 3/13/1880; and Seymour [1960], 104–17).

George Wright sat out the 1880 season, and the reserve rule has been a bone of contention between professional baseball players and club officials ever since. Although the players have a legitimate gripe, some people have had a hard time sympathizing with their plight. On October 10, 1879, the *Cleveland Plain Dealer* claimed that the rule was necessary for the good of the game. Players were "killing the goose that laid the golden egg" by demanding salaries which ranged from $1,000 to $1,800 a year, "more money for six months' play, three or four days in the week, two hours each day, than ninety-nine out of every hundred men can earn by twelve months' work, six and seven days in the week and from eight to twelve hours a day." On the other hand, there were also some people who thought that nothing was too good for the players. In 1883 the city of Detroit was reportedly selling bonds to raise money to give each player "a house and coach and four." Mayor Thompson had issued an order requiring the citizens to raise their hats when passing the honorable aggregation, while schoolchildren were taught to sing "The Conquering Hero" when one of them approached. This may have been exaggerating things a bit. But when Boston won the Players' League pennant in 1890, the fans presented Captain Mike Kelly with a house near Cape Cod, a carriage, and four magnificent horses, so the "king" could travel in style. It was truly an age of heroes. Come to think of it, what other age could have produced a ballad like "Casey at the Bat"? (Seymour [1960], 106, 325; and Voigt, I:200–201.)

PART II
College Days

CHAPTER 8

Introduction

You talk about painting a town red.
If anybody wants to take a few lessons on this point let them apply to the Harvard boys.
The Sporting Life, *May 27, 1885*

Harvard's class of 1885 has to be regarded one of the most distinguished crews that ever graduated from America's oldest university. This was the class that included Ernest L. Thayer, Sam Winslow, captain of the undefeated 1885 nine and one of the greatest team leaders in the history of intercollegiate athletics, and, by rights, William Randolph Hearst, the future founder of a vast publishing empire, and the first to publish "Casey." Technically, Hearst was a year behind the two Worcester products, and never received a diploma, but he was vice president of the Base Ball Association, worked with Thayer and Winslow on the *Lampoon* and the Hasty Pudding Club play, and left the Yard when they did, at the express invitation of the faculty, who were getting a little tired of his bonfires and practical jokes (*HUC*, 1 [1886]: 20–34; and Vermilyea and Moore, 43).

Jokesters they were, too; not just Hearst but Thayer, Winslow, and the entire *Lampoon* staff. They brightened things up at the Yard in the early 1880s, and made things hot for a faculty faced with the challenge of educating the recalcitrant students, and at the same time trying to control a new athletic program that seemed to have only one goal in life: beat Yale.

Thayer entered Harvard in the summer of 1881, graduating with honors in English composition and philosophy in 1885. In his freshman year he began writing for the *Lampoon,* America's oldest humor magazine, and after serving a two-year apprenticeship was exalted to the rank of president of the *Lampoon* board, a post that he occupied with dignity during his junior and senior years. Thayer also belonged to Phi Beta Kappa, Delta Kappa Epsilon, and the Fly Club. On October 23, 1884, in the fall of his senior year, the popular Worcesterite was elected Ivy Orator of his class, and delivered the Ivy Oration on Class Day, June 19, 1885, one year before Harvard's 250th anniversary.

Another honor was accorded to Thayer during his senior year, when he

Charles Eliot in 1853 (courtesy of the Harvard University Archives).

was selected to write the Hasty Pudding play. Founded in 1795, the Hasty Pudding Club was the most important college society at Harvard. It was the custom of the club to admit into its membership the most prominent men not only in athletics and good fellowship but also in literature. Among the members in Thayer's day were the captains of the baseball and football teams, leading athletes in other sports, the presidents of the *Lampoon, Crimson,* and *Advocate,* the three college papers, and other men, Hearst for example, who had become prominent in one way or another. Thayer took Joan of Arc for his subject, an appropriate choice for a school that was quietly beginning to accept women students at the Annex (now Radcliffe) (*NYT*, 2/23, 4/7/1885).

Charles W. Eliot, president of Harvard from 1869 to 1909, personified the *mens sana in corpore sano,* and was the most influential leader in the educational circles of his day. He had rowed on the 1858 Harvard crew, and in 1869, at the age of 35, became the youngest president in the school's history. In his inaugural address of October 19, 1869, Eliot emphasized that Harvard was "intensely democratic in temper," but added that there was an aristocracy to which the sons of Harvard belonged, "the aristocracy which excels in manly sports, carries off the honors and prizes of the learned professions, and bears itself with distinction in all fields of intellectual labor and combat." When the students attempted to carry excellence in athletics too far, in proportion to their mental development, Eliot took the historic first steps toward the regulation of intercollegiate athletics. To encourage freedom of thought and action among the students, and promote intellectual diversity, he developed the "elective system," which, as he said in 1894, "has proved to be the most generally useful piece of work which this university has ever executed." Undergraduates were given a free choice of studies offered by the college which they could pursue to the completion of a course for the first degree. Freedom was the key word here, but within limits, since all of the studies offered had some cultural value, were nonvocational, and were therefore considered to be part of the liberal arts and sciences (Eliot [1869], 49; Ralph B. Perry [1931], 73; Ronald Smith, 164; Morison [1930], lxix–lxx; and Morison [1936], 341–46).

As with any progressive reforms, sizable obstacles had to be overcome before any meaningful progress could be made. Governing boards, a small but vigorous minority of the college faculty, and a number of old grads opposed the movement away from the classics, philosophy, and mathematics toward modern subjects such as English, French, German, history, economics, and the natural sciences. But Eliot was young, and could wait. "He had the patience of an Indian," as Harvard historian Samuel Eliot Morison has said, "and the perseverance of a beaver." With some minor exceptions, required courses for seniors were abolished in 1872, for juniors in 1879, and for sophomores in 1884, when Eliot announced the "practical completion of a development which began sixty years ago." There were now no required courses except freshman English and French (or German), two half-year lecture courses in physics and chemistry, and sophomore and junior themes and forensics.

One of Thayer's first articles for the *Lampoon* gave students an inside view of the elective system. In the late spring of 1882, at the end of his first year at Harvard, it was time for the students to decide which courses to take in the following year. Some poor souls could not make up their minds. Thayer then interviewed a number of professors, and President Eliot himself, to ascertain their views on the best courses to take, and presented the results of his survey in an article called "Help Yourself."

> As the time approaches when we are obliged to signify the electives which we intend to take next year, it may be of use to some whose minds are not wholly made up to hear the opinions of some of the Professors with regard to making a choice.
>
> Prof. MacEmerton, on being asked what he considered a liberal course of study, said: "I think there is nothing which tends so much to educate a man and fit him for practical life as a study of human history. I should therefore advise all young men, who wish to spend their time profitably, to take courses 1, 2, 3, 4, 5, 6, 7, 8, 9, 10, 11, &c., &c. in History, and not to waste their time upon any frivolous and useless courses which may seem more entertaining."
>
> Profs. Whitewin and Goodyer say: "We cannot conscientiously recommend any courses now given at Harvard, except those which fall directly or indirectly under the supervision of the Greek Department. It is evident to all who know anything about the requirements of a University course, that the Latin department is lamentably weak. Fine arts, as a natural outgrowth of the Greek, is allowable, as are also the histories of Greece and Rome. But it is extremely inadvisable for any young man to devote much time to the study of modern languages, which afford little or no mental discipline, and whose only advantage lies in their practical usefulness."
>
> Prof. Bone, on being interviewed concerning the best plan to be pursued, said: "I have noticed with great distress the increase of the study of Physics and Natural History in this University. I do not see how any conscientious person can consistently pursue a course in these branches. Geology and Biology are the inventions of the Devil, and Darwin has gone to be rewarded according to his deserts. Herbert Spencer and J.S. Mill have had such an effect upon the minds of students, that they have become entirely deaf to argument, and it is almost impossible to find one who is not more or less tainted with the doctrine of Heredity and Evolution, which are the plague spot of modern science. If studies which touch upon these questions are strictly avoided, I see little objection to any other courses."
>
> The Professors of the Law School said the best practice for a lawyer was to learn the sharp practices of mankind, and that the sharpest practice men could get here was to go out on Jarvis Field and practise with the nine.
>
> The Professors of Mathematics declared that there was a singular lack of mathematical ability in the College at present, some lower class men being so slow that they had to count on their fingers; but these were not so bad as those who counted on winning the Class races.
>
> Finally, the President declared that it was quite possible for any man of ordinary ability to take all the courses in the Elective Pamphlet during the four years, and he strongly recommended Freshmen to adopt this plan early in their career, in order to avoid such an accumulation

> of work during the last few days of the Senior year as might, if they happened to row on their crew, and the race were postponed on account of bad weather, make it necessary to call a class meeting, and consider the advisability of withdrawing the crew from the race, because of their being over-trained,—in order, that is to say, to catch the four o'clock train,—particularly as they had wanted to row on Tuesday, and would have done so if '83 had not had an hour examination, which caused Wednesday to be out of the question for '85, when '84 was unwilling to consent to any such agreement as that. What do you say? [*Harvard Lampoon,* 5/25/1882].

The new curriculum called for corresponding reforms in the methods of teaching. Eliot disapproved of the old-fashioned daily recitations, and in 1880, after ten years of coaxing the faculty, he was able to report that recitations had "well-nigh disappeared," except for elementary languages and mathematics courses. Lectures, discussions, and "Socratic" colloquies between teachers and students had become the prevailing methods, creating a more democratic atmosphere in the classroom. Emerson, inspired, no doubt, by Harvard's baseball victories over Yale, drew an analogy between the ideal class and a baseball club. In an essay on Plutarch's *Morals,* first published in 1870, the Sage of Concord described the relation between the philosophers of ancient Greece and those who came to them for instruction: "This teaching was no play nor routine, but strict, sincere and affectionate. The part of each of the class is as important as that of the master. They are like the base-ball players, to whom the pitcher, the bat, the catcher and the scout are equally important" (Emerson, 291).

William James (1842–1910), the philosopher and psychologist, was one of Thayer's professors at Harvard, and awakened in the young student a lifelong interest in the deeper problems of life. In 1861 James entered the Lawrence Scientific School at Harvard, where Eliot was then teaching chemistry, and then went on to the Harvard Medical School in the fall of 1864, receiving his degree, after mixing his studies with some travel in Europe, in June 1869. Three years of reading and reflection followed, and in 1872 he was appointed instructor in physiology in Harvard College. Seven years of teaching prepared him for the course on "The Philosophy of Evolution," which he inaugurated in 1879. Though many people were somewhat skeptical of Darwin's theory, the behavior of baseball fans made the new philosophy at least seem plausible. The wonder was not so much that the monkeys could actually be our uncles but that the jungles were so far removed from the bleachers (Ralph B. Perry [1932], 590).

Francis J. Child (1825–96) was probably the biggest influence on Thayer's development as a writer and poet during his college years. Harvard's first professor of English, Child was appointed to the position in 1876, and taught up until his death in 1896. He published a monumental collection of English and Scottish popular ballads, with extensive commentaries, from 1883 to 1896, and also founded the American Folklore Society in 1888. A number of Child's students have paid high tributes to their old teacher, both as a scholar and as a man. Francis Barton Gummere called him "the keenest, soundest, most loved of American scholars." Morison remembered him as "the most beloved of teachers," while the James brothers, Henry and William, were among his warmest admirers. Henry described Child as a "delightful man, rounded character, above all humanist and humorist." To which William added, "He had a moral delicacy and a richness of heart that I never saw and never expect to see equalled. . . . I loved Child more than any man I know" (Genzmer, 67; Morison [1936], 278; and Jones, 27.

A native of Boston, Child graduated from Harvard in 1846, and after a brief stint as a tutor at Harvard, went to study comparative philology in Germany. There he was brought into contact with the work of the Brothers Grimm, and imbibed the Romantic theory, *Das Volk dichtet,* the people make the poetry. The word "ballad," according to Child, signifies a narrative song, a short tale in lyric verse. In his view the *popular* ballad is a distinct and very important species of poetry. Such poetry is always an expression of the mind and heart of the people, taken collectively, and never the personality of the individual poet. The fundamental characteristic of popular ballads is therefore the absence of subjectivity and self-consciousness. Though they do not "write themselves," as William Grimm had said, and though a poet and not a people has composed them, still, says Child, "the author counts for nothing, and it is not be mere accident, but with the best reason that they have come down to us anonymous" (Child, 464; Hart, 784; and Wells, 250–59).

Thayer's ballad may be measured against the standards laid down by Child. While it may not have come down to us as anonymously written, it is certainly a *popular* ballad, expressing in lyrical terms a tragic experience which, sad to say, has been all too common with the American people. It is also true that the author, for a good many years, at least, "counted for nothing." What about the other criteria established by Child? The true ballad, he says, tells a story. It may be mythical or historical, humorous or pathetic, so long as the subject matter is of purely popular origin. At its best, it is brief. The geography is seldom specific, although in some cases the attention given to the setting adds much to the poem. Child cites the example of the ballad of Robin Hood and the monk, where "the landscape background of the first two stanzas has often been praised, and its beauty will never pall." On each of these counts, and especially the brilliant Mudville landscape, "Casey" clearly meets the test.

Harvard's influence on Thayer has been well summed up by Daniel Lothman. In 1935, when the class of 1885 celebrated its fiftieth anniversary with a dinner at the Algonquin Club, in Boston, he delivered a moving recital of "Casey," and afterward added a few well-chosen remarks:

It may not be amiss to recall some of the circumstances that led up to Thayer's writing the kind of poem he did. With an innate poetic instinct, Thayer fortunately had a training in English at Harvard that was conducive for developing that instinct as well as his literary ability. Besides, in spending four years at a college that stressed baseball, a sport in which he took a deep interest, he acquired both a technical knowledge of the game and a great enthusiasm for it. So, you see, at college Thayer had lived in an environment that was ideal for developing the qualifications of a writer of baseball. When the opportunity presented itself, this training bore fruit in the writing of "Casey at the Bat" [*HUC*, 10 (1935): 368–74].

CHAPTER 9

Life on the *Lampoon*

Lampy is the sagest . . . the same blithe, hearty rollicker he has always been; quick-witted, jovial, tart, but never bitter, never coarse . . . first and foremost a Harvard Jester.

John P. Marquand on
Lampy's 40th anniversary (1916)

The *Harvard Lampoon,* America's oldest humor magazine, traces its long and illustrious history back to the centennial year, when four Harvard students met in the room of Samuel Sherwood, 1876, to start "a College Punch." A sketch celebrating the paper's twenty-fifth anniversary identifies the instigators as Sherwood, a talented draftsman, his brother Arthur, 1877, "the life of every party which he joined," Ralph Curtis, 1876, an editor of the *Harvard Advocate,* and John Tyler Wheelwright, 1876, who suggested the name that was finally adopted–though he had also proposed the Harvard Harpoon–"a weapon difficult for folly to escape" (Kaplan, 59).

The first edition was ready on February 10. Sam Sherwood and Billy Otis, 1878, the business editor, got up at dawn and plastered posters all over the Yard advising the students that a new era was about to begin. Twelve hundred copies priced at 25 cents each were put on sale at Whiton's cigar store, at the corner of Main and Holyoke streets, and sold out at once. With a start like that "Lampy" went right on bouncing merrily along, through the good times and the bad, and is now older than the oldest living graduate, and a good deal friskier at that. It was a custom at *Punch* that each issue should be preceded by a dinner, and so for a while there were *Lampoon* dinners at different places around the Yard, until, in 1885, a sanctum was provided on Brattle Street by that "munificent keeper of the purse strings, Billy Hearst." Professor Charles Eliot Norton, a cousin of President Eliot, was invited to the dinner before the second edition, and assured his hosts that their hearts were in the right places, even if their drawing was crude, and their humor not the most refined.

The appearance of a humorous publication on the Cambridge campus was an event a long time in the making. "To the thinker," Thoreau had written in the 1840s, "all the institutions of men, as all imperfection, viewed from the point of equanimity, are legitimate subjects of humor." "Whatever is not necessary," he contended, "no matter how sad or personal, or universal a grievance, is, indeed, a jest more or less sublime." Humor, then, is not merely the province of a few writers and critics, but a common feature of everyday life, a sign of health in the young and the old alike. There are neighbors, he continued, whose salutations and conversations consist mainly in "the mutual play and interchange of a genial and healthy humor, which excepts nothing, not even themselves, in its lawless range," while the child, best proof of the point, "plays continually, if you will let it, and all its life is a sort of practical humor of a very pure kind, often of so fine and ethereal a nature, that its parents, its uncles and cousins, can in no wise participate in it, but must stand aloof in silent admiration, and reverence even." Nature herself, thought Thoreau, "is observed to have her playful moods or aspects, of which man seems sometimes to be the sport" (Thoreau, 150).

While Thoreau was philosophizing on the nature of humor, writers like Artemus Ward, Bret Harte, Mark Twain, James Russell Lowell, and Oliver Wendell Holmes were capitalizing upon it, and beginning to create a new and distinctive type of humor that by the 1870s would come to be regarded as "the one complete revelation of the national character." As George T. Ferris noted in 1874, "America has of late years bristled with humorous writers, as does the porcupine with quills." Mark Twain was pronounced the most representative type of American humorist, because he embodied "the peculiar style of the average American journalist." He had recently moved to Hartford, and was in the prime of his life and power. In the five years which had elapsed since the issue of *The Innocents Abroad,* the sale of his books had reached 241,000 copies, for which the gullible public had paid the astonishing sum of $950,000. Plus, starting in January 1876, the *Atlantic Monthly* was running his series of sketches about "Life on the Mississippi," and paying a handsome fee for them too. Perhaps it was a good time to start a comic periodical (Ferris, 16–17).

In 1908, when the public finally woke up and began to take an interest in the author of "Casey at the Bat," Thayer was interviewed by Homer Croy for the new *Baseball Magazine,* and told him a few things about his college days on the *Harvard Lampoon,* recalling his old friends on the staff as "a splendid corps of men." Besides Thayer and Winslow, there were Willie Hearst and Genie Lent, the "Western Barbarians" from San Francisco; Fatty Briggs of Springfield, Massachusetts, "one of the best men that ever graced the staff"; Tommy Sanborn of Concord, son of Frank Sanborn, poet; Conway Felton of Philadelphia, great-nephew of Cornelius Conway Felton, president of Harvard and the Normal Institute of Physical Education; George Santayana from Madrid, the well-known philosopher; Adams Crocker of Fitchburg, Massachusetts; Owen Wister of Philadelphia; and W.W. Baldwin of Baltimore, later assistant secretary of state under President Cleveland.

After graduation Briggs, Lent, and Thayer made up the "Harvard Brigade" that Hearst brought out to San Francisco to help him run the *San Francisco Daily Examiner* (Croy, 10–11).

Santayana was one of the *Lampoon*'s artists. He never wrote for the paper, even the text for his sketches was usually supplied by the others, but in his autobiography he left a fine sketch of his Harvard days and the *Lampoon*. As he described it, the Harvard Yard, both in its architecture and its manners, was "distinctly Bohemian," not in the Parisian sense, but of the "red-brick lodging, tavern and stable-yard Bohemia of Dickens and Thackeray." Sanborn, who sat next to Santayana in classes where the freshmen were arranged in alphabetical order, and became his closest friend at Harvard, was described as "a poet of lyric and modest flights but genuine feeling," not naturally in harmony with the transcendentalism of Concord, where his father was a conspicuous member of the Emersonian circle. There was more of Chaucer in him, Santayana thought, than of Emerson or Wordsworth; even Shakespeare – except in the songs – he found too heavy and rhetorical. Felton and Baldwin, on the other hand, were "not New Englanders, rather Southern, without crotchets and with unaffected old-fashioned literary tastes, leaning towards the sentimental and the nobly moral." Their room, number 1 Thayer, was a *Lampoon* sanctum where Santayana met with them to compose their parts of the upcoming edition. They loved Thackeray, and Felton would read aloud, "Wait till you come to forty-year." Santayana regarded Baldwin as "an engaging person, who inspired trust and affection, and I recall the circle in which we moved with the warmest pleasure" (Santayana, 197–200).

Although Hearst and Thayer traveled in different circles, Santayana seemed to know them well enough to form some lasting impressions. He spoke of Hearst's independence, attributing it to the fact that his father was a millionaire and a senator from California, his long cigars, which he considered "bad form in the Yard," and his budding powers as a newspaper owner and manager, which made him invaluable to the *Lampoon*. "He not only knew how to secure advertisements," recalled Santayana, "but he presented us with a material sanctum, carpeted, warmed by a stove, and supplied with wooden armchairs and long tables at which all the illustrated comic papers in the world were displayed as exchanges for our little local and puerile 'Lampy.' How easily a little cool impudence can deceive mankind!"

If the philosopher kept a distance from Hearst and his cigars, and remained aloof from *Lampoon*'s smoke-filled inner sanctum, he knew Thayer and his work well enough to form some interesting impressions. There was nothing inherently wrong, mind you, about the business of manufacturing fine woolen goods, so long as the sheep did not mind; in fact, it was both practical and profitable. But perhaps Santayana expected something more from the president of the *Lampoon*. Without so much as mentioning the immortal

"Casey," he contrasted Thayer's brilliant work for the *Lampoon* with the comparable dullness of his later career:

> The man who gave the tone to the *Lampoon* at that time was Ernest Thayer, not one of our group. He seemed a man apart, and his wit was not so much jocular as Mercutio-like, curious and whimsical, as if he saw the broken edges of things that appear whole. There was some obscurity in his play with words, and a feeling (which I shared) that the absurd side of things is pathetic. Probably nothing in his later performance may bear out what I have just said of him; because American life was then becoming unfavorable to idiosyncrasies of any sort, and the current smoothed and rounded out all the odd pebbles [Santayana, 197].

Mercutio is one of Shakespeare's most remarkable characters. A friend of Romeo and kinsman of the Prince of Verona, he has been called the epitome of Renaissance man, Shakespeare's ideal man, a great poet, and an actor's dream. As the Roman god Mercury was a god of oratory and eloquence, so Mercutio was very fond of talking. When the Nurse asks Romeo, "I pray you, sir, what saucy merchant was this, that was so full of his ropery?" Romeo replies: "A gentleman, nurse, that loves to hear himself talk, and will speak more in a minute than he will stand to in a month." Mortally wounded in a sword fight with Tybalt, Romeo's foe, Mercutio still manages to fire off a pun: "Ask for me to-morrow, and you shall find me a grave man."

The critics have been unusually generous in their praise of Romeo's loyal companion. "Shakespear," according to the poet Dryden, "show'd the best of his skill in his Mercutio, and he said himself, that he was forc'd to kill in the third Act, to prevent being kill'd by him." Another distinguished poet, Coleridge, outdid Dryden in his admiration for the unfortunate swordsman. "Mercutio," says the author of the *Ancient Mariner,* "is a man possessing all the elements of a poet: the whole world, as it were, subject to his law of association. Whenever he wishes to impress anything, all things become his servants for the purpose: all things tell the same tale, and sound in unison. This faculty, moreover is combined with the manners and feelings of a perfect gentleman, himself utterly unconscious of his powers." As a final tribute to the departed punster, perhaps the most touching of them all, here are the thoughts of the poet and essayist, Alice Meynell: "With Mercutio vanished the light heart that had given to the serious ages of the world an hour's refuge from the unforgotten burden of responsible conscience; the light heart assumed, borrowed, made dramatically the spectator's own" (Quennell and Johnson, 185–86; and Meynell, 69).

Thayer teamed up with artist "Fatty" Briggs on some of the *Lampoon*'s finest productions of the early 1880s, notably the editorials, stories, and feature cartoons concerning the Harvard Athletic Committee. Briggs also painted the playbill for Thayer's *Joan of Arc,* and played a conspicuous part in that harrowing production. In 1890, after an attack of the grippe developed into a case of pneumonia, his promising career was brought to a close. Thayer composed a fine sketch of his friend which was published in one of the class reports:

> As a caricaturist, Mr. Briggs was certainly the most talented of the men of his time at Harvard. He drew familiar faces with humor, and many of us, doubtless, still have in our possession his ingenious likenesses of John the Orange-man, Oscar Wilde, Henry Irving, Langtry, Theo, and of several members of the Faculty. We must all remember with pleasure the double-page cartoons of Mr. Briggs. Collectively they would form almost a pictorial history of the significant events of our day, and we will particularly recall his treatment of the French opera, which we all went wild over, the return of our victorious ball-team, and the first outrages committed by the Athletic Committee.
>
> The life of Mr. Briggs was not eventful, but, the writer has been told by one who knew him better than any one else, singularly happy. He was born in Springfield, July 13, 1862, the son of Albert Dwight Briggs, a civil engineer, and later, one of the Massachusetts Railroad Commissioners, and of Caroline Clapp Briggs. He received his early education at private schools in Springfield, and fitted for college at Adams Academy, in Quincy, Mass. His father died before he came to college.
>
> The circle of Mr. Briggs' acquaintances in Cambridge was not large, but the few who enjoyed the privilege of knowing him well, always found in him a most agreeable and interesting companion. He possessed a memory of rare retentiveness, remarkable critical acumen in matters pertaining to art, and, for so young a man, a profound knowledge of the world. Unusually gifted as he was, vanity had no place in his character, and he showed for the work of other men, whom a less generous nature might have regarded as rivals, the keenest and heartiest appreciation. Mr. Briggs was not a hard student, but it seemed to the writer as if he remembered every line that he read in books, and this would not be quite incredible of one who could come away from an evening at the opera with a good part of the score, words, and music, in his head.
>
> Socially, Mr. Briggs was in the main affiliated with the members of the "Lampoon" board. He drew continuously for the "Lampoon," from the third number that appeared after his entrance into college to the very last issue of the paper in his senior year. He also belonged to the Hasty Pudding Club, for which society he painted the excellent play-bill, commemorating '85's performance of *Joan of Arc*, which now occupies a conspicuous place on the walls of the new theatre [*HUC*, 3 (1892): 17–18].

Once Thayer had become oriented to Harvard life, he started contributing articles and poems to the *Lampoon*. His first two published items, both poems, were probably written for Halloween and appeared in the November 17, 1881, issue, pages 32 and 36, no doubt somewhat later than he would have preferred. Still, it was something for a mere freshman to waltz onto the campus of America's most prestigious university and have his work published in the *Lampoon* right off the bat. The title page of this volume credits most of the writing to five seniors and four graduates, among whom was J.T. Wheelwright, one of the founders of the *Lampoon*. No sophomores and only one junior and one freshman (Thayer) were represented. One of the seniors was Owen Wister. His famous novel, *The Virginian* (1902), combines frontier humor with adventure, and introduces the brave, quiet hero who became the model for the popular image of the cowboy.

Thayer's first poem was addressed "To May":

Tell me, pretty cousin May,
Have you power as, gossips say,
In a scarce forgotten day,
        Beldams had?
Power of a mystic rite
That possessed such magic might
As to drive a luckless wight
        Nearly mad?

Have you, by this secret art,
Made an image of my heart,
Into which you poke a dart
        Here and there?
If to this you answer no,
Tell me that where'er I go
Makes each thought of you a throe
        Hard to bear.

In the depths of those brown eyes
'Neath the lashes' long disguise
Such a witching power lies
        At your beck,
That one prays with every pang
(As the folk of witches sang)
May she meet her fate and hang–
        Round my neck.

PH.

In the same issue, a few pages after this curious poem to May, was a fantastic composition entitled, "A Soldier's Prayer." Somewhat longer than its companion piece, this one was signed, "P.T. B-RN-M," after the famous showman, Phineas T. Barnum, who had just joined with James T. Bailey to form the Barnum and Bailey Circus. Fortunately, or unfortunately as the case may be, the title page gives Thayer's full name, otherwise it could easily have been overlooked. This, the second of Thayer's two Halloween poems, is a bizarre, nightmarish blend of a thrilling incident involving Miss Arabella Deane, the beautiful bareback rider, whom Thayer had apparently seen in action under Barnum's big top, and a common, everyday occurrence which any Harvard student could relate to.

If someone were to tell you that the dinners served at Memorial Hall, where the freshmen took their meals, consisted of macaroni soup, baked haddock, boiled turkey (with oyster sauce), roast rib of beef, cottage pudding and apples, you would probably say, Why, this is excellent. But it sounded better than it looked, and it looked, needless to say, much better than it tasted. In addition, there was a monotonous recurrence of the same dishes. To make matters worse, Memorial Hall was one of the principal objects of interest to strangers visiting Cambridge. One of the galleries of this establishment was thrown open to spectators, and the public was invited to come and "watch the animals eat." It must have been a horrifying experience for all concerned (*NYT*, 12/25/1882).

The Soldier's Prayer
An Incident of the Ring
By P.T. B-RN-M

It was, indeed, and that's the truth, a most heart-rending scene,
Which happened in the year we hired Miss Arabella Deane.
Miss Arabella Deane, now, we engaged that year to star,
And had you sought her equal you'd have gone almighty far.
A splendid bareback rider, – she was most divinely fair,
And had, if you'll believe me, an enormous head of hair.
Now, with this head of hair, sir, the performance that she made
Threw other circus novelties way back into the shade.
After we had shown the lions, the clown a song would sing,
And Arabella's charger was brought into the ring.
To help her mount her stamping steed the clown gave her his hand,
'Mid the plaudits of the crowd, and the music by the band.
Then, swiftly round she rode whilst unbinding coils of hair,
And as each coil was loosened it stood out in the air;
Until the lengthening tresses the full circuit had made,
And 'neath the hairy canopy the clown sat in the shade.
With her teeth she seized the ends 'mid thundering applause;
And round and round the ring she flew, a mass of hairy gauze;
Then, leaping light, she rose and stood upon the golden train,
Until her panting charger once more came round again.
Such was her performance, and it packed the tent each night,
Till people came from far and near to see the wondrous sight.

One eve, as Arabella, high mounted on her steed,
Had urged her gallant charger to attain his highest speed,
And as around the ring she drew her mass of golden hair,
A dreadful cry of horror burst through the evening air.
The hearts of all stood still, and every voice was hushed,
While, bursting through the sawdust ring, an armless soldier rushed.
His eyeballs wild stood out with fear; quick came his struggling breath;

His hair stood rigidly on end; his face was pale as death;
And standing in a frightened pose, he stretched to heaven his arm,
While all the listening audience was filled with strange alarm.
Not a sound, not a whisper low, the awful silence broke,
The while, in faltering accents, the armless soldier spoke:
"I've fought in many battles, yet never once have fled;
And I've looked without trembling on wounded and on dead.
I've met with dreadful dangers upon both land and sea,
But never was aught dangerous that had alarms for me.
Yet now a nameless horror my very blood doth freeze;
That this may never come to pass, I pray upon my knees.
I pray,–but e'en the prayer, sirs, puts my heart in anxious flutter,–
I pray that I may never find such hairs within my butter."
A sympathetic shudder ran throughout all the tent,
As the armless soldier's plaintive prayer to heaven above was sent.
And though since this scene happened 'tis from ten to twenty years,
I can't even look at butter without bursting into tears.

A final note on P.T. Barnum. Since Thayer took his nickname, and later his pen name, from "the great American showman," a sketch of Barnum's life may also throw a sidelight on "Phinney." Phineas Taylor Barnum was born in Bridgeport, Connecticut, on July 5, 1810. As a young man he did odd jobs, kept store, tended bar, ran an abolition newspaper, and was selling tickets for a theater when opportunity in the person of Joice Heth knocked on his door. Heth was a hymn-singing black woman, believed to be the nurse of George Washington, 161 years of age–as verified by the papers in her possession, signed by Augustine Washington, the father of George. Barnum became her agent, and on August 10, 1935, arranged a reception for her in Niblo's Garden, New York. Gifted with an amazing memory, Heth could recall all the details of Washington's youth, including the nursing of the illustrious infant, and the cherry tree incident (which, however, she thought was a peach tree). The people flocked to see her, and from this early experience Barnum drew one of his life's great lessons, "There's a silver lining in every crowd" (Paxson, 636–39).

After that, Barnum's future was in show business. In 1842 he opened the American Museum, featuring Niagara Falls; the woolly horse; the Feejee Mermaid; General Tom Thumb, the celebrated dwarf; the bearded lady; and the "Egress." Many patrons hurried through the halls in pursuit of the elusive "Egress," until they found themselves outside the museum. In the late 1860s Barnum began to organize "The Greatest Show on Earth." With three rings under the big top he brought his circus to Madison Square Garden in 1871. After ten profitable years there he joined forces with one of his rivals, launched the firm of Barnum and Bailey, and opened under the new name in New York on March 28, 1881. The following spring he brought Jumbo, a huge African elephant, to New York, billing her as "The Only Mastodon on Earth," and "The Gentle and Historic Lord of Beasts."

A number of humorists drew upon Barnum and his menagerie for some of their materials. The great showman himself was one of the originals for Mark Twain's *Connecticut Yankee* (1889), while Jumbo's arrival in America inspired his hilarious short story, "The Stolen White Elephant" (1882). Edward S. Martin, one of the founding editors of the *Lampoon* included a sketch of Barnum in the first volume of *Life*, the national humor magazine he founded in 1883. Any resemblance between Barnum and Thayer, or any other writers or artists on the *Lampoon* staff, past or present, is, of course, purely coincidental.

P.T. Barnum

Of Phineas T. Barnum it is told, that when a malevolent person sent a couple of large snakes to destroy him in his cradle, the infant crawled to a bird-cage which was opportunely hung upon the floor near by, and opening the door induced the reptiles to enter and pasture upon the captive bird. Once in, he had them, and was found by his mother upon her return from the sewing circle, exhibiting his boas to the babes of the vicinity at one cent per babe.

Although the bent of his genius exhibited itself thus early, it was not immediately recognized. Opportunities for following his instincts were rare, and for lack of a better opening he contemplated, and for a time practiced literature as a profession. In imaginative writing lay his chief strength, and without unusual effort, he soon produced tales which at once took rank with Munchausen and the Arabian Nights. Then appeared the originality of his mind, for not content with the manner of publishing in vogue, he had his stories printed on great sheets of paper in parti-colored letters, illustrating them with pictures more astounding, if possible, than the text, and gave them to the public through the medium of paste and bill boards. Finding the cost of this to be too great for his resources, he went into the show business, which his great fame enabled him to conduct with such success that he became rich and universally respected, and was made Mayor of his native place [*Life*, 4/19/1883].

CHAPTER 10

The Harvard Athletic Committee

The close of Thayer's first year at Harvard was marked by an event that had a far-reaching significance for the future of intercollegiate athletics. On June 15, 1882, the Harvard Athletic Committee was organized to oversee and regulate all the athletic clubs on campus. The three men on the committee, all faculty members, were Charles Eliot Norton, cousin of President Eliot and professor of fine arts, John W. White, professor Greek, and Dr. Dudley A. Sargent, director of the Harvard gymnasium. Later in the year the committee adopted a set of rules that are the basis of our athletic regulations today. Formulating the first set of rules was no easy task. But the hard part was persuading the students, and particularly the faculties and administrators of other New England colleges, to go along with them. There must have been times when Norton, Sargent, White, and their successors wished that they had confined their activities to the classrooms. For, as Morison said, the 1882 baseball schedule "precipitated a reluctant Faculty into a policy of oversight and regulation that for nigh fifty years afforded that learned body more grief than any learned subject" (Morison [1936], 410; and Ronald Smith, 127).

Up to this time the control of Harvard's athletic clubs had been left to the students. They had organized the first crews and baseball clubs in the 1850s, and in 1874 founded the Harvard Athletic Association (HAA), the first organization of its kind in the country, to supervise all the athletic clubs on the campus. Andrew Davis, who studied the clubs at Harvard and published his observations in the *Atlantic Monthly* in 1883, was struck by their "wonderful organization." Not only were the various crews and teams under the leadership of captains, but each game had its representative association, which in turn formed part of the HAA. This tendency was also shown in the systematic character of the gymnastic exercises and various athletic contests, "restrained by rule, and managed with generalship and strategy, which had crystallized out of the rude and boisterous games which boys formerly played for fun and for exercise." The Harvard Base Ball Association elected officers, hired coaches and trainers, took in gate receipts, spent them, and made its own schedules. There were no eligibility rules, except that a player must be enrolled in some department of the university (Davis, 677; Morison [1936], 409; and Ronald Smith, 119).

Opening with a three-game series against the New York Mets at the Polo Grounds, Harvard's 1882 baseball club played a total of 28 games, including 11 with professional clubs, and 19, more than half, away from Cambridge (see Table 1). This was quite a change from the customs of 1655, when the Laws of Harvard College stated that "noe undergraduate upon any pretense of recreation ... shall be absent from his studyes [for] he shall studiously redeeme his time." Another thing that apparently concerned the Harvard faculty was the alarming increase in betting among the coeds at the Annex.

Table 1: 1882 Harvard Baseball Schedule

Date	Place	Opponent	Score
April 5	New York	New York	2–3
6	New York	New York	3–17
10	New York	New York	2–10
15	Boston	Boston	7–8
18	Boston	Boston	2–4
22	Worcester	Worcester	12–18
26	Lowell	Lowell	12–6
28	Boston	Boston	1–24
29	Providence	Providence	1–7
May 2	Cambridge	Tufts	23–2
6	Cambridge	Brown	7–6
12	New York	Stock Exchange	20–1
17	Cambridge	Dartmouth	8–11
19	Princeton	Princeton	4–9
20	Princeton	Princeton	14–13
27	New Haven	Yale	10–7
29	Amherst	Amherst	18–8
30	New York	New York	4–12
30	Staten Island	Stock Exchange	3–2
June 3	Cambridge	Princeton	3–9
5	Cambridge	Princeton	9–5
9	Cambridge	Amherst	10–0
12	Providence	Brown	17–13
14	Cambridge	Beacon	24–9
22	Cambridge	Yale	4–5
23	Cambridge	1877 Harvard Nine	18–0
26	Hanover	Dartmouth	10–11
July 5	New York	New York	4–5

Won 13, Lost 15 (overall)

Won 12, Lost 5 (amateur games only)

On May 18, 1882, the day before the first big game with Princeton, the *Lampoon* came out with a cartoon on the cover, "What Shall We Do with Our Girls?" "Well, Belle," says Amy, "How are you fixed for the College championship?" "I've got fifty on Harvard, Amy; but I *do* hope Princeton will win!" "Why?" "O, they've such a sweet little fellow that plays back-stop" (see illustration on page 100). Maybe the *Lampoon* was just having a little fun with Princeton's fine catcher, W.S. Schenck, who had been around for some time. He became the club's regular catcher in his junior year, 1879, graduated in 1880, and caught for a couple more years after that. In any event, the score of the big game was Princeton 9, Harvard 4. Belle was out $50! (Presbrey, 137; and Ronald Smith, 9.)

On top of complaints about the schedule and allegations of gambling at the Annex, there was a controversy about putting up a fence around Jarvis Field and charging admission, just like a professional ballpark. Proponents of the fence argued that since the club's expenses were paid by the students on a voluntary basis, and since some of the more thrifty students were watching the games for free, a fence would help solve the club's financial problems. But the *Crimson* thought that a fence would destroy the amateur atmosphere. On May 19, 1882, while admitting that many of the spectators were "deadheads," who watched the play from outside the railing, the paper objected that the fence, if built, would stand so near to the diamond that balls would be continually knocked over it. More importantly,

> [T]he unprofessional and chivalrous nature of our sports will be entirely destroyed by the sight of a regulation, unpainted, rough board fence, bristling with inverted nails. The Yale man's envy, that lovely sweep of green, extending almost uninterruptedly from the Gymnasium to the further side of Jarvis, will be hideously broken, and out athletic grounds will lose the generous, open appearance which betokens the broadening influence of college life, and become characterized by the mercenary and grasping aspect of those wooden bandboxes, the hired tracks.

No fence was built that spring, but some people obviously were up in arms over the mere suggestion of a fence.

Faced with the challenges to Harvard's athletic program that arose during the 1882 baseball season, the Athletic Committee examined methods of conducting sports, conferred with students, and reported before commencement that a standing committee ought to be appointed to regulate athletic sports, and that President Eliot be requested to ascertain if Yale, Brown, Dartmouth, Princeton, and Amherst (members of the Collegiate Base-Ball League) would unite with Harvard in prohibiting games with professional clubs. Eliot wrote to the presidents of other New England colleges in September, indicating that Harvard was prepared to take action on its own, but believed that common action would be more effective. All but Yale agreed. The New Haven school's policy at this time, and for many years to

THE

HARVARD LAMPOON.

SERIES II. VOL. III. CAMBRIDGE, MAY 18, 1882. No. 7.

WHAT SHALL WE DO WITH OUR GIRLS?

"WELL, BELLE, HOW ARE YOU FIXED FOR THE COLLEGE CHAMPIONSHIP?"
"I'VE GOT FIFTY ON HARVARD, AMY; BUT I *DO* HOPE PRINCETON WILL WIN!"
"WHY?"
"O, THEY'VE SUCH A SWEET LITTLE FELLOW THAT PLAYS BACK-STOP."

(*With all due respect to our artist, we would suggest, as a title to this picture,* "THE BAD HABITS OF OUR GIRLS.")

Our Girls (courtesy of the Harvard University Archives).

come, was summed up by their brilliant athletic adviser, Walter Camp. "Managers and captains," he said, "are absolute in their power, the rest of us bearing ourselves with proper modesty and decorum in offering here and there bits of advice" (Eliot [1881–82], 16–18; and Ronald Smith, 135–36).

Undeterred by Yale's reluctance to go along with the new rules, Harvard took unilateral action. The Athletic Committee fired Coach Robinson, the professional baseball coach who had been hired by the students, banned all Harvard clubs from competing with professional clubs, and denied professional trainers access to the college grounds. On October 7, 1882, the committee published the following regulations:

1. No college club or athletic association shall play or compete with professionals.

2. No person shall assume the functions of trainer or instructor in athletics, upon the grounds or within the buildings of the college, without authority in writing from the committee.

3. No student shall enter as a competitor in any athletic sport, or join any college athletic club as an active member, including baseball, football, cricket, lacrosse, and rowing associations, without a previous examination by the director of the gymnasium, and his permission to do so.

4. From the beginning of the college year 1883-84 no person shall be admitted as a member of any class or university crew unless he knows how to swim.

5. All match games outside of Cambridge shall be played upon Saturday, unless permission to play on other days is first obtained from the committee (Hartwell, 124–25).

At first, Harvard students took these developments in stride. In an editorial of October 21, 1882, the *Harvard Crimson* threw its support solidly behind Eliot's policy, expressing its regret that Yale was not willing to go along with Harvard's "crusade against professionals," and encouraging Harvard clubs with the words, "We'll just have to work a little harder, boys." With the baseball season still more than six months away, there was no reason for anybody to get too excited about what effect, if any, the new rules might have on the club's performance:

> The gentlemen who govern Yale honestly differed, no doubt, from President Eliot in their views upon professionalism, the influence of which their decision would make us believe they consider harmless. We are sorry that Yale will not join us in our crusade against professionals; but as she will not, we shall be obliged to get along as best we can, and must try to compensate for the advantage she will have over us by harder work in the various branches of our athletics.

In his annual report for 1881-82 Eliot reviewed Harvard's new policy, and stated the reason for the faculty's action. "Ball-games and boat-races," he said, "were in danger of losing that amateur quality which should always characterize the bodily exercises and sports of young men who are in training for intellectual pursuits." At the same time Eliot renewed his commitment to a strong, well-balanced athletic program that would benefit all students. The president stated that increased attention had been given to exercise and athletic sports within the past 25 years, and that the results, on the whole, were of great advantage to the University. The average physique of the students was sensibly improved; the discipline of the college was easier and more effective, and the ideal student was "transformed from a stooping, weak, and sickly youth into one well-formed, robust, and healthy." Eliot also recognized that "the perseverance, resolution and self-denial necessary to success in athletic sports turn out to be qualities valuable in business and other active occupation of after life." This was a significant observation, and would be echoed by President Theodore Roosevelt and many others in the years to come (Eliot [1881–82], 16–18).

On November 4, 1882, the *New York Times* published an editorial on college athletic sports, hailing the action of the Harvard faculty and urging other colleges to follow their example:

> Harvard has led where other colleges may wisely follow in framing college laws for the control of the athletic sports of the students. All college Faculties have, of course, the right to regulate the conduct of the students under their charge in athletics as in other matters, but, so far as we know, there has hitherto been no attempt to establish a body of written laws upon the subject, or to create by Faculty action what may be called a policy of athletics. ... Abuses of all sorts have been introduced, and the unchecked growth of the muscular department of our colleges has visibly diminished the students' store of available time and energy for books and blackboards. ... It goes without saying that up to a certain point proficiency at the oar and bat is conducive to a better comprehension of Greek words and tenses and a clearer conception of the sublime truths of the calculus. But excessive development of the biceps generally results in atrophy of the thinking faculties. The Harvard Faculty have not interfered a moment too soon, nor will serious students or wise parents accuse them of an unreasonable abridgement of the liberties of their charges.

As the *New York Times* admitted, however, a number of students objected to the first rule forbidding any college club to compete with professionals. "This rule has greatly displeased the students," said the editor, "and this very fact is a proof of its wisdom and timeliness." The intense rivalries that had developed had carried college athletics beyond their proper sphere. Great skill was developed by contests with professional ballplayers, but was not essential to a college player. "Assiduous practice will make a man an expert at billiards, and unremitting study will make him a well-read lawyer, but an attempt to combine the two processes will result in a poor billiard-player and an ignorant lawyer." After applauding the wisdom and prudence of the Harvard faculty in adopting rules 3 and 4 (a Columbia oarsman had drowned the previous summer while training for a race with Harvard), the *New York Times* noted that the age of senseless severity in college discipline had long passed. Jack in pursuit of a diploma was no longer in danger of coming out a "dull boy" through the policy of "all work and no play." The danger now, concluded the paper, "in these later times of regattas and tournaments and trainers, is of the contrary kind."

A few months later, before the 1883 baseball season began, the public discussion over intercollegiate athletics continued with an article by Dudley A. Sargent in the *North American Review.* He addressed the widespread misapprehension as to the amount and the system of physical training in American colleges. The tone of newspaper comment, which, as he admitted, was "often humorously intended, to be sure," was nevertheless misleading to readers. Athletics, gymnastics, and aquatics were not the chief subjects of college instruction, as certain editors would have readers believe. He wanted to correct this mistaken notion, and to call the attention of educators to the urgent need of some system of physical exercise in our higher institutions of learning (Sargent, 166; and Mott, 3:221).

Outside of the crews, said Sargent, very little rowing was done by individual students. At Harvard, Yale, Columbia, and Cornell less than 5 percent of the students rowed regularly, while in the smaller colleges, unless a regatta was coming up, the boathouse was hardly opened at all. The same was true for baseball. Only 18 students could play at a time, and two regular nines were all that the largest of the colleges maintained. The game, therefore, was limited to a class of experts, and only those who were members of the nine received the benefit of systematic training. At the same time gymnasts, as a separate class, had been rapidly diminishing in numbers. The gymnasium was used, regularly and systematically, chiefly by the boating men and the ballplayers as a means of keeping up their strength and skills during the long winter months (Sargent, 167–69).

The problem with college students of his day, thought Sargent, was that they tended to look upon college athletics simply as a field for rivalry. Of all the students in the country – outside of Harvard, Yale, and some other larger Eastern schools where there was a more general interest in physical training – not more than 10 percent gave any attention whatever to physical exercise, and less than 6 percent participated systematically and regularly as a means of culture and development. The solution, he thought, was a return to the gymnasium, to the harmonious cultivation of the student's mental, moral, and physical nature. If college faculties should permit a class of students to devote two, three, and four hours a day to physical culture, would it not be well, he asked, to make some provision for those who are not athletically inclined, but are more in need of exercise? This could be accomplished only by furnishing every school and college with a well-equipped gymnasium, by making its exercises a part of the regular curriculum, and by having them executed under the supervision of a competent instructor. Sargent described a course that was essentially practicable, and was being pursued at Harvard (*ibid.,* 170–79).

Arthur G. Sedgwick next took up the subject with an article on "Sports in and out of Colleges," which appeared in the *Nation* on March 29, 1883. Sedgwick, who had graduated from Harvard in 1864 and was a brother-in-law of Professor Norton, began by quoting a letter of President James McCosh of Princeton. There was a pretty widespread impression, said McCosh, that "the *enthusiasm* of college life" tends in the direction, not of literature or science, but of "muscles and bones"; and he told an anecdote of a father who, on the occasion of his son's graduation, bitterly remarked to a professor that he had sent his boy to college to become a scholar, but that what he had learnt there only fitted him for a position in a circus. "Certainly," McCosh continued, "the ambitious boy with a big body and a little mind feels it to be a mighty reward when he gets, because he has performed a feat, a cheer from 10,000 people assembled on the field in which Yale and Harvard are fighting for the headship." As the worst consequence of this spirit, the idlest fellow in his studies becomes the hero of his class, is feted, and gets the honors which his class has to bestow while the fine scholar is not appreciated, and is spoken of as a plodder, and branded with similar opprobrious epithets. Another thing McCosh disapproved of was that some students, "not satisfied with seeing the pure display of agility, wish something more stimulating, and bet on one side or the other," ending, in some cases, "if not in bankruptcy of fortune, in bankruptcy of character." Admitting the challenge posed by college athletics, McCosh said that the true way to meet it was that already taken at Harvard – for the colleges to undertake the supervision and regulation of college sports.

Sedgwick, agreeing in the main with the course taken by Harvard and Princeton, also wrote in defense of the students, reminding his readers that the *enthusiasm* for sport was not confined to college students, but was a feature of modern life outside as well as inside the colleges. "As a matter of fact," he added, "it runs a much wilder riot outside of them than it does inside." It was not college students who were responsible for the profound interest taken by the public at large, stimulated by the press, not merely in races or baseball matches, but in six-day walking matches, starving contests, quail-eating against time, and "events" which are of positive injury to the human body. Any student who reads the newspapers, Sedgwick argued, must infer from the space devoted to such contests that it is at least an open question whether the honor and glory to be obtained by success in this field is not as great as that to be achieved by distinguished services in the church, or at the bar, or in public life. Considering to what amazing excesses the love of "sports" of all kinds tends in the adult world, Sedgwick thought it was rather surprising that the college sports were, on the whole, still confined to "honest boyish contests of bone and muscle." And he found comfort and reassurance in the promise of leading colleges to supervise and regulate these contests. This type of supervision could check the spread of the feeling among the students, which adults do so much to encourage, that a man who can walk 500 miles in six days, or live without taking food for a month, or "jig" 20 steps in 17 minutes, "is a great public character, who reflects credit on his country and age, and whose memory will be cherished as a precious possession by generations to come."

Sedgwick took it for granted that colleges and universities ought to encourage athletic sports. It was useless to say, as some did, that athletic exercise was a good thing, but that athletic contests ought to be taboo. Anybody who would try to picture what sort of a place a college would be if the students pulled in wherries, exercised on parallel bars, ran, walked, and played ball solely for the purpose of physical "culture," and without any idea of rivalry, or of being found worthy of a place in a racing crew, or of holding a position in a college nine, would at once see that races, matches, games, and contests of all sorts are what give to college athletics 90 percent of their impetus.

Andrew Davis, another Harvard man, wrote on college athletics for the *Atlantic Monthly* in May 1883. The general interest taken in sports was so great, he said, that the question as to what extent college faculties should encourage athletic contests and intercollegiate games had become a subject for public discussion. As for the critics who denounced the policy of encouraging sports in colleges, Davis invited them to "play the good fellow, and come and see some of our matches," and not only the matches, "but the daily outpouring of the students into the green fields, where they can breathe the pure air of outdoors, and for the moment forget their books, and with joyous excitement obtain that bodily exercise which all need, but many neglect." To gain distinction in any of these sports, critics should remember, the members of teams and crews who enter upon a course of training voluntarily adopt methodical habits of life, content themselves with a simple diet, abandon all forms of indulgence which are condemned by sanitary authorities, keep early hours, and in general conform their lives to just the model that would be selected for them by their well-wishers. Nor do the hours adopted for their daily exercise necessarily interfere with the maintenance of a good standard of scholarship. If we admit that there are young men who overdo the thing; that the contests stimulate a tendency to back up the college by betting; that the travel to play matches during term time interferes with the studies of those on the teams, and that the games ought to be arranged to prevent this – still, the weight of these charges is partially offset by the stimulus which these games give to the great health-giving system of athletics, and which keeps our young men boys for a year or two longer, and will lengthen the lives of many of them by a decade. The effort should be not to prevent the games, but to regulate them so that the attendant evils would be avoided, and all their good influence exerted.

In the spring of 1883 the Princeton faculty, following Harvard, passed a resolution prohibiting the baseball team from practicing with professional teams. As soon as he heard about this John S. Harlan, captain of the nine, decided upon a diplomatic maneuver. After some correspondence he got hold of a baseball nine out of a patent pill manufactory in New Jersey, nonprofessionals, and, on the whole, he said, "fairly decent fellows." Just before the practice game started Harlan told the company captain about his troubles with the rule against professionals, and asked if he and his men could make a suitable demonstration. He had previously sent complimentary tickets to the faculty, telling them that he had succeeded in getting a nonprofessional nine for a practice game. Many of the faculty came. Harlan recalls the scene:

> I presume they never saw such an exhibition of ruffianism as those good fellows gave us. The pitcher came out in a red under-shirt, and with one shoe off; and the way they howled and quarreled among themselves, and with the umpire, and with me, was astonishing. The result was so convincing that when I appeared at the next Faculty meeting, with a copy of the rules adopted by the professional league, parts of which forbidding swearing, card playing, gambling, and boisterous conduct, etc., I carefully read, the Faculty unanimously rescinded the rule made a few weeks before. The result was that practice games with professionals again became possible, and Princeton made an excellent record for the season [Presbrey, 141].

Harvard was not so fortunate. As no other college adopted the rule against playing professionals, this put the school under a severe handicap. After a few practice games against exclusively amateur competition, the nine were not as well prepared as they might have been for a road trip to New Haven and Amherst early in the season. On May 12, 1883, Harvard was "whitewashed" by Yale, 8–0. Two days later, the club scored only once against Amherst, losing 8–1. On May 16, when the club got back to Cambridge, the *Harvard Herald* took the defeats as evidence of "the disastrous effect" of the antiprofessional rule on Harvard athletics. The club's play in the field in both games was all that could have been wished for, said the student paper,

> but it is folly to expect the nine to win games without being able to bat, and it is equal folly to expect a nine to be able to bat without any practice. Our nine enters the championship contest this year heavily handicapped from lack of practice in batting good pitchers. This practice has been acquired in previous years by playing professional nines or by being under a professional coach through the winter. Every other college nine has had the benefit of one or both these methods of practice this year; but Harvard has been forbidden to use either. Consequently, in beginning the college games, we find ourselves confronted with pitchers

> a great deal better than any we have batted before. The result is defeat. Undoubtedly if the championship series were long enough we should in time learn to bat effectively; but the series consists of only eight games, and in all probability by the time we shall have become able to do any batting the season will be at an end. In the meantime, while we have been getting the practice the other colleges will have been getting the games.

It was too late, continued the paper, for any change in the rule against professionals to have any effect on Harvard's chances for this year, but it was essential for the success of the nine the next year and for coming years that the rule should be repealed, and the sooner it was repealed the better.

The *Harvard Crimson* agreed. Reversing the stand taken the previous October, the paper said on May 19 that the editorial in the *Harvard Herald* should convince the faculty of the "injustice and folly" of their antiprofessional rules, and joined with the "college at large" in asking for their repeal. The faculty had meant well when it made the rules, and was upheld to a certain extent by the opinion of the college, but the *Crimson* was now firmly convinced that they had gone too far, and, if they persisted in their course of action, would provoke a "crisis" involving not only students but the graduates of the college:

> We believe that so far as the Faculty pass measures calculated to do away with the evils of professionalism, they have the undergraduates with them, to a man; but as soon as they deprive us of the benefits of professionalism, the very opposite is the result. . . . Now if there is anything we deprecate, it is a collision between Faculty and students; but it is evident to the most blind that where measures calculated to destroy Harvard's athletics are persisted in, such a crisis is sure to come; and, as we say, not only will it involve the students themselves, but a large majority of the graduates, to whom Harvard athletics are dear. Nor could such a crisis fail to harm the University, for it would be no petty grievance but a real and widespread discontent. We cannot too earnestly beg the Faculty to give careful consideration to their action before they persist in maintaining it to the bitter end, for it is a question of the greatest moment, and cannot be carelessly disregarded.

After a start like that, things could only get better. And they soon did, as the nine, home at Jarvis Field on May 23, rebounded with a victory over Brown by the score of 14–2. A week later, on May 30, Harvard turned the tables on Amherst, 6–4; and the next day, June 1, they won a big game with Princeton by the surprising score of 13–4. Although the nine won only 12 games out of 28, under the circumstances, it was not a bad season (see Table 2).

Table 2: 1883 Harvard Baseball Schedule

Date	Place	Opponent	Score
April 14	Cambridge	Beaon	2–7
19	Cambridge	Whiting's Nine	6–1
21	Cambridge	Holy Cross	17–5
24	Cambridge	Whiting's Nine	12–7
28	Cambridge	Beacon	5–0
May 1	Cambridge	Bowdoin	6–3
3	Newton	Newton	8–4
9	Cambridge	Beacon	10–18
12	New Haven	Yale	0–8
14	Amherst	Amherst	1–8
16	Cambridge	Beacon	5–6
18	Princeton	Princeton	5–6
19	Princeton	Princeton	4–13
23	Cambridge	Brown	14–2
24	Cambridge	Dr. Pope's Nine	6–5
26	Cambridge	Yale	1–5
30	Cambridge	Amherst	6–4
June 1	Cambridge	Princeton	13–4
2	Cambridge	Princeton	3–5
8	Cambridge	Hub	20–0
13	Cambridge	Beacon	9–3
16	Cambridge	Newton	5–8
20	Providence	Brown	5–10
21	Cambridge	Yale	1–4
23	Cambridge	Brown	2–1
25	Holyoke	Holyoke	2–3
26	New Haven	Yale	0–1
30	New York	Yale	1–1
July 2	Staten Island	Staten Island	2–1
3	Philadelphia	Young America	20–14
3	Philadelphia	Yale	9–24

Won 12, Lost 15

CHAPTER 11

Editor at Work

Phinney became an editor of the *Harvard Lampoon* in the fall of 1882, at the beginning of his sophomore year, joining Fatty Briggs, who had been made an editor the previous spring, and Felton, who was promoted at the same time as Thayer. Lent and Santayana were admitted to that select circle in February 1883, followed by Hearst, Sanborn, and Winslow in the fall of 1883. With his freshman year behind him now and a course of electives decided upon, Thayer's contributions to the paper became much more numerous, and he began to concentrate on prose, exercising his pen upon a wide range of subjects. Among the 33 items he wrote that year, all in prose, were "Physics Applied," "An Amoozin Adventur" (after Artemus Ward), "Mary's Little Dog," "Big Poker," and "Der Gustoms of Der Country." As a sample of his best work, four stories are included here.

The first is another horror story about the food at Memorial Hall. The tale turns on an ill-timed pun which caused an adventurous student, Charley Ross, curious about how food was prepared at the Hall, to become "Lost in the Kitchen." The inferno-like setting for the descent into the subterranean windings beneath the Hall shows the influence of Dante. Perhaps Thayer was studying the great poet in one of Professor Norton's classes at this time. Norton had lived in Italy for some time after graduating from Harvard in 1846, and published a prose translation of Dante's *Vita Nuova* in 1859. In addition to his professional responsibilities at the university, where he was professor of the history of fine arts from 1875 to 1897, in 1878 he invited a small group of scholars to meet regularly with him at his home at Shady Hill for reading and discussion of the works of Dante. In 1881 that group inaugurated the Dante Society of America, with Longfellow its first president. Thayer, as we shall see, visited Italy himself after graduation, and read Dante all through his life. "Lost in the Kitchen" appeared in the *Lampoon* on December 15, 1882 (Xiques, 187–90).

The second story, "Silent Communication," published May 18, 1883, concerns the mobility of the human features and their peculiar ability to supplement, and, on occasion, even surpass, the powers of speech. The third item is "Game Law Reform," from the issue of June 1, 1883. Summer vacation was a dangerous time for undergraduates. In increasing numbers they were coming back to Harvard in the fall as engaged men. This caused sadness and anxiety in their classmates, some of whom had more important things to think about than the athletic reforms of the faculty. The fourth story, "One of the Class Autobiographies," was published on June 29, 1883, as a tribute, no doubt, to one of the departing seniors.

Lost in the Kitchen

Note. – The following account of a daring exploration of the subterranean windings beneath Memorial Hall, which disastrously terminated in the loss of the explorer, was discovered attached to one of the dumb-waiters which communicate with these regions.

Search parties have been sent out, and every effort will be made to discover the wanderer. Slight hopes, however, are entertained of his ultimate rescue. If, indeed, he has not already succumbed to fatigue, it is feared that the powerful odors which pervade this locality, and the utter absence of digestible food, will have resulted in the death of the brave fellow. The narrative in his own words is as follows.

Always fond of adventure, I early conceived the idea that an exploration of the kitchen of Memorial Hall, while satisfying my craving for excitement, might, if intelligently prosecuted, be of inestimable value to science and remarkable interest to the world at large. This desire increased as I reached what is called the age of discretion; but which in my case, alas! must be termed rather the age of imprudence.

At last I resolved to undertake the exploration. Procuring the services of a native guide, I equipped myself with a dark lantern and provisions for four days; then, after devoting a few moments to prayer, we plunged into the abyss. On reaching the bottom, I was disappointed to find that a strong odor of boiled cabbage had shut out the view, which, on a fine day, is said to be extremely magnificent. Strange noises reached my ear, which excited in me an inclination to turn back, and a tendency on the part of my hair to rise. Swallowing my fear, however, I boldly followed the guide, at the same time carelessly displaying a seven-bladed jack-knife in my belt.

A deep roar, hitherto so blended with the other noises as not to excite my particular attention, grew constantly more distinct as we proceeded. I looked to my guide for some explanation. He responded that it was only the sausage motor. A slight shiver loosened my front teeth; but quickly recovering, the guide did not notice my alarm.

"Yes," said he, "it is a very powerful machine; it turns out fourteen miles a day. We run it on the co-operative plan."

"I don't understand," said I.

"I will explain. In the dining-hall, directly over the receiver of the motor, is a nicely poised trap. When a member of the association steps on this, he drops through, and undergoes a very interesting process which ultimately terminates in sausage, having a market value of from 13 @ 17 cts. per pound. An instructor fell in the other day, and _____"

"The result was all that could be desired?" I interrupted.

"He was one of the so-called hard men," continued the guide, without noticing my question. "At the time of his entrance to the receiver, the steam-gauge registered a pressure of 120 pounds to the square inch. 'Twas all in vain. The cylinder-heads were all blown out, and the motor was otherwise seriously damaged. There is one consolation, however."

"And what is that?" asked I, trying to swallow my cruel disappointment.

"Why, I hear that the instructor has been reprimanded by the faculty for meddling with the apparatus in the kitchen."

We had now proceeded about fifteen miles, and as night was rapidly drawing on, we selected a spot for our bivouac under the spreading branches of a clothes-horse. After partaking of the frugal contents of our knapsacks, we built a fire to scare off wild beasts, and then lay down to rest.

Next morning I awoke much refreshed. It was partly owing to my untimely mirth that I am now where I am. Many curious sights caught my eye as we walked along. I remarked [about] two men who were engaged in emptying flour and water into the top of a huge oaken cask. Another person was drawing off pure Jersey milk from an orifice in the bottom. Huge rolling-machines were mellowing the beef-steak. Especially interesting was a small factory where artificial clams were in the process of manufacture.

We had now nearly reached the limit of previous explorations, and were resting a moment in the chamber where the butter was stored. Mountains of this substance were piled up before us. It was a melting sight. I was so unfortunate as to remark that all the cakes of butter were stamped with an S.

"Yes," said the guide. "It is called Samson on account of its strength."

Then it was, wretched creature that I am, that I saw an opportunity to give rein to my brilliant wit. "Perhaps," I said, "like Samson, it would lose its strength if shorn of its hair."

A wild, low cry, a rushing sound, and I was alone; alone in that wilderness. My brain reels; I'm burning with fever heat; the sausage motor dances all horridly before my eyes. Send aid to me.

Charley Ross
(December 15, 1882)

Silent Communication

The mobility of the human features enables mankind to express much, in a delicate and expeditious manner, which, if rendered into speech, would seem at best clumsy and prosaic. Novelists have long been accustomed to make their characters convey to one another by means of their eyes meanings too fine and subtle to be expressed by word of mouth. Indeed, this silent means of communication has in the field of fiction attained a degree of perfection which appears almost incredible to one accustomed to couch his thoughts in the tame realities of ungrammatical English and swear-words. The following quotations, for example, taken from some works of the day, seem to exceed the limits of the possible.

"The stern old man rudely unwound his daughter's arms from her lover's neck; but as the disconsolate suitor motioned to depart, Estella bent upon him one last look, which said, 'If you'll call round again about eight o'clock, when the old man has gone to the caucus, I'll let you in at the cellar door, and we'll have some peaches and cream in the kitchen.'"

Here is another: "They were sitting at dinner alone. She did not speak; her heart was too full for utterance, but for one moment she flashed upon him her glorious orbs. He read her soul in the glance, which said far plainer than any paltry words could say it, 'Gimme plenty of stuffin' and lots of gravy.'"

It does, to be sure, seem improbable that any modification of the features would accurately express "plenty of stuffin' and lots of gravy"; but my personal experience in the efficacy of a single look warns me not to be unjustly critical.

I particularly remember one occasion at home on which there was company at dinner. When the dessert was placed upon the table, and I was eying the delicacies with pleasant anticipations, my mother directed upon me a warning look, which said just as plain as print that it wouldn't be safe for me to call for pie more than twice, unless I wished to subject my skin to an unnatural inflammation.

At another period, much later in life, I remember presenting my father with a number of unpaid bills. My sire examined them. He did not say a word, but he looked a whole folio volume with an appendix. The drift of the information conveyed by his glance was to the effect, that I would bring the gray hairs of my parents with sorrow to the grave; that this kind of thing had been going on about long enough; that to-morrow I would begin work in the store; that I had gone several stages on the road which leads to *crime;* and that hereafter I must go to church on Sundays and pass my evenings at home.

A look is often more effective in argument than all the words in an unabridged dictionary. However drunk a man may be, it is difficult to make him admit that he is drunk. You may reason with him as long as you please, he will claim that he is perfectly natural in his action and speech; that whatever peculiarities there are, are due to his bringing up; and that he can walk a straight line just as well as you can. But you take that man home and let his wife look at him, as wives are accustomed to look in such cases, and the poor fellow will feel in an instant that he has been drinking more than is good for him, and the old woman knows it.

Among the lower animals, also, silence is often more communicative than speech. The twinkle of a bulldog's eyelid will make a thinking man cross the street, while the barking of a Newfoundland dog will only make him swerve a few feet from his course.

Silent communication is capable of extensive development, and if properly cultivated might be made to supersede language in expressing many trite ideas, such as, It is a fine day, Bad weather, Going to clear off to-morrow? etc. The more intricate affairs of life, such as the Star Route Trial and the Tewksbury Almshouse Investigation, must continue to be interpreted verbally.

(May 17, 1883)

Game Law Reform

The following recent enactment of the State Legislature will be of interest to those students who propose to spend the vacation at some popular summer resort.

"*Whereas* the race of bachelors has of late years diminished with alarming rapidity; and

"*Whereas* the said diminution has been greatest in the summer months, owing to the pitiless ardor with which the said bachelors have been pursued and brought down at that time; and

"*Whereas* the said bachelors, being led on by such bait as *picnics* and *rowing by moonlight,* have been lured into pitfalls and ambuscades, and then ruthlessly fallen upon and annihilated; and

"*Whereas* it is of interest to this Commonwealth that the race of bachelors, being so necessary to the ornamentation of our parks and public squares, should not be exterminated, –

"*Be it enacted,* that whosoever shall be detected and convicted of hunting the said bachelors, or any other bachelors, either with snares, nets, fishing-tackle, or in any other manner whatsoever; or whosoever shall be discovered with a bachelor in her possession between the months of June and October inclusive, shall be fined not more than $5,000 nor less than $50, or imprisoned not more than twenty-five years, nor less than three days; and furthermore

"*Be it enacted,* that between the months of November and May inclusive, the pursuit of bachelors shall be lawful and proper, provided such pursuit be practised for the purpose of profit or support. But whosoever shall be detected and convicted of maliciously maiming or mutilating a bachelor for the sake of ungodly amusement, and leaving their victim thenceforward to lead a crippled existence, shall be liable to the same penalties which have hereinbefore been stated.

"Passed by the Legislature of this Commonwealth, and with the approbation of His Excellency the Governor, on this twenty-fourth day of May, in the year of grace one thousand eight hundred and eighty-three, New Style."

(June 1, 1883)

One of the Class Autobiographies

Seven cities claim the honor of being my birthplace, and any of them, I am confident, would be glad to bury me at the public expense. Where I was actually born I am unable to say, and my age would likewise be wrapped in obscurity were it not for the fortuitous circumstance that I have a twin brother, from whose age I am able to calculate my own. My twin brother was born in East Somerville.

With regard to my early life it may be said that I evinced unusual precocity. I was but four years old when I smoked my first hay-seed cigarette, and but nine when I kissed another boy's sister. In the following year I called my brother a darned fool. The popular verdict was that I was very old for my age.

Not having known my mother previous to her marriage, I am unable to say why my father married her; but at all events he afterwards regretted the act: for had it not been for her, I should never have been born, and father was always extremely sorry that I and my twin brother ever happened.

Until I was ten years old father's business was to take care of me, and he had to work about eighteen hours a day. He died in 1871, simply because I didn't know it was loaded. Next time he'll know better than to fool round when I'm playing soldier.

I attended numerous academies before I came to Harvard, but none of them were capacious enough to give my ardent temperament free play. So finally I went a few terms to the reform school, whence I graduated with high honors. I never thought of going to College until the Faculty offered me a reward to stay away. Then I gave a proctor three dollars, and was admitted with eight honors. I was absent from College during the greater part of the course, spending much of my time in calm rural retirement.

During my Freshman year I broke about every pane of glass in the College buildings, and though I cannot say that I was editor of any College paper, I supplied the basis for about 97 percent of the news. I took little interest in any branch of study, and was in the habit of passing my examinations by proxy.

Finally, I should say that during these four years I have had a real nice time, and whatever my future lot may be, wherever my path in life may lie, there will be one tie ever linking me to the seat of my Alma Mater,—I refer to that bill at Pike's.

(June 22, 1883)

CHAPTER 12

President of the *Lampoon*

Still a bachelor, Thayer returned to Harvard in the fall of 1883 to begin his junior year. After his outstanding work as a sophomore, he was the natural choice for president of the *Harvard Lampoon,* and assumed his duties at once. Briggs, Hearst, Lent, and Santayana had already joined the staff, and Phinney convinced his best friend Sam Winslow to be *Lampoon* secretary, a position unknown on earlier staffs.

After seven years of a semi-precarious existence the *Lampoon* was rumored to be on the verge of extinction. The *New York Times* noted that there was "talk of discontinuing the *Lampoon,* Harvard's *Punch,*" adding that some of the editors of the *New York Life,* a popular humor magazine, had graduated from the college paper. "The sole reason assigned is a lack of subscribers, and it seems a pity that a paper of its recognized brightness should be given up."

In his first editorial as president, October 19, 1883, Phinney assured his readers that although the *Lampoon* had spent the last two weeks "hovering on the brink of the grave," he had "decided to linger on; and to-day, accordingly, he greets his fifty thousand seven hundred and nineteen readers – only three of whom have paid their subscriptions – in the full possession of that faculty for sparkling, gushing humor which has done so much towards filling up Mount Auburn Cemetery." He was particularly happy with the large freshman class:

> We are pleased to see the multitude of bright and happy faces, glowing with the ruddy bloom of youth, whose wearers have nestled down among us so confidingly. We like this confidence – this simple, unquestioning trustfulness, which has enabled us to borrow eleven hundred dollars already. We are delighted, dear Freshmen, to behold evidences of your extraordinary frequency; for what do your numbers tell us? They tell us that our dear old University is annually spreading her influence wider and wider; that her educational facilities are ever growing better and better; and that we can work your class for about fifty more subscriptions than usual.

A cartoon by Fatty Briggs in this issue commemorated the 1883 nine. It shows a tombstone with a catcher's mask and crossed bats engraved over the inscription, "Sacred to the memory of the '83 nine." Above is the caption, "Non-professionalism did it." Thayer editorialized on the nine's summer trip, which included a Fourth of July game with Yale played at Philadelphia, and won by Yale, 24–9.

> It behooves us here to make a few remarks with regard to what our ball nine has been doing since our last issue. We will try to average up the general disability of the players in as few words as possible. Several of the players have perfect fielding records, having sought every possible chance to make an error, and uniformly succeeded. Several of the nine also have perfect batting records, having missed all the balls pitched to them, with unerring precision. The rest of the players were something less skilful, some of them occasionally knocking a foul tip, but they retrieved the disgrace at other times by striking out with the uniform regularity of an eight-day clock. Few, perhaps, have heard of the internal dissension with which the nine was threatened during its summer trip. In the fifth inning of the game at Philadelphia, one of the fielders, in a moment of forgetfulness, caught a fly. The unavoidable consequence was, that a man was put out. This fielder was naturally regarded with coldness after this display of insubordination; and, though no direct demand was made to him for an apology, he could hardly avoid seeing that any such practical jokes would not be countenanced by the rest of the nine. The man being conscious that though he had erred he had done so unintentionally, and not wishing to provoke any ill-feeling, frankly acknowledged his fault, and promised in the future to abstain from any such ungentlemanly conduct. The general good-feeling was thus restored, and we are pleased to say that from that time till the end of the trip not another fly was caught. With as good a nine next year, it seems as though we might secure the last, instead of the next to last, position.

Thayer also had a few more serious words to say. With the close of the previous year the main strength of the *Lampoon* went out in the senior class. Unless men come forward to write for it and draw for it, he said, the impossibility of continuing the paper was quite apparent. "We appeal, then, to all readers of the *Lampoon,* who derive any amusement from its columns, to untie some of the humor confined in their brains, that it may go abroad and do for others what the humor of others has done for them. . . . In short, we should like college men to contribute from their brains as well as from their pockets; for such a double support is necessary for the welfare of the paper."

Still no response. His editorials began to contain pleas for help on a regular basis. Without Phinney's prolific writings and Hearst's substantial allowance, the *Lampoon* might not have remained in print during this time. On December 7, 1883, in his first editorial after returning from Thanksgiving vacation, Thayer wrote:

> It has again become a disagreeable necessity for us to solicit the college for contributions. We cannot believe that there are no men in the University at the present time who possess the ability to write articles of such a nature as the *Lampoon* is accustomed to publish. If there are men who can write,—and we believe that there are,—it seems as though they might individually do a little towards enlivening a paper which displays such a meagre variety of talent as, we regret to say, the *Lampoon* at present displays. We desire above all things that men should try to write, and that they be not discouraged if they do not succeed at first. Hereafter we shall endeavor to return all rejected contributions, stating the reasons why they were declined. The *Lampoon* has in the past been considered enjoyable reading by the students; whether it shall be so regarded in the future or not, depends on the students themselves.

Phinney's modest assessment of the talent on the *Lampoon* ought to be weighed against the compliments of the *Yale Courant,* which Thayer reprinted in his December 21, 1883, issue: "The *Lampoon* is as good as ever. Its cartoons and satire are no longer confined to college absurdities, but everything capable of being burlesqued is handled fearlessly, and the defeated aspirant for governor comes in for his share. The prose and verse is uniformly excellent. The time should soon come, when Yale will feel sufficiently strong in humorists and satirists, to open a new field for honest rivalry." To which Thayer added: "There is a touching truthfulness about the above that moves us."

Fried salt codfish for Thanksgiving dinner? Not exactly the traditional fare, but this is what Phinney claimed he had in his editorial of December 7. In a sentimental aside, he finds Memorial Hall, with its infamous butter, and the Yard much the same as when he left them:

> The Thanksgiving vacation has come and gone, and now it seems as though it were only the day before yesterday since we left Cambridge. It is over now; that dinner with its wealth of fried salt codfish is now only a sacred memory. Time has dealt kindly with the college during our absence: only a few more gray hairs on the butter at Memorial, only a few more wrinkles in the table cloths. . . . We went into the yard, and there also everything was much the same; same old beech trees, same old buildings, same pristine flow of iron bitters from the Massachusetts pump.

Phinney snuck another solicitation for subscriptions into his Christmas editorial, with some advice on what to "take home to mamma." It was an excellent idea. No need to include any modest disclaimers in this one. Here Thayer glories in the past accomplishments of the *Lampoon,* and lets loose with a good sales pitch:

> Beautiful snow and the Christmas season have arrived together, and along with them comes the great question of what shall we take home to

> mamma? After long and deep meditation on the subject we can think of no gift so tasteful, so elegant, and so universally appropriate, as a year's subscription to the *Lampoon.* The *Lampoon* caters for all ages and for all tastes; it is always in season, and considering that it is so full of spice, we may truthfully say that season is always in it. To the gloomiest household it brings one happy day in every fortnight, and makes the most dismal garret bedroom a bright and cheerful home. Many a man cast down and meditating suicide, has read our columns just in time, and exclaimed, "There is still something to live for"; many a despairing mother with a drunkard husband, a large family, and no cash, has gathered fresh courage and strength through reading a copy of our paper found in the ash-barrel. The series of *Lampoons*, for the year 1884, will contain sketches from the most eminent American artists and literateurs; and Lampy's past reputation for unequalled excellence will be jealously guarded in the future.

The main issue during Thayer's term as president of the *Lampoon* (October 1883–February 1885) was the control of intercollegiate athletics. In his annual report for 1882–83, President Eliot said that intercollegiate contests become absurd when some of the competitors employ trainers, and play with professional players, while others do not. Further regulation was therefore needed by agreement between the colleges (Eliot [1882–83], 22–23). In the fall of 1883 the Harvard Athletic Committee sent letters to more than 20 leading schools inviting them to meet in New York on December 28 to discuss the control of athletics. The schools that were represented at the conference were Amherst, Bowdoin, Brown, College of the City of New York, Columbia, Cornell, Dartmouth, Harvard, Hobart, Lafayette, Lehigh, Princeton, Rutgers, Stevens Institute, Trinity, Tufts, Union, University of Pennsylvania, University of Vermont, Wesleyan, and Williams. Yale was not represented. The following letter was issued by the conference:

> The object of physical training is to confirm health, correct morbid tendencies, strengthen weak parts, give a symmetrical muscular development, and secure as far as possible a condition of perfect physical vigor. In order to accomplish these desirable ends, young men are encouraged to take exercise and to enter into the general practice of athletic sports and games. If, however, the object of physical training be lost sight of, and the desire to win the championship or to attain the highest degree of excellence in these sports be made the *paramount* aim, then the practice of athletics is likely to be attended with evils that demand consideration [Hartwell, 125–27].

Some of these evils, the report continued, had already begun to make themselves manifest in the practice of college sports. With a view to correcting them, and of making athletic exercises an aid instead of a hindrance to the cause of education, the conference recommended the adoption of the following resolutions:

1. That every director or instructor in physical exercises or athletic sports must be appointed by the college authorities, and announced as such in the catalogue.

2. That no professional athlete, oarsman, or ballplayer, shall be employed either for instruction or for practice in preparation for any intercollegiate contest.

3. That no college organization shall row, or play baseball, football, lacrosse, or cricket, except with similar organizations from their own or other institutions of learning.

4. That there shall be a standing committee, composed of one member from the faculty of each of the colleges adopting these regulations, whose duty it shall be to supervise all contests in which students of their respective colleges may engage, and approve all rules and regulations under which such contests may be held.

5. That no student shall be allowed to take part in any intercollegiate contest as a member of any club, team, or crew for more than four years.

6. That all intercollegiate games of baseball, football, lacrosse, and cricket shall take place upon the home grounds of one or other of the competing colleges.

7. That no intercollegiate boat race shall be for a longer distance than three miles.

8. That the students of colleges in which these resolutions are in force shall not be allowed to engage in games or contests with the students of colleges in which they are not in force.

In support of the first resolution, it was stated that physical training should form an essential part of a collegiate course; that the person selected to superintend this branch of education should be a man of character and ability, and that the dignity of his position should be recognized by giving him the moral support of the appointing power of the college. There was general agreement on this regulation, and on most of the others, but the second and third were more controversial. As a result, when the recommendations were distributed to the faculties and administrations of the colleges for discussion and ratification, there was no general agreement. Sedgwick reported in February 1884 that Harvard and Princeton had adopted them; Brown would probably refuse; there was no chance that Yale would accept them; and even if Columbia and Wesleyan did, the defection of Yale would make any attempt at union nearly impossible. Furthermore, as Sedgwick noted, the idea prevailed among a considerable body of students that the regulation of sports was something that the faculties of colleges had nothing to do with. Nevertheless, the faculties must have a voice in it, as long as they had a voice in college discipline at all. The health of students, the occupation of their time, and their morals were all affected, and unless the colleges were going to abdicate all their disciplinary functions and convert themselves into lecturing and examining machines, they would always have to exercise some supervision over sports (Sedgwick [1884], 182–83).

The *Lampoon* took a somewhat different view of the matter. Fatty Briggs created a special Valentine's Day card to the faculty from "Ye *Professional*," a professional baseball player, for the February 15, 1884, issue. Two weeks later, on February 29, Thayer wrote an editorial in which he lamented the fact that, judging from the actions of the faculty, "we have relapsed into a state of second childhood." Accompanying the editorial was a sketch of Professor Norton – always a favorite with the *Lampoon* staff – holding a babe on his lap and feeding it with a large spoon:

> We cannot speak too highly of the action which the faculty have taken in this matter of athletics, and we are wise enough to avoid a dismal failure in attempting to do so. We are now quite convinced of what hitherto we have hardly dared to hope, that the University tendency at Harvard is progressing steadily – backwards. Within the past few years the choice of electives has become free, and attendance at recitations is free to a certain extent. We have many liberties unknown to our predecessors of a hundred years (and less) ago; we can go where we please and to bed when we please, we can dress how we please, and eat what we please. We can smoke brands of tobacco and drink brands of whiskey not prescribed by the faculty. In fact, nothing has been left compulsory except salvation, and at times there have been indications that that also would become voluntary.
>
> Parental authority once removed is now being again imposed upon us, and so it must be presumed that we have relapsed into a state of second childhood. The question now is how far should the restraints on our conduct be carried. Some restraint is certainly necessary, for we are too thoughtless to be trusted with the responsibility of our own actions. We feel this to be so. With a mother's fostering hand to guide the spoon or pin a bib-tucker about our neck, that elaborate pattern of mock-turtle soup would never have obscured the naturally beautiful texture of our green silk cravat. We, therefore, call upon the faculty, – piteously, pleadingly, – either to superintend the feeding of the students personally, or appoint capable and efficient deputy feeders.

On a more serious note, there was also some discussion of the issue in the *Harvard Herald-Crimson*. Most of the students and alumni seemed to be opposed to the regulations. On Monday evening, March 3, a mass meeting of undergraduates was held in Holden Hall and filled that building to overflowing. Five resolutions were read and carried unanimously, asking for a reconsideration and revocation of the regulations which the faculty had recently passed. In response, the faculty met on March 4 and resolved that it desired a further consideration by the conference on intercollegiate contests of the proposed regulations. There were no further considerations that year. On March 13, however, the *Herald-Crimson* reported that Professors Sloane of Princeton, Sargent of Harvard, Van Vleck of Wesleyan, Goodwin of Columbia, and Merton of Harvard had met at Columbia on March 11, and addressed a circular to each college interested to the effect that as there was no prospect that the details of the plan would be received with general favor, no further move would be made by the committee.

President Eliot must have been very disappointed with these developments. He had the interests of the students at heart, not just the few who had the ability to participate in varsity sports, but the many who did not and who therefore needed a good democratic system of exercise and sports such as the one championed by Sargent. On April 25, the day Brown arrived for an exhibition game with Harvard, President Eliot ventured the opinion that nobody derived any healthful exercise from baseball except the pitcher and catcher. The other players, he suggested, simply exposed themselves to taking severe colds by wearing thin garments in the open air without any opportunity to put their blood in active circulation. The *New York Times* responded by portraying Eliot as a "hopeless theorist," and recommended that he take a class in baseball, and play shortstop and first base for a week (*NYT*, 4/26/1884). Thayer, on the other hand, found some real inspiration in the president's remarks. He invented a new indoor baseball game, which was advertised in the May 30 edition.

Lampy's Automatic College Base-Ball Nine

Our automatic base-ball nine is made up as follows.

For basemen we use three large panes of glass which readily permit all balls to go through them and can be easily rattled. A shadow fills the position of shortstop, being recommended to our notice by its power of seeming to do a good deal without accomplishing anything. Any small inconspicuous object which will not stand in the way of the backstop serves admirably for a catcher. Our pitcher consists of a rotary-motion glass ball trap with a forty-foot rise, and for outfielders we employ skylights neatly pasted over with tissue paper.

Owing to the inability of the fielding nine to bat, it was found necessary to provide one extra machine for the position of batsman; this may be secured from us at a slight additional expense. Our batsman consists of an ingenious arrangement by which a barrel hoop is fastened at one end of the periphery of an eccentric, propelled by a crank.

An experiment was recently made in which two nines of the above construction were pitted against each other, and the results were gratifying in the extreme. The score at the end of the fifteenth inning was 0 to 0, neither side having made a base hit nor an error.

We are now prepared to supply western colleges with base-ball nines at the following prices:

Nine No. 1. Consists of hard pine woodwork, ordinary window-glass basemen and a homely but durable shadow. All iron work is of best quality, finished plain. Put up complete in a pasteboard box; price, $26.50.

Nine No 2. Consists of varnished black walnut woodwork, ground glass basemen, ornamental shadow. Iron is all handsomely painted. Complete in a tin box; price, $42.50.

Nine No. 3. Consists of polished mahogany woodwork, French plate glass basemen, and a gilt-bordered shadow. All exposed iron work nickel-plated. Put up in a brass box; price, $63.00.

All our nines are warranted for one year, and all breakages which occur during that time will be repaired by us *free of charge.*

N.B. The batsman should be carefully oiled before each game.

Harvard's 1884 nine was a good deal more active than the *Lampoon* automatic nine. Rebounding from the catastrophic 1883 season, the club compiled a respectable record of 18 victories and 9 defeats, including 2 wins each against Dartmouth, Princeton, and Yale, and finished the regular season in a tie with Yale for the college championship. A crowd of over 4,000 howling spectators attended the deciding game, played in Brooklyn on June 27, which was described by the *New York Sun* as "the most exciting contest at base ball by college nines ever seen in the metropolitan district." The final score – Yale 4, Harvard 2 – is a score Harvard men have never quite forgotten (Blanchard, 198, 300).

The 1884 club was led by L.V. LeMoyne, a senior outfielder, and the veteran W.H. Coolidge, who was playing second base for his sixth and last year, and was getting to know the position pretty well. Winslow, a junior, and Edward H. Nichols, a sophomore, took turns in the pitcher's box, which in those days really *was* a box, 50 feet from the plate, while Herbert T. Allen, another sophomore, handled the catching chores. The first college game on the schedule was with Brown, played at Jarvis Field on May 1, and won by Harvard with the score of 8–1. Amherst visited Cambridge a week later and won a close one, 9–8. Then Yale came to town for an exhibition game on May 10, won by the visitors, 8–1. Winslow and Nichols shared the pitching in this game. Two days later, when Princeton played in Cambridge, Winslow went the distance as Harvard rebounded to defeat the Tigers in 13 innings, 5–4. And this one counted for the championship. Thayer's editorial comments in the *Lampoon* of May 16 indicate how seriously the students took even an exhibition game with their arch rivals. He also mentions a delegation from nearby "Muckerville," perhaps Somerville, which attended the concert celebrating the win over Princeton.

Well, Yale has done it again, and the spring influx of gold to New Haven has fairly set in. They do say that Yale men are brutal; but if brutality will enable us to wear diamond shirt studs, flowered waistcoasts, and patent leather shoes, in heaven's name let us be brutal. We are tired of seeing Yale eat fruit while we eat husks, drink wine while we drink water, sing when we sigh and laugh when we weep. If our teams would cuss, hoot, kick, fight and *win,* every mother's son of us would say Heaven bless them as we incidentally took the money from the stake-holders. They tell us to back the nine. We have tried this for three years, and now we intend to back out. If the nine think backing is indispensable to success, they can try backing us a little while. That is what the Yale nine does; the Yale nine is board and lodging for half the sports in college. Dozens of men go to Yale without a cent in their pockets, and work their way through college in luxurious style by uniformly staking their money on the home team. There is nothing wicked about this sort of gambling; the element of risk is entirely absent; winnings are the reward of honest toil, not the uncertain spoil of gamesters. When the Yale nine come to Cambridge, they bring along an iron safe to carry home the valuables in; and we will say for the benefit of such men as contemplate visiting New Haven this week, that there is a society there, founded in 1732, for forwarding destitute Harvard men to their homes.

Still there is some consolation, we "fit" the tiger successfully; but it ought not to have taken thirteen innings to do so. For the first time within the memory of the oldest undergraduate, the Glee Club celebrated a Harvard and not a Princeton victory. The Brass Band lent a great deal of assistance to the jubilation of the evening. We noticed, however, that the men with the big horns blew cautiously and with apparent timidity. They will, no doubt, conquer their bashfulness before the next public performance.

Never has such a large audience attended one of our open-air concerts, proving effectually the wisdom of a low and uniform price for admission. The delegation of muckers from Muckerville as usual displayed their keen critical taste by their discriminating applause; hereafter we hope that lemonade and sandwiches will be provided for the entertainment of these appreciative guests. Unless additional inducements are extended to them, they may cease to come, and the college can ill afford to lose their interesting society. When we get a good thing we should learn to keep it.

Everybody seemed to be happy Monday evening, and in a mood to cheer vociferously and impartially all the toasts proposed, saving one which no one ventured to offer – The Athletic Committee. We hope for many happy returns of the day.

Thayer probably accompanied the nine to New Haven to play a return game with Yale on May 17, this one to count in the college championship. The train stopped at Hartford, and a chest protector invented by William Gray, a Hartford man, was brought on board for Allen, the Harvard catcher. None of the nine had ever seen one before and it was looked upon as quite a curiosity. The next day, before the game, the members of the team tested this contrivance by throwing balls at Allen, who was wearing it. The test was so successful that he wore it in the game, and thereafter. Allen's catching, Winslow's pitching, and the superb outfield play of Tilden, Nichols, and LeMoyne were the features of the game on the Harvard side, as the visitors from Cambridge won a hotly contested game by the score of 8–7. Down by 7–4 going into the ninth, Harvard rallied for four runs to pull it out of the fire. Said the *Boston Globe*: "The Harvard delegation hugged their nine till the bones cracked, while the disconsolate countenances of the Yale showed plainly their disgust at Harvards crawling through such a small hole." Three more victories, over Amherst, Princeton (by the score of 15–3!), and Williams, rounded out the merry month of May, and made more palatable a defeat by Brown, at Providence, 10–6. Thayer commented on the nine's accomplishments in his editorial of May 30:

> Fresh victories, fresh cause for rejoicing, and more sleepless nights for conscientious proctors. Who can blame us for illuminating our joy with crimson fire and sounding it abroad by aid of cannon crackers? Yet the parietal committee attempted to put checks on our effervescing gladness.
>
> Our faculty have displayed their usual poverty of tact in the matter of these celebrations. The Brown faculty know how to manage these things; they possess a better knowledge of human nature. When Brown wins a victory the President makes a speech of congratulations to the students—something like this, probably: "Gentlemen, you have won to-day a great victory, and you have therefore my heartfelt thanks. Your success and the success of the college are indissolubly united; every victory you win adds prestige to the institution which you represent. When at some future time a member of that glorious nine observes the increasing wealth and influence of what will then be, perhaps, Brown University, he can proudly put his hand upon his heart and say, 'I done it.' Now, gentlemen, I want you to feel that the present occasion is an eventful one in our history. I want you to commemorate the day; I want you, as a particular favor to me, to make Rome howl, and tint this orderly city with a delicate shade of red. You must have a bonfire, and nothing I can think of will make a better one than the elegant coupe which I have recently purchased, and which, I assure you on my honor, has never yet been used. In order to make the coupe burn more fiercely, I have provided half a cord of excellent kindlings and a half-barrel of pure astral oil. The Dean has been instructed to distribute unlimited fireworks to all who apply, and the parietal committee will lend you all the assistance in their power in making night hideous. A full line of choice liquors has been placed at your disposal by the registrar; and, in fact, nothing will be found lacking that is needed upon such an occasion."
>
> Having finished, the President, we may suppose, ignited a fuse connected with a small barrel of gunpowder, and then retired to the bosom of his family.
>
> What was the effect of this speech? The applause that greeted its conclusion was feeble. The students were stricken with a feeling that any demonstration whatever would please the faculty. Accordingly, only the more pacific and law-abiding element in the college applied for fireworks, and their gayety was spiritless through lack of heart. The strong anti-rule party which usually predominates at such times obstinately went home and to-bed. By half-past ten every light was out in the dormitories.

On the other hand, how much was added to our celebration by the opposition which it encountered, every student knows.

In 1883 the Harvard Athletic Association, with the help of a grant of $1,000 from the corporation, had graded the northern portion of Holmes Field for a new baseball ground and quarter-mile track. It was on low ground and was late in drying out in the spring, so that all games were played on Jarvis Field until June. Dartmouth and Harvard played the first college game on this field on June 11. The pitching of Winslow quieted the Dartmouth bats sufficiently for Harvard to win, 6–1. The same teams met again on the same field on June 14, with a similar result: Harvard 14, Dartmouth 2 (Blanchard, 198, 300).

Under the circumstances, unfortunately, the student delegation from Dartmouth had little opportunity to exercise their lungs with their distinctive college yell, "Wah-hoo-wah!" This had been devised by Daniel A. Rollins, a senior, with the valuable assistance of Professor Proctor, his Greek professor, in the fall of 1878, a few months before Dartmouth visited Harvard to play the first baseball game between the schools. According to Henry Melville, a classmate of Rollins who was personally drilled on the proper way to articulate the yell, the second syllable was soft – "hoo," and somewhat prolonged, preparatory to a mighty bark with the final "wah!" As John King Lord has said, the wah-hoo-wah combines "a rare degree of sentiment and sound, for while it seems to suggest by a kind of whoop the Indian tradition in the founding of the College, it also possesses the true excellence of an effective cry, a rhythmic cadence and a great volume of sound. When properly given with slow and sonorous utterance it will in the mouths of a hundred men overpower any other known cry given by twice as many." William Byron Forbush, of the class of 1888, recalled it well: "That college cheer – how much it brings back to me! Its savage 'wah-hoo-wah' rings in my ears, even as I heard it when last I gave it to bid my classmates farewell, in those days when college dreams were all there was of life and when BASE-BALL was its noblest conflict" (Dartmouth College Archives; and Seymour [1990], 145).

While the effectiveness of the yell is no mystery, the exact origins of the words have been obscured by the passage of time. John B. Stearns, a professor of Greek and Latin at Dartmouth, has traced them back to an Indian named "Wahowah," sometimes spelled "Wohawa," whose English name was Hope Hood. In the 1680s he was chief of the land from Exeter to Salmon Falls. It is supposed that he died of his wounds received in the fight at Fox Point in 1690, and his friends brought him across the river and buried him on the point of land which bears his name, Hope Hood's Point. Mary P. Thompson has located this point on the "western shore of Back River, above the three creeks," and adds: "It is a spot as wild and solitary as it was 200 years ago, covered with thickets where the wild grape runs from tree to tree and where, it is affirmed, the groans of the Indian warrior are still to be heard among the moaning branches." It is perhaps worth noting that Harvard lost two of the first three games played with Dartmouth at the Hanover campus in 1880, 1881, and 1882, and then waited a good ten years to go up there and play them again (Blanchard, 299–302).

A trip to Providence on June 18 for an exhibition game with Brown resulted in another victory for Harvard, 12–3. Three days later Yale came to Cambridge for a big game at Holmes Field. Harvard jumped out to a 7–0 lead after two innings, and won going away, 17–4, as Winslow and three other players collected three hits each, while Nichols proved to be very effective in the box. Harvard and Yale finished the regular season locked in a tie for the college championship, setting the stage for a showdown in Brooklyn on June 27 (*ibid.*, 263).

Although the price of admission was double the professional charge, there were 3,000 spectators present when the game was called at 4:00 P.M. The gathering of ladies on the grandstand was especially noteworthy, as hundreds of bright eyes and smiling faces added a rare charm to the place. They enjoyed the game thoroughly, although they did not allow their spirits to overflow so hilariously as did their male escorts. Their cheers and college cries startled the neighborhood, as it was the first time in some years that a real college game had been played in Brooklyn. If a man went out on strikes or even got a single strike called on him it was sufficient to start an Indian whoop from the opposite side which shook the neighboring buildings. The *New York Herald* reported the scene as follows:

> Prior to the decisive Yale-Harvard game yesterday the Brooklynites imagined they knew something about enthusiasm, but now they are perfectly satisfied that they never had the slightest inkling of the definition of the word. The style in which the collegians carried on would have set the Feejee Islanders to the blush. If a man went out on strikes or even got a single strike called on him it was sufficient to start an Indian whoop from the opposing side which fairly shook the neighboring buildings. The free seats contained about 1,000 spectators, who seemed pretty evenly divided between the admirers or representatives of the two colleges, and the din that was kept up from that quarter reminded one of the braying of a thousand blood hounds. The Harvard delegation gathered on the west end of the stand and the Yales took up their position on the east end, and when the one end of the stand was not trembling under the frantic yells of the boisterous students it was because the other end had the call.

From other accounts, about 100 young men wearing light suits and straw hats and carrying crimson banners and ribbons made their headquarters at the lower west end of the grandstand. They were led by young Goodwin, the fast half-mile runner who seemed to have as strong a pair of lungs as he had legs. Whenever he wished the Rah! Rah! Rah! of Harvard to be heard, he would jump down in front of the stand, wave his arms up and down, and the spectators, knowing what was coming, would put their fingers in their ears to shut out the terrible din that would surely follow. The main delegation from Yale, under the leadership of Louis Hull, "the well-known college athlete," was seated near the center of the grandstand, while the rest of the Yale contingent went to the east end of the grandstand, and the rival parties contended for two and a half hours to try to drown each other's voices. Neither succeeded, and only the spectators appeared to suffer.

The Game

The umpire, Mr. Daffners, tossed the coin promptly at 4:00 P.M. Harvard won and took the field amid fierce, loud, and prolonged shouts of "Rah! Rah! Rah!" Hopkins and Terry, Yale's first two batsmen, were disposed of under "a perfect storm of applause" from the Harvard forces. The next batter, Bremner, doubled, and the Harvard shouts were drowned in the enthusiastic cheers of the boys in blue. Then, on a wild pitch, and a base hit by the cleanup hitter, Souther, Yale scored their first run and the yelling became deafening. Harvard went down one, two, three, and the first inning ended with the score Yale 1, Harvard 0.

In the second inning the Yales were retired for a blank, and Harvard took up the cheering. After Tilden had retired, Nichols and Allen made clean hits, and both scored on a wild throw by Souther with Winslow at the bat. The Harvard crowd shouted themselves hoarse as the Crimson took the lead, 2–1. From the style in which both clubs went about their work it was evident that it would be a close and stubbornly played game, and it proved to be so. Both clubs put forth their utmost exertions during the third and fourth innings, but the fielding was too sharp to allow any runs to be scored. The wildest kind of excitement prevailed in the fifth inning when Yale tied the score. Brigham opened the inning with a clean base hit. McKee followed with a base on balls. Odell forced Brigham out at third base, but Hopkins came to the rescue with a two-bagger, sending McKee home and tying the score. Odell also tried to score on the same hit, but was thrown out at the plate.

Yale took the lead in the top of the sixth. Terry led off with a base hit, Bremner followed with another, and both advanced a base on an error by Coolidge at second base, amid a burst of cheers from Yale throats. Then it was Harvard's turn to holler, as Souther and Booth were both retired before any runs could be scored. Stewart went to the bat next, and with two out, brought Terry and Bremner both in with a base hit, as the Yale crowd sent up a perfect storm of applause.

This was the end of the scoring, but Harvard had a brilliant chance for a rally in the bottom of the eighth. Smith opened with a base hit, Le Moyne drew a base on balls, and both runners were forwarded a base by a wild pitch. Coolidge was then given a base on balls. With the bases loaded and no outs,

Baker advanced to the bat with a perfect opportunity to tie the game. But Odell, the Yale pitcher, rallied in his position and struck Baker out. Smith was forced out at home by Phillips for the second out, and Tilden, the cleanup hitter, was finally caught out, leaving three men on bases. The game was intensely exciting at this point. Yale sent up a sigh of relief, and then another burst of applause as the third man was retired. And so ended one of the most remarkable ball games in college baseball history, with the score: Yale 4, Harvard 2. (This composite account of the game is taken from the *New York Herald, Sun,* and *Tribune.*)

CHAPTER 13

Winslow's Nine

Our Sam of the Nine
Was a captain fine,
And a fine good cap was he,
He called for his bat,
And he called for his ball,
And he called for his basemen three.

Each player he was a very good player,
And a crack at the game was he;
With Elis bold they draped the mould,
And the score was good to see.

Menu, Class of 1885
Twentieth-fifth Anniversary Dinner
Algonquin Club, June 28, 1910
[*HUC,* 8 (1915): 161.]

Ten straight! An unbroken chain of ten straight victories without a defeat against the best college clubs in the country, that was the record of the amazing 1885 Harvard nine captained by Worcester's Sam Winslow. It was the first (and last) time that a club in the Intercollegiate Base Ball Association went through a season unbeaten. Bill Sullivan, sports editor for the *Boston Globe,* said they would go down in baseball history as the "ten-straight" team. "To win the college championship was not glory enough," he said, "they were to be satisfied with nothing short of a clean record of inter-collegiate contests." Overall, the team won 27 of 28 games, with the one loss coming early in the season to the Cochituates, a strong amateur club in the Boston area—and Winslow turned that one into an important learning experience for the club (*BG,* 6/21/1885).

Harvard had a great team that year, they could all play ball, but Winslow's leadership was recognized as the single biggest factor in the club's success. "It is not an exaggeration," Sullivan told his readers, "to say that Harvard owes the championship mainly to Sam Winslow." Of course, one man cannot win the game alone, he admitted, but the 1885 season proved conclusively to all Harvard men that a captain is a large part of a nine. In short, Winslow "has

made the nine play ball in its broadest sense, a thing which has not been done at Harvard effectively since the time when Thayer held the reins," referring to Fred Thayer, 1878. The final score of the last game–Harvard 16, Yale 2–was almost enough to make a Harvard man forget the frustration and disillusionment of beating Yale twice during the regular season the year before, only to lose the playoff game by that infamous score of 4–2.

Captain Sam Winslow was born on April 11, 1862, the son of Samuel and Mary Weeks (Robbins) Winslow. He was educated in the public schools of Worcester, including the Classical High School, and at the Williston Seminary in Easthampton, Massachusetts. Very little is known of his baseball career in Worcester, but he must have learned something about the game and played it pretty well, since when he entered Harvard in 1881 he was elected captain of the freshman nine. As a sophomore he was good enough to play for the varsity. The next year he pitched and played the outfield for Harvard's second-place club, but his big chance came in the fall of his senior year in 1884. Phillips, a junior and an outstanding second baseman, was elected captain of the varsity, but was badly injured in the head playing football. His injuries were so serious that for a time his life was in danger. Winslow was named acting captain in his absence, and under his direction the candidates for the nine worked out regularly during the long winter months in the gymnasium (*NCAB*, 29 [1941]: 452; Blanchard, 198–200; *NYT,* 4/24/1885; and *BG*, 6/21/1885).

Sam had probably watched the professionals work out during the winters in Worcester, and put the experience to good use. Instead of the usual routine of practicing batting and catching in the "cage" of the gymnasium (a large open portion of the basement partitioned off from the rest of the room with strong wire screens and furnished with a dirt floor), he introduced the game of handball which the professionals practiced in the winter. "This game," according to the *New York Times*, "brings out agility and rapidity of motion in the players, trains the eye, and is beneficial in many ways." Besides handball, Winslow put the nine through regular exercise on the chest weights and running track, varying their work on occasion with dumbbells and Indian club swinging. Phillips, in the meantime, gradually improved, and when he got well enough was ordered to go to the South by his physicians, and to give up any hope of playing baseball in the coming season. Winslow was then unanimously elected captain, and the management of the team was under his control (*NYT,* 4/24/1885).

According to Sullivan, Winslow had a very simple theory which he put into practice, namely, "that batting wins ball games." As soon as the men could get outside in the spring several nets were set up. These served as back stops

Opposite: **Winslow's Nine (back row, from left) Elderly, Tilden, Winslow (Capt.), Smith, Foster, Willard; (front row) Wiestling, Claflin, (Mgr.), Nichols, Allen, Litchfield, Beaman (courtesy of the Harvard University Archives).**

for batsmen who stood in front of them, and practiced hitting all kinds of pitching. The advantage of this system was that several players were able to practice batting at the same time. Enough men were found in the college who could curve the ball, more or less, and no catchers were necessary. That the Harvard boys were determined to win the pennant was evident from the unusual zeal with which they practiced. Hours were spent on the diamond during this season, whereas in comparison the practice time of former seasons could be measured by minutes. And the extra practice appeared to by paying off, as they won all seven of their practice games in April, playing all of them at home against MIT, Dartmouth, Brown, Bowdoin, and amateur clubs in the Boston area. Still, no one was overly optimistic. As the *New York Times* reminded its readers, the rules of the faculty prohibited Harvard from playing with any professional team or with any amateur team which was considered more or less "tinged with professionalism." Since there were few strong amateur nines in the vicinity of Boston which the faculty deemed "suitable to play with Harvard," it was difficult to get practice games against strong pitchers, and even to arrange any games at all (*ibid.,* 4/24/1885).

The Harvard nine was averaging ten runs a game until they met the Cochituates on May 4 and faced their fine pitcher Bent, who held them to one run while his club scored three times. Captain Winslow found in this game that his men could not bat drop pitching. Bent's style of delivery was similar to that of Odell of Yale, and consequently it was the very thing Harvard needed to work on the most. As Sullivan said, Winslow's next move was one of the keys to his success (see Table 3). He immediately induced the Cochituate twirler to go to Cambridge each afternoon, so that the boys could have a chance to bat his effective pitching. As Bent was an amateur there was no objection to Winslow's plan, and as a result the members of the team learned to bat drop pitching. The players persisted in this kind of practice all through the season, and as a result they could hit any pitcher in the college league. In fact, after they defeated Yale at New Haven on May 16 by the score of 12–4, the boys acquired such confidence at the bat that the pitchers of the other teams were apt to get rattled when they faced Harvard's heavy hitters (*BG,* 6/21/1885).

Replacing Phillips at second base was another big challenge for Winslow. Litchfield, a sophomore, was given a shot at the position in April, and when this did not work out C.W. Smith, a junior, was shifted from first to second, and Waldo Willard, a sophomore, was stationed at the initial portal. The rest of the club was as follows: Allen, 1886, catcher; Nichols, 1886, pitcher; Beaman, 1885, third base; Wiestling, 1887 short stop; Tilden, 1887, left field; Foster, 1887, center field; Winslow, 1885, right field. Allen, Nichols, Smith, Tilden, and Winslow were regulars from the year before, Beaman was a substitute, Willard and Wiestling had played for the freshmen, and Foster was a walk-on who had played ball before coming to college, but did not try out for the freshmen team, waited until his sophomore year to try out for the

Table 3: 1885 Harvard Record

	Opponent	Place	H.	Opp.
April 11	MIT	Cambridge	11	4
16	Dartmouth	Cambridge	3	2
18	Roxbury	Cambridge	16	0
22	Brown*	Cambridge	9	1
25	MIT	Cambridge	19	5
28	Bowdoin	Cambridge	6	2
30	Picked Nine	Cambridge	9	8
May 4	Cochituate	Cambridge	1	3
5	Cambridge	Cambridge	20	1
7	Amherst	Cambridge	13	2
8	Tufts	Cambridge	4	1
9	Brown	Providence	3	1
11	Trinity	Cambridge	4	2
13	Picked Nine	Cambridge	3	1
16	Yale	New Haven	12	4
18	Amherst	Amherst	15	5
20	Tufts	Medford	13	11
22	Princeton*	Princeton	6	5
23	Princeton	Princeton	15	6
27	Dartmouth	Cambridge	12	5
June 1	Princeton	Cambridge	13	4
2	Princeton*	Cambridge	13	4
6	Dartmouth	Cambridge	9	3
10	Williams	Cambridge	8	0
15	Brown	Cambridge	3	2
17	Brown*	Providence	15	2
20	Yale	Cambridge	16	2
23	Dr. Pope's Nine	Cambridge	12	3

*Exhibition games
Source: Blanchard, 300.

varsity, and "somewhat to the surprise of the college succeeded in winning the coveted prize" (*NYT,* 4/24/1885; and Blanchard, 200).

Thayer was probably one of the more than 200 Harvard men who went to New Haven on May 16 to support their nine. A large assemblage of about 4,000 people attended the game. The grandstand was crowded, while the double line of ropes on each side of the diamond was lined deeply with carriages and coaches, to make no mention of the people lining the most exposed portion of the wire fence. The Harvard men were gathered around some crimson flags in the right field. Captain Winslow showed great coolness and self-possession on this occasion in dealing with the unruly crowd, and in this respect he bears a strong resemblance to the mighty Casey. According to the account in the Philadelphia *Sporting Life,* the game was prolonged to 3 hours and 20 minutes, "owing to the incessant yelling of the Yale sympathizers to disconcert the Harvard players. Every time an uncalled for demonstration of the nature occurred, Captain Winslow stopped his men until quiet was restored" (*SL,* 5/27/1885).

The game was close for four innings, with Yale leading 2–1 going into the top of the fifth. Harvard then rallied for 7 runs to take a commanding 8–2 lead, and won going away, 12–4 (see Table 4). "The jubilance of the Harvard men was unbounded," said the *Boston Herald,* "and cheer upon cheer followed the scoring of their nine." Willard and Winslow each went 3 for 5 to lead Harvard's 12-hit attack, while "much credit" for the victory was due to Nichols for his pitching and Allen for his catching, which was without an error (*BH*, 5/17/1885).

Table 4: Inning by Inning Score of
Game Played on May 16, 1885

	1	2	3	4	5	6	7	8	9
Harvard	0	0	0	1	7	0	1	3	0–12
Yale	0	1	1	0	2	0	0	0	0–4

From New Haven the Harvard nine next went to Amherst on May 18. The club's hard hitting continued as they won their fourth straight game in the College Association by defeating Amherst, 15–5. Yale and Princeton were tied for second place with three victories and one defeat. The *Sporting Life* described the team's triumphant return to Cambridge:

> You talk about painting a town red. If anybody wants to take a few lessons on this point let them apply to the Harvard boys. They did some very bright painting last Monday night, and laid the paint on thick. The return of the victorious college nine, after defeating Yale and Amherst, was received with music and fireworks at the Albany depot, and the members of the team were escorted to Cambridge by about 200 students, headed by the college band and members of the glee club. The route of the procession was lighted the entire distance by fireworks of every description, and when the company arrived at Harvard square the entire body of students were out to receive the ball players, although it was nearly midnight. The players were carried around the yard on the shoulders of their wild classmates, who cheered everybody and everything, until they were literally tired out [*SL*, 5/27/1885].

To give Nichols a rest Winslow pitched a couple of exhibition games on the road, the first with Tufts at Medford on May 20, a close one won by Harvard, 13–11, the second with Princeton on May 22, also won by Harvard, 6–5. The next day Nichols was back in the box for a game with Princeton that counted in the conference championship. Harvard's heavy hitters won this one handily, 15–6, and followed it up with two high-scoring victories over Dartmouth, 12–5 and 9–3, and another over Princeton, 13–4, to keep Harvard unbeaten and preserve her one game lead over Yale in the college conference. In one of the games with Princeton Winslow swatted a memorable home run that Willard remembered almost 40 years later, and described for the *Boston Transcript*: "Winslow, in a Princeton game, hit the ball so far that the Princeton left-fielder was content to mark down the spot where the ball stopped rolling and made no effort to field the ball in. I remember this very well, for, as Winslow rounded third on his way home, I coached him to slide. This he did very accommodatingly, and his home run was finished in a cloud of dust and blaze of glory" (*HUC*, 1 [1886]: 60; *BT*, 6/19/1923; and *HUC*, 9 [1915–25]: 194–95).

On June 12, with three big games coming up against Brown and Yale at the end of the season, Winslow had to suspend one of his best players for repeatedly breaking the training rules. This was the first time anything like that had happened at Harvard, and President Eliot called Sam into his office for a little heart-to-heart talk. One of Winslow's classmates tells the story:

> Winslow had a great team in 1885, but business and discipline had a great deal to do with the success of the crimson during that year. He showed what he was made of by suspending one of the best men on the team just on the eve of two decisive games because the player had repeatedly broken the rules of training laid down by Captain Winslow. Shortly afterwards "Sam" got a summons from President Eliot. He had never spoken to the President before and didn't know what it meant. President Eliot opened the interview by asking him why he had taken such extreme measures in suspending a player, a thing that had never before happened at Harvard. "Sam" related all the circumstances, and when he had finished President Eliot said: "Winslow, you did just right, and you deserve to win!" [*HUC*, 8 (1915): 130–31].

And Harvard *did* win. But the first of these games, played with Brown at Cambridge on June 15, was the closest conference game of the year. Although outhit, 11–3, Brown was tied with Harvard at 2 all going into the top of the ninth, when Harvard scored a single run to win the game (see Table 5). This clinched the championship for Harvard, since with two losses it was impossible for Yale to tie. The feature of the game was the fine work of Harvard's battery. Nichols struck out 20 men, while Allen chalked up 7 assists and 16 put outs.

Table 5: Inning by Inning Score of Game Played on June 15, 1885

	1	2	3	4	5	6	7	8	9
Harvard	0	0	0	1	0	1	0	0	1–3
Brown	0	0	0	0	0	0	1	1	0–2

At the end of the game the champions were borne off the field on the shoulders of their companions. They headed toward the gymnasium, where the students gathered in a body and cheered each member of the nine and the championship they had brought to dear old Harvard. Later in the evening there was a general celebration in the Yard, with the band, glee club, and fireworks playing a prominent part. But there was a matter of one more game yet to be played. Maybe it didn't matter so much now that the championship had been won, but Yale was coming to town on June 20. And that was always a big game (*SL*, 6/24/1885).

The grounds at Holmes Field were completely packed with people. There were about 6,000 spectators within the grounds, while the total number of people who witnessed the game was at least 8,000, among whom were nearly 1,500 ladies. And the Harvard boys gave them plenty to cheer about as they romped to a 16–2 victory. Winslow, hitting second in the order, reached second base on a fly ball to right field that was muffed, and came around to score Harvard's first run. Nichols scored right after him, giving Harvard a 2–0 lead before Yale had a chance to bat. Then Elis came back with a run in the bottom of the first, and that was all the scoring until the fifth, when Harvard rallied for 7 runs, presenting Nichols with a practically insurmountable 9–1 lead. Harvard finished with 16 runs on 18 hits, while Nichols held Yale to 2 runs, the second scored in the ninth, on a total of 4 hits. The headlines in the next day's *Boston Globe* read: "Harvard Hoarse with Cheering. The Wonderful Record of Captain Winslow's Nine. Old Cambridge Painted Crimson, so to Speak." The crew also won that day, which added to the occasion:

> Fire crackers, fish horns, Roman candles and bombs, backed by the exuberant voices of hundreds of excited students gave the college grounds at Harvard square last evening a Fourth of July appearance. Such a crushing defeat as was administered to the New Haven men yesterday afternoon was unexpected, even to the most hopeful of Harvard's sons. The enthusiasm at the close of the game was comparatively mild, but by nightfall the reaction commenced, and before supper time a strong corner had been made in the stock of all fireworks to be found in the square. When the news of Columbia's defeat reached the college yard the excitement knew no bounds. Cheer after cheer rent the air, first for the ball tossers and then for the victorious boat crew. As the stars came out, so did the fireworks. In front of Matthews' were gathered some 400 students, who employed their time in burning up powder and in shouting. Colored lights were burned in the square. From the windows of the neighboring dormitories Roman candles were set off in profusion, while an occasional rocket hissed spitefully on its way southward, as if on a journey to tell the crestfallen crew of Columbia and the vanquished Yale men that this is Harvard's year. During the evening the streets and neighboring sidewalks were crowded with the townspeople, whose interest in the matter of celebration was occasionally manifested by the lighting of a stray fire-cracker or applauding in an undertone the stalwart figure of some player as he passed by [*BG*, 6/21/1885].

The *Boston Globe* included a long account of Winslow's work throughout the season under the headlines, "Playing Under a Leader. How Captain Winslow Put His Men in Form and Overcame All Obstacles." The battery also received a good share of the credit. Nichols was "the terror of all batsmen." Few pitchers in the country delivered the ball more swiftly, and his curves were perplexing. Probably the only college catcher in the college league who could hold him was Allen, his regular catcher. "The way in which Allen has stood behind the bat and taken Nichols' rifle-shot delivery has been, indeed, remarkable." Besides doing most of the pitching, Nichols was also the top hitter on the club with an even .500 average for the ten championship games.

But the long and the short of it was, as Sullivan wrote in *Sporting Life,* "Sam Winslow has made the boys play ball." He set out from the start to get nine players who could hit the ball, and succeeded beyond all expectation. "The Harvard players are hitters, and hard hitters at that," said Sullivan. "The way they pound the ball is something astonishing." They won their games with the bat, hitting a phenomenal .306 as a team, compared to .144 for the opposition. Winslow's average was a respectable .295. His real contribution to Harvard's offense, however, was reflected in the team batting average, which was in no small degree the result of his superb coaching and leadership (*SL*, 6/24/1885).

In the 1920s, when he wrote the baseball chapter for John Blanchard's history of Harvard athletics, William T. Reid put the 1885 season in perspective. "The year 1885," he said, "remains one of the outstanding years in Harvard baseball history for all time." And it certainly helped Harvard men get over the 1884 season – at any rate, *most* Harvard men (Blanchard, 200).

CHAPTER 14

The Ivy Orator

On Class Day, June 19, 1885, four days after Winslow's nine brought the baseball championship back to Harvard, Thayer rose to deliver the Ivy Oration. He began by recalling his boyhood days in Worcester, conjuring up fond memories of his Irish nurse, the green fields, the leafy groves, and the sparkling waters of Lake Quinsigamond. He recounted a lesson he had learned one day when a picnic at the lake was ruined by noble thoughts. And he assured his hearers that he would not repeat this mistake, and ruin their picnic. In speaking of the faculty, he remarked that the purpose of the university was to afford them amusement. But the faculty played only one game. When the students got tired of playing that game, and took up "base ball, foot ball, boating and other unhallowed sports," the faculty appointed a "committee plenipotentiary." The committee prosecuted its work with great diligence, but when the ball nine piled up one victory after another, the committee began to get discouraged, and was permitted to retire (Ronald A. Smith, 129). Thayer wanted to say something about the man who was greeted by the infant populace with cries of "that's Sam," but could not rob the Class Poet of a means of livelihood. Sam Winslow was the hero of the hour. And yet, if it had not been for the Athletic Committee, and their rule against professional coaches, Winslow–or, for that matter, any other student–would never have gotten a chance to lead the Harvard nine. But why ruin a picnic?

Ivy Oration

DEAR CHILDREN,–It gives me great pleasure to address you to-day, for in the presence of a kindergarten I cannot help remembering that I was once a boy myself, and joyful recollections of that delightful period come over me with a rush. I call to mind the boyish sports and the boyish trials which you know so well. I call to mind my kind instructors who never suffered my wandering feet to go astray, who kept from me the corrupting influences of evil men, whose smiles were my reward, whose frowns were my punishment. I call to mind the bluff-hearted janitors who used to take in charge my little pocket-money, who never tired of playing with me that fascinating game, Button, Button, who's got the Button? in which, for a button, we generally used a gold watch and chain or some other trinket of merely nominal value, and I was always "it." I call to mind the gentle ministrations of my nurse, the goody, whose children I so strikingly resembled; who filled my young soul with indignation at the wrongs of Ireland; who, when by some unaccountable accident my most valuable pieces of *bric-a-brac* were shattered to bits, never failed to sooth me with soft, pleading words of comfort. These memories, my friends, overwhelm me as I stand in your presence to-day.

Before preparing my remarks for this occasion, I considered two problems; the first was, how long can I speak before you begin throwing things at me; the second was, how long can I continue after this before you get the range? These, according to the eminent Mr. Dougherty, are the two great questions of oratory. Now I know very well that a speech of any kind is distasteful to young people, but I still believe that some kind are more endurable than others, and that whereas I might goad you to desperation in a few seconds, I may escape positively fatal injuries for full twenty minutes. A children's speech has two requirements: it must be graphic; it must contain no moral; for nothing more exasperates the childish heart than a sermon in disguise. Now I merely wish to amuse you; I do not care whether you become useful citizens or not. I do not care how often you call for pie. You cannot shock me by looking upon the wine when it is red. You cannot wrench my heart-strings however much you may indulge in the poisonous weed. When you reach a man's estate, you may not get up to pray at half-past eight every morning; you may even come to look upon professional sports without a shudder of horror. These moral back-slidings I can contemplate in perfect repose of spirit. I never dream in the stilly watches of the night that some poor misguided child has kicked a blind man, and then wake up in tears. You see, therefore, that I differ on all points from most Sunday-school superintendents.

But, you will say, you may not preach, but you will certainly spring some noble thoughts upon us. You will begin with, "A stately ship, her white sails glistening in the morning sun, rode proudly in the offing"; or you will talk about getting shoved off the dock into the turbulent Back-bay of life; or you will rave on the flowery meads of prosperity and the darksome blind alleys of adversity. My young friends, your suspicions do me wrong. Too many joyous childhood days have been embittered, too many fresh young hearts have been seared and withered by the untimely utterance of noble thoughts. Moreover, I remember too well the baneful influence which noble thoughts exercised over my own early life. I cannot forget one particular picnic. It was a beautiful day, there were scores of children, and everyone was happy. The sandwiches knew no limit, the lemonade flowed like water—a good deal like water; the green fields, the leafy groves, the sparkling waters of the lake afforded ample means for the innocent enjoyments of youth. Shouts of glee awoke the hillside echoes. Some rolled their hoops along the velvet sward, some played at hide-and-seek, some launched to sea their tiny craft. Others, like myself, of a more romantic turn of mind, sought the inner recesses of the grove, where they ate green apples and smoked five cent cigars.

Suddenly the horn which had summoned us to lunch blew again, and all the merry horde came trooping in, thinking in their guileless hearts that there was something more to eat. It was not so. When we were gathered together a morose-looking creature came forward, and asked, "What is life? Is it picnics?" he went on, "Is it play? No, it is work. Look at the ant. Does the ant go to picnics? Does the ant go in swimming? Does the ant play Drop the Handkerchief and London Bridge Is Falling Down?" Tears rose in the orator's eyes as those noble sentiments fell from his lips, and we could not help feeling that he was weeping for us. The light went out of our hearts, a settled melancholy came over us, our day's pleasure was ruined.

Now, my young friends, I wish that this day may always be remembered by you with pleasure, and so, as far as I am concerned, it shall be untainted by any noble thoughts. What, then, shall I say to you? Shall I recount the unique adventures of Jack, the Giant-killer? Shall I tell you of the pathetic misfortunes of Little Red Ridinghood? No, that might be carrying a joke a trifle too far. I will give you, then, as far as possible in words of one syllable, some account of a great institution. This institution is called Harvard University, and it is situated in Cambridge, near the banks of the Charles.

Almost four hundred years ago to-day Columbus discovered America. He, therefore, is entitled to the honor of having discovered Cambridge; for, if America had not been discovered, Cambridge, it is likely, would have languished in obscurity. This is the foundation of that great moral axiom which a certain tramp once regarded from another point of view. He said, "I cannot waste my time in searching for flies in the milk till I have found the milk." It does not at all detract from the fame of Columbus that he never saw Cambridge; you ought not to traduce his memory on that account. Remember what he had suffered already. You owe a great deal to Columbus. You owe it to him that you are American citizens and not the cringing subjects of some European despot. You owe to Columbus the proud privilege of waving the torch of liberty in a Democratic procession, and then voting the straight Republican ticket at the polls. You owe to him your seventy-five cent broadcloths, your white cotton gloves, your Waterbury watches, your celluloid collars—whatever is distinctively and peculiarly American. It is with pain, therefore, that I see the influence of an effete European civilization corrupting the natural simplicity of our customs. My young friends, never be ashamed to eat with your knives, for I greatly fear that the word American will eventually lose its significance, and that the name of Columbus will be sunk in oblivion.

I shall not attempt to trace any further the history of the origin of Harvard University. When you have once found your continent, it is easy enough to build things on it. Harvard University stands to-day, and that should suffice for any one excepting the victims of a morbid curiosity. But I cannot go on conveniently without saying something of the town in which this University is situated. For it might, very naturally, be asked why Cambridge was chosen for its seat to the neglect of

Chelsea and Lynn. Cambridge is eminently fitted for a university town; it is old, it is quiet, it is slow. There are no happenings, no excitements there to distract the minds of students. The resident population consists principally of aged men who walk a block in the forenoon, and brag about it all the rest of the day. The lives of these people hang by slender threads, which the slightest jar is apt to break. It is manslaughter in Cambridge to kill a dog, for the master will inevitably die of grief. Many foul murders have been committed there by maliciously ringing front-door bells at one o'clock in the morning. Owing to the extreme weakness of the inhabitants, the students in the University, when on the street, are obliged to speak in whispers and walk on tip-toe. Some years ago, on an occasion of universal rejoicing, many students forgot themselves so far as to indulge in a display of fireworks. This is known in history as the Cambridge massacre. The number of those actually killed was only 479; the number of the paralyzed could not be correctly ascertained, because, as a rule, it is difficult to decide whether a Cambridge citizen is paralyzed or not. The Faculty were placed in a very delicate position by this catastrophe, for among the killed were several of the city's heaviest tax-payers, who are known to have protested strongly against the large amount of untaxed property owned by the University. Hence there were some suspicions of a plot in which the Faculty, through the proctors, their menials, were seriously implicated. It is alleged that the proctors fiendishly stimulated the students to prolong the work of destruction. For my own part, even in the face of strong circumstantial evidence to the contrary, I am inclined to doubt that the Faculty were the guilty authors of this horrible tragedy.

It will be inferred from what I have said that the climate of Cambridge is peculiarly conducive to uneventful lives. This is the fact. Lightning never strikes there, horses never run away, dogs never fight. Burglars, pickpockets and circuses shun the town. There is no chance in Cambridge for the young man of heroic intentions. Such a young man had best not moodily pace the streets at midnight. His heart-beats will not be suddenly interrupted by piercing female shrieks. He will not pause an instant to discover whence they came, and then rush boldly into a mysterious looking house with the blinds all closed in front. He will not find in a back room on the third floor a maniac dragging by the hair a fair young girl. He will not fell the maniac with one well-aimed blow and then turn his attention to the now fainting maiden. The devoted parent will not pile up stairs when the danger is over, call our hero the savior of his child, and bestow upon him all the small change he has about him. The gallant preserver will not cast the glittering coins upon the floor and cry, "Old man, I have your daughter." This sort of thing doesn't happen in Cambridge. The man who locates a story like that in Cambridge has not, you may depend upon it, lived there four years, and tried to brush up a little excitement by betting on the number of hacks in a passing funeral. It is very evident, therefore, why Harvard University is situated in Cambridge. Cambridge is a good place for a studious and contemplative life; it is a good place to enjoy the pleasures of self-communion.

I should like to speak at length on the Faculty of this University, but the subject is too sacred, and must not be dealt with lightly. I cannot, however, explain the purpose of the University without referring indirectly to that august body. Now the purpose of the University, as near as I can discover, is to afford the Faculty amusement; the Faculty are very fond of play. But they only play one game, and in order to play this it is necessary to have a university. This game is called forfeits; it consists in guessing riddles, and if you fail to guess correctly you have to pay a forfeit. The Faculty always propose the riddles, and the students always do the guessing. The Faculty made this rule, I suppose, because they did not care to spend the pleasant Indian summer of life in paying forfeits. If the students wish to do their part in this game creditably, it is necessary for them to keep in strict training. They must go to prayers every morning, and refrain from playing on the piano after nine o'clock p.m. Of course it is absurd to suppose that any one who does not begin the day with prayer can guess any – even the simplest – conundrum.

Now it so happened a great many years ago that the students became tired of playing forfeits exclusively. They took up base ball, foot ball, boating and other unhallowed sports; and as the Faculty refused to take part in these games, the students played with each other and with students from other colleges. The Faculty naturally felt grieved at this because it was not for such purposes that the University was founded. "Play with us," they cried, "play with us"; but the students, flinty-hearted creatures, disregarded the piteous appeal, and continued in their own naughty, independent ways. When all entreaties proved powerless to stop the growing evil, the Faculty determined upon sterner measures; they felt that if things went on as they were going, there might as well be no University at all; something, therefore, must be done in self-defense. Accordingly a committee plenipotentiary was appointed. Concerning this committee the verdict of history is that they meant well, but that nature had been unkind to them. This committee prosecuted its work with great energy and intrepidity, but it soon found that it was dealing with a seven-headed hydra – it no sooner cut off one head than another sprang out in its place. So the committee began to get discouraged, and when the ball nine piled up one victory upon another, it became evident to the committee's anxious friends that they were pining away. The committee, accordingly, was permitted to retire, and the Faculty began to despair of saving the University. Still the efforts of the Faculty have not been wholly without results. These results can be seen in the added significance given to that motto which Harvard foot ball enthusiasts appreciate so well; that motto which reads, "Only students of Harvard University are allowed to play upon these grounds."

Leaving the University in this critical condition, let me briefly call your attention to a class of men who have made the University remarkable, who, during the four years they were connected with it, industriously employed themselves in manufacturing history, – sedulously digging their heels in the sands of time. For four years they vainly sought to conceal their light under a bushel, and then, in answer to the world's plaintive cry for help, went forth. I should like to tell you of the individual achievements of these men, but life is short and the night is coming on. I should like to tell you of that remarkable crew which lost a race by rowing too fast—the boat found it impossible to keep up with its cargo. I should like to tell you of him who led the torch-light procession to victory, whom men called the Centaur because they were unable to decide where the horse left off and the man began. I should like to tell you of him who was greeted by the infant populace with cries of "that's Sam," who pulled to the top the crimson banner that had long languished at half-mast; and yet, my young friends, according to Dr. Sargent's tests he could not pull himself up to his chin but once. All these things I should like to tell you; but I cannot conscientiously rob the coming poet of a means of livelihood.

And now, my children, that you have quietly suffered me to go on so long, and that the time which I have allotted myself is drawing to a close, I am tempted to trespass on that ground which I forswore at the outset. Tolerate me for only one minute longer, and then you may go hear the band and chew peanut candy. But let me warn you that the days for enjoying bands and peanut candy are drawing to a close. On Wednesday next you will become men, on Thursday you will begin to run this country. You cannot of course realize yet the responsibilities of manhood, and I shall not waste my time in enumerating them. But I can, I think with profit to yourselves, give you a few points on ambition. Aim high! Do not be content with sitting on the fence; yearn to sit on the roof. Do not rest satisfied with the position of a college tutor. Push on! Push on! Be a brakeman. Hold your standard always in the front and let that standard bear these glowing words, "I'm pushing." Never sit down and say I have enough to eat, enough to drink, enough sleep, enough shelter; therefore I will do no more work. Keep adding to your possessions; add on anything that is left lying round by mistake. Follow this counsel, my young friends, and you will be rich, respected, happy.

I have nothing more to say excepting, by way of compliment, that I believe the ivy which is this day planted will prove inadequate to supply the demand for chaplets which will shortly begin to flow in. Now, children, you may run to your parents [Harvard University Archives].

CHAPTER 15

Papers of the President

There is no substitute for a trip to the Harvard Archives, where the friendly, efficient staff keeps all the back issues of the *Harvard Lampoon,* and gladly brings them out for anybody who wants to read them. You can sit there for days, if you have the time, and read the entire file dating all the way back to 1876. Our selection has to be limited to nine items Thayer wrote for the magazine while he was president (1883–85). The first, "A Lapsus Linguae," features Hollis Holworthy, the college dandy. Somehow he manages to secure a date with the beautiful young Rosalie Roseleaf, but a slip of the tongue ensures that it will be his last. In "A Lampoon Christmas Dinner," an Irish poet works corned beef into the verses knowing full well that corned beef is not one of the dishes that will be served, then flatly refuses to rectify his mistake, insisting that corned beef conforms better to the flow of the iambic trimeter. "Wit vs. Strength," the only poem in the assortment of nine, claims that "the modern maid by wit is stormed and carried," and that "poor, dullard strength, for her, may go unmarried." Thayer took up the subject again in one of the ballads he wrote for the *San Francisco Daily Examiner*.

All humorists have to contend with the fact that once people begin to appreciate their humor they are never taken seriously. Jackson, the humorist of "The Incomprehensible Joke," is annoyed by this, plays a cruel practical joke on his friends, and later, overwhelmed by remorse, repents – but only after the damage has been done. Midway through his junior year, as "The Semis" were approaching, Phinney offered this advice to his readers: "Knowledge is fleeting; make the most of it while you have it." It was a subject dear to his heart. He returned to it in 1895, when he addressed his classmates at their tenth annual dinner.

The next piece, "Mary Ann Stubbles," concerns a young lady whose ideal type could be found boating on any lake, but most likely Thayer had known a real Mary Ann Stubbles back home in Worcester, and was boating on Lake Quinsigamond himself when the accident occurred. The Valentine's Day editorial appeared on February 15, 1884, in a leap year, when Phinney was deluged with store-bought cards from his countless admirers. Although from Worcester, the center of the valentine card industry, Phinney warns his readers against buying one of these fancy, readymade cards, and instead recommends the romantic approach. "The sender of a valentine," he says, "must compose it and write it himself, or he is no true lover." Phinney claims that after reading his editorial, no good young man will ever send his sweetheart a store-bought valentine again. He may have been taking a cue here from his two older brothers, who were both married later that year. Ed married Florence Scofield, of Worcester, on July 10; Albert married Josephine Ely, of Newburg, New York, on December 4 (Crane, 4:154).

In "Half-Minutes with the Poets" Thayer defines poetry as "the mysterious divulgence of the ineffable," and proceeds to show how the hidden beauties and pathos of a familiar line may elude the grasp of the general public, but not the connoisseur. The modest subtitle, "By a Professional Critic," cannot fool anyone, for only a professional poet could arrive at the insights afforded us in this provocative essay, and there is no question that the poet is Thayer himself. The ninth and final item, "The Artificial Rain-Starter," is in some ways the most revealing of them all, for Thayer begins this one by remarking that a daily paper is "one of the great popular educators." For once he was not kidding. His firm belief in the educational power of the newspaper, archaic as it may seem to some people today, was shared by many of his contemporaries. Henry Ward Beecher, for example, remarked in his *Proverbs from Plymouth Pulpit* (1870): "Newspapers are the schoolmasters of the common people. That endless book, the newspaper, is our national glory" (Carruth and Ehrlich, 300).

Whether he knew it or not, Thayer was about to go to work for a daily paper. And as all real baseball fans know it was that paper, the *San Francisco Daily Examiner,* published by his old Harvard chum William Randolph Hearst, that first broke the story of "Casey at the Bat."

A Lapsus Linguae

> Miss Rosalie Roseleaf, who is beautiful and sentimental, was sitting one summer's evening with Hollis Holworthy on the verandah. The moon was shining brilliantly. Silence had reigned for some moments, when Rosalie who, as the books say, was not a thousand miles away from Hollis's purple cravat, looked up suddenly in his face, and sighed,—"I must go in at ten; is it ten yet?" "No, dear," said he, looking at his watch, "it is only ten minutes of ten." A soft restful expression spread over Rosalie's face at these words, and she said,—"Then we may stay here ten minutes more; ten precious minutes here together in the beautiful moonlight," and her head again returned to a point not a thousand miles distant from Hollis's purple cravat. Then poor Hollis, just as if the whole affair was a purely business transaction, blurted out, "But my watch is ten minutes slow." Poor, prosaic Hollis lost by a slip of the tongue the sweetest girl this side of Cambridgeport.
>
> (December 7, 1883)

A Lampoon Christmas Dinner

Unquestionably the greatest social event of the season was the *Lampoon* dinner which occurred at Young's Hotel last Saturday evening. The Papyrus club attempted to give a dinner on the same date, but the affair proved very stupid, and the thoughts of the guests were evidently elsewhere. The hour for the *Lampoon* dinner had been set for seven o'clock, and promptly at eleven minutes of eight the company sat down to table. Seventeen gentlemen, now or formerly editors of the *Lampoon*, were present, and an attractive menu was offered for their discussion.

It had been our first intention to have the menu written in verse, and our versatile poet was charged with the execution of the plan. The production which he handed us, however, proved unsatisfactory. He had mingled corned-beef and fried liver with the game, and Bermuda onions with the fruit. We told him that, not to mention his having put these dishes in the wrong departments, we would rather dispense with the Irish cuisine anyway. We agreed to accept his work if he would rectify these mistakes. But the poet flatly refused to make any corrections. He said that any changes would mar the symmetry of the whole poem; that it wasn't a question of whether we pined for corned-beef, liver, and onions or not, it was only a question of what would beautify his verses, and what wouldn't. In conclusion he said that it was simply outrageous to sacrifice art to the vulger demands of the palate. We reverence our poet highly, but we are not going to eat corned-beef in place of canvas-back duck, simply because the former delicacy better conforms to the rhythmic flow of the iambic trimeter. We had commissioned him to suit his verses to the dinner, but he insisted on suiting the dinner to his verses. 'Twas ever thus with genius. So we composed our menu in the best English and French prose, mixed in about equal proportions. There is a sinister cruelty in making one read a menu when he is not to taste of its contents – it is the meanest kind of brag – and we have too much regard for the feelings of our readers to publish that wonderful list of dishes in these columns.

Of course there was a great flow of spirits at the dinner – in the vicinity of twenty-three bottles. Bubbling mirth was present on all sides, and the waiters were so overcome with laughter that they had to be removed on shutters by the committee on repairs. The dinner was followed by toasts and songs. The company finally adjourned to the parlors, and after an hour of pleasant conversation on literary and other topics, an evening of great enjoyment was ended by the departure of the guests.

(December 21, 1883)

Wit vs. Strength

I.

Once maids were won by strength of arm, and deeds
Of war and might. The man of words must needs

Content himself as counsellor or fool.
Wit goes unmated when the strong men rule.

II.

The modern maid by wit is stormed and carried;
Poor, dullard strength, for her, may go unmarried.
The jester Time has wrought a change extreme,–
Now strength's the bachelor, and Wit's supreme.

III.

Wives able champions for their mates desire,
And different weapons different times require;
Once swords were used, and strength to wield them needed;
But now wit's mightier, and the sword's succeeded.

(January 4, 1884)

The Incomprehensible Joke

"You know," said Jackson, "that I always had the reputation of being something of a humorist; everybody felt bound to laugh at whatever I said, fearing that wit might be lurking even where they failed to see it. One day it occurred to me to test the honesty of my friends; so when a number of them were gathered about me, I slyly and smilingly made a remark which possessed neither wit nor meaning. All immediately burst into a roar. But a few minutes later I noticed a thoughtful expression steal over their faces; the conversation flagged; everybody became wrapped in meditation. Everybody thought all except himself thoroughly understood the joke.

"Pretty soon my friends departed one by one. Each hoped to find a clue to the meaning by telling the joke elsewhere. So they retailed it about as 'Jackson's latest,' and wherever it was told, it excited the most boisterous laughter. Thus everybody was confirmed in his suspicion that he alone could not comprehend the joke.

"In a short time the joke was all over town; it was put in a weekly paper over my name, and clipped all over the country. Everyone laughed at it at first, and then went home and thought it over. For a while I enjoyed the results of my experiment, but presently I saw that I might have been unintentionally cruel. Everyone was fretting himself sick over that joke; everyone felt disgraced for being unable to understand a joke which had been so heartily enjoyed all over the country. Brilliant men were chagrined because they could see nothing in a joke which the populace appreciated so hugely.

"It was impossible now to reassure everybody; the joke had spread too far. So I thought I would let it run its course. In a short time the joke crossed the ocean, and paralyzed all Great Britain; from there it took the regular continental tour; thence it proceeded by the Suez Canal to

India and Australia, finally completing the entire circuit of the globe. Mental prostration everywhere followed its path: whole nations were enfeebled and made unfit for work. Several deaths occurred through its influence. All peoples were agitated by my careless remark. Remorse overwhelmed me; and now I never make a statement of whatever nature without adding in brackets, 'This is positively no joke'."

(January 18, 1884)

The Semis

The Semis are upon us, and consequently, we suppose, we must go under. We have always doubted the wisdom of the examination system, anyway; examination knowledge like a dress suit is put on the for the occasion only. We looked through the back numbers of our blue books the other day, and were truly surprised to find how much we had forgotten and how well we had done it. Knowledge is fleeting; make the most of it while you have it. Just at this time we are men of learning; by the middle of next month we shall have returned to a blissful state of ignorance. Now is the time to show yourself to your family and friends. We know of a man who used to go home for a day or two in the midst of the examinations, and seize every opportunity to show how much he knew. He would get his father by himself in the library, and unload upon him the principal parts of all the German irregular verbs. Then he would go and whisper to his mother the most important events of later Roman history, and the date of each. Then he would confidentially inform his sister of many mechanical formulae. Three weeks later the same man would go home and say that above all things he despised pedantry.

(January 18, 1884)

Mary Ann Stubbles

Mary Ann Stubbles was the most consecutive talker I ever knew. She would talk along hour after hour without a pause, and apparently without drawing in a breath. She was a remarkable woman. She never wearied of talking. Other people would get all worn out by just sitting still and listening to her; but this wonderful woman never displayed the slightest symptoms of exhaustion.

One day Mary Ann was out rowing when the boat tipped, and Mary fell in and sunk. A hush seemed to steal over nature as she went under. The gentleman who had accompanied Mary Ann of course felt it was his duty to save her, even at the risk of destroying the calm which had now settled down on the world. With a sigh of relief, he failed in his efforts to succor her.

He then started off to find a drag. To do this he had to go eight miles. A party of men returned with him, and the lake was dragged over the spot where Mary Ann was seen to go down. At night-fall they had not succeeded in recovering the body. Next day they tried again, and about two o'clock p.m. (don't shudder, dear reader!) the drag caught on to something. Mary Ann was recognized by the feel. They pulled her to the surface. She shivered slightly as they lifted her into the boat, but she didn't speak. For the first time in her life Mary Ann Stubbles was winded. She afterwards admitted that she didn't believe she could have held her breath five minutes longer.

The mill is now running again on full time.

(February 1, 1884)

A Valentine from Lampy

Valentine's Day has called our attention to the fact that this is leap-year. We were awakened at half-past eleven yesterday morning by the rumbling of a heavy wagon which apparently came to a stand in front of our sanctum. Presently there was a great thumping on the stairs quickly followed by a loud knocking at the door. Curious to learn the cause of the disturbance, we rose and opened the door. Thereupon eleven men, each bearing a large, well filled bag on his shoulders, filed into the room. Having made a bin of four chairs, a table, a lounge, and fifteen Dresden china cuspidores, they emptied into it the contents of the bags, and then filed out again. The contents of the bags were, of course, valentines from the limited circle of our lady friends. It will be seen that the demand for us is considerably greater than the supply. It was naturally gratifying to be assured that the want of us is so universally felt, but we must ask even the Queen of Tahiti and the Princess Infanta of Spain to look elsewhere. For the many society belles, whose proposals we fell called upon to reject, we are truly sorry; if it will be any consolation, we can assure them that we will always be like a brother to them; that is to say, we will always freely borrow money of them when we feel the need of it. To the many thousands of ordinary young ladies who have made us the focus of their affections, we must gently but firmly say no. We hope they may be happy sometime and somewhere, but we shall certainly not be present at that time nor in that place. We beg all our lady correspondents to believe that we are grieved to render so many feminine lives thenceforth desolate, be such a general incentive to ruin and suicide, but we must do it. We are marked out by destiny to be a more dreadful disaster than the earthquake at Ischia. We cannot satisfy all; to gratify one would be cruel. What could one poor woman do were she the object of jealousy for seven or eight thousand despairing fellow creatures? Ladies we decline you all, for thus it is best.

Lampy intends this number to be a tribute to St. Valentine. The number is, in fact, a valentine from him to his readers and more particularly to his readers among the gentler sex. To each of these latter the verses contained herein are specially directed; Lampy loves them all with the strictest impartiality. Should any young lady who is not now a reader be made jealous by this declaration, and pine for an equal share of his affection with her sisters fair, she is at perfect liberty to procure the priceless boon by squandering the modest sum of twenty cents upon this current issue. She may then apply the verses to her own particular case without any extra charge.

We feel that modern valentines are not what they should be. Nature never intended tin foil, tissue paper, perforated cardboard, decalcomania and mucilage, to be the emblems of love. Yet combinations of these elements in different proportions and disfigured in different degrees, are the marketable incentives to the tender passion. The sender of a valentine must compose it and write it himself, or he is no true lover.

The modern valentine is too business-like; it is always bought ready-made. What verses there are on it are usually hidden away where you can't read them without rupturing something. Moreover, when a man buys a valentine, the verses and their sentiments are to him a very secondary matter; he invariably purchases the valentine which supports the greatest area of floral decoration proportionately to the size of the foundation. The consequence is that the receiver must possess considerable curiosity, backed by a good deal of ingenuity and detective skill, to discover any verses at all. She may, perhaps, by a painstaking search, find a crack somewhere through which she can read, by dint of much squinting and facial distortion, a portion, or possibly the whole, of a verse of which the purport will probably be vague and unsatisfactory. It is no pleasure to a black-haired girl to be congratulated on the possession of a wealth of auburn tresses, nor to a one hundred and eighty-five-pound girl to have the climax of a verse turn upon her willowy form. A young lady who is so modest that she dare not raise her eyes to a gentleman's face can surely cull no gratification from a valentine which slyly salutes her as a naughty flirt, and requests her "not to do so no more." All verses are not universally appropriate.

There! Now we feel sure that no good young man will ever send "boughten" valentines any more.

(February 15, 1884)

Half-Minutes with the Poets
(By a Professional Critic)

Poetry may be defined as the mysterious divulgence of the ineffable. This first sentence, for example, is of a poetic cast. If you can tell what you mean, use prose; if not, use poetry. Many persons, through ignorance of this simple rule, cannot understand poetry; they do not know that they must let their thoughts wander away from the literal meaning of the words into the fields of the infinitely beautiful which words cannot describe.

Take that awfully pathetic line from Casabianca:

"The boy stood on the burning deck."

Of fifty persons I have questioned not one could perceive the reeking pathos contained in those seven words. But I behold in them the perfection of the poet's art; if the author had written nothing besides that single statement, I should have recognized in it a master's hand.

Mark that third word "stood"; at this point the truly poetic mind begins to wander, and by the time the word "deck" is reached, it is quite out of sight. Does the reader see no pathos in the junction of the verb "stood" with the participle "burning" and the noun "deck"? If not, let the reader ask himself if he is accustomed to stand when he can sit. In his vague, mysterious way the poet wishes to express that the boy couldn't sit; the deck was too demnition hot. This is not namby pamby sentiment, this is genuine pathos.

The songster doubtless had this verse in mind when he wrote,

"Ye gentlemen of England who *sit* at home at ease,
How little do you think upon the dangers of the seas."

Which is as much as to say, if you had a red hot deck under you, gentlemen, you wouldn't sit, not long.

Who can read the words of Antony to the Romands,

"I came to bury Caesar not to praise him,"

without picturing to himself the horny-palmed old orator, with a spade in one hand and a pickaxe in the other, preparing to dig a grave.

In my mind the finest verses in the English language are those beginning:

"Give me three grains of corn, mother,
  Only three grains of corn;
'Twill keep the little life I have,
  Till the coming of the morn."

There is a heart agony in that word "only" which operates on me like a peeled onion. How feelingly it depicts the alarms of the poor wretch lest his mother, acting from sinister motives, should give him more than three grains. He was hungry but cautious; he knew that the corn would swell.

The poet does not say whether the mother gave her son the corn or sent him to bed supperless; but since we have now switched off into the ineffably infinite, we may as well suppose that she did give it to him, and we may imagine the youth as he drops into a calm and peaceful slumber, softly murmuring,

"The corn is swelling fast, mother,
The corn is swelling fast," etc.

The story of "Little Mabel" who looked out across the night and saw the beacon light a trembling in the rain, is good, but fanciful. How far, gentle poet, do you suppose it is across the night? twelve thousand miles, certainly; and it is rather improbably that Little Mabel could see the rain so far as all that. It seems as though the poet might have found a beacon light nearer home which would have answered his purpose quite as well. But perhaps he had an interest in the manufacture of some patent duplex burner and inserted these lines as an advertisement of its intense illuminating power; please send a two cent stamp for circular.

(October 17, 1884)

The Artificial Rain-Starter

We learn from a daily paper, one of the great popular educators, that a device has been invented for bringing rain by artificial means. The nature of the contrivance is as follows: A balloon containing a can of dynamite connected by fine wire with the earth, is sent up into the clouds. When the balloon has risen to a sufficient height, the electric current is turned on through the wire; this explodes the dynamite, and the rain, the inventor declares, immediately begins to fall.

This is certainly a wonderful invention, but after mature deliberation anyone would probably decide that it is best to rely on nature for the grateful, cooling rain. Some like rain one day and some another, and nature is perfectly fair to all. But if he who desires rain can bring it by simply sending into the sky a balloonful of dynamite, he is taking an unfair advantage of the man who does not desire rain; for although a little dynamite may start a shower, no dynamite can stop it.

Supposing I wish to get up a picnic. If the weather is fair, or if there are only a few clouds in the sky, I should naturally say, "This is a good day for a picnic;" and I should stand an equal chance with all the rest of mankind of being right. But if every evil-minded citizen owns a patent rain-starter, what chance have I against the crowd. In case some such person in the vicinity of the picnic grounds should take it into his head to have a rainy day, and blast water out of the clouds, the picnic would be spoiled. The only way to act under such an order of things would be insert a notice in the papers to this effect:

"To the Citizens of Suffolk County

Greeting: On Tuesday, the 17th day of the current month, all citizens in this county are particularly requested to let the weather alone, as the undersigned desire to picnic on that date."

Then follow the signatures of the prospective picnickers.

There must be, however, a sort of fascination in the feeling that you can bring rain even though you may not care much about having rain, and many doubtless would try the experiment for fun.

This invention does away with the necessity of using a garden hose. If a man wishes to water his lawn, he comes out after supper, takes his balloon off the rack, loads her up with dynamite, and lets her go. When the balloon enters the clouds, he coolly turns on the electricity, and then scoots for the house. The rain comes down in torrents, and the couple opposite who were spooning over the gate, are obliged to break off their sweet discussion and streak it for shelter.

Of course laws would have to be passed to prevent all indiscriminate rain-getting, and to forbid unauthorized persons sending up dynamite balloons except in case of fire. Otherwise the rain would rain every day. Some people would be mean enough to make it rain on Sundays, so that they would not feel obliged to go to church. If Miss This-and-that proposed to have a lawn party, and Miss So-and-so should be jealous of its success, she might maliciously tamper with the weather, and then gloat over her rival's discomfiture. The moral man could get in an effective check on horse-races, and the immoral man could retort by precipitating the fountains of heaven upon camp-meetings. In short, people would make it wet for one another. "If you rain on me," says one, "I'll rain on you, so there!"

The man who invented the rain-starter ought to be suppressed.

(November 28, 1884)

PART III

Thayer and the *Examiner*

CHAPTER 16

Europe

Phinney's Ivy Oration was a huge success, and for months after Class Day his parents received congratulations from their friends on having developed such a bright and amusing offspring. Phinney and his best friend, Sam Winslow, were given European trips as graduation gifts. They sailed with Will Smith on the Cunard Royal Mail Steamship *Aurania* from New York on June 26. Mr. Thayer wanted Albert to see his brother off, so he sent a telegram telling him when Ernest was coming in on the train. His work kept him busy past Ernest's 3:30 P.M. arrival time at the station; Albert rushed down to the steamer as soon as he could, but he was too late to see his young brother before the ship sailed. He wrote Ernest a note, and in addition to wishing him a bon voyage, advised him to see a doctor about the danger of smoking as much as he did. "When I was home father had an idea that you were smoking a little too much. I speak of it merely because he wished me to but he thought that if I held up before you my own melancholy example I might have some influence." After describing the digestive trouble he developed from smoking, Albert apologized. "Excuse this little lecture, which is really father's. Goodbye" (AST to ELT, 6/26/1885).

Ernest was well aware of the dangers of smoking cigarettes; thanks to Mehitable Croaker he was privy to

The True Story of Obejoyful Binks

> Next to money the cigarette is the root of all evil. Since the introduction of cigarette-smoking there has been more crime to the tenement house than ever before. Wherever the cigarette is fostered, there crime finds its peculiar home; no man is so good, no man so pure, that the diligent use of the cigarette will not fit him for a career of crime.
>
> I have in mind the sad case of Obejoyful Binks. He was a sweet youth: good, kind, respectful to his elders, loving all and by all beloved. He never lied, nor swore, nor did anything wicked; but he ranked high in his Sunday school, and spent all his spare time in performing acts of charity.
>
> One day a dreadful street boy maliciously gave Obejoyful a cigarette, and told him how to use it. The street boy envied Obejoyful because he was so good and pure, and in this way he trusted to make him a tainted

sinner. Obejoyful accidentally smoked the cigarette in the privacy of his chamber, and immediately he began to change. He proceeded at once to let out his suspenders two inches all round.

Then Obejoyful went and bought a whole package of cigarettes. Having smoked them in rapid succession, he hurried to find his little sister. When he found the dear innocent playing with her dolls in the nursery, he went to work without delay and broke all the dolls; then he pulled his little sister's hair. This was the same little sister for whom he had been in the habit of staying in doors to amuse, when she was sick, on beautiful sunny holidays for which he had planned excursions with some dear boy friends. But he always gave up these excursions. When the boys called for him, and he heard their merry shouts and ringing laughter coming up the driveway, he always went to meet them with a brave cheerful look on his face, and said in a manly tone: "No, dear friends, I cannot go; I hope you will have a very nice time."

Then he would return to his peevish, fretting little sister; and during all the day while his thoughts were running on the green woods, and the purling brooks, and the sports of his dear boy friends, he never allowed a single unkind word to escape him; always he was gentle and forbearing. Mark the change which a single bunch of cigarettes has wrought. Now he delights to pull his unoffending sister's hair.

On the following day Obejoyful bought another bunch of cigarettes, and when he had finished them, he made haste to inquire where he could find a poor helpless blind man. Having found out, he rushed off. When he caught sight of the blind man painfully feeling his way along, Obejoyful said, "Ha, ha!" Then he went up to the blind man and asked him where he wanted to go. The blind man's face lit up with pleasure to think he was going to have some one to guide him to his destination; but when he had explained where he wished to go, Obejoyful told him to take the second turning to the right and follow up the scent. When the blind man said he couldn't see, but was a poor helpless blind man, Obejoyful said he was grieved to hear such an old man lie like that, and felt it his duty to punish him. So he took the blind man into the muddy street, laid him rudely down, and rolled him back and forth. Where the mud failed to stick on itself, Obejoyful consicienciously rubbed it on with his hands. Then Obejoyful said "Ha, ha!" some more, and let out his suspenders two inches.

This was the same blind man whom Obejoyful had taken home two days before, though to do it he had to go four miles out of his way. Throughout those four miles he had not allowed a single unkind word to pass his lips. What a change!

The next day Obejoyful bought and smoked two bunches of cigarettes. No sooner were they all gone, than he ran with all his might to a hardware shop where he purchased a bowie knife with six blades. Then he ran to an intelligence office and asked where he could find a good old woman who lived all alone, four miles from the nearest man. Then he hired a light buggy and a fast horse, and packed the bowie knife under the seat. He drove rapidly to where the old woman lived, and having

> hitched his horse at the front gate, entered the house without knocking. He found the good old woman sitting with her cat in her lap, dozing over her knitting needles, a picture of calm contentment. Then Obejoyful said "Ha, ha!" and let his suspenders out an inch and three-quarters. He poised his knife—but we will omit the horrible details. This was the same old woman for whom, only a few days before, Obejoyful had walked nineteen miles to bring a small pot of raspberry jam; and all the way home, in spite of his tired limbs, he had worn a bright, happy smile.
>
> We will not follow Obejoyful Binks any further, for he was hanged last Friday, and the road he took after the performance is too hot and dusty and suit the popular taste. Obejoyful Binks is but one of the countless victims of cigarette smoking. His case was unusually light.
>
> (*Lampoon*, volume 6, December 21, 1883)

Ernest, Will, and Sam visited Ireland and Scotland first. While in Ireland, Sam sent a letter to the SPY—Worcester's leading newspaper—in which he described the local people in a less than complimentary way. The letter upset Worcester's large Irish population. Samuel Winslow, Sam's father, who aspired to the position of mayor of Worcester, was thus placed in an awkward position. Sam's close ties with the *Harvard Lampoon* writers might have tempted him to try his hand at some humorous writing, but he laid an egg that time. Ernest's mother wrote in August, commenting on the reaction to Sam's letter ("It seems it was too truthful to suit the Irish"), and added her usual request that Ernest try to improve his penmanship ("We received your letter of Aug. 3 at breakfast time yesterday, which Nellie was fully half an hour deciphering, while your father and I were patiently waiting eager to get every word. I think you might with a little effort write more plainly.") She mentioned that they were having "very nice sweet corn" from their farm. Ernest and his siblings used to spend parts of their summer vacation on their Mendon farm (EMT to ELT, 8/16/1885).

His first prose contribution to the *Lampoon* had been a tale of making ends meet on a small farm; it was

Henrietta's Story

> My name is Henrietta. I am red-haired and freckled. My father is the owner of a house, a farm of two and a half acres, and four shares in the new liberty pole. Our live stock comprises a hen, and a bovine, albeit of the male persuasion. Our ancestors possessed some notoriety. One of them, a judge, died on the circuit. Another was judged, and died on the gallows. Still we are not proud, and permit a certain degree of familiarity on the part of our neighbors.
>
> My grandfather, the judge who has already been mentioned, was a man of considerable property. On his death, he bequeathed my father the hen and bovine referred to as constituting a portion of our little means.

> The hen, being of somewhat advanced years, only produced eggs at rare intervals in the summer months. These being too good for us to eat, and too few to sell, we resolved to advertise for boarders. Our advertisement dwelt particularly on a shade tree in the back lot, a huckleberry pasture within fifteen minutes' walk, and plenty of fresh air—and eggs.
>
> We awaited developments. They came. He was a tall, thin young man, with a pale face and a red nose. On the day after his arrival he inquired if there was a tavern in the vicinity. On being answered in the affirmative, he expressed much regret. When told where it was, he said he would get its bearings in order to avoid it in his future walks. It took him some time to find it. One afternoon, as I was engaged in my usual occupation, waiting for the hen to lay, our boarder approached me. I was much surprised, at the time, to notice that he came from the direction of the tavern. He emitted an odor suggestive of about three fingers of rum. His nose was red. I eyed him sternly. Thereupon he called me his night-blooming cereus. I was shocked. What would my ancestry think of such conduct.
>
> This repulse forced him to retire, and he sought the shelter of the shade tree in the back lot. Simultaneously—a curious coincidence—our bovine also repaired thither.
>
> Our bovine was a gentle creature on ordinary occasions, but he abhorred red. He abhorred our boarder's nose. I am confident it was the nose he wished to destroy. Personally our boarder was not obnoxious to him. Our bovine hurriedly approached our boarder, who turned to flee. There was no fence convenient. Our boarder was not insured.
>
> Henrietta.
>
> P.S. *The hen has laid.*
>
> (*Lampoon,* volume 2, December 1, 1881)

After visiting Edinburgh the friends split up; Will returned to America and Sam and Ernest went to France and set up quarters in Paris. It was cholera season, which upset Phinney's mother, but France had not reported many cases. She passed on Aunt Abbie's advice to wear two pair of socks during the winter months. The friends spent the winter holidays there, then Sam returned to Worcester to face the music, and Phinney remained in Paris. (Despite Sam's gaffe, his father became Worcester's mayor in 1886.) With the birth of Albert and Josie's first child, Ellen, in mid-December, Ernest became an uncle for the first time (EMT to ELT, 8/23, 9/25, 12/10/1885; Erskine [1981], 95; Crane, IV:154).

There was no way to communicate with the folks back home except by letter, but this posed no problem for Phinney. He had been known as a facile letter writer since his high school days (EMT to ELT, 8/10/1880); at Harvard he had felt confident enough to give

> Hints on Letter Writing
>
> In beginning a letter do not be bashful about saying *dear*; it means nothing—a man will address even his mother-in-law as *dear*.

If addressing a professional gentleman you may say "Dear Doctor," but never "Dear Lawyer" nor "Dear Minister." There is no telling why this should be so, probably it is merely one of the whims of fashion.

Do not address your creditors as "Dear Sir;" you might be suspected of sarcasm. Yet it would not be advisable to go to the opposite extreme and say "Cheap Sir" or "10-per-cent-discount-for-cash Sir." No, sir!

When writing to a lady friend always underscore the *dear*, or say "My dear" or "My dearest" or "My dearest darling." But never permit yourself to be carried away by your feelings and to say "Most dearest."

In concluding a letter never be afraid on conscientious grounds to say "Yours truly," though in point of fact you are not his nor hers nor anybody else's *truly*.

There are other ways of ending a letter besides "Yours truly," as "Yours sincerely," "Yours obediently," "Yours affectionately," etc., whatever the case may not be. These expressions are never strictly true. When a man really is somebody's *truly* or *sincerely* or *affectionately*, he feels obliged to go a step farther and launch out into "Your faithful darling" or "Your ever loving Charles."

Every letter writer is more or less of a deceiver. Still we are not going to change a custom which has prevailed for several years past.

(*Lampoon*, volume 6, February 1, 1884)

When signing his name to a letter, Phinney always used his first and second initials and his last name, even when writing to family members (ELT to EMT, 5/8, 10/23/1886, et al). Thus he acknowledged his middle name, even though he suspected his parents had cost him a life of fame and recognition by tagging him with one, as he wrote

Concerning Middle Names

A journal of reputation recently called our attention to the fact that George Washington, Daniel Webster, Henry Clay, Abraham Lincoln and numerous other American gentlemen of good social standing, were distinguished by the lack of middle names. "How tame," says this paper, "would George S. Washington or Daniel P. Webster, sound!" This is a startling truth. If George Washington had borne a middle name is it likely that his claims to be the father of his country would ever have been generally recognized? Could any one proudly refer to Daniel P. Webster as his country's greatest statesman? Perhaps it is fortunate for George and Daniel that they were never put to the test.

The prevailing absence of middle names in the names of our great men leads us to question if anybody could attain the pinnacle of fame and take a middle name along with him. We know we couldn't, because we know we haven't; and we've tried mighty hard. With all due acknowledgement of our obligations to our parents, we must condemn their lack of forethought in pinning us down by a middle name; a passing whim for literary composition ruined our prospects.

There was never but one great John Smith—he of Pocahontas fame—and doubtless he owes his position to the prudence of his godfather or godmother. All succeeding John Smiths have had middle names, and have been punished accordingly.

There is a tradition that George Washington was born with a middle name, but the affair was hushed up by his parents and friends who saw him with it on; they knew from experience that it would be futile for the boy to struggle along with such a crushing burden. It is also told that later in life George was informed of his early deformity; and ever afterwards he was subject to fits of melancholy. He always secretly felt that he had become the champion patriot by fraud. At times he was tempted to make a public declaration of the cheat that had been practised on his trusting fellow-citizens; but he ever hesitated, and meantime the canker kept eating away in his heart. Finally, after lingering on for about forty-nine years, he died of mental exhaustion.

Glancing for a moment at the men of our own day, we feel assured that Chester A. Arthur, James G. Blaine, Richard Grant White, and many more of our well-meaning but crippled fellow-citizens, are doomed to an early oblivion; but we can promise Dennis Kearney, John Kelley, and Paddy Ryan, that a golden future is waiting for them somewhere.

Having carefully considered this matter, and having observed the misery and want that middle names have caused, – the brilliant geniuses that they have ruined, we have resolved to start our offspring along without the disadvantage under which we have labored, and give them a fair chance.

(*Lampoon,* volume 6, February 1, 1884)

Samuel Heald Clary, stepson of the Thayers' neighbor, Alonzo Whitcomb, became Ernest's brother-in-law when Nellie married him on January 21, 1886. Ernest's mother later wrote: "They are all mated now but you, and there is no knowing how soon you will be bringing a wife home" (SBHS; EMT to ELT, 9/19/1886).

Phinney's fellow Lampooner, Will Hearst, was chipping away at his father, mine owner George Hearst, trying to persuade him to turn his political organ, the *San Franciso Daily Examiner,* over to him. The elder Hearst's political career had yet to take off, though he was a heavy contributor to the Democratic Party and used his editorial pages to promote the party's views. He left the running of the paper to others, as his time was taken up with the source of his wealth – his mining interests in Utah, Nevada, the Dakotas, and Montana. George Hearst had always hoped that Will would take over the large Hearst ranch in Mexico or get interested in running a mine. When Will said he wanted the *Examiner*, his father exclaimed, "Great God! Haven't I spent enough on that paper already? I took it for a bad debt and it's a sure loser. Instead of holding it for my own son, I've been saving it up to give to an enemy" (Swanberg, 33–34).

Although a few months older than Phinney, Will's academic odyssey had caused him to be a year behind his contemporaries at Harvard. As Hearst had been invited by the Harvard faculty to enter its murals no more, he considered his formal education at an end in the spring of 1885. He took off on a camping trip with his best friend Eugene Lent to the Black Hills of South Dakota that summer, then took a position with Joseph Pulitzer's *New York World* to learn the newspaper business the Pulitzer way. Journalism was the one activity that really captured Hearst's interest, and he wanted the *Examiner* to reflect his views of what a newspaper ought to be – a persuasive, creative, energetic force for fair play. "And to accomplish this," he wrote to his father, "we must have – as the *World* has – active, intelligent and energetic young men; we must have men who come out West in the hopeful buoyancy of youth for the purposes of making their fortunes and not a worthless scum that has been carried there by the eddies of repeated failures." He was so impressed with his acquaintances on the *Lampoon* that he foresaw a cadre of them joining him in San Francisco and adding their lively style of writing and illustrating to the *Examiner*. To this end – with the assumption that he would eventually get his way – he made arrangements with the *Examiner*'s managing editor to print travel letters that Phinney would send from Paris (*ibid.*, 30, 34).

Phinney's first epistle was dated January 11 and printed in the *Sunday Examiner* on January 31, 1886. In "French Pride" he concluded that the French believe the rest of the world – if it cannot fashion itself exactly in France's image – exists solely to cater to France. Other ideas, other customs, other likes, and other dislikes are looked on as absurdities. The French do not understand how a foreigner can love his country, serve it, defend it, and honor it. They do, however, understand a foreigner's willingness to overthrow the government of his nation, and his desire to become a French citizen. "The French – it will be understood, of course, that I refer to the masses – believe that the Creator made their country, the rest of the world was patched up from the waste pieces. – E.L. Thayer" (Croy, 11).

If this was Thayer's audition for the managing editor, he performed beautifully. Early in February the *Examiner* offered him a journalist position. Thayer later said he was more interested in seeing the West than in becoming a newspaperman, but he did accept the job without hesitation. He wrote letters to his mother and to Nellie on February 16 to let them know the good news. They were happy for his good prospects, but not for the distance it would put between them for who knew how long. Nellie complained, "Our family seems largely of a roving disposition. I don't like to think that I have got to 'stick to the bush' all alone." Ernest wrote to Albert about a week later; Albert was very impressed and thought Ernest could eventually compete with the Paris correspondent of the *New York Times* and do a better job. His parents, while "both pleased and proud that you have succeeded so well in your first effort as a newspaper correspondent," did not like the idea of his locating in San Francisco. "It is a good ways from home. . . . I hope you will get a position nearer home," his mother stated emphatically (ETC to ELT, 3/7/1886; EMT to ELT, 3/8/1886; and AST to ELT, 3/14/1886).

His next letter, dated January 25, a Valentine's Day entry in the *Sunday Examiner,* described "A Paris Café":

> Paris owes its position as the capital of the pleasure-seeking world to the ante-republic days, when it was the seat of the most joyous court in Europe. Then it was even more frequented by foreigners than it is to-day, for there were more fetes, more grand balls, more brilliant attractions of all sorts. In those times every young prince of Europe came to Paris to sow his wild oats, and of course something had to be done to provide for his entertainment. That Paris still maintains her reputation is due to the Parisians themselves. They are a pleasure-loving people, and in providing for themselves they invite the assistance of others. . . . The English are essentially a stay-at-home people; they are cold, reserved, phlegmatic. The Frenchman lives out of doors, in the cafés, where he can find associates and unburden his mind. He always seems to be saying come and play with me; he can endure anything more easily than solitude. The Frenchman does not stay at home and listen to the cricket on the hearth; he does not bow down and worship the household gods; his family circle is apt to be ruptured by his absence. It is a curious fact that the French language contains no word for *home.* You can say at my home, at his house, at her house, but the nearest you can come to the meaning which the word house by itself calls up in our minds is domestic fireside (*foyer domestique*). It is certain, I think, that home does not have that deep significance among the Latin that it has among the Anglo-Saxon races. Our beloved song, "Home, Sweet Home," would arouse no particular yearnings in the heart of a Frenchman. If the lines ran, "Café, Sweet Café," he might grapple the sentiment and shed tears.
>
> It may be supposed that the cafés of Paris are numerous. On the Boulevards, the principal streets, there is an almost uninterrupted line of them. The cafés must not be confounded with the restaurants, for although the two are sometimes connected as institutions, they are quite distinct. The word café (coffee-room) seems to imply something to eat, and the appearance of the establishment, with its many little round tables and its army of white-aproned waiters, supports the illusion in the mind of an American stranger. In point of fact these places deal entirely in drinks, using the word in that restricted sense which does not include water. They are the equivalents of our American barrooms, but at the same time of a widely different character. The American bar is, so to speak, merely a watering-place on the busy journey of life; the Parisian café is the retreat of leisure hours where drinking is simply not frowned upon. In an American bar you may be the only customer, and yet there may have been a dozen thirsty travelers in as many minutes preceding your arrival. In a café all these men would be there when you came; yes, and a good many who had come two hours before; even one or two, perhaps, who dropped in day before yesterday. And yet it is possible that none of these guests of the house have taken more than one glass.
>
> When a Frenchman enters a café he first looks about him in quest of a

friend or an acquaintance. It is probable that he will be successful in his search, for all Parisians have their favorite cafés, where they go every day. Well, the Frenchman finds his friend, and sits down at the same table with him. When the two have mutually informed themselves of each other's health and have exchanged whatever original ideas they may entertain as regards the weather, they come down to the real business of conversation. The Frenchman loves to talk, and he is as confidential as a child. He does not need to keep a journal for the reception of his secret thoughts. He has no secret thoughts, no more than a barber. He tells you everything: He tells you how he would run the Government if the people had enough consideration for their own interests to make him king; then he tells you his meerschaum is coloring and what remarkable intelligence his dog displayed the other day. After perhaps fifteen minutes, perhaps an hour, of this mental unloading, the Frenchman will have a happy inspiration. It occurs to him that a little moisture will do something towards keeping his tongue afloat. He calls the waiter and orders a drink, not such a drink as we are accustomed to order at home, but a French drink. The French drinks appear to the novice innocent beverages, but they possess withal the iron will—the indomitable strength of purpose of our forty-rod whisky. Some of them are very sweet to the taste, not unlike melted sugar peculiarly flavored. The French drink a good deal of what we call cordials at home, and vermouth and absinthe. Curacoa, mixed either with brandy or bitters, and water is a general favorite; also, hot claret and water, with sugar and a slice of lemon. *Grog Americain,* a French adaptation of rum punch, is not without its admirers. Nowadays beer is drunk in growing quantities. A few years ago it was almost unknown in Paris.

When our Frenchman gets his drink, he takes a sip of it, and he takes another sip of it whenever the conversation lags. The drink always seems to be the last thing that he thinks of. How such conduct would wound the feelings of a Kentuckian! At last it may occur to monsieur that he would like to play cards, or checkers, or backgammon, or dominos, or chess. The material[s] for all these games are furnished gratis by the establishment. Well, he sets to it. When a game is finished he thinks that he has forgotten something. He finds on reflection that he has forgotten something—he has forgotten to take a sip. He repairs his negligence, and the next game begins.

A Frenchman feels no more compelled to drink in his café than an Englishman or American does in his own parlor at home. The café is a place for recreation, a clubhouse free to all. If you have a mind to wait so long, you will see men who stay there for hours, and during all that time order but a single drink. In America, when a man goes into a saloon, you know what he goes there for; and if he doesn't come out within an hour, you may expect, with a certain degree of confidence, to see him fall out. I have never met a single case of intoxication in a Parisian café, and I will venture to say that if the café system were introduced in America, there would be much less heavy drinking than there is to-day.—E.L. Thayer.

"French Families" were discussed in Phinney's letter of February 1, which was published in the *Sunday Examiner* on March 7:

> The subject of the French in their family relations has never been treated expansively by our most popular authors of Sunday-school literature. On the other hand, the so-called sensational novelists have made it the basis of certain moral reflections of a rather dubious cast. When, as in France, marriages are contracted in most cases purely from motives of personal interest, one can predict that connubial misery will be more common than connubial bliss. Still the French family life has its good side, for, however much domestic broils may sunder husband and wife, the relations between father and son and between mother and daughter are usually of the most intimate and amiable character. The children of a French family pass the early stages of their existence under the tutelege of a nurse. Apparently when they are out of bed they are out of doors, for the parks of Paris, particularly the Champs Élysées and the Tuileries gardens, are crowded at all seasons of the year and at all hours of the day with nurses and their charges. During the tender age the child sees about enough of his parents to know them when they pass him on the street. The French believe, – I will not say wrongly – that that squalling, ungrateful bit of humanity, a baby, is more of an annoyance than a blessing. The French sentiment is, if this offspring of ours wants to pull hair and to screech like a locomotive whistle let him work off his irrational spleen on someone who is hired to submit to such indignities; we pass out. I can see nothing heartless in this, although many, especially among my fair countrywomen, appear to think otherwise. Have the baby brought in to be kissed, when he is good and inoffensive, by all means, but when he is bad and bellicose, take him away. The baby does not mind whose hair he pulls; all he wants is hair, hair simply, hair in the abstract, real or false; then let him try the nurse's. No more does he care who spanks him. He accepts the smart as one of the evils of existence, without considering from what source it comes or harboring any thoughts of vengeance. Then let the nurse do the spanking. A nurse is usually reliable in this respect. The French love their children just as much without uselessly making themselves martyrs to persecution.
>
> When a child has outgrown his nursing, at the age of five or six years, he becomes a regularly installed member of the family. If a boy, the father takes him in charge; if a girl, the mother assumes the chief control. Childhood, such as we know it, does not last very long in France. When a boy has graduated from the parks and simultaneously from the care of his nurse, he is more or less secluded from companions of his own age and thrown into the society of older people. A boy does not have the run of the town nor the golden privilege of picking out his own companions. He is always under a surveillance, which is less obnoxious to him because he has never known anything else. When his parents are willing to accord him a holiday he is taken formally to some house where the young people are irreproachable, then he is told to pitch in and have a

rattling fine time. Consequently his mirth has a false ring to it, like the laughter of a man who, in the presence of spectators, has sat down on a freshly painted fence. The French boy at play is an eyesore to a well-educated American. He has none of those grand old sports–baseball, football, bar-up, hare and hounds–so familiar to our own youth. He plays whiptop and battledoor and shuttlecock, and an insipid game of tag, in which nobody is it.

The French boy is thrown so much in the society of his elders, and his relations with his father are of such an intimate character, that his manner becomes grown up long before he is promoted to the dignity of men's clothes. He is not shoved off to the second table when company comes to dinner; there is no fear of his being so indiscreet as to call for a second help of pie. The French father treats his son as an intelligent and reasonable creature, and not like a plaything. In America a father never has a serious conversation with his darling boy, except when he is holding him by the ear. If he wishes to discuss religion on its less practical side he chooses older associates. We have a saying that children should be seen and not heard. In France children are not throttled in this peremptory manner.

Up to the time when a French boy enters the university or is in some other way emancipated from a continual surveillance he has reason to be cautious in claiming that his soul is his own. Certainly, he is never made to feel the responsibility of the trust. A French boy usually lacks independence, spirit and that savoring of cussedness which no well-regulated boy should be without.

He is as good as gold and about as elastic as lead. He is one of those exasperatingly perfect boys who always say "Thank you" and "If you please," and are always eager to run errands for their grandmothers, and never abuse their sisters and never accept a stamp without asking leave from papa. . . . I must say, in justice to the French youth, that when his years have caught up with his education he is not half a bad fellow. As a child he is a failure, but as a young man he is a gratifying success. He is easy in his manners, light-hearted, and endowed with many agreeable accomplishments. . . .

Although the son seems to command a good deal of parental attention, the bright particular star in the French family is the daughter. It is the ruling ambition of every right-minded father and mother to marry their daughter well. The child's training, almost from the day of her birth, is guided by this desire. Three things are essential in order to bring about a successful marriage. The girl must have all the feminine accomplishments in a greater or less degree. She must have a dot. She must have a spotless reputation. The mother is chief manager of her daughter's education. She teaches her all that she knows, herself, and provides her at an early age with instructors in music and dancing. Mother and daughter are almost constant companions, and the latter soon learns to appear easy and collected in the society of older people. French girls have no gawky age. Meanwhile the father is working his best to provide the dot. The dowry is a grand necessity, for Frenchmen do not fall in love in earnest without a cash inducement. When they give up a life of celibacy they expect to receive some indemnity. In order to guard her reputation, the French girl is never allowed any companions of the opposite sex; she can go nowhere without a chaperone; she cannot receive a gentleman caller tête-à-tête; she cannot even go by day on the streets of Paris without at least the attendance of a maid. Several years of her education are generally passed in a convent in the strictest seclusion. The French girl, I may say, is kept in almost perfect ignorance of the horrid men till she has married one of them. She will probably marry young, and her husband will be from eight to fifty years older – old enough, at any rate, to have seen all that there is to be seen in the world, and a Frenchman is never too old to retrieve his fortunes by marriage.

In courtship, as everyone knows, the first thing requisite is to get permission from the parents to hunt on their premises. In America a designing father would not dare to demand the intentions of his daughter's suitor; he would be afraid of frightening him away. In France, a suitor is not allowed to call repeatedly on a young lady without defining his position, for if he should turn out lukewarm, the young lady's sensitive reputation would be compromised, and her future chances would be diminished. Practically, therefore, a Frenchman has to marry on sight; he has little opportunity of testing the temper of his choice. He knows the size of her dot and he hears her put through her catechism of accomplishments; he must take the rest in faith. It is not strange, then, that in France man and wife often fall apart even before the honeymoon has commenced to wane. And there is another more potent reason for a lack of harmony in the marriage state. The girl, when she enters into wedlock, is likely to be as fresh as a new-blown rose, while the husband is steeped in worldliness, and a disenchantment must soon come for the former, which may result in disastrous consequences.

French girls have little to say in the selection of their mates. In this matter they yield docilely to the wishes of their parents. They are educated to think of marriage as the main thing and of the husband only as a necessary ingredient. Their seclusion from male society during maidenhood usually leaves them – sentimental novels to the contrary – heart-free when the wedding-day comes round. The bride must feel a certain gratitude toward her groom, for he is, in a sense, her liberator. Marriage for her means emancipation, a larger and freer life in the world. For this reason, I should hesitate to say that a girl would prefer a young husband to a baldheaded patriarch. The patriarch is likely to be rich, and the happiest woman in France is a rich young widow. She has all the freedom of a married woman without the incumbrance of a husband. – E.L. Thayer.

Phinney's last submission to the *Examiner* concerned "French Cookery," in which he recounted a dining experience he had in a high-class French restaurant. Dated March 22, it appeared in the newspaper on April 29:

> Paris always has an immense floating population, and a large part of the permanent residents do not eat at their lodgings. One may live very cheaply at the ordinary restaurants, the competition is so great; but among the swell resorts of the high *bon ton* competition seems to have the effect of sending prices up. This is natural, perhaps, when one considers that many men judge of the excellence of a thing by what it costs. The expensive restaurants are usually situated on the principal boulevards and for this reason they often draw into their toils the unsophisticated traveler. I know this from dear experience. The first time that I dined away from my hotel in Paris I collided with one of these restaurants and was impressed with the aristocratic stillness of the place, with the half score of haughty waiters standing idly about, and with the utter absence of customers. One menial took my hat, another my cane, and a third my overcoat. I knew then that I was a victim, but when I saw the prices on the bill of fare I turned pale. Soup was very cheap, only sixty cents. I wondered if they would let me off with a soup. I decided to order a soup and when finished with it to remember with visible agitation that I had another engagement. The head waiter came up to me, and in order to inspire confidence and to put the establishment off the scent I commanded a seventy cent soup. "And afterward?" said the head waiter. My game was up and I swallowed a sob which was a square meal all by itself.
>
> I tried to skip the fish, but the head waiter wouldn't have it; he withered me with scorn. I was obliged in the end to take all the courses that are prescribed by French custom. Then the head waiter left me and the butler took his place. The butler asked me what wine I fancied. I fancied a pretty cheap wine and I named it. "And afterwards?" said the butler. I crawled. Pending the arrival of the soup, a waiter expressly detailed for this service covered my table with what the French call *hors d'oeuvres,* little nothings to whet the appetite, radishes, sardines, prawns, butter, etc. I fell to and devoured most of these delicacies, supposing that they were thrown in. I was mistaken. The bill for these items added up to ninety cents. Butter was one franc. Strangers in Paris will do well to beware of the *hors d'oeuvres*. They are always put on the table in the better class of restaurants with the manifest purpose of extorting money. The bill took my breath away. I will not state the amount, for people might think I was bragging.—E.L. Thayer.

Nellie's eagerness to read her brother's articles led her to write to the *Examiner* and request that copies be sent to her in Worcester. "We all wanted to see your letters and I saw no other way of getting at them but to go to head-quarters," she wrote. When she finally received them, she wrote to Ernest that she enjoyed his writing, but the drawings accompanying his work were ridiculous: "I think if I were you I should rather object to the pointless illustrations scattered through some of your letters." Unbeknownst to Nellie, Will Hearst had already complained to his father and the *Examiner* editor about the poor quality of the newspaper's illustrations, "if you may call them such, which have lately disfigured the paper. . . . Illustrations embellish a page; illustrations attract the eye and stimulate the imagination of the masses and materially aid the comprehension of an unaccustomed reader and thus are of particular importance to that class of people which the *Examiner* claims to address. Such illustrations, however, as have heretofore appeared in the paper nauseate rather than stimulate the imagination and certainly do anything but embellish a page." Young Hearst's recent exposure to the excellent original art work by George Santayana, Fatty Briggs, and others in the *Lampoon,* and the creative illustrators at Pulitzer's *World* added to his disgust with the cuts used in the *Examiner,* which he suspected were Cuticura soap advertisements rather than original drawings (ETC to ELT, 4/5/1886; and Swanberg, 29–30).

In that same letter to her brother about the need to write to the *Examiner* to acquire his letters, Nellie added: "I suppose the next thing [is] I shall have to write to the photographer's when I want your photograph and buy it of them. I think you act very grouchy about giving any of your family your photographs. Last summer you were very thoughtless of us, and if you really have had your pictures taken again without remembering me with one, when I have reminded you so often of sending me one, I shall think you are indeed an unnatural brother" (ETC to ELT, 4/5/1886).

Having a picture taken in those days meant sitting with a frozen pose until the exposure was completed. The ordeal was tiring and the result was often gruesome to look at. Phinney had discussed photographic and other types of smiles in a *Lampoon* article:

Concerning Smiles

> Philosophers tell us that man is adequately described by the term, "laughing creature"; because man alone of the members of the animal kingdom is able or inclined to laugh. The term "smiling creature" has a somewhat broader extension. There are two zoological organisms that smile,—men and clams. If a clam is held in a strong light, horizontally, with the mouth towards the observer's eye, an unmistakable smile will be seen to lurk about its pensive and elastic features. Hence comes the comparison, "happy as a clam."
>
> It may, however, be doubted that a smile is always indicative of happiness. I have known a man to smile on discovering that he had been sitting on a fence recently painted, but he was not exactly happy. His mouth smiles, to be sure; but his eyes wore a wistful, far-away look, as though he were wondering how he could turn his trousers inside out without taking them off.
>
> Moreover, as he walked home through the least frequented streets, endeavoring to obscure two square feet of oil and turpentine with the small available area of hand, and at the same time appear easy and unconcerned, one could perceive that the smile was a hollow mockery, a transparent veil which failed to conceal the underlying care and anxiety;

care because he had a wife, and anxiety to know if benzine would take it out. No, he was not happy.

Different men are often of widely different temperaments. Thus it happens that the same incident may not seem equally amusing to all. A gentleman of my acquaintance, for instance, once sat down on the wrong end of a tack, and although the circumstance struck me as well deserving a smile, he failed to see the point, which, nevertheless, he felt with the greatest distinctness. (The tack was one inch long.)

Smiles are of two kinds, cheerful and lugubrious. Now, it is a matter which nearly concerns the annual death rate, that all persons should discover to which of the two classes their facial contortions belong. The test, however, must be made with great circumspection, and never without consulting a physician. A victim of imprudence in this respect has recently come under my notice.

This personage, having remarked the depressing effect which his smile always had upon his jovial associates, foolishly endeavored to discover the cause by smiling at a plate-glass mirror; he immediately fainted away. Consciousness indeed returned, but only to be succeeded by a severe illness, from which he never completely recovered, being throughout his life, which was happily short, a melancholy, broken-hearted man. His was a lugubrious smile.

Some people should never smile; it is crime. A man who cannot smile without giving his Adam's apple a prominent position in the social scale of mundane existence, and discovering his nasal calibre to an incurious public, should overcome this nervous tendency, and study for the ministry. A man who has lost an incisor should never smile till after dark on a cloudy night. In the broad light of day, the general effect is that of a picket fence with a hole for the cat to go through.

Some men, I have no doubt, fail to smile creditably for lack of proper instruction. A smile, for instance, catches some men without warning; the next moment they are as sad as if a hand-organ were chanting Old Hundred in the immediate vicinity. Smiles should not be thus; they should dawn gradually, and disappear slowly, like a June bug up an apple tree.

When a man has drunk a certain quantity of champagne he begins to smile, and he continues to smile as long as he remains in that particular condition. This is a smile that you can rely upon; it requires neither food nor drink; it is the outward manifestation of pure joy; you can put a stamp on it, and mail it to any quarter of the globe with a surety that it will arrive fresh. This smile has no particular object, but it is a smile that will keep out the cold; a smile that will have a fine moral effect at a camp-meeting; but it is a smile very hard to bring home safe on a dark night, and put to bed without waking the old man.

One more smile and I am done. It would be inexcusable in an article of this nature to make no allusion to what may be called the photographic smile. This is a disagreeable task, to be sure, but a sense of duty compels me to make mention of it. The photographic smile is an anomaly in nature; one of the saddest results of modern invention,—a wild, weird,

> ghastly thing. There is a fixed intensity, a stern resolve about this smile which, while it makes one admire the subject's indomitable will, vaguely conveys the impression that he has eaten too liberally of a colicky watermelon. Doubt as to what could occasion such a smile is very apt to induce in the observer cold feet and a sick headache. No reliable cure for it has as yet been discovered. Inoculation has proved fruitless, and transfusion of blood alike unavailing. We may, however, look forward to a time when this disease shall be extirpated, and the photographic smile regarded as one of the horrors of the past.
>
> (*Lampoon,* volume 4, November 10, 1882)

Ernest's European vacation was coming to an end. Feeling that he had said everything he wanted to say with regard to the French culture, he thought about his impending trip to San Francisco and hoped to get instructions and travel money from Will Hearst. It was getting so near his sailing date Ernest sent Hearst "a very urgent letter" and got a cablegram back which informed him that money and a letter were on the way. Relieved by the wire, Ernest wrote his mother on May 8. He told her there wouldn't be any more *Examiner* letters and that he was going to work on improving his French fluency for the rest of his stay. He was writing in French three hours every day; he avoided speaking English by staying away from Americans as much as possible. A Norwegian youth who was staying at the same hostelry made a good companion; since neither knew the other's native tongue they were forced to communicate in French (ELT to EMT, 5/8/1886).

After sailing for home at the end of May, Thayer spent a month in Worcester visiting with family and friends and getting ready for his big adventure in the West. He went to Flushing to visit Albert and Josie and to see his infant niece Ellen (AST to ELT, 4/30/1886).

CHAPTER 17

Crossing the Country

Thayer left for San Francisco by train in late July, steering clear of any "travelling Hannahs" who might be on board. Luckily for Phinney, he had been forewarned of such women by *Lampoon* staffer Owen Wister (1882) (who later wrote *The Virginian*) in his

Railroad Idyls

I wonder what her name is?
  The brim of her hat should be wider;
But I think my little game is
  To manage to sit down beside her.

The side I am on is sunny;
  Her side of the car is shady;
So my movement doesn't seem funny
  To this simple-minded young lady.

Our silence at first is oppressive,
  And a subject to start on is needing;
So I venture, "Our speed is excessive;
  Don't you think it's too rough for reading?"

The ice broken, we soon become bolder,—
  We talk of the meadows and thickets;
When the Conductor taps my shoulder,
  And softly murmurs, "Tickets!"

"O dear! I must have mislaid it,"—
  And she searches about in confusion;
I find out the fare, and have paid it,
  Begging pardon for such an intrusion.

Soon we stop at a station,
  She sees several people enter,
And leaves me in some trepidation,
  With, "I must change for Canaan Centre."

An old man who saw my adventure
  Leans forward: "That's travelling Hannah,"

He says, "and she merits some censure,
For she often gets rides in that manner."

(*Lampoon*, volume 2, October 4, 1881)

Phinney had written a railroad yarn of his own in 1882. He told the story through an offspring of Artemus Ward, Charles Farrar Browne's alter ego of 15 years earlier. While on the train Ward, Jr., fell into

An Amoozin Adventur

I hav bin exhiberting my onparaleld show in the town of Springfeald, Illinoy, and hav met with overwhelmin success. The Kangaroo is in good Helth, and continners 2 B the funniest little rascal you ever see.

Havin sent my Wax Figgers on ahed, I took the Trane for Chicargo. On the Trane I had a most amoozin adventur.

A female came up unto the seat whereon I was reposin, and sed, "Is this seat okkerpide?"

Sez I, "Summat."

I notised as how she had a Babe in her arms, and experients has tawt me that thare is no room for me and a Babe on the same seat. Not bein naterally crooil, when she axed me, "Ma I set down here?"

I replide, "2 B sure."

When the Trane started, the Babe begun to cri. This sot me to moozin. I thawt like this. Wy is it that a inphunt alwaze crize on the cars, whereaz in a nice lonely ten aker lot it will keep its luvly mowth shut tite? Thare's Moses; Moses in the bull-rushes. In spite of enything the Bible ma say to the contery, I manetane that Moses in the bull-rushes was as dum as a stun post. Bi the wa, sum peple wud like to know whare was Moses when the lite went out; but wat I shud like to know is, wat did Moses do when the bull rushed (impromptu goak). If old Pharo's dawter had put Moses on a litnin express trane, Moses wudn't hav cride then, wud he? O, no! Certingly not 2 B sure. (This is sarkastic. I don't mean this.)

Whilst I was thus moozin, that female unto me did say, "Kind sir, I think my child wud like to pla with yure watch."

My hair riz! When I recuvered suffishently as to be able to sit down, I indignently exclamed, "Mam, yure child ma B essenshally goldarned, but never shall its recless grasp cloze on my valooable gewelry. Yure ear, mam; I wud not that sum theaf shud hear wat unto you I say. That watch cost sixteen dollars!"

Whereat she was suffishently impressed. "O, how," cride she in teres, "O, how shall I suth this inphunt's vois?"

Sez I, "I shud recommend a gag."

"O crooil, crooil man!" sed she. "Hast thou no hart?"

"Mam," sez I, "I hastest, leestwize, thare is sumthin in the rejun of my seventh rib wich I hav bin led to suppose was a hart. Dowtless it is a liver. Very likely. Of course. That's so!" (This is a wa I hav of goakin.)

Prezently that pestiferus female spoke onct agen. Sed she, "Ma I maik so bold as to ax you to hold the Babe, whilst I from the lunch cownter a sandwich do obtane?"

"Perhaps you air not awair," I replide, "that my life is not inshured, and that Ime the only support of a wife and a twins. Sutch bein the case, I am 4ced to decline."

"O crooil, crooil man!" sed she.

"Jes so," I sez. "Ecsacly!"

"O, sir," she then did unto me exclame, "my child is all I hav!"

"Then," sez I, "you air destitoot indeed."

"Can you, a father, speke like this?" she cride.

"Yes, mam," I sed, "I can. I can do a grate many other things 2. I can taik a grown person's dose of corn whiskey, and get home alone."

"Think of that twins of yures," sed she, "yure blited wife."

I alwaze think of Betsy Jane," sez I. "2 soles with but a single thawt, 2 harts that beet as one." (Poeckry.)

"Ile waist no more wurds on sutch as you." So saying, she lade the inphunt on the seat, and went a sandwich to obtane. (This sounds like poeckry, but it aint. Its the moosic in my sole.)

Prezently the trane started. The fack that the parient of that pesky little fule had not cum back, scared me sum, I am free to confess. (To the editor: put some stars here.)

The inphunt is now on my hands, and he will be a valooable addishun to my menajery of livin wild beests. I shall call him the howlin hieena.

Trooly yures,

A. Ward, Jr.

P.S. My Kangaroo is the funniest little cuss you ever see in all yure bawn daze.

A.W.

(*Lampoon*, volume 4, December 15, 1882)

Standard Time. We take it for granted today, but before 1883 it did not exist, and before cross-country rail travel it really wasn't an issue. For at least 30 years before 1883 the railroads had been lobbying the government to establish a uniform system of time zones in the United States and Canada so their timetables wouldn't be such a nightmare to develop. Every locality had its own "time zone"; noon was determined by the moment when the sun was at its highest point. A person traveling East to West or West to East on the train was constantly passing through new time zones, each a few minutes off from the others. Each railroad established its own time standard; by 1880 there were 50 different ones. Finally, a system of time zones, each an hour behind the one just to the east of it—developed largely by Charles F. Dowd, principal of Temple Grove Ladies Seminary in Saratoga Springs, New York, and Canadian Sandford Fleming—was adopted by the U.S. and Canadian governments. William F. Allen, secretary of the General Railway Guide, managed to get all the railroad executives to agree to the compromise standard. The new time standard took effect on November 18, 1883, at noon. Boston had to put its clocks back by 16 minutes, Worcester 15 minutes 44 seconds. Washington, D.C., clocks were put ahead 8 minutes, and so on (Southwick, 83–84).

As Phinney crossed the country, and changed his watch three times at most, he might have remembered his *Lampoon* article assessing the advantages and disadvantages of

The New Time Standard

> We have heard numerous protests against the proposed introduction of one standard of time for wide strips of country, contrary to the intent of Nature. Some people are impressed with the belief that they will have less leisure with the same amount of work. There is a prevailing misconception that on and after the 18th of this month the sun will begin to run on an entirely new plan, by special request of the American Academy of Arts and Sciences. This is not so. The sun will still adhere to its old twenty-four hour schedule; but in some places, instead of calling it noon when the sun is at the meridian in those places, they will call it noon when it is at the meridian somewhere else. Hence it may be noon when the sun is before the meridian, and it may be noon when the sun is after the meridian. One is in the wrong to suppose, however, that because it is expedient to call it noon when the sun is past the meridian, on that account he must run any faster to catch a train.
>
> There are certain curious features of the new arrangement which it is interesting to consider. Suppose, for instance, a house of which the threshold of the front door is on the dividing line of two strips of country differing exactly by one hour in time. A man would be obliged, in such a case, to leave his front doorstep promptly at twelve in order to get home at one; but going in the opposite direction, he could easily start from his house, and reach a point four miles distant in less than thirty-seven seconds. It will be hard on the poor husband who lives in such a locality; for though he started for home as early as eleven o'clock P.M., he could not possibly get there before the early morning hour. The lovely daughter of the house, moreover, cannot sit on the bars later than nine o'clock, or her mother will scold her for not getting home till ten. There is an advantage on the other side for the eligible young man, who, after spooning in the parlor till twenty minutes of one, can reach the nearest saloon in time to get one more drink before the store is closed. A sharp business man of this vicinity who could get a job to saw wood by the hour, could do a day's work in ten minutes. It would only be necessary to adjust the centre line of the stick of wood over the division line of the country, and however fast the man might work, his saw blade, starting from one side of the stick, say at seventeen minutes of twelve, could not possibly get through till after seventeen minutes of one. It would thus take more than an hour to saw one stick once; hence it follows that it would take ten hours to saw

through wood thus placed ten times. *And the whole thing might be done inside of ten minutes.*

From what has been said above it will be readily seen that this stepping from a region of time-to-get-up into one of breakfast-is-ready, will cause considerable confusion; and we should not be surprised if the country on either side of the dividing lines became deserted for miles, all moving to places where they could get unsnarled.

There will be indubitable advantages in having wide strips of country regulated by the same standard of time. It has always made me feel sad when I am through with a good dinner to think that a man in Cincinnati is just sitting down to the attack. Henceforth we two will have an even start, and more friendly feelings will prevail between us. Then under the former system, if your darling happened to be a thousand miles away, you could only tell her to think of you sometimes. It was impossible then, as now, to define the exact time when she shall think of you, so that you can think back simultaneously. Now you can tell the dear girl just when you wish her to throw you a kiss, and you can dress yourself up to receive it. With watch in hand, you can determine to a second when to let the thrill of pleasure slip down your *chorda dorsalis,* and the receipt of the kiss may be duly acknowledged by the next mail.

Finally, it is pleasant to imagine all the persons of regular habits throughout one of these broad strips, rising, dressing, eating, drinking, working, going to bed, and sleeping, together. This unity of action will doubtless knit more closely the ties of patriotism in each time-district, though men may feel estranged from those who live across the dividing lines.

(*Lampoon,* volume 6, November 16, 1883)

CHAPTER 18

Baghdad by the Bay

On his arrival in San Francisco at the end of the month, Phinney checked into the Baldwin Hotel at 14–16 Ellis, near Market Street. After settling in, and before reporting for work, Thayer no doubt took a look around the city. If he was looking for a place completely different from his home town he found it in San Francisco. Worcester, Massachusetts, a mill city of 80,000, was an old, well-established Eastern city that had always been satisfied to grow slowly. San Francisco, in less than 40 years, had attained a population of about 350,000; an accurate total was hard to ascertain because of the numbers of "municipally nomadic" persons (residents without residence) who eluded the enumerator. The city was stretching and growing toward its limits every day. It was unnoticeable by the time of Thayer's arrival, but much of the northeast part of the city had once been part of the bay. According to a *Scribner's Monthly* article, "The City of the Golden Gate," (July 1875):

> The pioneer loves to dwell on the changes that have taken place in the physical aspect of the city. He will tell you that the greater part of the business portion of the town has been reclaimed from the sea; that where mighty warehouses now stand ships rode at anchor; that where the Babel of commerce is loudest the peaceful crab had his home and the festive dolphin disported; that the tide swashed against the sandy shore on the present line of Montgomery street; that where now stands the Cosmopolitan Hotel, towered a sand-hill seventy feet high. [ELT to EDT, Sr., 8/5/1886; ETC to ELT, 2/11/1887; 1861 *SFCD* 15; and *Scribner's Monthly,* 269].

About a week after Thayer checked into the Baldwin, reigning middleweight champion Jack (Nonpareil) Dempsey checked in with his wife and set off a flurry of speculation as to whether he was there to fight. He claimed to be retired from the ring for the present, and in the months he planned to stay in the city he would fight no one for less than $1,000 a side. Although the Baldwin was a nice place to stay, it was not San Francisco's landmark hotel. The ten-year-old Palace Hotel, located on Market Street at the foot of Montgomery Street, was the source of pride for the San Franciscan, "who never fails to boast of this hotel as the most stupendous thing of its kind in the world," according to William Henry Bishop in his article "San Francisco," published in *Harper's New Monthly Magazine* in May 1883. The nine-story building, "so studded with bay windows that it has the air of a mammoth bird-cage," was especially enchanting at night, when its electric lights were turned on, striking the many tiers of white columns. A band performed twice a week in the music gallery. The focal point of the hotel was the glass-roofed court, where guests could sit and listen to the music or look at the tropical gardens. They could also promenade in their choice of galleries on the different levels above, or look over the balustrades to the ground level of the court, to gaze at the gardens or watch the comings and goings of carriages in the circular asphalt driveway (EX, 8/9/1886; and Bishop 818).

Two blocks north of the Palace stood the financial district. The two-block area was bounded by Bush Street on the south, California Street on the north, Montgomery Street on the west, and Sansome Street on the east. The influential banks and stock exchanges were here, including some with foreign connections never seen in Worcester: the Alaska Commercial Company, the Bank of British Columbia, and the Hong-Kong and Shanghai Banking Company. The most important banks were the four-story Nevada Bank, from which the weightiest decisions involving mining matters supposedly emanated, and the two-story Bank of California, "whence the brilliant Ralston rushed forth in his trouble to drown himself in the bay," after the flow of gold from the Comstock mines slowed to a trickle and creditors descended upon him. The Merchant's Exchange was an ornate, City Hall–looking building, and the Stock Exchange, which dealt in mining stocks exclusively, was centrally located on Pine Street. The exchanges were relatively quiet in 1886; the boom in mining stocks had peaked in 1875, then collapsed, which burst the bubble of many a would-be millionaire and caused Ralston's rash act (Bishop, 816–17).

Vestiges of the depression remained. Real estate values were a fraction of their inflated levels of ten years earlier. Many ships came in ballast to pick up wheat from the interior since the market for exchange goods was so depleted; as a result, shippers charged exorbitant fees to transport the wheat. The alleys between the financial blocks were dotted with small refreshment places, such as "The Dividend Saloon," "Our Jacob," "The Comstock Exchange," and "The New Idea." Bootblacks were found here, too, dressed in neat uniforms, unlike in the East; they set up their easy chairs on platforms in rows under attractive canvas awnings (*ibid.*).

If Thayer had gone to San Francisco by boat, he would have experienced a most impressive view of the Golden Gate. The narrow strait, which was often shrouded in fog, opened into a wide bay that was more like an inland sea with a commerce of its own going on among the cities and towns on its shores and inland. This natural harbor ensured that San Francisco would be important as a collection and storage point for the produce and goods being shipped from the interior and a distribution point for goods and machinery coming in from other parts. It was also the main shopping, financial, and entertainment center for the area. The San Francisco Bay was over 70 miles long, 10 miles wide, and its circumference, including San Pablo and Suisun bays, was 256 miles. Suisun Bay received the waters of the Sacramento and San Joaquin rivers, and the boats that plied those waters. Ferries had regular schedules to carry people between the city and Oakland. The San Francisco waterfront held goods ready for export, such as redwood lumber from the north and grain from inland. South of the waterfront was the site of heavy commerce in fruits and produce. Battery and Sansome streets were lined with large wholesale dry-goods houses. Kearney Street was the center of retail shopping, though in recent years it had lost its place of prime importance to the wider and longer Market Street. Still, dry goods, jewelry, clothing, and other articles were available along the street (*ibid.,* 813, 815–16).

Worcester was surrounded by hills, but San Francisco was built on steep hills, of sufficient elevations to offer spectacular views of the city, bay, and ocean from the top, but a backbreaking climb from below. Bishop wrote, "To ascend is like going upstairs, and nothing less." California Street in the vicinity of Taylor Street was known as Nob Hill, and was the location of the mansions of the city's most prominent residents, mainly the railroad magnates such as Stanford, Crocker, and Hopkins. Nob Hill was 300 feet high, Telegraph Hill about the same, and Russian Hill – another area of fine residences – rose 360 feet. The method of reaching these residences and points on the lesser elevations was by cable car, "one of the very foremost in the list of curiosities," according to Bishop, who gave this description of the contraption:

> It is a peculiar kind of tramway, quite as useful on a level, but invented expressly for the purpose of overcoming street elevations. Two cars, coupled together, are seen moving, at a high rate of speed, without jar and in perfect safety, up and down all the extraordinary undulations of the ground. They have no horse, no steam, no vestiges of machinery, no ostensible means of locomotion. . . . The solution to the mystery is an endless wire cable hidden in a box in the roadbed, and turning over a great wheel in an engine-house at the top of the hill. The foremost of the two cars is provided with a grip or pincers, running underneath it, through a continuous crevice in the same box as the cable, and managed by a conductor. When he wises to go on he clutches the always-moving cable, and goes with it; if he wishes to stop, he simply lets go and puts on a brake. Fortunately, there is no snow and ice in this climate to clog the central crevice, which, by the necessities of the case, must be open.

Bishop repeated an old story relating the astonished comment made by a Chinaman observing this marvel for the first time: "Melican man's wagon, no pushee, no pullee; all same go top-side hill like flashee" (*ibid.,* 814, 824).

Most of the ordinary houses in San Francisco, as in Worcester, were made of wood. However, unlike the grand residences in Worcester, which were often of brick or stone and used wood as a feature, the mansions in San

Francisco, though enormous and expensive, were usually built of wood. The moist, cool climate and irritating regularity of earthquakes made wood the practical choice for homes, whether extravagant or modest. Bishop observed: "To prepare sites for habitations on these steep hills has been an enormous labor and expense. The part played by retaining-walls, terraces, and staircases of approach is extraordinary. The merest wooden cottage is prefaced by works of this kind, which outweigh its own importance a dozen to one" (*ibid.*, 824).

So many wooden structures meant fire was always a hazard. The fireman was a hero in those days and was often eulogized. Phinney had once honored a man who never failed to respond to a fire alarm in

The Energetic Fireman

The fireman figures prominently in every community; the fireman's ball, and fireman's muster (or competitive squirt) are known wherever the wooden frame house flourishes. But the fireman is chiefly remarkable for his bravery; his bravery has long been the theme of prose and verse, and of telegraphic brevities in the daily papers. The fireman is always being praised not only for what he has done, but for what he would do if he had a chance. There have been cowardly soldiers and cowardly sailors, but no one ever heard of a cowardly fireman.

I wish to-day to speak of one who stands out prominently in a profession where prominence is not easily attained. Need I say that I mean John Smith? John was a very energetic fireman; you rarely met him when he wasn't going to a fire – at any rate I never did. John owed me $4.00.

Often when John was peacefully working in the shop where he was employed, quietly amusing himself with filing iron castings, he would hear the solemn clang of the fire-bells. Then there was no craven hesitation on the part of John Smith, but with a brave, cheerful face, away he would rush to certain peril – perhaps to death – in the nearest gin shop. Sometimes it would be eight hours before he could get back to his work – sometimes, if not oftener, three days.

John was a very generous man. He would frequently invite two, maybe three or four friends, to liquor up at his expense. After his friends had filled their glasses five or six times, John would be startled by an alarm of fire, awful sound; and thinking a human life might be in danger, he would bound away, leaving his pleasant companions to settle for the racket. It grieved John deeply to be compelled to do such a thing as this.

I remember another occasion upon which the highest and noblest feelings of John's nature were wrung by an alarm of fire. He had been engaged in an altercation with a burly expressman. High words were followed by blows; just at this point John heard the fire-bells. For a moment he was swayed between a sense of duty and of honor; two passions were struggling within him. Suddenly it occurred to him that a woman who would remind him of his mother might be in danger. With a sigh of farewell to honor, he fled.

> One cold winter's night there was a great fire in town; millions of dollars in property were destroyed; hundreds of lives were lost. For two days and nights the brave firemen fought the flames, until at last the progress of the conflagration was checked. On the next day the roll of the fire-department was called; many brave men were missing; among the number was John Smith. A search-party was at once organized, and after laboring four days, all the missing were found except John Smith. Late on the following night they brought in his lifeless body. They had found him in a back alley—*frozen to death.*
>
> (*Lampoon,* volume 6, January 18, 1884)

Worcester was a city of old families—many, like Thayer's of English origin—steeped in tradition, conservative and careful. San Francisco, which sprang up as a result of the gold rush of 1849, continued to attract immigrants from all over the world, most of whom came because they were gamblers, risk-takers willing to try their luck at hitting the financial jackpot through rash speculation. San Francisco society, far from tradition-bound, was creating a new milieu out of the heterogeneous individuals who had become wealthy through orthodox or unorthodox avenues. Bishop described San Francisco society as having "an understratum of unexceptionable refinement," though there were those who were "a trifle bizarre in the use of . . . newly acquired wealth" (*ibid.,* 818).

Phinney's earlier lampoon, which did not seem so farfetched after he encountered the nouveau riche of San Francisco, described the

American Aristocracy

> We ain't no poor despicable American aristocrat; not much. We wants it distinctly understood that we eats pie with our knives, and drinks our soup right out of the tureen. We don't imitate the cold reserve of the English; if we wants to borrow four dollars, we says so. There ain't nothing English about us, not even our grammar; no, sir. We're all wool Americans.
>
> When we goes to an evening party, we don't try to look disgusted and bored like those blamed English, and the bloated American aristocrats who imitate them. We always shows a live and healthy interest in all about us; we tries to make our host feel easy. We asks him, for instance, what he suspects the layout's going to tax him, and whether he cleaned them fish himself or got the hired man to do it. That's the genus of light-hearted-man-of-the-people we is.
>
> It ain't safe for no bankrupt English Princes to come moseying round our daughters. We believes in marrying our female offspring to the good, plain, old-fashioned American who knows how to make his feather weight sugar do a heavy weight's work. This is the only kind of a creation that woman can really love. We don't believe in none of your marriages *de convenance,* as the French say; we wants the divine fire and nothing shorter.

> We would also remark that although we are one of the people, we are the only one; American aristocrats ain't shucks side of us. Some people feel all-fired smart and stuck up, but we says we're the only people that's got any claim to be stuck up; and we thinks we can do it gracefully.
>
> We have yet to find our equals.
>
> (*Lampoon,* volume 6, January 18, 1884)

San Francisco had well-developed arts and literature, and a school of design that was turning out talented graduates. The group that comprised the best intelligence in the city was the Bohemian Club. The leading professionals and amateurs in arts and literature were found in this group, and they put their creative minds together for a monthly "Jinks" and an annual get-together called the "High Jinks." The High Jinks was an excursion into the country with a nighttime entertainment in masquerade costume among the Big Trees – the redwoods of Sonoma County. "The ceremonies on this occasion are as wild and weird as the humorous invention of a couple of hundred bright intellects can make them," wrote Bishop (*ibid.,* 818–19).

One of the San Franciscan's favorite leisure-time activities was a carriage ride out Point Lobos Road to the Cliff House and Sutro Heights. In the 1870s there had been a dozen turnouts where carriages could stop so passengers could take in the ocean view; after the economic downturn those turnouts were no longer maintained. At the Cliff House, visitors could have a meal and watch the sea lions on the rocks below. Sutro Heights had gardens, and platforms with telescopes set up for viewing the ocean (*ibid.,* 816; *The Overland Monthly,* 242; *Harper's New Monthly Magazine,* 820; and *West of the West,* 416).

One didn't have to leave the center of the city for amusement, however. San Franciscans could always go downtown and watch the construction of the "New City Hall," located on a triangular lot – an ancient burial ground – bounded by McAllister and Larkin streets and Park Avenue, which ran parallel to Market Street. The cornerstone had been laid in late 1871, and construction had been going on since then; the end was not yet in sight. The city would not go into deficit spending on the project, so when the allocated funds for a given year were depleted, work on the domed complex ended until the next fiscal year. Business was being conducted from the finished portions of the New City Hall. The old City Hall at Kearney and Washington streets – which was built as the first Maguire's Opera House and sold to the city – was retired from active civic duty. After 15 years of this stop-and-go construction, San Franciscans were probably calling the building the "Old New City Hall" (*Scribner's Monthly* 269; *The Overland Monthly,* 133; and 1872, 1879 *SFCD,* 16).

Another long-term project was Golden Gate Park. It was started in 1870 and covered 1,013 acres between the ocean beach and the northwestern area of the city. What was originally a windblown wasteland had been made viable for trees, shrubbery, lawns, and botanical gardens. There were paths for equestrians and pedestrians as well as a paved road for carriage drives. According to the 1872 *San Francisco Directory,* the park possessed "all the requisites of hills, vales, lakes and arable lands to render it a delightful resort as well as a picturesque ornament." By the time Thayer arrived, a Sunday stroll through the park was considered a local tradition. All in all, San Francisco was a solid city with a varied economy; it was hardly the wild, lawless, uncultured outpost it had been in its early years. It now had a strong governmental structure and fine cultural institutions, and was already famous for its hundreds of restaurants with their variety of menus and prices (Oscar Lewis, 164; *The Overland Monthly,* 561; and 1872 *SFCD,* 17).

Baseball in San Francisco

> In this city very worthy and muscular baseball clubs are numerous as man-traps in the pavements or horse and wagon traps in the driveways. They are so numerous that if some convulsion of nature were to strike dumb every "church-going bell" in the city, yet would every passer-by know the blessed day by the baseball playing in every vacant lot and by the uninterrupted line of spectators seated on the fence, with coattails interrupting the fence legends of St. Enoch's Grease or other peerless palliatives of pain [*San Francisco Chronicle,* 4/16/1883].

Bay Area baseball was thriving by the time Thayer arrived. In fact, 1886 was one of the liveliest years area baseball had seen in the 26 years since the first official games were played. The California League was an impressive organization starting its eighth season. President John J. Mone, a capable 37-year-old attorney, had seen the league through some dismal times since 1882, when he took control. Through his strenuous efforts and strict enforcement of high standards he raised the league, and therefore area baseball, to a plane of respectability. There were actually two baseball seasons every year, the championship season and the winter league season. California players on Eastern rosters during the summer came home to play the winter season. They were often joined by out-of-state players, for whom California was, according to the *San Francisco Chronicle,* "the asylum, gymnasium and hospital . . . in the winter." Team rosters were rounded out with local players; those squeezed out by Easterners felt slighted. Apparently, management felt the rarely seen players were a better draw at the gate (Vermilyea, 39; and *CHRON,* 5/16/1887).

The year 1886 had started smoothly enough on the surface. The winter season was being played mainly at Central Park, San Francisco's ballpark that was valued at $1.5 million because of its prime location downtown, bounded by Market, Seventh, Mission, and Eighth streets. Some games were played at the Oakland Grounds, at Fourteenth and Center streets in Oakland (*CHRON*, 11/18/1884).

Behind the scenes, Mone was negotiating with the Central Park Association for the upcoming championship season. Mone found the terms offered by association superintendent D.R. McNeill to be unacceptable, and he wondered what McNeill was up to. Then, on Valentine's Day, McNeill bumped the regular winter league game between the local Stars and Haverlys to allow two femi-nines – the Red Stockings of Chicago and the local Blue Stockings – to play at Central Park. The winter league game had to be switched to the Oakland Grounds; Mone was so furious with McNeill that he decreed the California League would never play at Central Park again (*EX* 2/8, 2/15, 3/22/1886; *CHRON* 2/15, 3/9/1886). Coincidentally, U.S. Senator James Fair, a baseball enthusiast, was just completing the construction of a new ballpark on Alameda Island. He leased his park, the Alameda Athletic Grounds, to Andy Piercy, the Stars' second baseman, and the California League reserved it for the season. Meanwhile, McNeill got busy and started up a new league to play at Central Park. He called his organization the California State League, commonly known as the State League to avoid confusion. Mone's arbitrary decision was not popular with the players; some of them switched to teams in the State League so they could continue to play in San Francisco (Vermilyea, 39; *CHRON* 3/9/1886; *EX* 3/22, 4/5/1886).

On a happier note, the first old-timers' game was held on Washington's birthday, the twenty-sixth anniversary of the first games played in California. The *San Francisco Chronicle* commented that the old-timers were "earnestly desirous of forging the link that will join the fading generation of ball players with the new." When the 1886 championship season started there were three San Francisco–based teams in each league – the Stars, Haverlys, and Pioneers in the California League, and the Knickerbockers, Californias, and Damiana Bitters in the State League. The Altas represented Sacramento in the California League, and the State League's fourth team was Oakland's Greenhood and Morans (G&Ms) (*CHRON*, 2/23/1886; and *EX*, 4/5/1886).

A controversy in May involving Piercy, pitcher Jim Mullee, and the Stars led Mone to expel Mullee and the Stars from the league. The G&Ms immediately left the State League to take the Stars' place in the California League; the State League continued its schedule with three teams. Stockton organized a team and took the fourth spot in the State League during Thayer's first week of work at the *Examiner*. The California League, with most of the veteran players, was able to attract large crowds to its games at Alameda and the Horticultural Park in Sacramento. The State League, playing at Central Park, was guaranteed a steady flow of spectators through the gates (Vermilyea, 39–40; and *EX*, 7/26/1886).

CHAPTER 19

Phinney the "Funny Man"

Thayer began work at the *San Francisco Daily Examiner* Tuesday, August 3, at 8:00 A.M. and worked until 11:00 P.M., taking notes on the activities of the touring Grand Army. On his second day he felt pressured at having but four hours to research the life of Samuel Tilden and write his obituary. Ernest planned to find permanent quarters soon after starting work, but his first days were so hectic he had no time to look for lodging. He couldn't afford to remain at the Baldwin Hotel; Will Hearst made arrangements with his mother for Thayer to stay at the Hearst family home at 1105 Taylor Street until he could find permanent lodgings (ELT to EDT, Sr., 8/5/1886; EDT, Jr., to ELT, 9/14/1886; EMT to ELT, 10/13/1886; and 1887 *SFCD*, p. 591).

Thayer knew that the Hearsts were well off because Will was getting an enormous allowance at Harvard, and he may have met Phoebe Hearst when she came to Cambridge to make sure her son was comfortably situated when he first entered that institution. Mrs. Hearst was just beginning to show her great philanthropic interest in education. She was very interested in making sure young people got a solid start in life, and she was happy to be of help to Ernest (Swanberg, 24–25; and *DAB,* 489).

George and Phoebe Hearst were one of San Francisco's more fascinating couples. In 1850 George Hearst had come to California from the family farm in Franklin County, Missouri, to seek his fortune. Born in 1820, he had two years of formal education and then was put to work in the fields with the family's four slaves. He also worked part-time at a lead mine near the farm. Mining captured his interest. He stumbled through every geology book he could get his hands on. He learned all he could from the lead miners he worked with and from studying the diggings, and eventually he gained such a feel for mining that neighboring Indians called him "Boy-that-earth-talked-to." He took his hard-won knowledge out West and became wealthy through what others perceived as pure luck in knowing where to find ore. He never looked wealthy, though. He remained unpolished throughout his life. When he was 40 he returned to Missouri to attend to his ailing mother. He visited his friends, the Appersons, and was quite taken with the way their 18-year-old daughter Phoebe Elizabeth had turned out. George remembered carrying her on his shoulders ten years earlier. Now she was a petite, lovely young teacher who spoke precise English and pretty good French. George courted Phoebe and, for whatever reason, she eventually accepted his proposal of marriage. His mother died. George and Phoebe were married on June 15, 1862, and after George settled his mother's affairs, they sailed for San Francisco. On April 29, 1863, their only child, William Randolph, was born in a bedroom at the Stevenson House in San Francisco (Swanberg, 3–7).

George bought Phoebe a house on Rincon Hill, set her up in housekeeping, and headed off to his Nevada mines. Phoebe took charge of her son's upbringing. She lavished all her attention and affection on the boy. She was determined that he would be well-educated, mannerly, and moral, and she would instill these attributes in the tyke by the use of reason, without resorting to punishment when he misbehaved. "Billy Buster," as his father called him, was an impish child. With loving bemusement, Phoebe put up with his mischievous pranks, and agreeably paid for damages when they traveled. Will was very bright. He soaked up knowledge like a sponge, but he wasn't willingly regimented into a classroom environment. He developed strong emotional ties to people he liked, but he was painfully shy and had a hard time mixing in with a group. As he got older he tried to buy or shock his way into the center of things. His best friend growing up was Eugene Lent, who went along with Will in many of his pranks. "Genie," though also from a wealthy family, was given much less freedom and a smaller allowance. His forays with Will were not the type of behavior he would have had the nerve to exhibit on his own (*ibid.*, 7, 9, 15, 25–27).

While in Paris, Thayer had developed a fondness for taking wine with his meals, and he made the mistake of mentioning it to his mother while he was in Worcester. As a supporter of the temperance movement, she was very unhappy about this. She showed her concern in her first letter to him in San Francisco, dated August 6, 1886: "Your talk with me about wine drinking has troubled me perhaps more than it need to, for I hope you were not in earnest when you advocated the daily use of wine. I am afraid you like it too well now, and am very sure it would be better for you in every way if you never tasted it again." In the same letter she mentioned the anxiety his father felt about his venture: "He says you are starting upon something you know very little about and that your work will be much harder than you anticipate. But I suppose you do not expect a bed of roses and have prepared yourself for a few thorns."

Sure enough, though, Ernest had a hard time adjusting to his new environment, the long workdays and lack of leisure. In addition to his own assignments he had to get stories that the veteran reporters considered boring or unrewarding. Even though he had a couple of fellow Harvard graduates at the *Examiner*—they were known collectively as the Harvard Brigade—he felt homesick and disillusioned. The day after his twenty-third birthday he wrote his mother a letter that reflected his frustration and unhappiness. The letter was passed around among the family; everyone tried to console him. He was reminded of how long and hard his older brothers had had to work and how much they had had to learn before they were established in their fields of endeavor – Albert in law, Ed, Jr., in owning and operating mills. They all thought him lucky to be starting out at a salary of $35 a week when his only writing experience was for school publications. His mother wrote to him on August 25, speaking for herself and his father:

> We received your letter of the fifteenth yesterday and were not surprised that you were a little disappointed, as writing for a living is very different from running a college paper. But we think you must not be so easily discouraged in your first effort. We think you have a talent for writing but nothing can be well done without experience. . . . No talent even of the first order is worthy anything until it has been cultivated. . . . We should have considered it a miracle if you had gone to the Examiner and stept into the traces with nothing to learn, and think a year's practice will only give you a superficial knowledge of your business. We think you have commenced under very favorable auspices and hope you will not get disheartened.

Ed advised him to get plenty of rest and to take it easy. Albert told him to stop agreeing to do the reporters' work. "I suppose they will shove all they can on you." About his homesickness Nellie offered, "It is only a natural and fitting sensation for any well-ordered being, set down among strangers 3,000 miles or so from his home and friends at hard labor." She added some news about two of his good friends: While in Kennebunkport, Maine, on vacation, Nellie had been introduced to Fatty Briggs, who was staying at the same hotel. "He seemed a very good-natured, lazy sort of a fellow," she wrote. "He spoke very highly of you and said he was extremely sorry not to have seen you after your return from Europe." Back in Worcester she had run into Sam Winslow. "He asked very particularly after you and showed me quite a little attention, in carrying an immense bundle for me, assisting me on to a car etc., all on your account." She finished with, "Sam is looking fat and well as ever" (EMT to ELT, 8/25/1886; ETC to ELT, 9/3/1886; AST to ELT, 9/10/1886; EDT, Jr., to ELT, 9/14/1886; and Swanberg, 54).

Despite the consoling letters, Ernest spent the rest of the summer in a depressed state of mind, missing his family and trying to work his way into a comfortable niche on the newspaper. His mother encouraged him to get out and socialize: "It will not do for a western newspaperman to be bashful," she cajoled in her September 19 letter. Ernest may have put a bug in Will Hearst's ear about offering Briggs the head illustrator's job at the *Examiner,* or maybe Hearst thought of it himself. At any rate, in late September Briggs showed up in San Francisco to draw for the *Examiner*. With his jovial friend, Ernest set out to find lodging; they settled on rooms across the hall from each other at 215 Post Street, near Union Square. Thayer thanked Mrs. Hearst for her hospitality and moved to Post Street on October 1 (ELT to EMT, 10/23/1886).

Unfortunately, the first thing he did in his new environment was catch a serious cold; he felt so bad he called in a doctor, much to his mother's relief. The only lasting effect of the cold was that his pay was lowered since he stayed home from work a couple of days and therefore wrote fewer articles. His father sent him $100 to help him get by. This was to be the first of several colds Thayer suffered from during his San Francisco stay. Like most people, he had a hard time adapting to the city's changeable weather. The temperature varied considerably at different parts of the same day. "A proper male costume for San Francisco is humorously said to be a linen duster with a fur collar," noted Bishop. When Ernest wrote home with his new address, he mentioned that Briggs was sleeping on his lounge, even though Fatty's room was right across the hall. Nellie told Sam Winslow about it; he laughed and said that was where he would be every time. Nellie said, "I should imagine from what I saw of him last summer that he might usually become such an attitude" (ELT to EMT, 10/23/1886; Bishop, 832; and ETC to ELT, 11/30/1886).

Ernest was sometimes ill at ease in public situations, but he greatly enjoyed being in private homes, and his soft-spoken, well-mannered way made him a favorite with the mothers of his former classmates. He was always welcome to dine at the homes of Mrs. Hearst and Mrs. Lent, Eugene's mother. Mrs. Hearst planned an evening's entertainment for charity at the Grand Opera, an immense theater which was closed except for special events. She commissioned Thayer to write a play – similar to the burlesques put on at Harvard – as the main offering of the evening. He wrote the play in good time, but was having real difficulty with rehearsals, so much so that he regretted having become involved at all. He wrote home on October 23:

> Well, this play has proved a very difficult undertaking, & although I am under certain obligations to Mrs. Hearst who has been exceedingly kind to me, I am very sorry that I accepted the task which she requested me to carry through. The young men out here are so utterly ignorant of everything pertaining to one of our college burlesques that the whole burden has fallen on my shoulders & – in that the writing of the play, which is entirely original, is done, I am obliged to superintend the rehearsals. If the thing succeeds, my labors will not of course be entirely lost, but I have so little experience in this line of work in which experience is particularly valuable, that I am very much afraid of a fizzle. I have not even a good troupe of comedians, as at Cambridge, who will make the very utmost of my production.... I shall take a minor part myself, so you see I am very busy. ... On the whole, however, I am rather enjoying myself. Every night bar none these two weeks I have dined either at Mrs. Lent's or at Mrs. Hearst's.

He preferred dining at the Lent's, he said, because he felt more at home there and found the company (which included Eugene's attractive sister) more interesting. Unfortunately, the Lents left for New York on October 26, which put a serious crimp in his dining options (ELT to EMT, 10/23/1886).

Thayer was also beginning to enjoy his work at the *Examiner*. He had been taken off reporting totally and was charged with writing special articles and editorials at $5 per column. This was where his talent and interest lay and he was much happier for it. His hard work on the play paid off, too. It was performed on Saturday evening, November 13, and was quite a success.

The day after the performance, while *Examiner* sports reporter Ted Bonnet covered the State League game at Central Park, Thayer joined the throng of 18,000 to 20,000 spectators who squeezed into the Alameda Athletic Grounds to see the famous heavyweight champion John L. Sullivan in person. The State League and the California League had vied with each other to get Sullivan to umpire a league game; the California League won. In 1884 Phinney had spoofed Sullivan's popularity in

Prince Fisticuff's Magnanimity

> The excellent John L. Van Sully, Prince Fisticuff, was one day hunting with his retinue in the Elliot St. close. In the excitement of the chase the noble gentleman became separated from his followers, and suddenly found himself alone. Thinking lightly of the danger which one of his rank must incur in going about alone, the Prince thought it would be royal sport to make a pretense of being an ordinary citizen; for he was tired of the pomp and splendor which everywhere attended his movements. With this purpose in view he entered the nearest bar-room, and called for Irish whiskey. The barkeeper, remarking the very ordinary appearance of his customer, handed out a bottle of a peculiarly vicious South Boston brand. The prince, however, thinking it was as good as ordinary men were accustomed to, pronounced it excellent.
>
> At this time one of the Prince's retinue, who on missing him had been filled with alarm, came into the saloon; for being acquainted with his master's merry moods, he had known where to seek him. This gentleman exclaimed, "Noble Van Sully, you are here then."
>
> On hearing the words of the new comer, the bar-keeper turned pale with fright, now knowing the rank of him whom he had treated so ill. Falling on his knees, he besought the Prince to spare his life. The Prince at once raised him to his feet, and smiling kindly upon him, said: "Have no fear, my good man." Then slapping him on the shoulder with his cane, he conferred on the bar-keeper the title of Lord Chief Sponger, the honor to revert to his heirs after death.
>
> The bar-keeper was deeply grateful to the Prince, and thenceforward, remembering how he had been rewarded, he always dealt out his vilest whiskey to strangers, hoping that they might be noblemen in disguise.
>
> (*Lampoon,* volume 6, January 18, 1884)

Baseball's popularity by the 1880s attracted well-known entertainers—actors, singers, pugilists, comedians, swordsmen, and jockeys, to name a few. Many of the them took part by handing out trophies and medals to players.

John L. Sullivan actually stood on the mound and hurled a few gopher balls for the new Providence team in the Eastern League on opening day. "Gentleman" Jim Corbett was such a good all-around athlete he signed an amateur contract to play center field and second base for the Alcazars of San Francisco (scouting report: "He's a heavy batter, good fielder and excellent base runner") and was expected by many to be signed by a local professional team in 1888. When the great John L. was in town it was to his benefit, as well as the California League's, to make an appearance (*EX*, 3/22, 11/15/1886; and *CHRON*, 3/10/1887).

Sullivan as an Umpire

> John L. Sullivan, the champion pugilist and pseudo ball-tosser, was the drawing card yesterday at the Alameda Grounds. It was believed by the management that the announcement that the Trojan would umpire the game between the Greenhood & Morans and Pioneers would attract an unusually large number of spectators, but the immense multitude that swarmed through the gates was not anticipated by the most sanguine. Ladies were charged admission, but escorts and quarters were not lacking. Members of the gentle sex were apparently the most anxious to cast their lovely eyes upon the handsome pug. They came as early as 11 o'clock, and an hour before the game commenced the grand stand was densely thronged with females. At 2 o'clock every seat on the grounds was occupied, and a complete circle was formed about the diamond. When the Pioneers started out to practice the fielders were prevented from taking their positions owing to the proximity of the throng. The sphere was driven far into the field by the batters for the purpose of forcing the people back, but this produced little or no effect. The 2 o'clock train from this city swelled the multitude and it soon became apparent that there would not be sufficient space in the field to play the game. The crush was so great that none of the spectators were comfortable, and nearly all distressed. The lack of foresight in the management in not having more than one entrance came nearly being the cause of many serious accidents which only the good nature of the crowd prevented. At one time nearly 2,000 people were struggling to get into the grounds through a gateway not three feet wide. Less economy and more thought for the public convenience should be the rule at these grounds. There should be at least five entrances.
>
> **Sullivan on Deck.**—At the regular hour for commencing the contest there were over 18,000 people on the grounds. The scene was a repetition of the one witnessed at the Polo Grounds in New York on Decoration Day. Men, women and children were scattered all over the field. The surrounding housetops, trees and fences were hidden beneath the weight of humanity. Finally the spectators became impatient, and began to yell for Sullivan, and all eyes were anxiously turned in the direction of the dressing-rooms, in which it was presumed the great gladiator was ensconced. Shortly before 2:30 o'clock the lilliputian form of President Mone was seen bounding over the fence in the rear of the homeplate.

He was followed by Pat Sheedy and the only John L. The latter was attired in a neat black suit, with Prince Albert coat, and baseball cap. He walked up to the homeplate, and when the people caught a glimpse of his stately form there was a grand rush in his direction. Men in center field struggled hard to make a home run across the pitcher's bag, and ladies at the initial and third bag made strenuous efforts to reach the same goal. In a few moments Sullivan was in the center of about 2,000 people. He quietly twirled his mustache and maintained a phlegmatic demeanor, while he gazed around like a Roman General surveying the excited and admiring populace upon his return trip across the Tiber at the close of a successful Punic war.

The ball-tossers, who were forgotten for the time, went into executive session at the outskirts of the throng. In the mean time the entire police force of Alameda, consisting of as many as seven men and a short but stout chief, was called out to quell the disturbance. They worked sedulously to scatter the mob, but all in vain.

He Lets the People Gaze on Him.–Fortunately President Mone scored an idea. He argued with himself and arrived at the conclusion that if Sullivan disappeared the crowd would fall back. He accordingly made a suggestion, and Sullivan disappeared. Then the people began to yell their disapproval, but lung power had no effect. Finally a general discussion was inaugurated, and it was decided to clear the field upon condition that the pugilistic novelty be escorted around it so that everybody could view his classic countenance. This proposition was made to President Mone and he acceded to the demand. Sullivan was informed of the demand and kindly consented. He soon afterward made his appearance in company with Sheedy, and the pair were escorted by a squad of officers around the circle in the field. A crowd of small boys followed and a peanut vender dropped in the rear. During the walk-around females flocked from all quarters and kept apace with the giant and his manager. When they arrived in front of the grand stand everybody arose and saluted the hero at the conclusion of the trip, and the people began to shout and the sounds of rejoicing continued for several minutes.

When Sullivan retired De Witt Van Court made his appearance and called game. The people however refused to move off the field, and despite the combined efforts of the police officers and ball-tossers the throng remained within twenty feet of the bases. The people in the grand stand shouted to those in the field to move off, and the latter replied with shouts of derision. The players were obliged to adopt the rule that a man would be allowed only one base on a ball in the field.

Morris and Carroll, the Pittsburg battery, appeared with the Pioneers. The pitcher was slugged by the Oakland boys, and gauged by nearly every batter. But, no doubt, he did not try to do any effective work in the box. As the spectators interfered with the players many errors were scored, and in consequence the contest excited little interest. Owing to these facts a detailed account of the game is not given [*EX*, 11/15/1886]. [This article was later modified and rearranged, with a box score affixed, and appeared in *The Sporting News* over Waller Wallace's nom de plume, "Gold Pen." There were no copyright laws then (*TSN*, 11/27/1886)].

Thayer had established himself as the *Examiner*'s funny man; now he'd be able to use the techniques he had honed at the *Harvard Lampoon*. The acclaim for his burlesque and the Sullivan article pleased Thayer so much that he thought of staying in the West for two or three years, and possibly marrying and settling down, despite his poor opinion of San Francisco society, so different from what he was used to in the East. He had been corresponding with Miss Lent while she was in New York, and he was interested in her (ETC to ELT, 2/11/1887).

Nellie responded immediately to this news: "I am very glad you are so satisfied with your work and are content in spite of the contempt which you express for San Francisco society. I have no doubt, though, that if you really should settle, as you speak of doing, for two or three years even in that city you will change your opinion of its inhabitants greatly. Probably the tenor of the society there is changing too all the time for the better." She added, "At any rate we all think here that it would hardly be safe to publish your present views as expressed in your letter to me, else we might stir up more of a breeze than Sam Winslow did with his letter from Ireland." Nellie had an opinion about her brother's thoughts of marrying: "It seems to me the greatest nonsense, to think of it at all. If you must do it too at the risk of inflicting upon us such a vulgar lot of new relatives, by all means don't. But if you stay out there many years you probably will not forever be able to turn up your nose at some one of those maidens with her supply of ducats to back her natural vulgarity" (ETC to ELT, 12/22/1886).

Ernest's letters home were read avidly, handed around among family and friends, but deciphering his handwriting continued to be an exercise in itself. His mother was always after him to write more legibly. Albert had no trouble reading the letters, she said, "but you know he is a N.Y. lawyer." She commented in mid–November on a letter Ernest had written to Will Whitcomb, Nellie's brother-in-law: "I do not know whether he has been able to read it yet; the last I knew the whole family were hard at work upon it. We all think you had better get a type writer." By the end of November, Nellie wrote assuring him that Will "at last account . . . had succeeded in making out all but a few of the words." Nellie facetiously suggested that the *Examiner* might make use of her services in translating his contributions, for "the credit is given me," she crowed, "of being best, and, indeed, quite remarkable at deciphering your letters" (EMT to ELT, 8/16/1885, 11/16/1886; and ETC to ELT, 11/30/1886).

Having become more enthusiastic about his work, Thayer started sending clippings of his work home. In his October 23 letter he had requested that his mother "preserve them carefully, for I cannot duplicate them, & I am now beginning to make a collection of all the articles I write." Family members were glad to see that he was striving for more variety of style, although Nellie missed his flair in the serious articles he wrote. They asked him to send them whole issues of the *Examiner* so they could see his items in place on the newspaper page (ETC to ELT, 11/30/1886; and EMT to ELT, 10/13/1886).

His mother worried that Ernest would have to spend Thanksgiving alone. Sounding like one of the people Bishop described as "Americans . . . who confine their interest in their own country to a small strip of its eastern seaboard," she lamented, "I suppose thanksgiving is not noticed much outside of New England." Mrs. Hearst showed how mistaken that notion was by inviting Ernest to a sumptuous feast, which he recalled in detail in a letter home at the end of November. His mother, impressed, wrote to him on December 7: "I thought we had a very good thanksgiving dinner but it sinks into insignificance in comparison with yours for we had only five courses & sat nearly two hours at table." She was happy that her young son had such a thoughtful friend as Mrs. Hearst, and told him, "I shall always feel grateful to her for her kindness to you" (Bishop, 819; and EMT and ELT, 11/30, 12/7/1886).

CHAPTER 20

Winter 1886-87

The big baseball news that winter was the mid–November arrival of the Louisvilles, one of the teams in the major-league American Association. McNeill had arranged for them to spend the winter playing games at Central Park against local teams; he hoped to lure California League teams back to his park with the Eastern bait. The players were all for the idea, but Mone would not condone it. The strong Louisvilles were too much for any of the State League teams, but California League teams were confident they could defeat the mighty visitors, if only they could get a whack at them (Vermilyea, 40; *EX*, 10/18, 12/27/1886).

Ernest's parents considered spending the winter in California, but it had grown too late in the season for an easy overland trip. Mr. Thayer had suffered for years from nettle rash when the weather turned cold, and this winter it was worse than ever. He decided his best hope of relief was "a course of baths at the Hot Springs" in Arkansas. Mr. and Mrs. Thayer hosted a family Christmas dinner on Sunday, December 19. They started their Southwest train trip on Wednesday, December 22. Mrs. Thayer was not looking forward to the trip, but thought her needlework would see her through for two or three weeks. Nellie wrote to Ernest on December 22: "Father endured his humor for some weeks but had to give in at last, and mother seemed to think it her duty to suffer martyrdom with him and go to that last resort and fountain of health and beauty." Nellie was left in charge of the house, the horse, and her parents' cat. "The first will not be a source of much trouble to me," she wrote, "as I have only to carry the keys. I have, however, to see that the horse is exercised and the cat is fed" (EMT to ELT, 3/8, 11/30, 12/15/1886; and ETC to ELT, 12/22/1886).

Ernest went overboard buying Christmas gifts for his relatives. They were not surprised when he acknowledged that the holidays had been very expensive for him. Nellie teased: "Considering how expensive you found the Christmas season this year, I judge you must now have attained the age when you no longer care to have Christmas every day in the year." Ernest had received some nice gifts, too, as he reported to his parents: "The clock which you sent me was very acceptable indeed. My watch is very unreliable, in fact so unreliable that I have stopped winding it up, and for the past two months

I have been guessing at the time. My other presents were a gold pencil from Albert, a pocket-book from Ed, a smoker's service from Mrs. Hearst & an ink stand from her son" (EMT to ELT, 1/9/1887; ETC to ELT, 1/11/1887; and ELT to EMT, 1/8/1887).

The Louisvilles, having wiped the mat with all the State League teams, were eager to try conclusions with teams from the superior California League. Since California League teams wouldn't play at Central Park, the games were set for the Alameda Grounds. On Christmas Day, the Louisvilles defeated the G&Ms in a close game, 5–4. The next day, to the pure delight of all Bay Area baseball enthusiasts, the league champion Haverlys won a well-played, low-scoring game, 3–2, and handed the Louisvilles their first defeat in the 20 games they had played since they started their winter trip (*EX*, 12/27/1886).

The *Examiner* printed this editorial comment (maybe written by Thayer) in its sports column on December 27:

> Never before in the history of the national game on this Coast has there been such excitement in baseball circles as has existed during the past two days. The meeting between the clubs of the California League and the Louisvilles has created a furor which promises to shower golden treasures on the players. The defeat of the visitors for the first time since they left their native heath, by the champion Haverlys, has created considerable comment, and the lovers of the sport find it difficult to restrain their enthusiasm. The members of the Falls City team naturally feel very sore over their defeat, and will no doubt play with a vengeance during the game against the Pioneers on Saturday next. The members of the latter nine are confident of victory, and offer to stake large odds on the result. The contest will no doubt attract a multitude of people to Alameda, and large amounts of money will change hands during the progress of the game.

Louisville made short work of the Pioneers and left the Bay Area soon after. The Louisvilles' financially successful trip to the coast was bound to encourage other Eastern teams to visit the West in the future (*EX*, 12/15/1886; and *CHRON*, 2/17, 3/10/1887).

Fast Company

In an early January letter Ernest wrote to his parents showing his ambivalence with being in the constant company of his fellow journalists:

> I have been leading a very quiet life since I last wrote you. I see nobody at all outside of my professional colleagues & I think that journalists are very much like cattle in that respect. They move in herds. As a rule they are very amusing fellows, for they have all had very varied experiences, & they are brighter & more intelligent than the average of

> men. Sometimes, however, I get very tired of their society, for with all their good points they certainly lack steadiness & respectability. They are wild, happy go lucky fellows, tied to nothing & nobody, as much detached from the laws of society as shooting stars are from the laws of the universe. That is what I dislike about it all, & when I see a methodical family man I feel that I am becoming something quite different from him.

His dining options were getting fewer and fewer. "Mrs. Hearst will start for the East to-morrow and I shall dine at her house for the last time to-night." In anticipation of Senator Miller's death and her husband's appointment by Governor Stoneman to fill the unexpired months of Miller's term, Phoebe might have been going house-hunting in Washington, with or without Mr. Hearst. "She will probably not return to S.F. for a year or more" (ELT to EMT, 1/8/1887; and Swanberg, 35).

A letter from Hot Springs arrived shortly thereafter and in it his mother wrote that his father "feels better every way than at home" and warned Ernest about working too hard. "You must consider that your health is worth more to you than anything else, and I hope you will take proper care of it. It is easier to get sick than to get well" (EMT to ELT, 1/9/1887).

Two of Ernest's coworkers were thinking of starting a magazine and asked him to join them. He would have to invest $1,000 in the venture; he wrote a long letter to his brother Ed, explaining the plan and asking for a loan. Ed answered before he even finished deciphering the whole letter. He was "willing and unwilling" to accommodate Ernest.

> I do not want you to lose the money and then have the load of having to pay it up. If you should lose it and father heard of it you know he would blame me for lending it to you. . . . Your project is a very rose colored one. You have met with two extremely unbusinesslike or very generous men, unless your modesty has kept you from saying or knowing some other reason for taking you into partnership besides the consideration of $1,000. If you wish to write for the magazines it would be much better for you to stay where you are until you get an opportunity to get a chance east in New York or nearby on some newspaper, and work gradually into work to your taste.

He enclosed a check for the requested amount. "I strongly advise you not to use this check; from what I know of human nature it cannot be a success" (EDT, Jr., to ELT, 1/13/1887).

Ernest made no mention of his risky venture to his parents in his next letter to them. His father abhorred speculation of any kind; having had to work hard from the age of 12 had taught him not to take any risks. Instead, Ernest told them about the latest phenomenon in San Francisco.

> Something very remarkable occurred here yesterday. . . . There was a snowstorm, the fifth one in forty years & the heaviest one within the

> memory of man. The snow fell thick & fast for six hours, but in the city not more than two to three inches accumulated owing to the moisture of the ground. The people here made all they could out of the unusual occurrence. Snowballing was carried on with a fury that I have never seen equalled. The most inoffensive passengers were attacked by mischievous boys, & it was as much as one's life was worth to ride in a streetcar or even in a carriage. The papers this morning gave from four to eight columns to the extraordinary event of which everybody is so proud.

That news must have amused his parents, who were in the South, congratulating themselves on having escaped the snow and zero weather in New England (ELT to EMT, 2/6/1887; and EMT to ELT, 1/15/1887).

Ernest never mentioned how he celebrated on New Year's Eve, but he described how the Chinese in the city celebrated their new year:

> The festivities are kept up for seven days & they consist in exchanging calls, high living, & the explosion of millions of fire crackers. The way the Chinaman sets off fire-crackers puts American boys to shame. He buys from 100 to 500 packages & jams them together in a long rope. This rope is suspended from a second story window & the end which dangles above the sidewalk is ignited. It takes from five to fifteen minutes for one of these ropes to fire themselves out, & the cost of a rope is from ten to one hundred dollars. Of course it is an amusement for the rich, but all Chinamen are rich at New Years, that is to say they do not scruple to spend all the money they have saved, & then to buy a rope of firecrackers numbers of them club together & share the expense. The noise the fire crackers make is deafening & the air for blocks around their quarters becomes dense with smoke.

Ernest had heard or read, and apparently believed, that February was "one of the warmest & pleasantest months out here." He found, however, that it was "exceptionally disagreeable & cold. The temperature has never gone down to the freezing point, but there is a north wind which is so moist & raw that it cuts one to the bone & makes one more uncomfortable than the severest of our Jan. days at home." Another cold had caused him to miss a couple of days of work, and his income fell to $20 for that week (ELT to EMT, 2/6/1887).

Nellie was constantly pumping Ernest about Will Hearst – was he engaged or not? Her friend Agnes had seen an announcement in a newspaper that a Miss Calhoun was to leave the stage in London and sail to America "with the intention of soon being united in marriage to a son of Senator Hearst." The story behind that item was that Will had fallen in love with Miss Eleanor Calhoun, an actress three years older than he, and they had become engaged. In order to get Miss Calhoun away from her son – for whom she foresaw marriage to some young lady from a distinguished family – Phoebe Hearst quietly arranged to sponsor Eleanor's acting lessons in London. Thus, by taking advantage of the actress's ambition to play Shakespearean roles, Phoebe had saved Will for a more suitable match. By the time Miss Calhoun was to return to America, Will no longer considered himself engaged to her (ETC to ELT, 2/11/1887; and Swanberg, 32).

The elder Thayers wended their way slowly back to Worcester. Unfortunately, their cat, which was entrusted to Nellie, became ill and was dying of the mange. Mr. Thayer was very fond of the cat, so his return to the cold weather in Worcester was doubly unhappy. The Thayers arrived in Worcester on Sunday night, February 13. They stayed at the Bay State House; Ed, Jr., had gone to his parent's home and started the fire under the boiler during the day Sunday, but by nightfall the house was not yet above freezing. Mr. Thayer kept a rousing fire going all day Monday, and by evening the house was warm enough to allow them to settle back into housekeeping. Mrs. Thayer was ill by the time they got back home. She was suffering facial pain and thought it was caused by a bad tooth, so she had two teeth removed. Because the teeth were so difficult to extract, the dentist advised her to have ether if she had any more pulled. "You must take care of your teeth," she wrote Ernest on February 19, "for I believe you have the Darling teeth that were never made to come out" (EMT to ELT, 1/30, 2/19/1887; ETC to ELT, 2/11/1887).

Good News and Bad News

On March 1 two events occurred which had a definite impact on Ernest's outlook. The first event was the birth of a son to Nellie and Sam; they named him Ernest Thayer Clary. Ernest received a telegram announcing the birth and then heard nothing more for three weeks (SHC to ELT, 3/21/1887).

The second event, whose impact was not so pleasant, was Will Hearst's arrival back in San Francisco to take over the *Examiner*. On March 4 Senator George Hearst was sworn in for a full term as U.S. senator and his son Will took over officially as publisher of the *Examiner*. Will Hearst's return had serious implications for Ernest's budding journalistic career, as he told his parents in a letter dated March 27.

> I have not been doing so well financially since I wrote you last – Will Hearst came back to Frisco the first of March with a determination to make the *Examiner* the greatest paper on the coast. Since then he has been gathering talent from all parts of the country, & I am getting gradually crowded towards the outer edge. Whether I shall get pushed over or not – I do not know, but it is one of the eventualities against which I must provide. My income has shrunk by depress from $35 to less than $25 a week & I am schooling myself to think calmly of the day when it will cease altogether. I am limited now to one special article a week & to a daily instalment of editorial paragraphs, & in case these should be shut down upon there will be one more human being out of a

> job. [He had developed a tougher hide in the seven months he'd been on his own.] I am not however so prone to despair as I was in the early part of my career as a bread-winner. It would not, perhaps, be such a colossal misfortune if I did turn out a failure in journalistic walks. Certainly there is not much money in it, however high you rise, & for me who is not to the manor born, the work becomes continually more exhausting & difficult. Still I shall not give up the profession so long as I have an excuse for clinging to it. Twenty-five dollars a week will not always be a reasonable excuse, but at present, I think, it is. Hearst is no longer a boy, but a man with a scrupulous regard for his own interests. He no longer concerns himself with pushing us along—not that I regret it, for it gives me a greater feeling of independence—but I have to struggle with the best of them. A good many of the old employees have been discharged since his return, & it would not quite take my breath away if I met with the same fate. My mind is made up on one point. If I cannot hold my own in my present position, that of an editorial & special writer, I will give up the Examiner entirely. I will not go back to reporting under any circumstances. The life of a reporter on a Frisco paper is one of a man accursed of God, & for me who am not only hard of hearing but somewhat sensitive about intruding where I am not wanted, it is a foretaste of what all good Catholics tell me I am to expect hereafter. So on the whole you need not be completely taken back if I turn up in Worcester one day. You will see me perhaps on Main Street before the leaves begin to fall, surrounded by a pack of barking dogs & humbly submitting to the jibes of the infant populace [Swanberg, 41; and ELT to EMT, 3/27/1887].

Being an eternal optimist, Thayer looked on the bright side:

> The weather has been marvellously fine for the past few weeks, & I should find it very hard indeed to get out of spirits when it is a pleasure simply to go out of doors & breathe; at least I have plenty of "breathing spells." I take advantage of the greater leisure which I now have at my disposal to read a little outside of the newspapers, but being troubled with my old weakness of the eyes I cannot read very much. There are at present four graduates of Harvard working on the Examiner [Thayer, Fatty Briggs, Cozy Noble, and Eugene Lent] & we usually dine together in the evening. We spend about two hours at table trying to get each other to praise our individual work. Hearst joins us three or four times a week & we tell him how to run a newspaper. He should have a great many excellent ideas on this subject by this time [ELT to EMT, 3/27/1887; and Swanberg, 54].

"I am anxious to hear some news of Nellie & the child & I do not quite understand why nobody has written to me of this important family matter," he wrote to his mother. "I hope that the new baby has not driven the old one entirely out of your mind, & I shall expect a long letter this week which will be a tribute of affection to both" (ELT to EMT, 3/27/1887).

Sam Clary, the father of baby Ernest, finally wrote Uncle Ernest a letter. He said that Nellie had got dressed for the first time the day before and that day she had come down to dinner and supper. Mrs. Thayer had been able to leave her house and come to see her grandson that day, too, after having been confined at home for almost two weeks with neuralgia. “She has suffered a good deal with it but Dr. Sargent says she will get over it all right,” he reported (SHC to ELT, 3/21/1887).

CHAPTER 21

The California League

The California League's move back to the city left Andy Piercy with an empty ballpark on Alameda Island. Asked what he intended to do with the Alameda Athletic Grounds, Piercy said, "I guess I will sow wheat or plant potatoes." Instead, he set out to sign some good available players with an eye to starting up a new league. With Gus Gumpertz of Stockton, D.R. McNeill, and some local businessmen, Piercy organized the Pacific Coast League on March 30 to replace the now defunct State League. The four teams – the Stocktons, Oaklands, San Franciscos, and Damiana Bitters – were to play at the Alameda Grounds and at Goodwater Grove outside Stockton. The directors took a strictly business approach to setting up the league. They paid the players a salary that was high enough so they wouldn't need outside jobs; that way they were available to practice regularly and concentrate on the game. Each player would be issued a game uniform and a practice uniform. The ambitious plan declined to address the overwhelming popularity of the California League; thus the new league lasted only until June (*CHRON*, 2/24, 3/28, 4/4/1887; and *EX*, 6/6/1887).

Stockton

> *No interior city of the State has so many advantages as Stockton. She is situated in the very center of the great valley. She is right square in the road from San Francisco, the queen city of the West, and the mineral wealth and magnificent scenery of our mountains.*
>
> (Examiner, *December 27, 1887)*

Stockton, a city of 18,000 incorporated July 23, 1850, is 82 miles east-northeast of San Francisco on a line that runs right through the main peak of the Diablo range. Mount Diablo, at 3,849 feet, is not high as Western mountains go, but rising above the flat, low San Joaquin valley it is an impressive landmark that can be seen for miles. In both Stockton and San Francisco, Mount Diablo was known as "the mountain" (*EX*, 10/19, 12/27/1887; *An Illustrated History*, 59; and Mount). "Standing up boldly in splendid isolation from a broad, level plain without other mountains to limit its height, a view of Mount Diablo is easily recognizable by its double summit and its regular conical outline, resembling that of a volcano" (Hoover, Rensch, and Rensch, 227).

Located just south of the delta where the Sacramento and Mokelumne rivers meet, Stockton had an early history of mud trouble. There were many sloughs – muddy, shallow-water areas – throughout Stockton. Some of the sloughs were drained to allow development of the city and stop the flooding and muddying of the streets, which planking did not help, except temporarily. In the winter of 1861-62 heavy rainfall flooded the whole San Joaquin Valley; Stockton was separated from every town but San Francisco by a barrier of mud (Tinkham, 14–19; Bishofburger, 88; and *An Illustrated History,* 59).

Stockton was considered crucial for the spread of baseball in California. It was vital that teams in the interior, away from the population center of San Francisco, put up some good ball. Although Stockton was San Francisco's business rival, its efforts in the baseball line were encouraged. San Francisco papers wrote glowingly of Stockton's new baseball team in 1887. The players were referred to as the Slough City boys. The Stocktons were a strong team; they were reorganized as the A&Gs and played exhibition games against California League teams during the 1887 season. Their strong showing not only caught the attention of California League directors, it was exciting for their local supporters (*SL*, 12/9/1885; *STIN*, 4/27/1888; *EX* 7/4, 8/15/1887; and *CHRON*, 3/21, 5/23, 5/30, 6/13, 7/4/1887).

Stockton always had a good chance to win games, which made a little more palatable the hazardous trip out to that "dusty retreat" called Goodwater Grove, where home games were played. The field was outside of town, and Stockton rooters had to brave "the discomforts of the street cars, the dusty road, and the jolting on and off of the crooked rails" to reach it. Away games were an even more scary experience, especially when the home boys didn't win. On the 5:00 P.M. train back from Sacramento after a disappointing loss to San Francisco's Haverlys there, a group of young men who were drowning their sorrows in alcohol "got on board and made the passage to Stockton extremely lively," the *Stockton Evening Mail* reported. "This particular crowd amused themselves by snatching off each other's hats and throwing them out of the car windows while the train was going at the rate of twenty-five miles an hour. The festivities wound up in a free fight in which several revolvers were flourished, a proceeding which caused the sober part of the passengers to get out on the platform and under the seats." One passenger rode all the way back to Stockton on the rear platform, because, as he said, "those revolvers on the train had an ugly look." Stockton was considered "the country" by San Franciscans, and seemingly for good reason. It still had rough edges; San Francisco hadn't had any pistol-shooting incidents at games in 20 years. "Bad blood" existed between the citizens of Stockton and Sacramento, and, according to the *Examiner* on March 21, "Sheriff Cunningham and posse were obliged to interfere during the progress of the Stockton-Alta game" (*STIN*, 4/27/1888; *STEM*, 7/25, 8/1/1887; and *EX*, 7/25/1887).

The Haight-street Grounds

The popularity of Golden Gate Park encouraged the Central Park Association to acquire land for a ballpark just outside the Stanyan Street entrance. The lot was bounded by Stanyan, Kate (now Beulah), Waller, and Shrader streets, just below the terminus of the Haight-street line of the Market-street railroad. When the railroad people saw the crowds that were attending the remote Alameda Athletic Grounds, their mouths watered to think of the profits that would be theirs with a ballpark in the vicinity of the park. The railroad directors agreed to put up the money to build the ballpark, and construction was begun with a March 27 opening date in mind. Completion of the Grounds, and therefore its opening, was delayed one week due to heavy California dew (*CHRON*, 6/8/1886, 3/10/1887; and *EX*, 4/10/1887).

On April 3 about 10,000 spectators showed up to see the new grounds and witness the opening game of the California League season. In an April 4 *Examiner* article Thayer wrote:

> The California League has inaugurated another season under the most auspicious circumstances. Yesterday the sphere was set in motion and the ash was wielded with a will, and ten thousand pairs of eyes gazed with enthusiasm on as interesting an exhibition on the diamond field as has been witnessed for many a day. If the hearty reception with which the opposing nines were received as they made their appearance, resplendent in new uniforms, can be accepted as a criterion of the future prospects of the league, then the magnates of that organization may justly feel proud of their success.
>
> The opening game was all that could be desired. It was beyond the anticipations of the most sanguine, and not even the bickering critic could find a flaw. Every player appeared in excellent trim after his brief vacation, but the work on the diamond displayed the fact that since the close of last season the tossers have taken considerable practice.

Each team was required to carry 12 players; those not playing on a given day were sent to the entrance to help take and count tickets. The players called this "playing the gate," and some were very good at it. According to the *San Francisco Daily Chronicle* on April 25, 1887: "Pope's gate play was splendid. Not a man escaped him, to say nothing of the ladies." When Eddie Lorrigan was scratched from the starting lineup one day, the *San Francisco Daily Examiner* covered for him: "Lorrigan was unable to pitch yesterday on account of sickness and not because he heard that Foreman was going to umpire as rumored. He made a success grabbing tickets" (*EX*, 4/2/1888).

Now that the California League once again had a ballpark in San Francisco it was a cinch to dominate the local baseball scene. The State League was reorganized as little more than a group of farm teams for the four California League teams. Crowds of 10,000 or more could be expected for League games at the new grounds. On days of big games cars were transferred from the other lines of the Market-street Railroad to the Haight-street line to transport people to the games. Even so, the cars were packed to overflowing with humanity. One such scene was described in the *Examiner:* "Men hung on to the poles supporting the roofs of the dummies and were as thick as monkeys in a South American forest. Women stood up on the car platforms tightly sandwiched between men whom they had never seen before, but it was no time to be squeamish or even particular, because all the cars were crowded, and the jam was increasing as the hour for the game grew near" (*CHRON*, 4/4, 8/22, 9/26/1887; and *EX*, 4/4, 7/25, 8/5, 10/3, 10/10/1887).

Hearst's Exploits

On Friday, April 15, Hearst arranged to have a huge hot-air balloon launched from home plate at Central Park. Dubbed "The Examiner," the balloon was to be a floating advertisement for the newspaper, while a photographer in the basket took aerial photographs of the city and vicinity. After the photographs were taken the balloon landed safely in a canyon near Crystal Springs, although the balloon and basket rebounded half a mile into the skies on one attempted landing. This was the first of many Hearst exploits in the name of journalism. Once he and his reporters rescued a fisherman clinging to a rock when the Coast Guard said the seas were too rough; he also faked an emergency to expose the lax rescue methods used by the local ferry company; he arranged for rail delivery of the paper to outlying areas; and, on slow news days, juiced up stories to fascinate readers.

He knew the *Examiner* shouldn't try to outclass the *Chronicle*; the best bet would be to build up the *Examiner*'s circulation from the vast numbers of Bay Area residents who didn't read newspapers on a regular basis. His goal was to have a paper "which depends for its success upon enterprise, energy and a certain startling originality and not upon the wisdom of its political opinions or the lofty style of its editorials" (*EX*, 4/16/1887; and Swanberg, 30, 46, 47, 56).

One of the greatest innovations Hearst made in West coast newspaper publishing was to increase and improve sports coverage, especially baseball. He had a regular sports page on Mondays that gave thorough coverage of the events of the previous weekend. Because of his coverage of National League and American Association games and standings—usually on the front page—he forced his competitors to follow suit or lose readers to the *Examiner*

(Swanberg, 30). Walter Appleton, director of the New York Giants, was quoted as saying, "The *Examiner* has knocked out all the other local dailies by publishing those National League scores. Such enterprise will surely be rewarded, especially on this coast, where I was surprised to see so many thousand people interested in the national game." Even the smug *Chronicle* felt threatened and moved the "Sportsman's Niche" from Thursdays to a Monday slot soon after Hearst became publisher of the *Examiner* on March 4 (*EX*, 6/20/1887; and *CHRON*, 3/21/1887).

Ernest Thayer still hadn't received the newsy letter he had requested from his mother. Nellie, not yet fully recovered from the birth of Ernest's namesake, finally wrote in mid–April, explaining that their mother still was bothered by the pain in her face and eye and the tickling in her throat. She called in Dr. Sargent, who "thinks she is on the mend now, but she has been and still is rather blue and discouraged. . . . You must write to mother often. She is not able to write herself. She does not even read much of any on account of having pain in her left eye. We all think that as soon as the weather warms up a little and she can be out more she will get her appetite back and so gain. I have been over to see her a number of times in the last week or two and hope to be able to get over there every day before long." Will Hearst's innovations were being noticed in the East: "Sam was reading in the 'Tribune' this morning about how young Hearst was changing the staid old 'Examiner' into a 'lively modern paper.' I have not much idea that Mr. Hearst will realize your fears in turning you out of his employ, but I must say I wouldn't feel very bad to see you on the streets of Worcester again." She added her favorite question, "When is your employer going to be married?" (ETC to ELT, 4/17/1887).

CHAPTER 22

Baseball, 1887 Style

Time Out

Thayer started attending all the baseball games at the Haight-street Grounds, but in mid–May he left for home. As he has predicted, he was on the streets of Worcester before the leaves fell, but it was not because of having lost his job at the *Examiner*. His mother, Ellen Maria Darling Thayer, died on May 16, one month before her fifty-eighth birthday. Contrary to Dr. Sargent's rosy prognosis, she never recovered from what he had diagnosed as facial paralysis. She was buried in the family plot at the Rural Cemetery in Worcester. On Wednesday, May 25, the *Worcester Evening Gazette* contained this notice: "Ernest Thayer of Harvard '85, and for the past year connected with the editorial staff of *The San Francisco Examiner,* reached home Monday evening on a visit to his father, Mr. E.D. Thayer, at 67 Chatham Drive" (Crane, IV, 154).

This would seem like the opportune time for Ernest and the *Examiner* to end their affiliation, but neither Hearst nor Thayer seemed eager to break the tie at this time. No doubt Ernest's relatives urged him to stay in the East and look for work closer to home. But he had left his heart in San Francisco: Miss Lent was still on his mind. After two or three weeks in Worcester he returned to the West and his job at the *Examiner*. The proposed magazine deal must have fallen through, or else it went ahead without Ernest. He might have had to use some of the money he had borrowed from his brother to get home (ETC to ELT, 2/11/1887).

New Rules

The one season in major-league history wherein a base on balls was considered a hit–derisively called a "ghost hit" or a "phantom hit"–and a time at bat was 1887. Five balls meant a walk, down from seven in 1886. Also in 1887 the three-strike strikeout was abandoned temporarily for the four-strike whiff. These rule changes were tried out in winter league games, but the California League was lukewarm, and decided to wait until these new rules had a good tryout in the East before adopting them. Every once in a while a sportswriter would take the league to task for fighting the tide of progress; these protests seemed a waste of time. If Thayer had written "Casey at the Bat" in 1887 needing four strikes, the poem would no doubt have died quietly, as it would have had no relevance after that year (*EX*, 4/4, 6/20, 7/4, 9/5, 10/10, 11/28, 12/19/1887; and *BENC*, 2853).

American League Plan

Never content to stand still, the Eastern major league baseball magnates were hatching a radical plan in midseason:

> Manager Spalding mentions a new project that is on foot among the leading baseball magnates. The plan is to drop the Metropolitans and Clevelands from the American Association, and the Indianapolis and Washington nines from the National League at the end of this season. Then the League and the Association will be consolidated under the title of the American League. The New Yorks, Philadelphias, Athletics, Bostons, Brooklyns and Baltimores will comprise the Eastern section, and the Chicagos, Detroits, St. Louis, Louisvilles, Cincinnatis and Pittsburgs will form the Western division. The Western teams will make one trip east, and the Eastern clubs will return the visit. Each nine will play six games with every other club in the league. There will probably be litigation if there is any attempt to bring about this scheme. Some clubs won't have it.
>
> *Exchange.*
>
> (Printed in the *Examiner,* June 13, 1887)

The California League season was a great aesthetic and financial success. Even the *Chronicle*, the last San Francisco paper that would go overboard, was getting into the baseball craze. A July 11 article described

> "Down-Town Interest"
>
> In the business houses, on 'Change, in the banks and insurance offices, the sole topic of leisure-hour conversation is baseball; and it is said that one of the reasons why employers assented so readily to the petition of employees for shorter hours on Saturdays was that they were all anxious to see the league games. Bank clerks and insurance men, grocers and ironmongers, all are bent on witnessing a good game, and to the field they come from all parts of the city.
>
> The ladies, too, are wild over the "diamond," and society's chief topic of conversation is upon this subject.
>
> "Did you see that daisy twirl of Incell's?" says Miss Nob Hill to Mr. Van Ness avenue, as they glide around in the meshes of the waltz.
>
> "That was nothing to what Knell did last Sunday," the gallant replies,

> and on they go, interspersing the chit-chat of fashionable life with bits of baseball slang.
>
> The old deacons of the church have the fever, too, and after Sunday's service many of them may be seen slyly slipping out to the grounds and looking around with eyes askant for fear that they may be seen. They are seen, however, and the good little Sunday-school boy has his quiet little thoughts about the matter that he communicates to "ma," and "ma" in turn communicates to the whole parish, so that it soon goes around:
>
> "Did you ever! Deacon Jones was out to a baseball match Sunday! Shocking!" and then they give a satisfied little chuckle that the old man had been caught.
>
> The craze has caught the schools, too, and the little "school-marm" cannot but sympathize with the little boys and girls who are talking about the interesting topic when they should not do so, for does she not know how they feel about it herself?
>
> In short "There's baseball in the air," and it must soon begin to wane, for the enthusiasm is too absorbing to be long sustained.

The California League's main problem seemed to be games at Sacramento. Visiting teams complained about the travel and the treatment they received there from spectators and the umpire, all of whom were much too one-sided to suit visitors. Sacramento had started the season holding California League games at the Agricultural Park, but it was considered inadequate for the baseball boom in that city, which was due to the strong showing the team made at home early in the season. On June 26 their new ballgrounds, Snowflake Park—located on the line of the Sacramento and Placerville Railroad between Twenty-eighth and Thirtieth, R and S streets—was thrown open to the public. It was built along the lines of the Haight-street Grounds. Buoyed by their success at home, the Altas took over first place early in the season. The last week in July, however, the Haverlys overcame them and moved into first place. The Altas' level of play slipped, and soon they were fighting to hold onto second place (*CHRON*, 5/21/1887; *EX*, 6/13/1887; and *CHRON* and *EX*, July, August 1887).

In early August it was announced that the St. Louis Brown Stockings and the Chicago White Stockings would be wintering in San Francisco and playing each other at Central Park. The Central Park grandstand had been damaged by fire and was in the process of being rebuilt. The whole configuration was being changed: the diamond was being moved toward Mission Street, which would add 75 feet to the width of the field area; the grandstand was being built along the Eighth Street side, closer to Mission Street than before (*EX*, 8/6, 10/3, 10/24/1887; and *CHRON*, 6/13/1887).

Casey Was at the Bat

On August 20 in Philadelphia an exciting ball game was played between Harry Wright's Phillies and the New York Giants. The *New York Sun* had a great writeup of the game, copied in part by *The Sporting News* on August 25. It was pretty colorful, even for those days. Its ninth-inning imagery, though in prose form, bears some striking similarities to Thayer's 1888 poem. Part of Thayer's job was to read other newspapers; chances are good that he read either the *Sun* or *The Sporting News* article, was struck by the imagery, got a kick out of the play at the plate involving former Woolies shortstop Arthur Irwin, saw the evocative phrase, "Casey was at the bat," and clipped it out for future use. Here is the first half of the *TSN* article:

> Philadelphia wanted two to tie when the inning opened. The crowd was very quiet when the home team came to the bat for the last time. But when McGuire lifted the ball safely into centre garden for one base there was a mighty shout. Irwin followed with a single to left and the crowd began to grow excited. Then Ferguson hit a slow bounder to Ward, and by fast sprinting beat the ball to first. Three on the bases. Everybody on the right and left field bleaching boards and over on the grassy terrace were on their feet. The occupants of the pavillion seats were bending forward, all with one hope. That the Phillies would win the game. Casey was at the bat. The excitement was intense. A subdued hush for once gave place to the wild enthusiasm which was ready to run riot. Then Casey led the dance. He poked the ball out into right field, and it fell out of reach of the fielders. Everybody ran. There was a mighty roar from the crowd, which was like unto a volcanic eruption. McGuire safely crossed the plate and Irwin was coming to third like a race horse. He gave a hasty glance into the field, and saw Dorgan and Richardson trying to pick up the ball. Then he started home. The enthusiasm of the crowd gave Irwin wings. He came up the path from third at his fastest speed, and at the same time the ball was travelling with all the rapidity that Richardson's muscular arm could give it. The crowd saw the point. Would Irwin beat the ball? Much depended on it, perhaps the championship. On came the ball. Irwin was still six feet from the plate when Brown put out his big hands and stopped its onward course. The noise was hushed. Irwin made a dive, he slid under Brown, and his hand was on the plate just as the catcher brought the ball down on his back.
>
> "Not out," said Umpire Sullivan.
>
> The score was tied.

Daniel Maurice Casey, 24-year-old left-handed pitcher, had been sold to the Phillies from the Detroit Wolverines before the 1886 season with his battery mate, catcher James (Deacon) McGuire. In those days a battery stuck together, unlike today when one or maybe two catchers handle a whole pitching staff and they all have separate careers. Harry Wright looked forward to having a left-handed pitcher (neither the Athletics nor the Phillies had ever had one). Wright said he liked left-handers because their pitches came in at an angle rather than straight in, thus making them harder to hit. (Within the year an eminent Philadelphia physician would advise another

Phillies' southpaw to give up pitching – that left-handers, as a rule, do not last long because of the strain on the heart.) Wright also expected his pitchers to be an integral part of the offense and defense. Casey was, in 1886, one of the two pitchers in the National League with the best defensive statistics, so he didn't let his manager down completely, but Casey and McGuire were considered the weakest batters on the Phillies. The Philadelphia *Sporting Life* said they would be called "feather-weight" batters in the West. The one time Wright didn't put Casey in the ninth spot in the batting order was when he put Casey eighth and McGuire ninth (*TSN*, 3/10/1938; 2/18/1943; *TRIB*, 8/14/1887; *EX*, 7/16/1887, 7/2/1888; *SL* 9/8/1886; *NYS*, 8/21/1887; and *EX*, 9/7/1887, 4/22, 4/26, 4/29, 5/11, 5/17, 5/22, 5/26, 6/2/1888).

Wright, by contrast, always batted Charlie Ferguson and Charlie Buffinton in the heart of the order when they pitched. Buffinton did bat ninth once: on August 10 Casey started a game and either split a finger in the second inning or broke it in the third; whatever happened, Buffinton was brought in to replace Casey and inherited his spot in the order (*EX*, 7/13, 7/14, 7/17, 7/20, 10/2/1887, 6/3/1888; and *TRIB*, and *EX*, 8/11/1887).

Casey was a left-hander who batted right-handed. In the game on August 20 he hit to the right side with men in scoring position, one of Wright's basic strategies. The fly ball that fell beyond the reach of the first and second basemen and the right fielder and scored the tying run was Casey's second hit of the game. Casey was probably aching when he started that game, because on August 4 he had been hit on the leg by a line drive off the bat of Chicago outfielder Marty Sullivan. Pitching with a sore leg on August 10, he had to leave the game with the finger injury. Casey's finger was still very sore on August 20, and Wright would not have started him, but "Maul's arm was lame, Devine was sick and Ferguson was afraid to trust his injured foot for a full game." No word on Buffinton (*BENC*, 1756; *TSN*, 8/25/1887; *TRIB*, 8/5/1887; and *NYS*, 8/21/1887).

Casey had blazing blue eyes and a friendly grin; he was known as "Irish Danny" by his fellow players. The *Philadelphia Press* called him "the smiling left-handed pitcher." Whether Casey ever had the nerve to stroll to the plate with pride and ease is problematical, but he most likely would have had a smile on his face (Mudville, 26; *EX*, 12/12/1887; *PP*, 9/28/1887; and Dunlop, 42).

Pills vs. Pleas

Thayer's special article, "Attorneys at the Bat" appeared in the September 4 number of the *Examiner*. Local lawyers and judges were getting into shape for a game against local doctors at Central Park on Admission Day for the benefit of the Boys and Girls' Aid Society. Thayer watched the members of the bar practice and was moved to paraphrase Hamlet's soliloquy:

> To play or not to play – that is the question!
> Whether 'tis better to look on and suffer
> The jealousy of seeing others playing,
> Or to take bat against some awful twisters,
> And by opposing knock them. To knock – to run –
> Aye, more! – and by a hit so say we end
> Inaction and the thousand natural features
> Of getting out – ah, 'tis a consummation
> Devoutly to be wished!

> It may seem strange, but it is nevertheless true, that the above effusion from a rival of the immortal bard, is an expression of the musings that have disturbed the massive brains of more than one member of the legal profession in this city during the last few weeks.
>
> There is no doubt that the dear old familiar game of baseball is an enchanting pastime, and has a firm grasp on the popular mind. There is something fascinating about the sport that defies resistance, even from dignified and patriarchal members of the bench and bar. No one pretends to know wherein this fascination lies. It may be the umpire, but this is only a faint surmise. At any rate, the men of to-day experience the same spell that enthused them when they were freckle-faced, saucy, barefooted urchins, over two decades ago.
>
> Then it lured them away from school; now it entices them from their work.
>
> This is particularly noticeable among lawyers and judges. The national game threatens to play sad havoc with the Bar Association, for many of its brightest members are on the point of deserting the profession, and it would not be surprising to see them earning a munificent salary by the sweat of their brow on the diamond field.
>
> During the past week several prominent attorneys have been seen walking around as if they were in urgent need of crutches. When asked if their limbs had been injured they would always mutter something about "Charley-horse" or "trying to steal to the middle cushion."
>
> George Washington Tyler is one of the men who, like Mike Kelly of Boston, has suffered from Charley-horse and he was never sold for $10,000 either. He has also been very hoarse of late and many of his friends thought that he had strained his voice while addressing a jury. But they were wrong. The famous attorney for the fair plaintiff has lately developed into a coacher and he has been giving imitations of Hugh Nicol of St. Louis on the Alameda diamond. He is quite a proficient ball-player and would make a success as a catcher if he could get a mask to cover his open countenance. It is true that he always notes an exception to the umpire's decision, but this is only the result of a pernicious habit acquired while engaged in a controversy with one W.H.L. Barnes.

Judge Hunt is another gentlemen who has been fascinated by the beauties of the great American pastime. He never misses a game at Haight-street park, and he gets many pointers in curve pitching from a secluded nook in the press stand. W.B. Mitchell often accompanies him and occasionally they swap stories before the game about the days of old when they distinguished themselves as ball-tossers. Judge Hunt always claims that ball was ball in those days. You couldn't stand around on bases until you took root and sprouted like a weed. Over the fence was out, and there was "no fair" hitting the ball with a cask of dynamite, nor the catcher didn't get $5,000 a year to stand behind the bat and have his nasal appendage fractured. It was a good, interesting, old-fashioned game, and the scores were not "one to nothing." It makes his Honor feel sad to see the club that had last inning go to the bat without saying, confidently, "We have got to make 30 to tie and 31 to win."

Judge Hornblower is also said to be an enthusiast on the national game, and he frequently "bats flies" to Prosecuting Attorney Coffey in a vacant lot in the rear of his residence in the Mission. Some time ago he knocked a fly that he tried to get himself, but in doing so he assumed about sixteen different poses on the greensward, which performance cost him a portion of his trousers. It was the next day that he fined an innocent small boy $40 for playing ball on the street. He has since regretted his severity on that occasion, because although he has been very anxious to witness a game at Haight-street Park his presence might create comment among people who had read about the heavy fine imposed on the lad.

Reuben Lloyd is gradually becoming fascinated by the ash and sphere. He is an ambitious player and can stop the hottest kind of grounder if he happens to be in its path, but the elusive leather always slips from his grasp. He has told a friend in confidence that his only objection to the game is that females cannot conveniently adopt it as a pastime.

Colonel J.J. Mone of the California League has been interested in baseball for many years, but he never attempted to master the intricacies of the sport until a few weeks ago, when Mike Finn induced him to catch a few curves in a vacant lot on Van Ness avenue. Finn wanted a little practise and he tossed them in slowly for a while, but when he got his arm in trim he sent in a hot "drop" that the little President dropped as if it were a ball of fire. Since then he exercises with a lad about his own size and Finn is allowed to sit on the fence and make suggestions.

There are several young lawyers in the city who are expert players, and they have organized a team to play a nine of physicians at Central Park on Admission Day for the benefit of the Boys and Girls' Aid Society. Before the game circulars will be distributed on the grounds requesting people not to shoot the umpire, as such an occurrence would delay the game.

Every afternoon these embryo ball-tossers can be seen engaged in practice at Central Park. Some of them have much to learn, while

> others are clever manipulators of bat and sphere. John Desbeck is an ambitious player, but he lacks agility. A few days ago he volunteered to catch a few balls delivered from the box by Captain Bell. John T. Dare wielded the willow in order to see if he could balk Mr. Desbeck. The latter appeared without a mask or the customary inflated breast-protector, and in consequence he got a foul tip which he missed. He got the ball somewhere below the diaphragm, and after taking a cursory glance at the surrounding landscape, proceeded to gradually and gently curl up like the petal of a tiger lily. Since then Mr. Desbeck has refrained from displaying his nerve as a catcher.
>
> There is no doubt that during the progress of the game on Admission Day there will be many exciting incidents that will be worth the price of admission.

The Pills outscored the Pleas, 43–29. Thayer wrote another long article describing the highlights of the game, complete with Fatty Briggs's illustrations of "remarkable feats of agility" by the ball-tossers (*EX*, 9/10/1887).

Miss Lent had married another. Ernest couldn't even tell Nellie, who knew best how he felt about Eugene's sister. He told Albert and let her find out through him. "That was sudden news to us," she wrote in a letter he received just about the time the Pills and Pleas were taking the field. She suspected Ernest was really hurt by it. "I hope it did not afflict you too severely." Ernest's recent telegram to their father made her think otherwise: "I don't know but that you may have had your head turned in some way." The telegram contained a request for $500 to buy some stocks.

> Father was very much astonished to think you wanted to speculate and he was a good deal disturbed too. Father wants you to stick to legitimate business, he says, and he can furnish you such help as is necessary in that direction only. Ed thought he might be more willing to send you the $500 if you were sure to lose it. And I am sure I think it would profit you more to lose in that game than to win. If you can't find anything better to do out there than gambling in stocks you had better leave at once. I have heard that people out there were going crazy on land booms and I suppose you were drawn in with the rest. You certainly must have been out of your head to ask father to assist you in any such scheme. He always talks very strongly against any kind of speculation. I trust you may have sobered down by this time and that I may get a sensible word from you soon [ETC to ELT, 9/4/1887].

Pennant Chase

The California League gave in and started playing by 1887 rules on October 1, probably to get the players used to them before the arrival of the Eastern teams, which now numbered four: the White Stockings, the American

Association champion Brown Stockings, the Philadelphia Phillies, and the New York Giants. The first three teams contracted to play at Central Park and the Giants were to play exclusively at the Haight-street Grounds against California League teams (*EX*, 10/2, 10/3, 10/9/1887).

The Pioneers, who had carried the target (been in last place) most of the season, had improved steadily to the point that, on October 9, they defeated the Haverlys to take over first place before a Haight-street crowd estimated at between 18,000 and 20,000 spectators. The *Examiner* described the crowd thus:

> No estimate of the number of people who watched the struggle for victory could be accurate. The gate-keepers could not tell even within many hundreds, not only because of the legion of lookers-on who got into the grounds by adopting the small-boy route (over the fence), but also on account of the throngs that made the adjacent sandhills and other elevations near by black with their presence. None of those occupying seats could make more than a rough guess at the number of people around them, since at no point save out in the field could all the crowd in attendance be seen. The strip of ground reserved for carriages was completely covered with vehicles. Thousands of men and boys lay on the green grass just inside the inclosure, making a line a quarter of a mile or more long, and thrice as many stood seven and eight deep up against the railing, trying to keep track of the game over one another's shoulder. They had to stand, since all the seats, which can hold from 12,000 to 15,000 persons, were taken even before game was called. There had been a crush outside the gates for more than an hour before 2 o'clock. Three cable lines—Haight, Hayes and McAllister streets—had brought an immense accumulation of humanity and many went out on the other Park cars and wended their way through the Park to the baseball grounds. The boxes of private parties and clubs that rise above the tiers of seats had their usual occupants, who were also accompanied by friends. In all, there were perhaps 18,000 to 20,000 men and women present.
>
> The ladies were far from few, and most of them were very enthusiastic. So numerous were they that all could not find seats in the grandstand. Lots of the girls stood up in consequence throughout the game. They found the best positions they could in the midst of the men, for many were so devoted to baseball that they came in twos and threes without any male escort, and made remarks and sharp criticisms about the players as the contest progressed. Others with parasols obtained seats on the benches that were unprotected from the sun, and the bright colors of their sunshades were as pretty and pleasing as the emerald hue of an oasis to the parched traveler in the desert [*ibid.,* 10/10/1887]. [This was part of a special article, separate from the writeup of the game, and was probably written by Thayer.]

The Altas slipped to third place, which pushed the Greenhood and Morans into the cellar. The Haverlys and Pioneers jockeyed back and forth, and on the next to last day of the season, tied for first, they played each other at the Haight-street Grounds. A new rubber home plate was laid just before the beginning of the game, officiated by Manager Robinson of the 1886 champion Haverlys. The game was won, 6–4, by the Pioneers, due in large part to the Haverlys' poor fielding, which brought an end to the Haverlys' notorious good luck. The young man who blew a fish-horn every time a Haverly run was scored concluded that Robinson had buried the Haverly mascot (good luck) and the Pioneer jonah (bad luck) under the new plate. Had the game been played on Sunday, the grounds would not have held all the spectators, but due to the six-day work week many were forced to miss the game. Even at that, the 8,000 in attendance comprised the largest Saturday afternoon crowd of the season (*ibid.,* 11/20/1887).

The Pioneers were about to go from last place in 1886 to first in 1887, but there was one game left to play, and the Haverlys could still force a playoff. The two contenders were scheduled to play the also-rans: the Pioneers played the G&Ms at the Haight-street Grounds and the Haverlys were hosted by the Altas at Snowflake Park in Sacramento. Both the Pioneers and Haverlys lost, so the Pioneers were champions, quite a feat for a team that was so weak in the first half it was written off for the 1887 season, except by a *Chronicle* reporter who had gone out on a limb way back on March 17 with this preseason prediction: "Last season the Pioneers carried the target. From present indications, at the end of the ensuing season it will fly the championship pennant" (*ibid.,* 11/21/1887).

The team that reporter was rating was quite a bit different from the one that finished the season. Mike Finn, Pioneers manager, was lucky to get Edward "Live" Taylor to play left field. Taylor, the "old man," signed to play at the Alameda Grounds, but changed his mind at the last minute. He returned to the Pioneers the second week of the season, which gave them the steady, popular outfielder – suspected of being about 60 years old – for practically the entire season. Finn had taken advantage of the demise of the Pacific Coast League to sign some of the phenomenal players who became available. He released his poorer players in midseason and picked up Eddie Lorrigan, an excellent pitcher, and the Smith brothers – "Big" at first and Hughey at short. Finn later added deaf catcher Jere Hurley and another pitcher, Joseph Purcell, whose real last name was Noonan (*ibid.,* 4/11, 5/16, 5/23, 10/31, 11/14, 11/21/1887, 4/25/1888).

> The baseball season now expires,
>   The captains cease to cuss,
> And insurance men don't rate umpires
>   As "extra hazardous."
>
> *Examiner,* November 14, 1887

The *Sunday Chronicle* gave a citywide, multicultural view of the popularity of baseball on November 27, 1887:

The Ruling Passion
(The Game of All Nations)

"I never saw anything that has taken hold like this baseball," said a pioneer merchant the other morning as he stepped off a street car just in time to have a hot liner off a ragamuffin's bat go whizzing within an inch of his hat. At the same moment an old lady strolling down the street with her thoughts fixed on the market price of a Thanksgiving turkey and her eyes on the rough sidewalk came into violent collision with the batsman. The old pioneer shook his stick threateningly, the injured matron emitted an ear-piercing yell and the juvenile athletes vanished down the nearest alley to remain in hiding till the aroused policeman had once more resumed the perusal of his morning paper under a friendly awning. Such scenes are occurring every hour of the day all over the city, and for that matter, throughout the Union. It is not remarkable, therefore, that an acknowledged champion of the noble art of sliding twelve feet on his stomach to a base, should be regarded as one worthy the homage due a hero. It is no unusual thing for the man who journeys to the suburbs without losing an eye on the way, to see a practice game of a nine-year old team watched with feverish interest by all the solid citizens of the ward. The match game of the Young Resolutes and Dauntless club, all under thirteen years old, was decided with such *eclat* on a western addition sandlot, the other afternoon, that half the assessment roll of the district was represented on the adjoining fences. A police judge peered anxiously over the eastern fence, while a dignified member of the Superior Bench swung his long legs from an adjacent chicken-house commanding a full view of the diamond. The owner of a block of brick buildings on Market street rested his gold-headed cane on the sidewalk to see the eventful test, while such ordinary individuals as stockbrokers, produce merchants, supervisors and City Hall officials hung from the surrounding trees and roofs like blackberries along a Sonoma county fence. That distinguished object of London admiration and present idol of the British aristocracy, John L. Sullivan, would have felt flattered to have such a delegation of wealth and statesmanship witness his proposed effort to reduce Jem Smith to the social status of an ordinary hospital patient.

In the Eastern States the heavens during the summer rain baseballs. The climatic conditions here for such a phenomenon are much more favorable and baseballs seen in more profusion in the air during the winter than the summer. The luxuriant growth of baseball players here demonstrates as conclusively as everything else the superiority of California. The hopelessness of the Eastern struggle to keep pace with us is shown in all things, whether indigenous or transplanted. There is a monotony of style and speech of the Eastern baseballist that is altogether wanting in San Francisco. Here the infinite variety in color, race and speech of the baseball enthusiast cannot fail to excite admiration. One need but to cross the city in a straight line from the Potrero to North Beach to see how hopelessly the East has fallen behind us in the widespread devotion to the national game. The Celt and the Anglo-Saxon combine south of Market street to keep up the batting averages to the championship notch. There the breezy accents of Cork and Galway mingle with the euphonious vernacular of the native batsman born with a cigarette in his mouth. One has to proceed northward but a short space before a marvelous transformation of players is seen. Pat Moriarty, Solomon Isaacs and George Washington Holmes and company disappear from the rivalry for championship honors, and Chow Cum Cook and his pigtailed associates occupy the diamond. Any Sunday afternoon on Stockton street one may see a team of rising Mongolians wrestling with the technicalities of the great American game, while affluent pawnbrokers, pork butchers and influential highbinders and their wives beam down approvingly on the athletes from the rickety balconies. The Chinaman has become an easy convert to the national game, as ball-playing has been from time to immemorial an honored pastime of the Mongolian. Feet and hands have been used, however, instead of bats; but the rising generation of Chinatown has unanimously adopted the American club, and the national game promises to make more work for the Celestial surgeons and oculists of Dupont and Jackson streets.

Leaving behind the odorous purifeus of Chinatown and still going in a straight line toward the bay, the observer finds the Latin races fallen under the sway of the American national game. Colorado Maduro, Jose Broncho, and their associates, with their piercing black eyes and straight hair, dark as the raven's wing, knock holes in the dusty shop windows and aggravate staid Mexican matrons by eccentric out-curves and dangerous liners. A few blocks further and the language of Gaul, so exhilarating to a game of baseball on the street corner, greets the spectator, as Pierre and Françoise and Auguste jeopardize their thumbs in the hope of becoming ornaments of some highly professional diamond. Still a few blocks further, and Antonio Spaghetti and Francisco Di Macaroni can be heard exhorting each other in mellifluous Italian, while several other noble Romans hold down the piles of bricks in the streets that do duty as bases. Here and there on the journey from south to north can be also heard the strong gutturals of Bismarck's dearest language and the fierce expletives that indicate that Bulgaria and Austria are engaged in bitter rivalry at the bat. Frequently, too, as the spectator nears the northern termination of his journey, he hears the sturdy shouts of Nicholas Goptolovsky and Alexander Hetkimoffsky when some juvenile Cossack makes a three-base hit, and the stake of a package of cigarettes against a rusty jacknife is trembling in the balance. Before the wide expanse of the bay unfolds itself at the feet of the spectator he shall have become convinced that while the Atlantic States may have made baseball the national game, it has remained for San Francisco to make it the game of all nations.

(*Sunday Chronicle,* November 27, 1887)

CHAPTER 23

Winter 1887-88

The last day of the California League season was the first day of the winter exhibition season at Central Park. Thayer wrote a special article describing the grand parade before the game:

> There was a mighty sound of brazen instruments tooted by enthusiastic musicians in the vicinity of the Russ House yesterday noon that fell upon the ears of the public, and invited their attention. Religious folk, who had been reverently listening to some lamb of the fold in their favorite churches, heard it, and felt impelled to draw near. Sporting men, lovers of the manly art, eye-glassed dudes, and the small street urchins, rushed toward the spot and set up a prolonged cheer.
>
> It was not a hero from the wars, a politician about to make a stump speech, or a funeral – it was the starting of the gay procession of baseball players, who were to toss the slippery sphere at Central Park, which was to be then reopened for the season.
>
> First came the brass band, then a hack containing D.R. McNeill, President of the Central Park Association, James A. Hart, manager, and C.B. Powers, the umpire. Next rode the Philadelphias, clad in white pants and shirts, red stockings and white caps ornamented with red stripes. After them came the famous St. Louis Browns, in red and white habiliments, while last rode the Chicagos, who wore suits of blue and white, with the blue almost washed out. Were it not that "beauty unadorned is best adorned" the Chicagos would have looked a dingy crowd.
>
> As the procession wended its way to grounds thousands of people, forgetting the teachings of their pastors and the sin they were going to commit, crowded the street-cars and sidewalks until when the park was reached there was a surging, howling, rustling mass of humanity ready to storm the citadel if any one sought to bar their entry.
>
> A small detachment of General Booth's brigade of the Salvation Army ineffectually sought to turn the wanderers from their ways with a cracked cornet, a big drum and four voices whose sweetness had long since fled. An enterprising vender tried to attract their attention by offering them packages of "genuine Arabian gum drops" for 5 cents, and an angel attired in white expatiated glowingly on the merits of "Boss candy, only 5 cents;" but the eager pleasure-seekers urged him to return

> to his celestial abode and consigned the gum-drop seller to a warmer region.
>
> At length the sidewalks began to be visible again, and inside the park one vast sea of human beings was visible. The estimates of the number present ranged from 10,000 to 15,000 persons. Every available seat in the grand stand, boxes and benches around was occupied, and thousands contented themselves with standing through the game rather than miss the sight. Even the tops of the high palings were pre-empted by small boys, who possessed the fly-like capacity of being able to climb a perpendicular ascent without breaking their necks.
>
> It was a big day for the Chicagos, who succeeded in waking the echoes by the way in which they disposed of their opponents, the Philadelphias.
>
> The players were a fine-built crowd. The Chicago girls are world-renowned through the alleged size of their feet, but if their baseball brothers have inherited a similar abnormal development of their pedal extremities it in no way interfered with their covering the ground when any chance of a run was visible. "Let her go, Gallagher!" shouted an interested sightseer, and let her go they did every time.
>
> Mullane, the Chicago pitcher, divided his time between sending in a red-hot balls and masticating a quid of tobacco, but Crane, the Philadelphia's pitcher, also did good work for his side, their defect being their inability to strike Mullane's balls to some region where a cold-blooded catcher was not waiting to receive them with open hands.
>
> Powers, the umpire, attended strictly to business, heedless of the admiring glances of the fair sex, who were sprinkled along the seats, as he ever and anon fiercely uttered the monosyllable, "Out!"
>
> At the end of the game a prolonged cheer went up, and the Philadelphias retired in hacks, determined to ride above their defeat. A cruel cynic muttered to a friend as they drove away: "Well, I guess you will have to walk back to Philadelphy if you don't play any better in the future than you did to-day."
>
> A St. Louis Brown man was of the opinion, however, that but for the immense crowd the scores would have been more even, as a number of balls that went close to the spectators would have been caught.
>
> Another cause of the defeat of the Philadelphias may have been, that although the sun streamed down so warmly as to cause many persons to doff their jackets, the only beverage allowed the players to keep up their spirits was—water [*EX*, 11/21/1887].

Still another reason for the Phillies' poor showing was that the contingent in San Francisco that winter was not really the major league Phillies. Harry Wright, manager of the Phillies, was against having the team go to California to play during the winter; he wanted his players to rest in the off-season and believed the trip would cost the Phillies the 1888 pennant. Many top Phillies players would not defy Wright, and this included practically the whole pitching staff. Despite all this, captain Arthur Irwin got four of his teammates to join him, and filled the roster out with "Eastern players picked up on the route to this city" (*CHRON*, 12/27/1887; and *EX*, 11/25/1887).

Meanwhile, the New York Giants were down in Los Angeles having some close calls with a team that had been beefed up with Eastern players. They arrived in San Francisco for a Thanksgiving Day doubleheader, while the "Phillies" fell to the Chicagos and then the Browns in a doubleheader at Central Park. The Giants beat the Haverlys, but lost a game to the G&Ms, who had carried the target in the 1887 California League season. The *Chronicle* teased, "It is hard to travel 3,000 miles to meet defeat at the hands of the tail-enders of a minor league." The Saturday after Thanksgiving the Giants played the highly touted Stockton club and routed them, 26–0. The Giants' lineup included four future Hall of Famers – Mike Kelly, Roger Connor, Tim Keefe, and Buck Ewing, all of whom were by then famous veteran players. The Stocktons had a 20-year-old first baseman who had not yet played in the major leagues, but Jake Beckley was destined for the Hall of Fame himself. His record of 2,377 games played at first base stood for over fifty years. His work in the few games he played with the Stocktons impressed team directors; Pittsburgh signed him during the 1888 season and he played major league ball for 20 years (*EX*, 11/21, 11/25, 11/27/1887; *CHRON*, 11/28/1887; *BENC*, 27, 651; and Appel and Goldblatt, 27).

Shortstop John Montgomery Ward – who was content to be known as Monte Ward early in his career before he went to law school – joined the Giants after the owners' meetings ended. That added a fifth future Hall of Famer to their lineup. Ward always fought for players' rights; he felt that the $10,000 Chicago received for the sale of Kelly to the Bostons should have gone to Kelly, not Spalding. Incidentally, the $10,000 check Boston used to purchase Kelly was on display in San Francisco along with the Beauty himself (*EX*, 11/28/1887, 9/9/1888; Appel and Goldblatt, 384; and *SL* 12/14/1887).

The "Joints," as the New York players were affectionately known to their California admirers, were given the largest buildup of all the visiting teams. Ballplayers have always been notoriously superstitious, and the New York players were no exception. In a special article on November 25, 1887, Thayer wrote about the various mascots and Jonahs of several individual players in "Giant Ideas."

> Some of the local admirers of the New Yorks can help them considerably in the coming contests if they choose. Several of the team have only to encounter certain objects to put winning out of the doubtful category and cause the laurel to prepare for descending on their brows.
>
> Per contra should any one desire to chase success away from the Giants it could be done very easily with the aid of a cross-eyed person or a funeral. There are other feathers in the wings of the bird of ill-luck, but the pair mentioned are too stout to fail under any circumstances.
>
> Roger Connor is intensely happy when he spies a load of barrels standing on end. If they lie on their sides no significance is attached, but

when the barrels stand on end Roger will bet money that he will knock out a home run, besides banging the ball for numerous little things like singles and two-baggers, and fielding without an error. This barrel business never fails, and friends of the big 'un have been known to hire a brewery-truck driver to stand his kegs on end and drive by Roger in order to put the kibosh on the opposition and enshroud him and his team in good luck.

Buck Ewing marks colored ladies as his mascots. Passing one on the street does him some good, being brushed by the skirts of one helps a great deal, but to walk between two of them makes fortune a sure thing. Buck's fancy inclines to the extreme night in point of color, and all luck is graded by the tint of the mascot. Light yellow is the mildest carrier of success, and coal black is the acme. Buck used to drive a brewery wagon, but does not side with Connor entirely on the barrel scheme.

John Ward religiously reads a chapter of the Penal Code of the State he is in before going on the diamond, and has fine luck when he does not forget it.

Beauty Kelly counts his success by the number of girls that admire him within his hearing. If the number is odd he is bound to achieve success with the stick; if even he will shine in fielding and base-running.

Richardson will mourn in the Far West, because he has not Governor Hill of New York to bless him before the game opens. The Governor and Richardson are warm friends, their relationship being formed while the ballplayer was a reporter.

Tiernan shakes possible flies off by sprinting the length of the tour of the bases. This warms him up, and shows any ill-fortune how speedy he is, and how useless it would be to attempt to light on him. Tiernan can run 100 or 300 yards like a quarter-horse, and the fact that he is one of the best sprinters in America adds to his income by considerable.

Tim Keefe has no pet belief in mascots, but takes notice of cross-eyed people with reluctance. His main reliance is in his cunning thumb and forefinger, and a "lucky mark" or white fleck on either is nursed as a pet as long as it remains. Tim writes shorthand and plays rink polo equally well, and both make him lucky through the winter. He likes to hear Roger Connor sing a little song mildly just before a game opens.

Denny and Brown have some pet ideas of their own, but they are too well known here to need repetition. They side in with the majority on burying a horseshoe under the home-plate, and mourn with the gang over the dead hard luck that cannot help but follow crossing a funeral procession. This is even more sad than an encounter with a cross-eyed girl with red hair and no white horse in sight.

Connor's Home Run

The right-field fence at the Haight-street Grounds was finally inaugurated – in the rain on December 4 – when Roger Connor hit the first home run over it. "King" Kelly predicted it and won countless bets he had placed on Connor's accomplishment of that feat. It didn't take long for Connor to take flight himself. His swift departure was attributed to several possibilities: one was that he had received word of his wife's serious illness in New York; another that he had got the better of former major leaguer Charlie Sweeney in a fight and Sweeney had gone after him with a pistol. Safely back at his home in Waterbury, Connecticut, Connor insisted that he had simply become homesick (*EX*, 12/4, 12/5, 12/15/1887; *CHRON*, 12/19/1887; and *SL*, 12/28/1887, 1/18/1888).

Dan Brouthers, the National League's other slugging first baseman, was asked to replace Connor. The *Chronicle* sympathized: "Our local twirlers heaved a great sigh of relief when they learned that Roger Connor had packed his grip and stolen silently away, but their poor hearts again sank within them when Walter Appleton informed them that he had sent for the heavy-hitting Dan Brouthers of the Detroits. Connor is certainly a heavy hitter, but the superior ability of Brouthers in wielding the ash is conceded by every one." Brouthers had his superstition, too. According to the *Examiner*, "He has a queer way of telling how many hits he is going to make in a game by shaking a dice from a box. If the dice turns up six Brouthers is very happy" (*EX*, 10/3/1887; and *CHRON*, 12/19/1887). (Brouthers didn't take the offer to join the Giants; he stayed home in upstate New York with his family.)

Back to Three Strikes

About this time the National League and American Association reversed themselves and changed the four-strike strikeout back to the three-strike rule. The *Examiner* provided this short history reviewing recent changes in batting rules:

> The new rules have been tried and it has been clearly proved that, as heretofore under the rules previous to the '87 season, the pitcher will become the most important player in a nine. Under the rules of '86 a batsman could call for either a high or low ball, the former meaning from the waist to the shoulder and the low ball being below the waist, no lower than the knee. Three strikes were out, providing the ball was caught by the catcher or fielded to first in time to intercept the runner on the dropped third strike. Six balls were allowed the batsman.
>
> This state of affairs was amended by the National League and American Association so as to become five balls and four strikes, a strike to be called on any fair ball thrown over the plate between the knee and shoulder. It was pretty hard on the pitchers, and there was considerable difference of opinion as to whether the rules would be a success. Much to the surprise of the Eastern baseball writers they were.
>
> A better or more successful season than the past both in the East and

> in this city has never been known in the history of baseball, consequent upon the heavy hitting and fine fielding occasioned by the change in the rules.
>
> The League, thinking to improve the rules for next season, make more amendments to the ball and strike rules by dropping one of the strikes and making it five balls and three strikes. This, of course, will give the twirler about 12½ percent more percentage over the batsman next season over last by taking off one of the strikes.
>
> During the few games that have been played in this city under the newly amended rules, they have clearly proved that the pitcher will be the most prominent personage in a ball team next season [*EX*, 12/19/1887].

On November 27, in one of the last games played under the four-strike rule, the Giants beat the champion Pioneers, 1–0. Thayer wrote the article that describes an at-bat by Mike Kelly:

> For the Giants $10,000 Mike, who is already quite a favorite, was greeted with a generous outburst of applause when he assumed his graceful attitude facing Lorrigan.
>
> None of the Giants were on their bench; they were standing up watching Lorrigan.
>
> "One ball," cried Sheridan, then "one strike, two strikes, three strikes." The beauty had not struck at the ball, and he was getting interested.
>
> The crowd encouraged Lorrigan to "Strike him out, Ed."
>
> Lorrigan stood facing Kel for the final effort. In came the sphere, the beauty made a lunge with his bat which met nothing but the air, and amidst the shouts of the crowd the "only Mike" retired to the bench [*EX*, 11/28/1887].

That at-bat had none of the tension of Casey's at-bat, and the crowd was with the pitcher not the batter, but Kelly's nonchalance until he was down to his last strike was just the same as Casey's in the poem written six months later. Lucky for Thayer the three-strike rule came back; four strikes lacks the drama of three, and would have made for an even longer poem, which Hopper found to be quite long enough when he sat down to memorize it in August 1888 (*HUC*, 6 [1905]).

Though they had been the main attraction coming into the winter exhibition season, the Giants, playing listlessly, were losing followers and causing dissatisfaction among those who continued to patronize them. At one point in late December, the *Examiner* observed, "The New York nine must have a poor idea of the patience of a San Francisco baseball audience." Mike "King" Kelly was the focal point for much of the jeering. In the December 26 game the *Examiner* reported, "Michael Kelly, the famous player from Boston, was the first batsman up for the Gothamites, and, so as not to break the record which he has so industriously struggled for since his arrival in San Francisco, struck out. His playing on first base was in keeping with his batting, as he did not seem to care whether he put a man out or not, for in the fifth inning he deliberately muffed an easy fly to obtain which he would not have had to take a step" (*EX*, 12/27/1887).

Kelly Skips

On December 29 Kelly shaved off his mustache, put on a certain brown shirt, and told his companions, "Whenever you find me with this shirt on, you may consider Kelly a scarce article." An *Examiner* reporter interviewed "The Only Mike" while he and his wife were waiting for a train heading East. Kelly assured the reporter that he had fulfilled his contract, but added that he was unhappy with the way the players were treated, and that he had been threatened with an injunction to coerce him into staying in the West. He intended to leave anyway, and he concluded, "It will take a mighty big deputy to bring me back." His departure caught the coordinators of the winter exhibition season off guard. California League President J.J. Mone was surprised, "but did not appear grieved when told that the erratic king had skipped." According to Mone,

> Mr. Kelly has been treated better than any ball player that has come here before, and he certainly has no cause to kick. Special bonus was paid to get him out here, and he made $900 since he came. He has a great reputation, but he has done nothing here to back it up. He hasn't played ball, and he has done more drinking than is good for him. He didn't pan out well, and we wouldn't pay such a sum again to get him. About all he did on the field was kick against the umpire. He has not filled his contract, and I shouldn't wonder if he had a lawsuit on hand when he gets back East. He has had some negotiations by letter about the management of the Boston Club, and perhaps that is the reason why he has returned. Possibly his wife thought this town was too speedy for the $10,000 beauty, and hurried him away for his own good. He is the only member of the team who has drank anything here. The rest have been very strict and have attended to business [*ibid.*, 12/30/1887, 1/2/1888].

In a conversation with a "prominent member" of the New York Club, an *Examiner* reporter was told that "Kelly's kicking was entirely unwarranted, and that if anything he had been treated better than any other member of the New York Club. As an example of the manner in which the aggregation was treated, handsome Tim Keefe stated that on one occasion one hundred newsboys were invited to attend the game and their entrance fee was charged to the New York Club at the rate of 25 cents each when they were probably admitted for nothing, the maximum charge for such boys being 10 cents" (*ibid.*, 1/2/1888).

The picked nine calling itself the Phillies was having a rough time of it. They really needed Dan Casey, and offered him a nice round sum to join them – $1,000 and expenses. He started out from Binghamton on Tuesday, December 13, according to the Philadelphia *Sporting Life,* but changed his mind either before or after he got on the train, because he never arrived in San Francisco. His catcher, Deacon McGuire, had returned East on the same train as Roger Connor; maybe Casey found that out. His alternative activity that winter was to act as best man at the wedding of his brother's brother-in-law in mid–January, and he was all decked out for it. "Imagine 'Dan' in a dress suit instead of a ball player's uniform," gushed the *Sporting Life* (*ibid.,* 11/28, 12/12/1887; and *SL*, 12/13, 12/28/1887, 1/18/1888).

The vigorous, animated style of play the St. Louis Browns were displaying excited the admiration of Bay Area fans, but in order to see them, cranks had to go to Central Park. This was soon to change. Attendance at Haight-street had declined steadily due to the Giants' weak playing, while Central Park was enjoying more and more business as the winter season wore on. Central Park, unlike the Haight-street Grounds, could tell exactly what its attendance was; the first turnstile in the West was installed there in early December. It made sense for the California League to invite the Browns to play at the Haight-street grounds, and throughout January some exciting games were played before a once again enthusiastic crowd. Members of the Eastern teams were leaving two or three at a time, so that midway through January no Eastern team was still intact (*EX*, 12/12/1887, 1/2, 1/16, 1/23/1888).

Rosters were being set for all the professional teams in the country; California players were in demand in the East, some by National League teams. The *Examiner* noticed that local players were not jumping at offers to go East:

> Already the shrewd Eastern manager is sending on telegrams to rising California ball-tossers, and as fast as they are received an answer is given that they will have to seek other spheres for "finds." The baseball business in California is on the rise, and ballplayers of any note are satisfied to stay at home. There has been a number of ball-tossers incubated this season in California that would undoubtedly make their mark in the East next season, if they could be induced to go, but they are strongly averse to going. One of them said the other day: "Why, what is the use of going East, when we can make more money by staying at home?" Regarding reputation, he said: "A person cannot live on that." There will be a very slight emigration of ball-tossers from this county this season, judging from the refusals so far by the local players. Ryan has refused a good offer from the Western League St. Louis Club; Shea had an $1,800 offer from Newark, which he disdainfully tossed over his shoulder; Borchers had tempting offers from Chicago, Boston and New York, but refused them all to sign with the G & Ms. Several others of the local players refused to go East, and the offers have just commenced to arrive" [*ibid.,* 1/3/1888].

The earliest baseball cards were created in a studio setting arranged to look vaguely like a baseball field. An artist or photographer would capture the subject in an awkward and unreal pose. The *Sporting Life* thought a little baseball expertise in the studio would improve the situation:

> There is one feature of baseball which is sadly behind the age, and that is the artistic branch. The soap business is boomed by the finest work of the engraver and lithographer, but base ball pictures are the ghostliest sort of failures. Players are made to assume all sorts of impossible attitudes, catchers are put behind the bat with bare hands and nothing but a mask on, while fearless umpires stand alongside of the catchers entirely unprotected from the assaults of the deadly foul tip. Considering the general interest taken in base ball, it would seem worth the while to engage an artist for the work who knows the difference between a base hit and a balloon on fire [*SL*, 2/8/1888].

By mid–February almost all the Eastern players had returned East. The only ones left in the Bay Area were the ones with homes there and Arthur Irwin, whose young son Herbert was too ill to travel. When the Haight-street Grounds were no longer in use, they were closed while a grass infield was installed and the old chairs and benches in the ladies' grandstand were replaced with opera chairs (*ibid.*, 2/15/1888; and *EX*, 1/23, 2/20/1888).

Stockton's New Ballpark

Gus Gumpertz had resigned as head of the Stockton A&Gs. The team was reorganized with stockholders and the name was changed to the Stockton Brown Stockings or, affectionately, the Browns.

Local cranks were eagerly watching the progress on their new ballpark, called the Banner Island Grounds. It was conveniently located six blocks from the Court House. In addition to baseball games, pedestrianism and foot racing would be accommodated by a cinder track 425 feet long, and there would be a bicycle track on the inner portion of the driveway, four laps to a mile. The main entrance was on Fremont Street near Otter. Local "kickers" were out in force. Stockton natives had a reputation for complaining every time a project of any kind was under way. The Stockton Base Ball Club was threatened with an injunction to prevent them from completing the fence around the ball grounds and also to prevent the building of a grandstand. "The threats have not frightened the managers, who were raised in Stockton and have become used to rubbing against kickers, and the work is being prosecuted as fast as possible," noted the Stockton *Daily Independent* on February 9 (*CHRON*, 5/23/1887; and *STIN*, 1/10, 2/9/1888).

Stockton played its first game as a member of the California League at the new Banner Island Grounds on March 26, 1888. The festive day was marred by a defeat at the hands of the G&Ms, but the game was close, 3–2, and well played (*STIN*, 3/27/1888).

Last Days on the Examiner

Thayer and Briggs spent their last weeks on the *Examiner* hard at work on the anniversary edition which detailed the numerous accomplishments of the newspaper in the year since Will Hearst took it over (*EX*, 3/4/1888). Thayer's last editorial column appeared on February 20, 1888. One of the items in "City Front News" read as follows:

> Yesterday being the first really pleasant day that has been enjoyed for some time, the promenades of the city front were as crowded as a popular Paris boulevard. Scores of young men treated their Sunday girls to an economical gaze upon the vast shipping interests, which to see properly and impartially entails a walk of about four miles. However, as walking was good and cheap, the maze of masts generally excites interest and forgetfulness all the way along. A party of four couples who had worked up from the Pacific Mail docks to Meiggs wharf had trouble when their beaux refused to take the North Beach cars to again return them to the city. The result was that the ladies abandoned the ungallant swains and took a car at their own expense, while they were being pelted with peanuts to the thrilling tune of "Chippy, Get Your Hair Cut," that was being whistled by those who had been deserted [*ibid.*, 2/20/1888].

On the same page was the news that Edward "Live" Taylor, "The Famous Leather-Chaser," left-fielder of the champion Pioneers and one of the most popular players ever to play in the Bay Area, had died the day before. "While in the East he contracted a lung complaint, and was never healthy thereafter." His age was given as "about 38." (According to the birthdate given in the *Baseball Encyclopedia,* Taylor had just turned 33.) (*EX*, 2/20/1888; and *BENC*, 533.)

John Montgomery Ward later commented, in an article discussing the life of a ballplayer: "It is a remarkable fact that a large percentage of the players who have died have fallen victims to some affection of the lungs, and I believe this to have been due, not to irregular habits and dissipation, as some have unkindly suggested, but to the frequent colds to which they have been subject" (*EX*, 9/9/1888).

The California League was preparing for its 1888 season when Thayer was leaving San Francisco. The league dropped Sacramento and Snowflake Park in favor of Stockton and the Banner Island Grounds. The Haverlys and Pioneers continued to represent San Francisco. Many San Franciscans thought one team called the San Franciscos would advertise the city better nationwide. The G&Ms, or Oaklands, filled out the four-team league (*ibid.*, 1/23, 2/20, 3/15, 3/19, 12/3/1888).

The Trip Home

On Washington's birthday, Will Hearst took half of his staff with him to Washington, DC, to publish a special edition of the *Examiner* full of arguments in favor of holding the Democratic national convention that summer in San Francisco. Thayer was able to see Mrs. Hearst again in the Hearsts' beautiful home at 1400 New Hampshire Avenue. When Will Hearst was ready to return to California, Thayer and Briggs left the others and went back home to Massachusetts – Briggs to Springfield and Thayer to Worcester. Thayer's full-time journalistic career thus came to an end (Swanberg, 52; and Croy, 11).

PART IV

Thayer and "Casey"

CHAPTER 24

The Creation of "Casey"

Back in the family home at 67 Chatham Drive, Thayer had hardly settled in when a monumental storm hit, on March 11–14, just before spring was due to arrive, on the calendar at least. Known from then on as "The Great Blizzard of 1888," the monster storm caused 400 deaths in New York and New England. After digging out from the blizzard, Ernest thought about his future. He knew he had to look for work or else join the family business, which his father had wanted him to do from the start. He owed Ed that money he had borrowed, so he went to work as a clerk at Ed's mill in Cherry Valley, a milling area next to Worcester. Although his interest lay in philosophy and literature, he had a facility with numbers and finance that came in handy in this work. He continued to send ballads and filler to the *Examiner* until his job at the mill began to take all of his time and energy (World, 520; Croy, 11; and *SBN-P*, 8/22/1940).

The last ballad Thayer contributed to the *Examiner* was "Casey at the Bat," which he wrote in May 1888. Phinney relished the annual changeable nature of that month. Back in 1884 he had written in the *Lampoon*: "To-day the bud; to-morrow the leaf. The man who strikes out to-day will make a base-hit tomorrow. Nothing fixed, nothing stationary, nothing certain; such is the month of May; such is life!" (Croy, 11; and *Lampoon,* volume 7, 5/2/1884.)

Many factors could have contributed to his inspiration to write a baseball ballad this time around. Ted Bonnet, who was a sports reporter for the *Examiner* at that time, later recalled that he and the other reporters were all looking forward to Phinney's upcoming baseball ballad, so maybe Hearst had requested one, or maybe Thayer told them that's what he would send next, or maybe Bonnet meant it had already been received and they were looking forward to seeing it in print. Sitting at home in Worcester in early baseball season, Thayer might have started reminiscing about watching the 1885 Harvard varsity's games; now that he was back in Worcester he was able once again to see his friend Sam Winslow, captain of that great nine (Peck, 950).

Watching the exciting 1887 California League pennant race at the brand new Haight-street Grounds gave Thayer plenty of subject matter for a baseball poem. Very likely he had taken the train over to Stockton to watch a game or two at Goodwater Grove. He would have been struck by the varied topography along the way – passing Mount Diablo, seeing the delta, and being in the great flat valley. The Giants' winter visit gave him the chance to see the $10,000 beauty, Mike Kelly, game after game and be awed on that rainy December day when Roger Connor sent the ball 460 feet over the right field fence. Yes, there was a plenty of fodder for a baseball ballad. Thayer might also have kept the clipping of that August game wherein the weak-hitting pitcher Dan Casey got a clutch hit to tie a game in the ninth inning, and thought of turning it upside down, with a slugger letting down the crowd by striking out in a similar clutch situation – an experience shared by baseball fans of all ages, but one they never really get used to or accept gracefully. Who knows? Thayer may have run into his old high school nemesis on Main Street in Worcester; Daniel Henry Casey was now a teacher at the Ledge Street Grammar School. Like Thayer, Casey still lived in the house where he grew up, at 22 Hill Street. Casey's name might have appeared in a Worcester newspaper and given the creative mind of the 24-year-old Thayer the spur it needed. Whatever caused the ballad to be written, De Wolf Hopper and an entire nation would be grateful (*WCD*, 1889).

The *Examiner* printed the poem on the editorial page on June 3, next to the announcement that Hearst had met one of his primary goals – the *Examiner* had surpassed the *Chronicle*, the *Call*, and the *Alta California* in circulation, with a daily average of 52,628 readers. The poem was signed "Phin," and was obviously written to amuse Bay Area readers, because the mountain, the valley, the flat, and the dell (delta) evoke Stockton – Slough City – Mudville, as do the names of the players.

Cooney

Billy Cooney played outfield for Stockton in 1887. He was a coacher when the Stockton team was at bat; the coacher's job was to rattle the opposing pitcher from the third-base coaching lines by yelling obnoxiously. On June 21, 1887, the *Stockton Daily Independent* commented: "Cooney's coaching is a caution. The beauty of his playing is that he is every bit as expert with his hands as he is with his mouth." He and two other players lost their female following with the suggestion that ladies start paying admission to Goodwater Grove so there would be more money for players' salaries. Cooney was released on July 25 for an unannounced infraction of the rules. He was reinstated the next week and released again in late August for weak batting (*STIN*, 5/12, 7/26, 8/23/1887).

Flynn

Dan Flynn played for Stockton in 1887 and part of 1888. He was a pitcher and a shortstop. As often happened in those days, when players were known by reputation but not looks, Dan was passed off as John (Jocko) Flynn – a sore-armed pitcher from the Chicago White Stockings – by Sam Morton's Base Ball bureau, from whom Manager Gus Gumpertz obtained him. Jocko Flynn's 24-6 record in 1886 gained him the top winning percentage (.800) among National League pitchers that season. Jocko, 23, was 5′6½″ and weighed 143 lbs. Dan, 24, was 5′8″ and weighed 160 lbs., according to the *San Francisco Daily Morning Call,* which did an article on Dan Flynn, reprinted in the *Stockton Daily Independent* on May 5, 1887. Both Flynns were right-handed pitchers, apparently, because left-handed pitchers were so rare their left-handedness was always mentioned. The *Call* said about Dan Flynn, "He is an unassuming individual, one not liable to talk or brag about his baseball record." Such restraint! (*STIN*, 4/19, 5/5/1887; *BENC*, 1857; and *LAH*, 7/10/1887).

Gus Gumpertz shocked all of Stockton on July 25 when he released Flynn for no apparent reason. Flynn had been pitching well, hitting well, and his base-running exploits never failed to excite the spectators. Flynn's salary was the bone of contention for fellow pitcher Eddie Lorrigan, who wanted more money. "He was originally brought out here as a change pitcher and he did very well," said Gumpertz during an interview, "but many in the club were dissatisfied because he was receiving double the salary of the other." When the other Stockton team directors learned of Gumpertz's move, they met, made the salary adjustments necessary and reinstated Flynn before they adjourned the meeting. The *Stockton Daily Independent* wrote in Flynn's defense on July 26: "Flynn is a quiet, gentlemanly fellow who is very popular, and has made many friends here, every one of whom protested against his release. He is a conscientious and skillful ball player, and all he needs is encouragement and proper support." While Dan Flynn was having his ups and downs in the West, Jocko Flynn was at home back East in Lawrence, Massachusetts – where he and Thayer were both born – trying to get his arm back into shape (*STIN*, 7/26/1887; *CHRON*, 8/1/1887; and *BG*, 7/13/1887).

Blake

There was no Blake on the Stockton nine or in the California League in 1887 or 1888, but there was a player named Blakiston who could be "Blake, the much despis-ed"; he played for Stockton in 1888. Blakiston was born Robert J. Blackstone in San Francisco. His name was sometimes spelled "Blakeston," so it must have been pronounced that way. Blakiston was called "Silent Bob" due to his incessant talking. Early in his career he was described this way: "Blakiston is a spasmodic and therefore not a reliable player. His every movement on the field shows a consciousness that 'every eye is upon him,' and that the spectator has but to gaze and witness a *rara avis* among ball tossers. The effect of his playing depends wholly upon the condition of his mind, as he is governed entirely by his moods." When he played on the American Association champion Philadelphia Athletics in 1883 he was presented a gold medal for his fine play. When he returned to San Francisco and the California League he always wore the medal and regaled anyone who would listen with his exploits of that 1883 season (*EX*, 4/18/1887, 4/8/1888; *BENC* 672; and *CHRON*, 4/5/1880).

In the poem Blake "tore the cover off the ball." Blakiston was quite a hitter; he often headed the batting list and had power. Billy Incell, one of the league's top pitchers, said that whenever Blakiston came to the bat he expected to see him knock the ball over the fence. A sailmaker by trade, Blakiston made the canvas bases for the Philadelphia Athletics and for the teams in the California League. Also known to be a hunter, yachtsman, crack pool player, and, of course, a raconteur, he was over 30 years old playing in a league where most of the players were in their twenties (*SL*, 3/24/1886, 11/30/1887; *EX*, 3/21, 3/28, and 10/3/1887, 2/28/1888; and *CHRON*, 7/11, 8/1/1887).

His maturity and good looks made him a favorite with the ladies, which further irritated the other players. A lady sent this "tender epistle" to the *Examiner* in early August 1887:

> August 4, 1887
>
> Dear Sir:
>
> Would you please announce in the columns of the *Examiner* that an admirer of Robert Blakeston was tempted to take off her sealskin coat and give it to him last Sunday, when he was shivering on the diamond. I just want him to know that he had at least one sympathizer in the grand stand.
>
> Please do this and oblige
>
> The Admirer

The *Examiner* responded: "The writer of the above is probably not aware of the fact that "Silent" Bob is hitched in the matrimonial harness (*EX*, 8/8/1887). (A baseball player shivering on the diamond and a spectator in a sealskin coat in mid-summer? It *must* be San Francisco.)"

Barrows

The other player mentioned – Barrows – is a mystery, although there was a player on the 1871 Boston Red Stockings named Frank Barrows. He might have made a deep impression on a Worcester lad of eight (*BENC*, 2588).

Thayer didn't think about the "Casey" poem after he sent it in. Little did he know the agony and ecstasy that awaited him because of his composition about a failed slugger. The *Sporting Times* printed the last eight stanzas of the poem on July 28, 1888, but substituted "Kelly" for "Casey." A subtitle acknowledged that the poem was "adapted from the *San Francisco Examiner*." Then, in August, an extraordinary thing happened that lifted "Casey" above the run-of-the-mill newspaper ballad that gains fame for a day – the one when it appears in print.

CHAPTER 25

Kelly at the Bat

Take him for all in all, we shall never see his like again.

–Boston Globe, *November 9, 1894*

Mike Kelly was one of the greatest all-around ballplayers that ever trod the green diamonds. The fun-loving Irishman from Troy, New York, was a familiar figure on ball fields from Boston to San Francisco, the game's first national hero, the first ballplayer to write a book about his baseball adventures, and one of the first old-timers elected to the Hall of Fame. A born actor, Kel was so full of life and animation that he could make headlines just by striking out. In fact, it was once believed that he had inspired, composed, and popularized the ballad of "Casey at the Bat" all by himself. True it is, Kel knew Casey's story by heart, recited it on a regular basis, and was about to deliver another stirring performance at the Palace Theater in Boston on November 8, 1894, when the "Great Umpire" called him "Out." And a surprising number of Mike's contemporaries believed that he had inspired the baseball epic. But to claim that he actually composed the verses himself might be stretching the truth a little too far–even for Kel.

The Boston star, known to baseball fans all over the country as "The King of the Diamond," "The Only Mike," and "The $10,000 Ball-Tosser," and to his friends as plain old "Kel," had just returned from a winter season in California with the New York Giants and was at the peak of his popularity when "Casey" made his debut in the *San Francisco Daily Examiner*. Jim Kennedy, editor of the New York *Sporting Times,* spotted the poem in the Pacific coast paper and at once noticed a remarkable similarity between Kelly and Thayer's hero. To give the poem a point, and bring it home for Eastern readers, he substituted "Kelly" for "Casey" and "Boston" for "Mudville," cut the first five stanzas, and published "Kelly at the Bat" in the July 28, 1888, issue of his paper, with an acknowledgment that the poem was "adapted from the *San Francisco Examiner*" (*HUC*, 7 [1910]: 219; and Vermilyea and Moore, 46–48).

Why, you might ask, did Kennedy cut the first five stanzas of the poem, after Thayer went to a lot of trouble to set the stage for Casey's appearance?

Maybe it was just a question of space. More likely, he thought that the poem had too much of a California flavor for an Eastern audience. Where was the mountain, for example, in Boston? Thayer probably had in mind Mount Diablo, "the silent sentinel of the San Joaquin Valley," the landmark that guided the first wagon trains to the Golden State in 1841, to the ranch at the foot of the mountain where Dr. John Marsh, a Harvard man, was awaiting the party with a dinner of pork and hot tortillas. Mount Diablo plays an important part in the history of Stockton, and was incorporated into the great seal of the city in 1851. Bret Harte introduced the mountain to Eastern readers in his first popular sketch, "The Legend of Monte Diablo," which appeared in the *Atlantic Monthly* in October 1863, about six weeks after Thayer was born. Besides the mountain, there were other matters for the editor to consider. Blake and Flynn, important players in Thayer's poem, were apparently named after a pair of well-known California League players from Stockton's Slough city nine. When they both come through with clutch base hits, the crowd of about 5,000 spectators sees Casey advancing to the bat, and shakes the whole Great Valley with their hurrahs! It was quite a scene Thayer had concocted for the opening act, with a spectacular California setting; but it did not go that well in a ballad about Kelly and Boston, so Kennedy cut it (Vermilyea and Moore, 44–46).

Kennedy's timing was perfect, as the Giants moved into a first-place tie with Detroit on July 28, (the day Kennedy published "Kelly at the Bat") and were determined to capture the first National League pennant in the club's history. The entire population of New York City came down with a case of baseball fever. Archibald Gunter, the novelist, probably read the ballad in Kennedy's paper, went to the *Examiner* for the original verses, and then handed them to his friend, De Wolf Hopper, for a benefit the actor was planning for the Giants at Wallack's Theater. Some of the people who heard Hopper recite "Casey" for the first time on August 14 had apparently seen the edited version in the paper, and thought that Hopper had changed "Kelly" to "Casey" so as not to offend the "King." As late as 1943, a letter to this effect appeared in the *New York Times* (*NYT*, 2/10/1943; and Murdock, 25–28).

Kennedy's editorial shenanigans must have annoyed Thayer a good deal, but they were nothing compared to the claim made by the *New York Sun* in 1895 that the "Kelly" variation was the original version, that it had first appeared in the *Sun,* and that "Kelly" had later been changed to "Casey" to give the poem a universal flavor. Hearst published a prompt rebuttal in the *Examiner,* but it apparently had little effect, for as late as 1935, according to anthologist Burton Stevenson, "many old-time devotees of the diamond still treasure it in its adapted form, believing it to be the original one." At about the same time, commenting on Kennedy's substitution of "Kelly" for "Casey" and the persistent popularity of "Kelly at the Bat," one of Thayer's old Harvard classmates explained that this was "easily understood by those who are old enough to remember that 45 years or so ago 'Mike' Kelly was by far the most conspicuous baseball player in the country. It may fairly be said, also, that, in spite of the reputation of 'Babe' Ruth and other notables, no player in all the subsequent history of the game has quite attained the heights on which Kelly stood" (*NBL*, Casey folder; Burton Stevenson, 119; and "Casey," 534).

Kennedy's keen critical powers and brilliant editorial work did wonders for the poem. He was the first to recognize Thayer's classic and bring it to the attention of an Eastern audience, serving as a sort of mediator between the poet and the people, interpreting the Mudville verses for the multitudes. Thayer, however, was surprisingly slow to appreciate the fine efforts that were being made on his behalf. To complicate the situation, Kelly apparently claimed the authorship of the stanzas for himself. Maybe he winked when he made that claim, and maybe he didn't, but the word got around that the "King" had claimed "Casey," and some people naturally took it seriously. After all, it was well known that Mike had developed a sudden taste for poetry in the spring of 1887, when he left Chicago and moved to the Hub. And he certainly could write, for he had written a book about his baseball adventures that was published in Boston on April 1, 1888, just a few weeks before Thayer wrote "Casey." In the late 1880s and 1890s, when nobody knew who the real author was and Eastern papers were reprinting the poem anonymously, a rumor like this was bound to be popular with the cranks, and get passed along, and there were always plenty of people around ready and willing to believe it.

The surprising thing is that Thayer took the claim seriously, and even complained about Kelly's "impudence" in a statement to the press. Replying to a letter from Joseph M. Cummings of the *Baltimore News,* he wrote on February 2, 1905: "There have been many claimants to the doubtful honor of having written 'Casey at the Bat'—among others, I believe, the late Mike Kelly of Boston, and it has never seemed to me to be worth my while to expose their impudence." This was the last time Thayer ever mentioned Mike Kelly in writing. The author never acknowledged, and for that matter never explicitly denied, that Kelly had anything to do with the ballad. In the letter to Cummings, who had asked Thayer about his reasons for writing the poem, he simply told him: "You ask me what incentive I had for writing 'Casey.' It was the same incentive that I had for writing a thousand other things. It was my business to write, and I needed the money." Albert G. Spalding, corresponding with Thayer from his home on Point Loma, California, where he was writing his monumental history of baseball, did not have much better luck. The author wrote to Spalding from Rome in 1909: "The poem has no history. It was written in the regular course of business when I was a journalist on the staff of the *S.F. Examiner*." Spalding published the letter verbatim in his book, with a photograph of the author. But he had to wonder, a poem with no history? Was Casey just a figment of the poet's imagination? Or was Thayer's puzzling answer just another prank from the past president of the *Harvard Lampoon*? (Murdock, 11; and Albert G. Spalding, 448.)

A poet to the end, Thayer did nothing to dispel the clouds of obscurity that gathered about the Mudville slugger as the years rolled by. In the 1930s, when a whole new generation of baseball fans was clamoring for "the truth about Casey," and Danny Casey of the old Philadelphia Phillies claimed to be the original Casey, the *Syracuse Post-Standard* and *The Sporting News* published a letter from Thayer, who by this time was getting a little exasperated by the question. The author was still unwilling to provide any relevant details, though he stated his position in slightly different terms: "About 'Casey at the Bat,' I am sorry to say there is no story connected with the writing of those stanzas. . . . The poem has no basis in fact. The only Casey actually involved, and I am not sure about him, was not a ball player." (*The Sporting News* left out the "not" when they printed the letter; and most later writers followed *TSN*.) Thayer, as he admitted, was not too sure about it, but the circumstances surrounding the composition of the poem suggest that there *was* another Casey involved–and there was certainly a ballplayer named Kelly (*HUC*, 19 [1935]: 373–74; *SP-S*, 9/3/1935; *TSN*, 3/31/1938; and Murdock, 28).

Mike had all the qualifications. He was Irish, as Irish as Paddy's pig; he loved the crowds, and the crowds loved him; he inspired the cranks to compose songs, verses, and stories of all kinds, mostly of a humorous character, which appeared in the papers from Plymouth Rock to the Golden Gate; he played winter ball on the Pacific slope when Thayer was writing for the *Examiner*; he was playing in Boston, near Worcester, both on the stage and on the ball field, when the author returned to his home and penned his immortal poem; he practically saved an umpire's life during his first year in Boston, and demanded fair play for baseball's arbiters in his book, *"Play Ball!" Stories of the Diamond Field,* which hit the stands just a few weeks before Thayer wrote "Casey" and undoubtedly influenced the poem; last, but not least, he struck out swinging one day in San Francisco when he wished he hadn't.

Mike Kelly

Michael Joseph Kelly was born in Troy, New York, on December 31, 1857. His mother and father, Catherine and Michael, were natives of Ireland. Mr. Kelly was a papermaker by trade, served in the Union Army during the Civil War, and moved his family to Washington, DC, after the war. Beyond that, little is known of them. We do know, however, that Mike was born at the right time. The first convention of baseball clubs was held in New York City in January 1857, and a club was organized at the State House in Albany that spring, signs of baseball's new status as our national game. The next year, Higginson's article in the *Atlantic Monthly* identified baseball as a native American game, and connected it with the national character. Playing baseball was a good way for immigrants and their children to become full-

Mike Kelly in 1887 (courtesy of the National Baseball Library & Archive, Cooperstown, N.Y.).

fledged Americans, and Mike took to the game like a duck takes to water. Before he was five years old he could catch any pitcher in town with his bare hands, throw to second on a line, hit the ball a mile, and run halfway to second before anyone heard the crack of the bat. Meanwhile, in 1862, the Atlantics, led by the O'Brien brothers, and other Brooklyn clubs were pioneering a new profession that seemed made for youngsters like Mike (*NYC*, 5/29/1880; Kelly, 10–17; Tuohey, 185–96; Starr, 309–10; Kaese, 41; Wittke, 270–1; Seymour [1960], 26, 48; and Appel and Goldblatt, 244–46).

Washington was alive with baseball when Mike and his family moved there in 1865. Government clerks in the nation's capital, following the lead of the Albany clerks, had organized their own baseball clubs even before the war, and President Lincoln used to go out and watch them play. The first baseball poster, published by Currier and Ives during the 1860 election, featured the president holding a bat in one hand and a ball in the other, and was entitled, "The National Game. Three 'Outs' and One 'Run.' Abraham Winning the Ball." In the summer of 1865 the Brooklyn Atlantics, champions of the country, were invited to come to Washington and play the Nationals, a club of government clerks. The morning after the game, which the Atlantics won, 33–15, a delegation of Nationals led by postmaster of the Senate Arthur Pue Gorman escorted the visitors to the White House where they were received by President Johnson. The president hoped that the Nationals would have better luck next time, and told his visitors: "Gentlemen, I thank you for the honor of your visit." And so baseball was given the highest official recognition as our national game. In the following spring Currier and Ives published a popular chromolithograph, "The American National Game of Base Ball," which showed the Atlantics at bat against their old rivals, the New York Mutuals (*Brooklyn Eagle,* 8/31/1865; Seymour [1960], 43; Voigt, I: 9–12; and Baragwanath, 80–81).

Kel was nine years old when he began his amateur career with the Keystones, a junior club, in 1867. The family moved to Paterson, New Jersey, six years later. By this time Mike was ready to organize his own club, and called it the Keystones, after his old Washington unit. In Paterson he met a lifelong friend, Jim McCormick, later a big-league player with Pittsburgh, and the two of them used to play ball and talk over their plans together. The 1870s were great years for American youngsters. The first professional league, the National Association of Professional Base Ball Players, was organized on St. Patrick's Day in 1871. After five years of increasing prosperity (13 clubs joined the association in 1875), the association was succeeded by the National League of Professional Base Ball Clubs in 1876. As Kelly recalled later, the boys narrowed it down to three choices: "We did not know whether we would become actors, ball players, or engineers on the railroad. These, to us, were the ideal professions." Mike's first job was as a paperboy. He used to get up at 4:00 A.M., go to New York, and return at 6:00 A.M. with his papers, which gave him a chance to "play ball" in the afternoon. In the winter of 1877 he went to work in a silk weaving factory. His friends advised him to stick to the work and leave baseball alone, but it was no use. "I was a crank on the game," said Kel, "and couldn't leave it alone if I wanted to. So I went at it again." He opened the 1877 season playing for a professional club in Port Jervis, New York, then jumped at an offer to catch for the Buckeye Club of

Columbus with McCormick as the pitcher. His fine play in Columbus led to an engagement with Cincinnati's National League club as their right fielder and backup catcher for Jim "Deacon" White in 1878. The rookie got off to a good start, hitting .281, playing well in the outfield, and backing up White in 17 games.

Kel's second season in the National League turned out to be a turning point in his life. Cincinnati split its first 8 games, then went on a disastrous road trip to the East at the end of May, losing 8 of 11 games at Troy, Syracuse, Providence, and Boston. Mike reached first base just once in 21 at-bats. Cal McVey, the manager, was thinking of dropping him and asking Jack Leary, then playing for Manchester in the International Association, to take his place on the roster. McVey telegraphed Leary to come down and play the last game in Boston on June 21, but Jack could not get there in time for the game. Kelly went 4 for 5 with 2 doubles, a triple, and a home run as Cincinnati won, 15–13, and Leary was never heard from again. Mike finished the season third in hitting (.348), third in slugging (.493), third in triples (12), fourth in runs scored (78 runs in 77 games), and tied for fifth in home runs (2). Later in his career, when he was sitting on top of the world, Kel looked back on that big game in Boston, maybe the biggest game in his life, and wondered:

> What might have been the result if Jack Leary appeared on the grounds in Boston? I would have been laid off, and returned to Paterson in disgrace. Perhaps I never would have had nerve enough to play in a league club again. That moves me to repeat the sacred thought:
>
> Great God, on what a slender thread
> Hang everlasting things. [Kelly, 12; and *BENC*, 68–69.]

Kelly in Chicago

When the 1879 National League season was over Mike joined the Cincinnati-Buffalo combination on a trip to San Francisco, where he gained a following on the Pacific slope. Chicago also went out to the West coast that winter, and signed the rising young star for $1,400. Mike opened the 1880 season auspiciously with a game-winning home run against his old Cincinnati club. On May 29 a sketch of his life, with a portrait, appeared in the *New York Clipper,* which told the story of how Chicago captain Adrian Anson first came to notice Mike's base-running abilities. In a game against Chicago in 1879, Kelly stretched a routine single into a double and got to the bag awfully fast, attracting quite a crowd as the entire Chicago club, led by Anson, gathered around the umpire at second base, and claimed that Kelly was out because he had allegedly skipped the initial portal. While the players were discussing the situation with the umpire, Mike, always on the alert, dashed off toward third, and from there, seeing no one at the plate, trotted on home.

Kelly appeared in Thayer's home town for the first time on June 16, 1880, when Chicago played Worcester's new National League club at the Agricultural Grounds before a large crowd of over 2,000 spectators (only the Memorial Day crowd of 2,700 drew more people that year). Hitting third, Mike scored 2 of Chicago's 7 runs as the "Westerners" overcame a 6–5 Worcester lead and "a perfect pandemonium of shouts" to win one of the most exciting games of the season, 7–6. Three days later Mike led off the game and scored 3 of Chicago's 8 runs as the visitors won another close one, 8–7. And so Kel turned in an impressive performance during his first visit to the Heart of the Commonwealth (*WG*, 6/17–6/20/1880).

As an all-around player, Mike has never had an equal. He usually caught or played right field, but he could and did play any position on the field, including pitcher. Kel's hitting, running, fielding, throwing, and most of all his spectacular base running sparked Chicago to five pennants (1880–82 and 1885–86) in his seven seasons with the club. When Mike got on base the fans would all stand up and holler "Slide, Kelly, Slide!" and Kel was sure to give them their money's worth. On top of his baseball abilities, the big, jovial, warm-hearted Irishman was one of the game's most colorful characters both on and off the field, and had a great many friends in Chicago and a few other cities besides. In the first issue of *The Sporting News,* which appeared on St. Patrick's Day in 1886, the paper's Chicago correspondent said that he had met Kel when he returned to the city after spring training in New Orleans, and that any further training would be wasted on "the king of base stealers." Mike was in midseason form, fit and trim, ready and raring to go. "Few people in this city can boast of the popularity Kelly holds," claimed the reporter. "He could get the nomination for mayor on either ticket without making an effort."

The year 1886 was a banner year for Kel as he won the National League batting title with a .388 average, scored 156 runs – a new league record – and led Chicago to the club's fifth pennant in seven years. It was the first time anybody had led the league in scoring for three years in a row, and it would be the last time a National League player would accomplish that feat for almost 100 years – until Pete Rose came along in the 1970s. But as things turned out, Kel's best year in Chicago was also his last. The trouble began on June 22, when the White Stockings found themselves trailing Detroit, 5–3, in the late innings of a game played in the state famous for its cranberries and white pine. Anson, "with defeat staring him in the face, began a series of grand, high kicks." At every close decision that favored Detroit, he kicked, and once the big captain walked up to Umpire Gaffney "in a very threatening manner, and Kelly, who feared some trouble, stepped between them. Gaffney fined Anson $50, and then added another $50 dose before he quieted down." The fines amounted to $110 in the aggregation, a goodly amount in those days. "Will I pay them?" Anson was asked. "Not I, not a dollar; not a penny. If Gaffney does not remit the fines I'll have him fired, or my name's not Anson" (*TSN*, 6/28, 7/5/1886; and Overmyer, 22).

About a month later, Chicago club owner Albert G. Spalding fined Kelly and six of his teammates $25 each for drinking – not to the extent that it interfered with their play, but as Spalding explained it, "they have been taking a glass of beer or a toddy now and then, and when seen by others the act was exaggerated and repeated to the discredit of the club." Among the "others" was a Pinkerton detective the owner had hired to follow the boys around for a few weeks and report back on their activities. As Spalding recalled it some years later, when he read the report to the team Mike broke the silence with one of his "characteristic drolleries," saying: "I have to offer only one amendment. In that place where the detective reports me as taking a lemonade at 3:00 A.M. he's off. It was a straight whiskey. I never drank a lemonade at that hour in my life" (*SL*, 7/28/1886; and Albert G. Spalding; 525).

That was typical of Mike, taking the heat for his teammates when they got into trouble, and trying to keep the club loose. As Jim Hart, later one of his Boston managers, said, (Tuohey, 188) "He was so big-hearted and so honest that it was a difficult task to discipline him in this one fault. He would always admit the truth, no matter in what light it placed him; and when other players were equally as guilty as he, in his story he only was the culprit. No player can truthfully say that Kelly ever shielded himself at their expense; in fact, when players on the team got into trouble it was always to Kelly they looked for help to extricate them."

Spalding's report gave Kelly a good opportunity to get in one of his jokes, but the fines took some of the fun out of the thing. And the players were not too happy about paying them. After all, as the owner admitted, they were just going out for a few sociable drinks, which did not detract from their performance on the field. Some of the players, Kelly included, even thought that a little drinking and socializing was good for them, and helped them to play more as a team. In any case, Spalding's arbitrary decision hit Mike the hardest, since in addition to the $25 fine, which he felt was unfair to begin with, he lost a $200 drinking bonus he had been promised on his contract. Mike went to Spalding and informed him of his belief that the Chicago management had not treated him fairly. Spalding smiled, and regarded it as just another Kelly joke. But this time Kelly was not kidding. He said, "President Spalding, at the close of the season I'm going up to Hyde Park, in New York, for the winter. My brother-in-law has a farm there. If I'm not a member of some other club next season, you will find that farming is good enough for me during the summer. I will not play again in the Chicago club, under any circumstances, and don't you forget it" (Kelly, 45).

After the season, the Eastern papers started harping on rumors of a disagreement between Kelly and Spalding, and the Chicago fans naturally wanted to know how things stood. "Did you have a quarrel of any description with him before he went east?" Spalding was asked. "Most emphatically, no," was the reply.

> We parted on friendly terms, though he may have felt sore on account of losing the money on his drink contract of 1886. He said to me that he had received a letter from his brother asking him not to sign for another year before he came East. His brother, he told me, wanted him to go into the horse business. I have only the kindliest feeling for Kelly, and if he can make more money in any other business no one will wish him success more heartily and sincerely than I.

As for the fines, the owner said that he did not like to fine the players, and in the five years he had been head of the club he had not fined them more than $300, including the $175 last summer. Spalding emphasized that he did not want to lose a man like Kelly if reasonable terms could be arranged: "He is a valuable man in a club, not only because he is a good player, but because he puts life in the game, and makes it interesting and amusing for the spectators. When himself he is full of life and animation, originates more new tricks than all the rest of the players put together, and he is a good man to steady young players and give them confidence in themselves" (*TSN*, 1/15/1887).

But Kelly's Chicago days were over. Boston wanted him in the Hub, Mike was having second thoughts about farming, and the final outcome of Spalding's one-man temperance crusade was that the Chicago club, which had won 6 pennants in the first 11 seasons of National League play, would not win another one for 20 years.

The King of the Diamond

The Nelson House in Poughkeepsie, New York, was the scene of the biggest baseball deal of the nineteenth century. At exactly 12 noon on February 14, 1887, Mike Kelly signed a contract to play with Boston. Bill Sullivan, a reporter for the *Boston Globe,* was there to witness the proceedings, and as the genial Mike laid down the pen, he turned to Sullivan and said, "Well, I am with you." Boston club treasurer Jim Billings then folded the contract, tucked it into his innermost coat pocket, and soliloquized in a meditative tone: "Good things come high, but we must have them." Featured in the *Globe*'s final edition for the day was the full story of the historic event, including a sketch of Mike's life, and headlines proclaiming "The Only Kell" as "A Born Baseball Player, and the Acknowledged King of the Diamond" (*BG*, 2/14/1887).

Tired of watching Chicago walk off with the pennant every year, the Boston club directors had taken a great interest in the rumors of Kelly's dissatisfaction with the management of the champion club. Money was no object. They were determined to sign the Chicago star at any cost, unless he wanted the earth and the North Pole thrown in. After negotiating with Spalding, the Bostonians paid Chicago $10,000 for Mike's release in early February, and in the meeting with Kel agreed to pay him $5,000 for the season. Since the salary limit was $2,000 by National League rules, the contract was drawn up for that amount, and then Billings said that the Boston club wanted a picture of their new player and would pay well for it, $3,000 to be exact. This brought the grand total Boston paid for Mike's services to $15,000 – more than five times what many governors made! (*Ibid.*, and Kelly, v–vi.)

Why did the Boston directors, who had built a reputation for frugality, shell out so much money for one ballplayer? Because, among other things, there was a lot more to Mike than just his record, remarkable though it was. As Sullivan said, no figures could possibly give any idea of Kel's "wonderful and almost ceaseless activity on the diamond, the phenomenal work he does, and the influence he exerts upon the members of his own team." If it were possible to strike an average for "steadiness at the bat, conscientious fielding, persistent kicking, skillful base getting and a knowledge of all the tricks that help to win, he would easily stand without a peer." Above and beyond his all-around ability, Mike possessed an indomitable spirit. "In victory," Sullivan concluded, "he is jubilancy itself, but defeat, no matter how severe, cannot crush him or dampen his wit and good-nature."

Henry Chadwick, perhaps the most competent and impartial judge of such matters, paid Kel the finest tribute that any ballplayer could be paid. In a feature sketch written for *Spalding's Official Base Ball Guide* in 1887 (published in April), Chadwick introduced Kelly as the league's top hitter for the 1886 season, and emphasized that he had never played for his own record. "On the contrary," said Chadwick, "Kelly invariably plays ball rather for the good of his team *and that his team may win,* than for the advancement of his individual fielding, batting, or catching record, and it has been this self same sacrificing spirit, coupled with a natural quickness of thought and execution as well as an innate talent and ability as a ball player, that has made him so valuable as a ball player to the clubs he has played with of late years." Without mentioning the drinking fines specifically, he put them in perspective by commenting on Mike's personal characteristics, both on and off the field: "Kelly has an individuality of his own, which is seen to a marked degree, both upon the ball field and in his social intercourse with his fellow Players. Genial, witty and intelligent, he is the life of the team, and to a great extent, the magnet which holds its members together." Finally, in reference to reports that Kelly was going to captain the Boston club, Chadwick praised his leadership abilities: "A great general in a contest; a clear strategist; well versed in every point of play, and competent to play any position himself; tricky, bold, and thoroughly experienced in his work upon the diamond; he is eminently qualified for the position he has attained in the profession, and is thoroughly capable of making any team he may connect himself with, an exceedingly uncertain quantity, if not a dangerous factor in a championship race" (Chadwick, 6–7).

The reaction to Kelly's loss in Chicago was predictable. Many of the fans there were so upset with the club for selling Mike that they boycotted the games, except when Boston came to town. "Well, well," said Ned Williamson, the veteran third baseman, "this just makes me tired. Kel was the life and soul of the Chicagos, and you can bet your sweet life the playing strength of the team will be greatly weakened by his departure. Why, Mike was an attraction, viewed in a commercial sense, who has brought thousands of dollars to the Chicago treasury, and Spalding will never again have a man in his team who will be to it what Mike Kelly has been." Williamson was asked if Kelly was now the highest paid player in the game. "Yes," he answered. "O'Rourke has heretofore been the highest paid player, his salary being about $4,000. This must make O'Rourke sick" (*SL*, 2/23/1887).

Outside of Chicago, Kelly's fans and friends around the country welcomed the news of his move to Boston. Wally Wallace, the California correspondent for the *Sporting Life,* wrote that the people of the Golden State "felt elated over the success of Mike Kelly," who was "an immense favorite here." Throughout the season the *San Francisco Daily Examiner* kept its readers informed of the Kelly boom. One report told of an intimate conversation between two cranklets at the Hub: "Boston Young Lady (to friend)–'I've come to ask a great favor, Penelope.' Penelope–'Yes!' Boston Young lady–'Yes. Some friends are to spend the evening with us, and I wish you would lend me your picture of Captain Mike Kelly for my album. Mine is being framed'" (*EX*, 7/16/1887).

Mark the day, Sunday, March 13, 1887. It was unquestionably one of the biggest days in Boston's long and illustrious history, since "the king of ball players" made his very first appearance in the city that day as a member of the Boston Base Ball Club. Mike was also a member of the New Orleans Lodge of Elks, and that afternoon, after registering at the United States Hotel, some brothers of the order took him to dinner at Perkins' for "a jolly good time." Word of Kel's presence in the Hub soon got around, and on Monday morning a dozen or more "enthusiasts" met Sullivan on the street and greeted him with the remark: "Did you know Kelly is in town?" "I rather did," said Sullivan, "but I thanked each one in turn for giving me the tip." Mike and the rest of the players went to Winslow's Rink that day and began working out. Kelly, "the ten thousand dollar player," showed up in a stylish light overcoat which fitted his splendid physique like the "paper on the valls," sporting a silver-headed cane and rosebud in his lapel that made him look like "a gentleman of leisure." He didn't intend to do much work the first day, "but he is so wedded to base ball that when he saw one flying around he peeled off his coats and caught, while Madden, the Portland youngster, pitched" (*SL*, 3/23/1887).

On St. Patrick's Day, while Sullivan stood in Winslow's Rink and watched the boys picking up grounders, "one of our cranks of the cranks hustled in, and almost before he had got inside the door he was winning games in his vivid imagination." The *Boston Herald* contributed to the spirit of the occasion by publishing a chart showing that "Kel" had averaged 100 runs a year since 1879, and had scored more runs than any other player in the National League (see Table 6).

Table 6: Leading Scorers of the National League

	1879	**1880**	**1881**	**1882**	**1883**	**1884**	**1885**	**1886**	**Total**	**Avg.**
Kelly	78	71	84	81	92	120	124	152	802	100
Gore	43	69	86	99	105	103	115	149	769	96
O'Rourke	69	70	71	62	99	112	119	105	707	88
Brouthers	–	–	60	71	88	80	87	139	520	87
Dalrymple	45	90	72	96	78	110	109	61	661	83
Anson	41	52	67	69	69	108	100	114	620	77
Hines	81	61	64	73	93	92	63	82	609	76
Richardson	53	43	62	61	73	85	90	125	592	74
Hanlon	–	30	63	66	64	85	93	101	501	72
Ward	71	49	56	58	76	99	72	80	561	70

A few days later, out on the West coast, the *Examiner* reported that within a week of Mike's arrival in the Hub the fame of "the $15,000 ball-tosser" had eclipsed even that of the great boxer John L. Sullivan:

> John L. is no longer the reigning favorite in Boston intellectural, esthetic and sporting circles. He has been superseded by Kelly, the $15,000 ball-tosser. He is still regarded as a curiosity by the bean-eaters, and wherever he goes is the nucleus of all eyes. Several nights ago he attended a performance in a hub theater, and when his presence was discovered, opera-glasses were leveled at him from all quarters, and scarcely any attention was devoted to the play [*EX*, 3/27/1887].

Kelly recalled the night of May 9, 1887, as "the most memorable night in my life." By that time he had made a number of new friends in Boston, and they wanted to give him a big welcome and make him feel at home. So they arranged a party for him after the opening day game with the Phillies, and invited Mayor Hugh O'Brien to come and make it official. Harry Wright's club won the game, 5–2, before a sellout crowd of 10,000 spectators at the South End Grounds. But there was still joy in Boston, and quite a bit of it at that, when John Graham, a brother Elk, went to Mike after the game and told him there was going to be a benefit for Dan Hurley at the Boston Theatre that night. "He is a fine fellow," said Graham, "and we want to give him a good house. Won't you have the Philadelphia and Boston clubs attend?" After the benefit, he added, there was going to be a little reception at the Elks club, and he hoped Kel could attend that too. Mike said he would, and went to the club after the benefit, accompanied by several friends. A splendid banquet had been prepared, and Kelly did not have the least idea what it was all about until he was introduced to Mayor O'Brien, and sat down next to him. O'Brien delivered a stirring speech, and on behalf of the Boston Lodge of Elks and other friends presented Kelly with a handsome gold watch, chain, charm, and pencil. Said Kel:

> For the first time in my life ... I was unable to make a speech. I had faced angry mobs on the base ball field, and had made funny speeches to them, but, like the Waterbury clock man in "She," my tongue was paralyzed, for the first time in my life. I said something or other, I don't know what. It was the first present I had ever received. I had been a member of the Chicago Club for several years, and was glad to draw just my salary. But I came to Boston, and the first day of my arrival was given a testimonial fit for a king. Well, there is only one city in the country where they do that sort of thing, and that's in Boston [Kelly, 17–18].

The day after the dinner Boston bounced back to defeat the Phillies, 17–4, as they sent 50 men to the plate against Dan Casey. Kelly collected 2 of his club's 19 hits and stole 3 bases. Boston won 15 of the next 20 games, for a total of 19 out of 27 in May, and kept pace with league-leading Detroit, which with a weaker schedule that month had won 21 out of 28. In a review of the first month's play, the *Sporting Life* noted that Kelly had strengthened the Boston club by his playing, "and especially by the spirit of emulation he has infused into the club." As a sidelight, Boston fans were following a running battle between the club and a piratical speculator named Sullivan who had erected a tower outside the grounds and seated people at cheap prices. The club had raised the fences five or six times and Sullivan had kept pace by raising his tower each time. A decoration day doubleheader with Detroit, with separate admissions for the morning and afternoon games, drew 27,000 spectators to the South End Grounds, compared to doubleheader crowds of 23,000 at New York, 17,000 at Pittsburgh, and 10,000 at Washington. Even with the unexpected competition from Sullivan's tower, the sum Boston paid for Kelly was returned twofold before the first month of the season had ended (*SL*, 6/8/1887).

Kel was the toast of the town, and the talk of the country. All kinds of stories, songs, and verses were penned about the Hub's red-hosed hero and published in the papers from coast to coast, chronicling the human side of the man as well as his triumphs and failures on the green diamonds. It would be hard to single out one production that would indicate the sort of reception Mike was given in Boston, and the enthusiasm he generated in the hearts of the hometown fans, but here is a tribute to Kel called "Beautiful Mike." Written by J.E. McCann, it was a baseball variation of a popular nineteenth century poem about that staple of New England life, "Beautiful Snow." This remarkable production appeared in the *New York Clipper*, a national sporting weekly, in the middle of the summer:

Beautiful Mike

Oh! Mike, beautiful Mike!
Sure, you know, it's you that we like
To see at the bat when the game is a tie –
To see you just go after knocking a fly –
Swiftly running, gliding along.
Beautiful Mike, you can do no wrong!
Stealing from first to second and third,
Skimming from there to home, like a bird!
Then, beautiful Mike, from Heaven above
Re-echo the shouts from hearts that you love.

Oh! Mike, beautiful Mike!
Hearts stop beating when you make a strike
At the beautiful sphere, that comes whizzing along
Like the rise and fall of Homer's great song.
Rising, falling, curving it comes,
And then out to centre it merrily hums –
And then, ere it touches the green, grassy ground,
You're at first, and second, and third, and around,
And the air is alive with rythmical yells
As you lift your cute cap to Boston's sweet belles!

How the wild crowd sends cheer after cheer
When you stop a hot grounder, and pick up the sphere,
And drive it to first as hard as you can,
And first sends it home, cutting off the third man!
Neatly, finely, speedily done,
Oh, wild, windy West's magnificent son!
So splendidly done that the clouds hurry by,
To give weary Sol a chance for to eye
The beautiful son of the beautiful West,
With Samson-like hair on his head, toes and chest!

Oh! Mike, beautiful Mike!
With old Boston town you can do as you like!
You're bigger than Lowell, or Parkman, or Holmes,
You're rarer than ruby-tipped tortoise-shell combs!
Rarer, fairer; precious as all
The pictures of dead men of Faneuil Hall!
From the North End to South, from the Hill to the Cove,
You can paint the town red whenever you rove;
And not one copy will your head dare to strike,
You exquisite, lovely, magnificent Mike!

And you were unknown to us, beautiful Mike,
Once, as the trout in the sash of a pike!

Unknown, unloved, with your genius and grace,
With your moustache and eyes and Raphael face!
Unknown, unsung, unhonored were you,
While playing with Anson's uncultured, rough crew,
While Morrill and Radbourne and Johnston and Wise,
We eulogized up to the infinite skies!
But they're shattered idols since we made the strike
(With ten thousand plunkers), you pearl of pearls, Mike!

How strange it would be, you beautiful Mike,
Should you not bring to Boston the pennant we like!
Should you let Messrs. Ewing and Ward, and the rest,
Take that beautiful silk from the beautiful West,
Why!–Hi!–By!–this and by that,
You'll be as dead as Hamlet's old "rat"!
But why borrow trouble? You're sure with your men
To bring the old pennant to Boston again!
And then–then! Arrah, sweet Mike!
It's you that we'll love, and it's us that you'll like!
[*NYC*, 7/30/1887; and Voigt, I:179.]

Strange though it was, Mike failed to bring Boston fans the pennant they wanted in his first year at the Hub. The club got off to a fast start in May, but was then slowed by a series of injuries to key players. On July 10, 1887 the *Boston Globe* published a front-page cartoon of "Our Broken-Up Nine," and advised the management: "Come, gentlemen of the triumvirate, send your crippled players to the mountains or seashore, and get some able-bodied men to fill their places while they are resting. It will be money in your pockets in the long run." But there were not enough first-class replacements available in the middle of the season to get the club back on track. Although Captain Kelly hit .322, stole 84 bases, scored 120 runs, and played at his usual furious pace in his first season with Boston, the club fell to fifth place, proving once again what Kelly knew better than anybody: baseball is not a one-man game. There was also a lesson in the fact that after shelling out $15,000 for "The King of the Diamond," Boston came nowhere near winning the pennant. As George Gipe has shrewdly remarked, we all know what happens to heroes who do not produce immediate results: "They are hissed and booed, made the butt of satiric jabs, even the subject of humorous poetry" (Gipe, 534).

Boston's fifth-place finish in 1887 may well have been a factor in the composition of "Casey at the Bat." But the Beaneaters improved steadily after that, climbing a notch to fourth in 1888, and jumping to second in 1889, a game behind the Giants. In 1890, when the Players League was organized, Mike signed with the new Boston team, became a player-manager, hit .326, caught 56 games, played 27 games at short, played a few more games at every other position except second base, and brought the old pennant to Boston again. Kel's legion of friends and fans did not want to wait too long to show their gratitude, so before the season was halfway over they purchased the former Dr. Harlow estate on Main Street in Hingham, just outside of Boston, and on August 12, 1890, Mr. and Mrs. Michael J. Kelly moved into their fine new home. The next summer, when the Players League folded, Mike rejoined Boston's National League club, which immediately went on an 18-game winning streak and overtook Chicago to win the pennant. Another Boston pennant followed in 1892, and when he retired in 1893 Mike could look back on a creditable record of playing for 8 pennant-winning clubs in 16 years of big-league ball (*Hingham Journal,* 8/15/1890; and Appel and Goldblatt, 246).

"If you had ever seen him play, you would have no trouble remembering him," said Boston Hall of Famer Hugh Duffy one day as he sat in Fenway Park. "Kelly was in a class by himself." Nobody alive today has ever seen Kelly play, but we have no trouble remembering him, thanks mainly to the National Baseball Museum and Hall of Fame in Cooperstown, where his records and all of the records of our national pastime have been carefully preserved. And after reviewing the records and testimonials, it's easy to see why Duffy made that assessment (Kaese, 41).

First of all, as a fielder, Kelly played all nine positions competently, wherever he was needed, had a terrific arm, and threw out more base runners than any other player of his time. In the 1880s, when Mike was in his prime, he won two National League batting titles and was among the league leaders in every batting and base-running category imaginable: hits, runs, doubles, triples, home runs, stolen bases, and total bases. In the spring of 1888, when "Casey at the Bat" appeared, Mike's career batting average was the second highest in the league, and he was seventh in career home runs. Kel always said that a man could hit a ball anywhere if he practiced long enough. And he had a simple explanation for his amazing success. "I call for a high ball," he said, "and bang away at anything I think I can hit" (Anson, 115; *BENC*, 71–111; and *SL*, 2/23/1887).

Since nobody thought to keep track of stolen bases before Kelly came along, we'll never know how many bases he stole in the early part of his career. But a check of the records from 1887 to 1890, the first years stolen base statistics were kept, shows why Mike's base running generated so much enthusiasm. In the 1880s, judging from the available figures, Kelly stole an average of 60 bases in every 100 games he played – a pace matched only by the astonishing Rickey Henderson in the 1980s. Mike's spectacular base running and sliding inspired the fans to rise from their seats and holler, "Slide, Kelly, Slide!" The famous chorus became a baseball legend, and inspired a popular recording and Broadway hit tune of the 1890s composed by John W. Kelly and sung by Maggie Cline. Boston artist Frank O. Small's dramatic painting of "Slide, Kelly, Slide!" (1889) captures the "sacrificing spirit" which writers like Chadwick admired in Kelly, as it shows Mike sliding head first into second, just ahead of the throw, while one of his teammates scampers home with another Boston run. In 1927, the year Babe Ruth belted a record-breaking 60 home runs, MGM was busy making a movie of *Slide, Kelly, Slide!* with William Haines in the title role (Seymour [1960], 357; Voigt, I, 48–49; Gardner, 186; Appel and Goldblatt, 244–45; and *BENC*, 1008–09, 1090).

Whatever his other accomplishments, Kel's real specialty was scoring runs. This is the oldest measure of a player's ability in the books, and in Mike's day was regarded the most important. Kelly was the first player to score 150 runs in one season, with 156 in 1886: not an easy act to follow, since the last players to accomplish that feat were Joe DiMaggio, with 151 runs for the 1937 Yankees, and Ted Williams, 150 for the 1950 Red Sox. Since then, only Rickey Henderson and Lenny Dykstra have approached that mark, Henderson with 146 runs for the 1985 Yankees, and Dykstra with 142 runs for the 1993 Phillies.

Kelly was also the first player to average 100 runs a year over the course of a decade. Modern-day greats like DiMaggio, Williams, Henderson, Stan Musial, Mickey Mantle, Hank Aaron, and Pete Rose have all followed suit, but to find players who matched or even approached Kel's pace of a run a game during a decade, we have to go back to Williams in the 1940s and Ruth in the 1920s. And they didn't run the bases like Kelly did (Deane, 18; and *BENC*, 593–1650).

Henderson, Ruth, and Williams have something else in common with Kel: they struck out quite a bit, once every two or three games on the average. But did Henderson, Ruth, or Williams ever go down swinging on the fourth strike, and make headlines for accomplishing that feat? Kel gained that dubious distinction in the fall of 1887, the year they experimented with the four-strike rule. Mike had donned a Boston uniform for the first time that season, doubled the attendance, then tagged along with the New York Giants for a winter trip to sunny California. The Giants were already loaded with future Hall of Famers like Roger Connor, Buck Ewing, and Tim Keefe; with Kel on the club, this was one of the greatest aggregations of professional ball-tossers ever assembled in one place.

Walter Appleton was the man who arranged the Giants' first trip to San Francisco, and invited the great Boston star as an extra added attraction. The New York club director went to the coast during the winter of 1886-87, and was impressed by the fans and ballplayers of the Golden State. He talked with California League President Johnny Mone about playing the Gothamites at the new Haight-street Grounds, and sent numerous telegrams and letters back to Manager Jim Mutrie and Captain Johnny Ward urging them to visit the metropolis of the Pacific. He told them about the baseball boom on the coast, and the "glorious climate," and was positive that the club would find the trip both enjoyable and remunerative. On July 20, when negotiations were completed, the *Examiner* broke the news that Kelly and the Giants were coming to California in November.

After a couple of tuneup games, the Giants were all warmed up and ready for a showdown with the San Francisco Pioneers, champions of the California League, at their new Haight-street Grounds next to the Golden Gate Park on Saturday, November 27, two days after Thanksgiving. The best in the East against the best in the West. Mike's picture was plastered on the cover of the *California League Score Book* that day, and as he advanced to the bat to lead off the game he was greeted with a generous round of applause. Kel was the picture of confidence as he calmly took three straight strikes, then struck out swinging in his tremendously graceful style, while a crowd of more than 10,000 spectators gazed upon the star batsman from their seats in the steep wooden stands. The Giants went on to win a close ball game, 1–0, and gained a good deal of respect for their California League opponents in the process. Kelly's first appearance at the bat was one of the big stories of the game. It must have been something to see, and for the cranks who were unfortunate enough to miss it there were five paragraphs and a headline, "Mike Fans the Air," in the sensational account of the game Thayer wrote up for the next morning's *Examiner* (see p. 224). The crowd was with the pitcher, mainly, and the names, the setting, and the game situation were not quite the same as the ones in the poem Thayer wrote for the *Examiner* six months later. But most of the basic elements were there: the saga of a hero advancing to the bat in a big game, in front of a big crowd, and striking out. This hotly contested ball game, matching the East against the West, must have been stored up with the rest of the poetic recollections Thayer drew upon when he composed his "Ballad of the Republic." There were others, of course, but the showdown in San Francisco, the big game next to the Golden Gate Park, on the shores of the Pacific, witnessed by a crowd of about 10,000 spectators, including Thayer, on a Thanksgiving weekend in 1887, was perhaps the most memorable.

Kelly and Buck Ewing made a big impression on the fans and reporters with their catching and throwing, and the players took the time to work with some of the kids and young catchers in California. The papers noticed this, complimented the Eastern stars on their fine work with the rising generation, and said that they had never seen any catchers who could throw like Kelly and Ewing. The trip also gave Mike a chance to renew his friendship with some old acquaintances from his first tour of the slope in 1879, and to make hundreds of new friends.

So far as is known, Mike never gave any thought to running for office, and thought only of running the bases. But the trip to the Pacific coast improved his political standing, and the next spring, O.P. Caylor told readers of the *Sporting Life* that Mike was "a good, true, level-headed Democrat," and added "it is about time the country knows it." He thought it would be a good idea while the country was casting its eye around for a suitable man to run with Cleveland for the vice presidency to give one glance at Boston. "Cleveland and Kelly would sweep the country," he predicted. The ticket would be particularly strong in Boston, Chicago, and California. "True," he admitted, "Kel would have to make some sacrifice in salary by the change, but his patriotism ought to carry him through." Mike was not the type to let this sort of thing go to his head. As Fred Pfeffer, one of his old Chicago teammates, described him, "geniality, good nature, and self-sacrifice were his strongest traits. The most famous and popular ball player of his day, it was a wonder to me that he didn't lose his head under the adulation and adoration showered on it. Feted, wined, dined, entertained, made much of, he never once ceased to be other than the plain, open-hearted, and unaffected Kelly" (*SL*, 4/25/1888; and *NBL*, Kelly folder).

Once Mike had moved to the Hub, it was only a matter of time before he tried his hand at writing a book. His intellectual powers had laid around dormant for several years in Chicago, but they were soon restored in Boston. "Everybody speaks all sorts of languages, and attends lectures, and reads poetry, and wears spectacles," said Kel in an 1887 *Examiner* report. "I hadn't been in the town more than two days before I got a craving for literature, and I couldn't get any peace until I had subscribed for the 'Waverly Magazine'." When he returned from California in 1888 and his Boston publishers pressed him for a book of his adventures, Kel obligingly put down the bat, took up the pen, and started writing. Pretty soon he was done, and his book was published in 1888. Mike's picture was on the cover, and above and below it was the title Boston had given him, in big capital letters, "The King of the Diamond." Priced at 25 cents, it was sold in cities all over the country, and at once established Mike as the brightest of Boston's intellectual beacons (*EX*, 7/16/1887).

Kelly had friends and fans all over the country, but he always had a special place in his heart for Boston. Chicago was the Hub's arch-rival in the early days of the National League, yet Kel was treated pretty well when the western club went to Boston to play ball. This impressed him. And, of course, they treated him like a king when he put on a Boston uniform. As he said in his book, Boston is "a great base ball city," in some ways the greatest:

> I always had a regard for Boston, and the people who saw the games in the Hub. This was on account of the treatment I always received at the South End grounds. Sometimes, perhaps, I would be "guyed" as strongly even as Anson, but, as a rule, I always received the very best treatment. This is saying a great deal, considering the fact that I was a member of a visiting club, and had the reputation of being a tricky man on the field. How a Boston audience would shout and roar, with mingled feelings of anger and joy, when I would cut the third bag on my way home. It almost reminded me of hundreds of insane people let loose. Yet, if I made a good play in the next inning, it would be greeted with shouts of honest applause. In that respect, Boston leads the base ball cities of the country. The spectators are more fair minded, and will applaud the visiting players heartier than in any other city in this country. I've been to them all, and know just what I'm talking about. It's a great city. It's a great base ball city. I am more than proud to be a

> member of the Boston nine. It makes me happy to feel that I'm Kelly of Boston, instead of Kelly of somewhere else [Kelly, 15–16].

Today's umpires may not always realize this, but they owe a great deal to Mike Kelly. More than anything else, it was his base running that dramatized the inadequacies of the one-umpire system. Nobody could umpire a ball game and keep an eye on Kel at the same time. But Mike was not just a trickster, trying to give the umpires a hard time. He had a genuine respect and liking for the friendless, solitary souls who back in the old days had to work the games alone. On more than one occasion Kel came to the rescue of an umpire who, by making one or two mistakes in the course of a couple of hundred calls, had incurred the wrath of the crowd. One day in 1887, for example, after his Boston club lost a close game at home with the Giants, a mob of irate Bostonians surrounded Umpire Jerry Sullivan. Captain Kelly rushed to Sullivan's side and practically saved his life, escorting him through the crowd with the help of a policeman. Kel's quick thinking and acting were never put to better use. It was experiences like this which inspired him to include a chapter on umpires in his book.

> To begin with, umpires are human. They have a heart, and the blood which flows through their body isn't any different from that which flows through the body of the ordinary man. Very many men who attend ball games, sometimes forget this. . . . Give the umpire a square show for his life. Don't howl at him. Don't imagine that you know it all and he nothing. Don't think that he is robbing your club of a game. Don't get mad. Don't think that he was appointed simply to give decisions to suit you. Don't do these things; and the result will be, that you will see better games of ball [*SL*, 8/24/1887; and Kelly, 56–58].

Some people will claim, of course, that it was just a matter of good business to make friends with an umpire who might one day be called upon to decide a tricky question; say, whether Kel had touched all the bases in his terrific rush to get home. As Pfeffer said, "He played the umpire as intelligently as he did the opposing nine. He would make a friend of him, engage his confidence, and in various ways get the best of close decisions." For an artist's opinion, take a good look at the umpire in Small's painting (see p. 262), and observe the expression on his face. Is there any doubt which way that call is going to go? (NBL, Kelly folder).

What did Thayer think of "Kelly at the Bat"? Maybe he saw the ballad in the *Sporting Times,* or heard about it from his brother Albert in New York, but he certainly knew all about it by the time Hearst published his rebuttal in the *Examiner* in 1895. And he was probably not too amused. Posterity, however, might view the matter a little differently, because, after all, if Kennedy had not recognized "Casey" as a classic, connected it with Kelly, and published it in his popular sporting weekly, there is a good possibility that Thayer's ballad would have suffered the same fate as countless other newspaper ballads. Kennedy introduced Casey to the East, where he really caught on, kept the essence of the poem intact, and did his work so well that in some places, at least, it's hard to see where Kennedy's version loses anything by comparison with the original:

> From the benches, black with people, there went up a muffled roar,
> Like the beating of the storm-waves on a stern and distant shore.
> "Kill him! Kill the umpire!" shouted someone on the stand;
> And it's likely they'd have killed him had not Kelly raised his hand.
>
> With a smile of Christian charity great Kelly's visage shone;
> He stilled the rising tumult; he bade the game go on. . .

CHAPTER 26

De Wolf Hopper Makes "Casey" Famous–and Vice Versa

"I owe a lot to Casey and I love him. He is the best friend I ever had."

–De Wolf Hopper, February 1935
[Park, 246.]

William D'Wolf Hopper was born March 30, 1858, in New York City near the Bowery, an only child. The family moved within a year to a brownstone at Forty-Third Street and Sixth Avenue. His father died when Willie was six, leaving an estate large enough to take care of Mrs. Hopper and leave a legacy to Willie when he reached the age of 21. Willie was pointed toward a law career but caught the acting bug as a teenager and that was that. He dropped the William from his name and changed the spelling of D'Wolf–his mother's maiden name–to De Wolf, so it would be pronounced correctly (NYT, 9/24/1935).

Hopper's first professional stage appearance was in the play *Our Boys* when he was 20 years old. He used the legacy from his father to start the Criterion Comedy Company, acting and producing plays until the money ran out. A serious railroad accident almost cost him his life, but it didn't change his jolly outlook on life. Next, this time with a partner, he started the Gosche-Hopper Company. Its star was Georgie Drew Barrymore, mother of Lionel, Ethel and John. Two seasons with this company wiped him out again, and he went to Broadway looking for work. Hopper stood 6'2" and had an athletic build, "with a thunderous voice that might set the back-drop shivering, to say nothing of the audience." His hair, when he still had it, was dark and curly. Later he wore an array of wigs and toupees (*ibid.*).

His stature and voice were ideal for tragedy, but he made a career out of comedy. "And he went about the difficult business of making people laugh with a subtle seriousness of purpose that was as unobtrusive as it was successful." He studied voice for a year, with a view toward singing opera, but his comedic talent sent him in the direction of parodying arias instead. He joined the McCaull Opera Company in 1885 with a six-year contract. In the middle of that contract he met "Casey" (*ibid.*).

He and fellow comedian Digby Bell, both baseball cranks (as fans were called in those days) proposed to Colonel John McCaull that the opera company attend the ballgame at the Polo Grounds and invite the members of the Chicago White Stockings and New York Giants to an entertainment the same evening at Wallack's Theater, where they were performing. It was agreed, and the notices printed. Archibald Clavering Gunter, author and former San Francisco resident, saw the notice and got the idea to offer Hopper the tattered copy of a baseball poem he had snipped from the *San Francisco Daily Examiner* when he was out West. Hopper recalled later that his infant son John was very ill with a diphtheritic sore throat, and the actor didn't think he had the concentration necessary to memorize anything new. He told McCaull about his son and added, "I can't commit this piece. I can't call my name until I hear how the boy is." Later, when he got word that the crisis had past, he took the rumpled clipping out of his pocket. "If 'Casey' is anything, it is a mile long." "I looked at it and I nearly fainted." He had it memorized in an hour, he said, "and kept it going in my mind" (*ibid.,*; and *HUC*, 6 [1905]).

All preparations having been made for the opera company to host the two baseball teams on August 14, this small notice appeared in the *New York Herald* that day: "The McCaull Opera Company will go up to the Polo Grounds this afternoon in three Tally Ho's, and this evening the New York and Chicago clubs will see the performance at Wallack's." The evening was described in Pulitzer's *World* the next day:

Comedian Hopper's Base Hits

> **The Ball-Tossers and Gen. Sherman Shed Tears of Laughter at Them.**—The Giants and the Chicagos, who had faced each other on the Polo Grounds yesterday afternoon, sat opposite each other in the boxes in Wallack's last night and listened to the McCaull Opera Company in Prince Methusalem. No one would have thought, to see them dressed so quietly in black, that they were the athletes they are. At the game in the afternoon the entire opera company, Col. McCaull included, sat on their tally-ho coaches and witnessed the contest, and the two clubs had come in the evening to return the call. The house was packed to the doors, and when the two clubs came in they were given an ovation.
>
> Just before the opera began Gen. Sherman, who is as fond of baseball as he used to be of forced marches, walked down the aisle to his seat in the middle of the house. He was instantly recognized by the ball-players in the boxes, as well as by the majority of the audience. Some one of Chicago's team began to applaud, and everybody took up the cue, and the old General bowed quietly to the impromptu reception.
>
> As might be expected, Hopper let himself loose on the subject of baseball, and the men laughed heartily at the bits that the comedian threw at them. In the second act, when he sang the "Dot on the I," the house roared from the beginning to the end. One of the favorite verses is about the victory of the Giants, and before he sang the verse Hopper

> turned to the Chicagos and said: "You have had the pennant long enough to stand this." At the end the usher carried down an immense floral baseball from the Chicago Club with "C.B.B.C." on it. In honor of the occasion he recited with brilliant effect that humorous poem, "Casey's at the Bat." The audience literally went wild with enthusiasm; men got up on their seats and cheered, while old Gen. Sherman laughed until the tears ran down his cheeks. It was one of the wildest scenes ever seen in a theatre, and showed the popularity of Hopper and baseball.

Ironically, the visiting Chicagos beat the home team Giants by a score of 4–2 that day, the same score the home team lost by in the poem. An additional irony is that August 14, the first recital of "Casey at the Bat," was Ernest Thayer's twenty-fifth birthday (*NY World*, 8/15/1888; *NYTRB*, 8/15/1888).

"Casey" was on his way; by October 15 – four months after the poem's first printing – the *New York Sun* was referring to it as "the time-honored 'Casey at the Bat'" (*NYS*, 10/15/1888).

The poem seemed to be a mascot for Stockton in the 1888 season. The Slough City boys oozed into a tie for last place on the very day "Casey" was published, but got new life and started a climb to first place. The season didn't end until late November; it was interrupted by a visit from the Chicago White Stockings and a picked nine called the All Americas – led by John Montgomery Ward – who embarked from San Francisco on the good ship *Alameda* for a baseball barnstorming tour to Australia. They had so much fun down under that they decided to expand their trip into a tour around the world (*EX*, 6/4, 11/5, 11/12, 11/19/1888).

Albert Spalding planned the excursion and got George Wright to go along as umpire. Actress Helen Dauvray, Ward's wife, designed the spiffy All-Americas' uniforms. The teams played a few exhibitions in San Francisco and Los Angeles while preparations were being made for the voyage. The players didn't put up their best game; the *Examiner* called it "Giant style," in reference to that team's efforts the winter before; it was no compliment. They were all on holiday, though, and were soon known collectively as the "Howling Wolves." Three thousand cranks waited on the docks of the Oceanic Steamship Company to bid the players adieu on November 18, then it was back to the business of finishing the 1888 championship season (*ibid.*, 11/5, 11/12, 11/19/1888).

Stockton ended up with the 1888 California League pennant. The Browns' great luck at home bolstered their won-lost record. Part of the reason they did so well at home was the inconvenience of travel for their visiting opponents. The city boys had more trouble adapting to the country town than vice versa. In a case of insult added to injury, in mid–July Mike Finn – manager of the 1887 champion Pioneers – missed the train that carried the team to Stockton and had to make an arduous trek to get there. He got to the team hotel just as his players were dragging themselves back from the Banner Island Grounds. Without Finn's exhortations on the field, the

Frank O Small

Pioneers had been victims of a no-hitter. Not only that, noted the *Independent,* "the manager of the champions rode from French Camp to Stockton muleback, and that evening took his dinner standing" (*ibid.,* 11/26/1888; and *ibid.,* 7/16/1888 from STIN).

Transitions

Ernest was still single, but he had plenty of relatives within close proximity. Albert's family continued to grow; he and Josie welcomed their third child and third daughter on August 21, 1889. She was named Josephine Ely after her mother. Florence, Ed's wife, gave birth to their only child, a son they named Scofield, on December 12 of the same year (Crane, IV, 154).

Frederick "Fatty" Briggs, the talented illustrator of the *Lampoon* and the *Examiner,* died of pneumonia in New York City on October 6, 1890; he was just 28 years old. The news hit Thayer hard; not just that Briggs was so young, but they had become even closer friends in San Francisco than they had been at Harvard, and Ernest had enormous respect for Fatty's artistic talent and believed he would have had a bright future. In the notice Thayer wrote for the third *Secretary's Report,* he noted that Briggs had grown frustrated with the limitations inherent in newspaper illustration and had returned to Springfield in 1888. He set his sights on a possible job in New York. "His health, however, had been much impaired by an attack of the grip, which left him nervously and physically exhausted, and, as it befell, he came back home only to lay down the life which, it is the conviction of his friends, contained the promise of a brilliant future" (*HUC* 3 [1892]: 17–18).

The comment about Briggs's illness raises the question of just whose poor health caused Ernest's resignation from the *Examiner.* Ernest went right to work in one of his brother's mills soon after he got home, so he couldn't have been too sick. Maybe he returned to Worcester because he knew Briggs would not be returning to San Francisco with the rest of Hearst's traveling band, and, with everything else going badly, he didn't want to be there without his easygoing friend.

Daniel Maurice Casey's major-league pitching career ended after the 1890 season. He went back to his home town, Binghamton, New York, and in 1892 notched a 4-3 record with the New York Yankee farm team in that city. He settled into a job as streetcar conductor for the Binghamton Railway Company (BENC, 1756; NBL, Casey).

Opposite: **"Slide, Kelly, Slide!" (courtesy of the Boston Public Library, Print Department).**

Senator George Hearst, who had been ill for some time, died in Washington, DC, on February 28, 1891. There was a funeral for him in the capital on March 5 and then the body was shipped to California and a second funeral was held at Grace Church in San Francisco on March 15. He was buried at Cyprus Lawn Cemetery. In the East, as in the West, "His abounding humor and emphatic honesty were long remembered." The reading of the will indicated that Billy Buster would still be on an allowance; all the Hearst money ($18 million) was left to William Randolph's philanthropic mother (*HARP*, 3/14/1891, 187; Swanberg, 61–62; and *DAB*, 488).

Nellie and Sam Clary had their second child, Ernest's fourth niece, Eleanor, on August 2, 1892. That completed their family (Crane, IV, 154).

Ernest fulfilled his periodic duty to Secretary Williams with this short note: "My life has been perfectly uneventful." He did admit that he was involved in the manufacture of woolens at Worcester (*HUC*, 3 [1892]).

Hopper and Thayer Meet

De Wolf Hopper continued to recite Casey at every opportunity; his symbiotic relationship with the poem made them both more and more famous. Hopper later claimed to have tried for four years to find out who wrote "Casey at the Bat," even to the point of writing to the *Examiner* but getting no response. Finally, one night late in December 1892, Hopper was performing at the Worcester Theater. The *Worcester Evening Gazette* described him thus: "His figure is tall and well made, his legs are beautiful, he has the art of what he calls 'ad lib,'–extemporaneous, spontaneous, witty side business–to perfection; and last but not least important, he recites 'Casey' as no other man can." Of course he was expected to recite the poem Worcester was so proud of (*HUC*, 6 [1905]; and *WG*, 12/22/1892).

According to the *Gazette,* Thayer went backstage between acts and had a "merry" chat with Hopper for 15 minutes. Hopper got ready to recite "Casey" after the performance of "Wang" and repeated encores; he introduced it thus: "The author of this piece that has done so much for me I never met until tonight. I had a faint idea who it was but to-night found out for sure and met him personally. He is a Worcester gentleman and his name is Mr. Ernest L. Thayer. I thank him from the bottom of my heart for what he has done for me." Hopper then recited "Casey" to thunderous applause, and afterward Hopper said: "Ladies and gentlemen:–Nine-tenths of this encore belongs to Mr. Thayer, and again I wish to thank him." Thayer hosted Hopper at dinner the following evening at the Worcester Club (*WG*, 12/22/1892).

Years later Hopper thought he met Thayer for the first time at the Worcester Club, not at the theater. There is another version of their first

Ernest Lawrence Thayer's Harvard graduation picture, 1885 (courtesy of the Harvard University Archives).

meeting that corresponds to his recollection. In that version, Harry Worcester Smith and William Scofield were in the audience at the theater. Harry Smith was the younger brother of Willie Smith, one of Ernest's closest friends in his youth. Will Scofield was the brother-in-law of Ernest's brother Ed. They approached Hopper after the performance and asked if he would like to meet the author of "Casey at the Bat." Hopper was tickled at the idea and accompanied the men to the Worcester Club on Elm street, where author and interpreter met for the first time. Hopper said he asked Thayer who or what inspired the poem and Thayer answered "Sam Winslow." Thayer was importuned to recite the poem himself, which he was loath to do, but he finally acquiesced. Hopper said later it was the worst recital of "Casey at the Bat" he had ever heard, and that included children forced into reciting it by their mothers. "In a sweet, dulcet Harvard whisper he implored Casey to murder the umpire, and gave this cry of mass animal rage all the emphasis of a caterpillar wearing rubbers crawling on a velvet carpet." Hopper and Thayer nevertheless became close friends after that night, thanks to "Casey" (Hopper and Stout, 85–87; Southwick, 77; *NYT*, 9/24/1935; and Croy 12).

CHAPTER 27

Thayer the Manufacturer

Thayer remained a clerk until 1894, when he and one of his relatives on his mother's side, A.W. Darling, took over the operation of the Bottomley Mill in Cherry Valley. He still lived at the family home (1895 *WCD*).

The third triennial anniversary of the class of 1885 was in 1894, and the tradition of reciting "Casey at the Bat" at the class dinner was begun that June when Roland Boyden did the honors. From then on the class considered the ballad "our 'Casey at the Bat'" (*HUC*, 4 [1895]; *HUC*, 6 [1905]; and *HUC*, 7 [1910]).

Class of 1885 Dinner

The tenth anniversary dinner of Harvard's class of 1885 was held at Young's Hotel in Boston on June 25, 1895. Thayer had written to Secretary Williams shortly before the reunion, "I eat hearty, and never wake before seven in the morning. I will attempt to speak at our decennial dinner, if I am not overcome with fright between now and then." When the date arrived, Ernest found that he was able to give the talk in which he remembered those who had died young and remarked on the ironic difference between the idealistic arrogance of youth and the practical necessities of living in the real world. It was a long speech, both humorous and thoughtful; here are portions of it:

> In my old age, now that I have forgotten pretty nearly everything I ever knew, and can, therefore, speak without bias, I am impelled to liken college training to vaccination: sometimes it takes and sometimes it don't. Sometimes it starts a man in a direction in which he can go on, and awakens tastes that always be to him a pleasure and a resource; and again, after crushing the little natural sense which its victim originally possessed, it uncoils itself from his person like a boa-constrictor from a dead hog.
>
> Both of the classes which I have just referred to are represented in my audience here to-night. I will name no names.

Now I wish to tell you that about a month ago, foreseeing that I might be asked to say something on this occasion, I put together a very neat little speech in a familiar style. Something that would make you plume yourselves on the advantages which you have received, something which would make you pity the outcasts—like, for example, the proprietor of this hotel—who never had any advantages excepting what they took. But the time for that kind of a speech is gone by. It would have been appropriate to a period ten years ago when a college education was the only thing you had, and was in your opinion the only thing worth having, but it would be entirely out of place to-day when, I am pleased to believe, a college education is about the only thing that you have not. It may be that in making these statements I am committing the error, the very common error, of judging others by myself. I know that I myself have been often taunted, and with fairness, on the ground that I could not pass with success the entrance examinations at Harvard; and this is true, notwithstanding the fact that if I did have to face that ordeal again, I would not need to know nearly as much to get through as I did need to know fourteen years ago. I have often wished of late years that no more serious obstacle than a proctor stood between me and success, and I cannot help thinking what very easy meat a proctor would be for some of you others, some of you statesmen, who can round up a thousand voters without any other claim to a nation's gratitude excepting that you need it in your business.

However, whether you have forgotten your college education or not, it seems to me that the old style of self-gratulatory remarks is not at all the sort of thing which this occasion calls for. We have not indeed forgotten that we went to college. . . . [A]nd this, I choose to think, is our best excuse for coming together at intervals and giving an account of ourselves. We no longer assemble as a congress of superior beings, possessed of a great deal of polish, which we have subsequently discovered will not cut ice, but we come here as plain citizens who have made the startling discovery that they are just like other people, united, however, by a common experience, a pleasant experience and one which I honestly believe has done us no harm. . . .

Fame and glory, these are beautiful possessions, but oh, ye famous and ye glorious ones, permit us others to believe that life of itself, even without glory, even with its unending disappointments, is a good thing; that it's a good thing to be in the world, a good thing merely to witness the righting of a wrong, a good thing to push a good thing along, however obscure you, the pusher, may be, a good thing to grasp the hand of a friend, a good thing to receive full in the heart the smile of a good woman, a good thing to come together as we have come here to-night, to sit among old comrades with good food, good wine, and excellently good conversation. Yes, life is full of good things, and here again mark how the years have wrought their changes. See how they have thinned the pessimists in our ranks. You remember our college pessimists, boys; the out-of-nothing, into-nothing, for-nothing gang. Look at them now. Look at their buxom wives, their fat children. Hear them talk in town meeting about the necessity of purchasing a new fire-engine. Visit them in the winter and see them shovel snow. Watch them when the baby has the croup. Try their cigars, and learn what a fatally weakening pessimism has brought them to pronounce good! No, there are no pessimists in active life, and we who are doing what we can in one way or another are pessimists no longer.

I have but a word more to say, and that is of those who began the morning with us but who have left us in the middle of the day. And once again, in speaking of them, must we acknowledge, I think, the marks which these flying years have impressed upon us, for have they not made for us the thought of death, if not less sad, much, much less terrible? There was a horror to many of us at the first loss of our classmates, men like ourselves, of our own age, a horror which crowded our grief aside, and for this reason, perhaps, as the years go by, those boys become not more but less forgotten. Who shall say when we think of them now that they are not with us more really than ever they were since first they were taken from our sides, that the spirit of their lives does not shine more clearly for us, that the influence they would have worked, the good they would have done, is not more true for us even than when we knew them in life? And as year follows year, and banquet succeeds banquet, those good friends of ours will be, unless we shall forget our own youth, more and more truly, more and more companionably, the partakers of our common cheer [*HUC*, 4 (1895); and *HUC*, 5 (1900): 90–96].

The Examiner *versus Dana*

The *San Francisco Daily Examiner* found it necessary to put the *New York Sun* in its place, and in the process get in a few zings at its owner, Charles Anderson Dana, when the *Sun* claimed that it originally published "Casey at the Bat" and called it "Kelly at the Bat." The 1895 *Examiner* article was published in the *Hoboken Evening World and Press* in 1898:

Comment on "Casey at the Bat." From the *SF Examiner*. The following is from Mr. Dana's New York *Sun*:

"After taking another retrospect of the native poetry of recent years worthy of contrast with the works of genius of other ages, we conclude that to the two poems mentioned by Mr. Dana in his recent address at Cornell University, 'High Tide at Gettysburg' and 'The Modern Romans,' there should be added another poem, probably more popularly known than either of those, entitled 'Casey at the Bat.' That poem was originally printed in *The Sun* as 'Kelly at the Bat,' referring to the famous Mike Kelly, who rose to fame in the right field of the ball grounds at Chicago. But it was immediately recognized as a work of quality too high to be left subordinate to any individual player, so the name of Casey was substituted as a more universal cognomen. 'Casey at the Bat' is a truly fine poem."

Old readers of the Examiner will readily recall the clever poem, "Casey at the Bat," upon whose theft from these columns Mr. Dana now felicitates himself, but for the benefit of newer ones we may mention that the verses in question were written by "Phinney" Thayer, one of the group of promising young men whose advent in the office of this paper created such a stir in San Francisco journalism in 1887. Mr. Thayer wrote the poem for the Examiner under the title, "Casey at the Bat." It caught on at once, and the unerring literary intuitions of the editor of The New York *Sun* did not fail to recognize its value. With a taste incomparably superior to that which he has since applied to the judgment of California wines, Mr. Dana promptly stole Mr. Thayer's work and published it as an original contribution to *The Sun*. In order to give it an Eastern local color he substituted the name of Kelly for that of the imaginary hero, Casey. And now, even after the lapse of seven years, he rolls the memory of this exploit as a sweet morsel under his tongue.

Mr. Dana is an old man, rich in honors and in coin, although he has not quite as many subscribers as he had a few years ago. But in the ordinary course of nature he will have to die some time, and we suggest the advantage of repentance before that melancholy event occurs. Otherwise we shudder to think where that venerable journalist, accustomed to ocean breezes and iced drinks, will go [*HEWP*, 1898, reprinted from *EX*, 1895].

William Henry (Harry) Wright

Harry Wright, "the father of professional baseball," died in Atlantic City, New Jersey, on October 3, 1895, aged 60. He outlived his wife by three years; she died after an operation in February 1892, having been an invalid for two years. Due to failing eyesight, Wright had retired as manager of the Phillies after the 1893 season. Ironically, the National League, taking account of his condition, created the post of chief of umpires for him. He filled the post until his death. Wright had been ill for some time; he had gone to Atlantic City as his last hope for recovery. He succumbed to pneumonia, and thousands thronged the streets of Philadelphia the day of his funeral. On April 13, 1896, "Harry Wright Day" was held by the National League to raise funds for a monument to the beloved baseball man. Veteran players came out of retirement to play commemorative games in various league cities. The monument at his grave in West Laurel Hill cemetery, Bala Cynwyd, Pennsylvania, was unveiled on June 26, 1897. The *Sporting Life* described it thus: "The monument is a bronze figure of Harry Wright in every-day dress, with his hat in the left hand, while the right hand grasps a pair of eyeglasses. The figure is six feet six inches in height, and is mounted on a pedestal of Barre granite seven feet six inches high, thus making the full height of the memorial fourteen feet."

Incredibly, Harry Wright was not inducted into the Baseball Hall of Fame until 1953, which was 17 years after the first selections (NBL, H. Wright [Seymour, Harwell]; *SL*, 2/13/1892, 6/26/1897; and *BENC*, 592).

CHAPTER 28

Hints of Immortality

As "Casey" began to make a stir, W.R. Hearst began to think of Phinney as one of those "top talents" he was always looking to engage. What a coup it would be to reinstall the author of America's favorite baseball poem as the *Examiner*'s funny man. That move would solidify in everyone's mind, too, that the San Francisco paper was the origin of the verses. In 1908 Thayer recounted to Homer Croy that, in 1896, "I received an urgent call to go to San Francisco which I did not accept." Hearst had recently bought the *New York Journal,* and Thayer did agree to go down to New York City for a short while; he wrote four ballads for inclusion in *The American Humorist,* the *Journal*'s Sunday supplement (Croy, 12).

That same year Thayer received a request from Samuel S. Green at the Worcester Free Library for a handwritten copy of "Casey" for the Worcester History Room. On July 10, 1896, Thayer wrote out the poem—with a few minor changes from the 1888 original—and sent it to Mr. Green with a short written note:

Leicester, Mass. July 10, '96

> Mr. Samuel S. Green,
> Dear Sir,
> In response to your very flattering request I enclose herewith a copy of *Casey at the Bat.* My handwriting is not easily legible, & I foresee some trouble for those baseball enthusiasts who desire to consult Casey in the original version.
>
> Sincerely yours,
> Ernest L. Thayer [WHR]

The changes he made in this poem were mostly cosmetic; the curious change is in the last line: "great Casey has struck out." That phrase is one of the most famous in the poem; most of us remember it as "mighty Casey has struck out," which is how it appeared in the original printing. The original sounds better and most reprintings over the years use "mighty Casey," despite Thayer's change. Thayer also dropped the subtitle "Ballad of the Republic. Sung in the Year 1888." He turned Flynn the lulu into Flynn the hoodoo, and he corrected the typographical error that changed Jimmy Blake to Johnnie in the *Examiner* original. (At least we assume it was a typo. Ball-tossers sometimes played under aliases to hide the fact they had been black-listed by another league, or sometimes so their parents wouldn't know they were playing baseball on Sunday or at all. Thayer might have exaggerated that indulgence by changing Blake's first name in the same inning! By 1896, when this was no longer so common, he kept the name the same. Or, he might have learned that Blakiston had changed his last name from Blackstone [which, coincidentally, was the name of Worcester's river and the village where Thayer's father was born] and so he changed Blake's first name.)

One word he did not change in any of his authorized copies was "clinched," in "his teeth are clinched in hate." Most editors have arbitrarily changed that word to "clenched," which is a more commonly used term today, assuming perhaps that "clinched" was another typo. Thayer's handwritten version, though, clearly shows the dot on the i. In the last stanza he made two changes besides the change from "mighty" to "great": he changed the spelling of "favored" to "favoured;" he changed the line "And somewhere men are laughing, and somewhere children shout;" to "And somewhere men are laughing, and little children shout" (*ibid.*).

After having lived at the family home for ten years, Ernest moved a few blocks away to the Hotel Newton, 5 High Street. In 1899 he moved to Leicester, nearer the mill and where Sam Winslow had been living for about ten years (1899, 1900, 1901 *WCD*; and *HUC*, 10 [1935]).

The Sporting News was one of the periodicals that received requests for reprints of "Casey at the Bat" at the end of every baseball season. In answering one of those requests in 1899, *TSN* called the ballad a classic:

> "Casey at the Bat" is a base ball classic. At the close of each season *The Sporting News* receives requests from all parts of the country for back numbers containing the poem. It is reproduced in this issue on page 6, along with its companion piece, "When Casey Slugged the Ball." The annual demand is easily accounted for. Its recitation is a feature of the testimonial to each year's pennant winners. The mere mention of it is enough to create a desire for it in those who have read and recited it, and the catchy title excites the curiosity of those who have its enjoyment before them. The daily papers have shelved it as a chestnut, but like wine it grows better with age and *The Sporting News* makes it a point to serve it up for its readers once a year. Requests for copies of it come at all seasons and from all quarters. It gives rise to many curious questions. Some want to know if the original Casey was related to the Brooklyn third baseman; others wish to be informed what position he played and on what team; a few express a desire for his photo and a great many inquire with anxiety whether he is still alive and if not, when and where he died. The following letter from California is a sample of the many similar requests received since the close of the

season. Mr. Schmidt not only knows and appreciates a good thing, but he manifests a most laudable desire to share it with his fellow fans. His letter follows:

Los Angeles, Oct. 31, 1899

Editor of *The Sporting News*:

I am aware that "Casey at the Bat" is regarded as something of a back number, but there are at least 10,000 young fans in California who have never seen it in print. One of our local papers, "the Times," has promised to publish it if I procure the copy. Will you help me out? Publish it just once more and it will be read by not only the young fans alluded to above, but by lots of us old fellows, who had rather see a game of base ball or read "Casey" than to annex a small "bot" and bird. We do not have National League ball here, but we all turn out to see whatever is given us and our games draw well. If consistent with your rules, please help us out in the above request and oblige,

Yours Very Truly,

Rudolph J. Schmidt [*TSN*, 11/11/1899.]

Fifteen years after graduation from Harvard, Thayer found he had very little to say to account for himself in his report to Secretary Williams for the *Secretary's Report.* By now, though, all his classmates were familiar with "Casey at the Bat" and the fact that their Ivy Orator had written it. Since Thayer was too modest, and, in fact, didn't want to remind himself that he wrote it, Williams began adding a note concerning its momentum toward becoming a classic. "Particulars had perhaps as well be omitted," Thayer wrote. "I begin to suspect that I am one of those plants which flower very late." Secretary Williams added, "There have been repeated requests for copies of E.L. Thayer's immortal poem, 'Casey at the Bat,' and of the philosophical address which he delivered at the Class Dinner in 1895. A copy of each is therefore appended hereto" (*HUC*, 5 [1900]).

CHAPTER 29

Will the Real "Casey" . . .

In addition to the popular choice, Mike "King" Kelly, and Thayer's named inspiration, Sam Winslow, there were a few others who claimed to be or were touted as being the inspiration for "Casey."

Daniel Maurice Casey

One day in 1900, in Binghamton, New York, streetcar conductor Daniel Maurice Casey, former National League pitcher and hitting hero of that game way back on August 20, 1887, banged his head on an overhanging trolley wire. When he came to, "memories" started flooding back on him. *He* was the "Casey" of "Casey at the Bat." It was a game on August 21, 1887, he recalled, and he struck out in an identical situation to the one in the poem. How was he to know that the little poem his good friend Ernie Thayer – a Philadelphia reporter – had written to tease him, would become famous nationwide? (*CR-H*, reprinted in *TSN*, 11/9/1901; *NYT*, 4/30/1935; and JBB to author 2/6/1988.)

Never mind that Thayer didn't know Dan Casey, was never a Philadelphia knight of the quill, was in San Francisco when that game was played, and that no one ever called him "Ernie," this is a good story. Casey said Mudville was a low-lying, muddy area near the Philadelphia ballpark. Maybe so, but having mud is not enough. Was it near a mountain, in a large valley on flat ground with a delta nearby? It's hard to accept Casey's recollections, when anyone who has ever known a baseball player or seen one interviewed has heard them recite their past glories in minute detail. How could Casey forget one of his few moments of heroism at the bat? He was close on the date; saying it was the next day makes one wonder if he or someone close to him had obtained a newspaper clipping of the game and confused the date of the clipping with the game date (*ibid.*).

Daniel Henry Casey

Daniel Henry Casey is the one Casey that Thayer thought *might* have subconsciously influenced him in the writing of the poem. When he wrote to

Dan Casey in the Dan Casey Day Parade, Binghamton, 1915 (courtesy of the Broome County Historical Society, Binghamton, N.Y.).

the *Syracuse Post-Standard* in 1930 he said, "The only Casey involved, and I am *not* sure about him." This is usually misquoted as "and I am sure about him." There were, of course, many factors working on Thayer's subconscious when he wrote "Casey at the Bat," but he was not sure if any one person was a conscious influence, although Hopper said he specified Sam Winslow. When people do write about Daniel Henry Casey they point out the subtle class distinctions at work in Worcester when Thayer and Casey were growing up there. Thayer is accused of being prejudiced against the Irish and of trying to show Casey up once more, as a sort of postscript to the *Monohippic Gazette* article of his high school days. Everyone who knew him and commented on Thayer's personality said that he was modest and gentle and wouldn't hurt anyone intentionally. He turned his barbs on himself as often as on anyone else. Daniel Henry Casey did have the physical stature of the mythical "Casey." He had the smile of Christian charity, according to his students in later years. He also had a temper that was shown vividly when he reacted to Ernest's article in 1880 with "big clenched fists turned white at the knuckles" (SP-S, 9/3/1935; and Casey 174, 191).

John Patrick Francis Parnell "White Wings" Cahill

John Patrick Parnell Cahill was born John Patrick Francis Cahill in San Francisco on April 30, 1865. Like many Americans of Irish descent, he adopted the name Parnell as his own to honor Charles Stewart Parnell, "the uncrowned king of Ireland," who led the fight for home rule in the 1880s. Cahill got an early start in the major leagues; he played with Columbus (American Association) in 1884 and with St. Louis (National League) in 1886; his last season in the majors was with Indianapolis (National League) in 1887. In addition to playing winter ball on Bay Area teams, Cahill played with teams all over the country. He was well liked everywhere, even though he wasn't a great ballplayer. If the number of nicknames given a player is a barometer of his regard, Cahill was indeed popular. Being a local product, the San Francisco press loved him and followed his far-flung career with great interest (*BENC*, 730; *World,* 332; *SL*, 9/29/1886; and *CHRON*, 5/25/1886).

The *San Francisco Daily Chronicle* proudly described his impact on Atlanta while he played there: "John Patrick Parnell Cahill (Patsy Carroll) made a great reputation playing shortstop for Atlanta. He was so popular there that they placed his picture in baseball uniform in the crevice of the cornerstone of the courthouse then being built, named a horse car after him, called a brand of cigars after him, and one enthusiastic admirer of the Atlantas named one of his children after him" (*CHRON*, 5/25/1886).

When he died on October 31, 1901, the *Oakland Tribune* paid him the ultimate compliment by claiming he was the inspiration for "Casey at the Bat":

> How Casey at the Bat Came to Be Written
>
> **A Reminiscence of the Baseball Game in which Patsy Cahill, the Well-Known Oaklander, Made a Memorable Hit and Saved the Day.**—"Casey at the Bat" is dead. Every baseball crank knows the poem and catches the rich humor of the climax when "Casey has struck out."
>
> Well, John Patrick Parnell Cahill, who died at his home here yesterday of consumption, was the original Casey of the comic poem, but oddly enough, the inspiration of that poem was not a strikeout, but a swat that sent the ball at a critical moment clear over the fence at the old Haight street grounds more than a dozen years ago.
>
> Cahill was a short, pudgy chap, with a jolly mug and a comical glance of his eye. He used to play with the old Greenhood and Morans who became the Oakland nine of the old California League. Whenever he took the bat it was the signal for all the bleachers to shout. Cahill was a popular player, but mighty "onsartin" about hitting the ball. Batting was not his strong suit. His best work was in the field.
>
> When a picked nine of Eastern players came out here with Kelly, the ten thousand dollar "Boston beauty," at their head, to play the cracks of

> the California League during a winter season, Patsy Cahill was a member of the nine that gave them the first taste of California ball playing.
>
> There was an immense crowd at the Haight street grounds that day, and the California boys put up a great game. At first, the Eastern men played with careless ease as if they felt they had a sure thing, but as the game progressed they found they had their hands full.
>
> But the California men could not score, although they kept their opponents from piling up runs. The end came with Patsy Cahill (Casey) at the bat, and a great day it was for California. It was the last half of the ninth inning. The Boston Beauty's men had two runs to their credit, while the Californians had stacked up a row of goose eggs. The bases were full, with two men out, when Patsy came to the bat. Everybody knew his uncertainty with the willow. The spectators felt their hearts sink, although a cheerful shout of encouragement went up from the bleachers.
>
> "One strike!" called the umpire.
>
> "Two strikes!" and the hearts of the crowd began to grow faint.
>
> Patsy jammed the end of his stick in the sand and took a firmer grip. He smote the ball like he wielded the club of Hercules. It went flying over the fence. Patsy made a home run and brought all the basemen in. The game was won. What a cheer went up! Patsy was a hero, for he had saved the day for California when everybody expected him to strike out.
>
> Watching him was a young writer on the *Examiner*, who had poetic talent and the gift of humor. The situation caught his fancy and inspired him to write "Casey at the Bat," which is a baseball classic to this day, although the author has long gone to his eternal rest. He was compelled to sacrifice the heroic culmination to the exigency which demanded a humorous climax to round out the poem.
>
> And that is how "Casey at the Bat" came to be written [*OTRIB*, 11/1/1901].

There are a couple of things wrong with these assertions: John Patrick Cahill was not in the lineup for the G&Ms in the winter games against the New York Giants (the "picked nine" the *Tribune* alluded to) in 1887. He did play, not for the G&Ms, and not even at the Haight-street Grounds; he sometimes filled in at third base for Tommy Burns on the Chicago White Stockings at Central Park. In fact, the game the G&Ms won from the New York Giants at the beginning of their West coast trip had no ninth-inning heroics by anybody; the game wasn't ever close. The G&Ms led 8–4 after eight and won 10–4. The *Examiner* headline the next day read "Bully Boy, Van–George and the Greenhoods Do up the Gotham Giants." George Van Haltren–the best ballplayer not in the Hall of Fame–pitched for the G&Ms that day, even though he was a rookie member of the Chicago White Stockings during the 1887 season. He wasn't playing with the Chicagos at Central Park because his contract was up for that season, and he was always welcome on the hometown team he left to join the White Stockings. Another thing the *Tribune* got wrong was its assumption that Thayer had already been issued a harp. His health abandoned him temporarily in 1892, but at 38 he was very much alive, and, though never robust, eventually got his health back (*EX*, 1/8, 1/19/1888; *BENC*, 1568, 2311; and *HUC*, 7 [1910]).

In response to the *Tribune* claim, the *Chicago Record-Herald* printed an article – reprinted in *The Sporting News* – saying in essence that this was just another of many claims, that any time a favorite local ballplayer died, that player was touted as the real "Casey":

Another Original "Casey"

John Patrick Parnell Cahill Dies of Consumption in California. – "Casey" is dead again – "Casey at the Bat" – the might "Casey" who set the world awry by striking out at Mudville. This time he is said to be totally dead, with no chance to appeal to the umpire of Destiny for a change of decision.

"Casey" has been dying at intervals ever since DeWolf Hopper made him famous by reciting that anonymous classic of the diamond, the "Beautiful Show" of base ball literature. But Casey would not remain extinct for any reasonable amount of time, so people have come to doubt the sincerity of his dying "stunts." Heretofore he has always had something up his sleeve or a confederate behind the wings.

His latest shuffling off was done at Pleasanton, Cal., which is bidding for some of the fame of Mudville. He didn't die under the name of "Casey" at all. On his coffin lid is inscribed the name "John Patrick Parnell Cahill." The cause of death, according to dispatches, was consumption. To clinch his claim to being the original of the poem, some of his friends have suggested that on his tombstone be cut these words:

Oh, somewhere in this favored land the sun is shining bright;
The band is playing somewhere, and somewhere hearts are light;
And somewhere men are singing, and somewhere children shout.
But there is no joy in Mudville, mighty Casey has "struck out."

And if it really be "Casey" whose soul went out with the tide on the sunny shores of the Pacific, what becomes of the claim of Daniel Casey, the street car conductor of Binghamton, N.Y.? Here was a gentleman of Celtic name, who was scalped something like a year ago when his head came in contact with an overhanging trolley wire. He said he was the original and only Casey, but he didn't die, and thereby his claim was much discounted, but not before Hopper and Anson and a few other old friends sent touching messages of condolence and Daniel had been advertised from Maine to Mexico.

The California man is really and completely dead. On that point all are agreed, but was he "Casey"? And if he were "Casey" and has "struck out" of the game of life, will the authorship of the verses never be established?

Chicago Record-Herald [*CR-H*, reprinted in *TSN*, 11/9/1901.]

Orrin Robinson (Bob) Casey

Here's a refreshing change–a man who claims *not* to be the subject of "Casey at the Bat." The people and the press of Syracuse, New York, liked to believe that former ballplayer O. Robinson Casey was the subject of the poem. "As a result of his great hitting ability there was for years discussion over whether 'Casey at the Bat' was written about him." Thayer's long letter to the *Syracuse Post-Standard* in 1930 explained that there was no ballplayer named Casey who was the inspiration for the poem. In a 1931 interview, Bob Casey said:

> My name is Casey and I played ball for twenty years, as catcher and third baseman, and several times I struck out with the bases loaded and two men out. But as for being the real, the genuine, the "immortal" Casey, the chances are 100 to 1 against it. The poem appeared first in the San Francisco *Examiner* on June 3, 1888. I was playing ball then on a semi-pro team in Syracuse, and it is most unlikely that the young man, fresh out of Harvard, who wrote the poem in San Francisco, ever heard of me.
>
> But when De Wolf Hopper began reciting "Casey" and everyone in Syracuse pointed me out as the hero, well, I let them build me up [*NYT*, 11/29/1936].

Roger Connor

"Casey" is always depicted as a giant of a man, a muscular, imposing warrior. Whether Thayer pictured him this way in his mind is a question, but if he did there were not many players in the 1880s who fit that bill. One of the biggest men playing at that time was Giants first baseman Roger Connor. At 6′3″ and 220 lbs. he towered over just about every other player and the umpires, too. Barrel-chested Dan Brouthers, at 6′2″ and 207 lbs. was in Connor's class. Mike Kelly was more the average sized player of that day, a bit above average at 5′10″ and 170 lbs. When Connor came to the bat in San Francisco for the first time, local cranks must have been amazed at his size, and when he hit the ball 460 feet over the right-field fence at the Haight-street Grounds, his legendary status was ensured. He was quiet and gentlemanly, though, not brash like "Casey." So if he was the inspiration for "Casey," it was for his size, not his personality (*BENC*, 783, 1090).

CHAPTER 30

Retirement

After two years in Leicester, Thayer moved back to Worcester in 1901 and took up residence at the Aurora Apartment House at 656 Main Street. He was tired of business in general and the woolen business in particular; he was in a financial position now to ease out of active participation in the Bottomley Mill, and his health had improved enough so that he longed to travel (1902 *WCD*; and *HUC*, 7 [1910]).

While he traveled in Europe during 1902, Thayer used the Worcester Club as his permanent address. In 1903 he spent a good part of the year in California. He went to the Hotel del Coronado in mid–February and intended to stay for two or three weeks, but ended up staying about seven weeks. The beauty of the seaside hotel, its golf course, and the southern California climate, which Ernest compared in a letter to Nellie as "rather better than the Riviera," delighted him so much that he told her after being there more than a month, "I . . . am so contented that I am not yet thinking of my departure." Ernest was playing golf (thanks to George Wright) three hours every day. "This game may be losing its popularity at home, but I think it must be because all the players have come to California. Here you will see fifty people on the links any morning. There are all kinds of tournaments" (1903 *WCD*; ELT to ETC, 3/1, 3/15/1903).

In addition to golfing, rowing, and sailing, he remarked that "Somewhere on the premises there is every kind of game you can think of – not to mention a monkey-cage & a tank full of seals." At first he was "furiously active" with golf, swimming, rowing or sailing every day, but as time went on he slowed down. He kept up his golfing but gave up most other activity. "I am lazier & lazier every day & put in a great many hours of pure loafing," he wrote Nellie after about a month there. Some prominent men stopped in while he was there – Marshall Field, General Merritt, John D. Rockefeller, "among others." Rockefeller's stop was a short one. "It was expected he would remain for some days, but something displeased him & he went back at once to his private car," Ernest wrote Nellie in late March, just before he left Coronado and headed for the Potter Hotel in Santa Barbara. His ultimate destination was San Francisco, but he was taking his time getting there. It was while he was on this trip that his father, Edward Davis Thayer, Sr., died in Worcester on May 12 at the age of 80 (ELT to ETC, 2/15, 3/1, 3/15, 3/29/1903; ELT to SHC, 2/25/1903 and *SPY*, 5/14/1903).

Nellie was probably tired of wondering when Will Hearst was going to get married by the time he did. One day before he turned 40, on April 28, 1903, he married Millicent Veronica Willson and they proceeded to have five sons (Swanberg 206, 321).

The Poem Becomes Famous

Thayer loved Europe, especially Florence, Italy, and he wanted to get away from the constant questions regarding the authorship and history of his now famous poem (*HUC*, 7 [1910]).

However, a letter from Joseph M. Cummings of the *Baltimore News* dated January 14, 1905, caught up with him in Rome. The letter remarked on the various people claiming to have written the ballad and requested some details that would prove Thayer was the author of "Casey at the Bat." Thayer's response was part of an article by Cummings printed in *The Sporting News* with the title "Author Discusses Claimants."

> Rome, Grand Hotel Du Quirinal, Feb. 2, 1905.
>
> To the Sporting Editor of the *News*: – Your letter of January 14, inquiring about the authorship of "Casey at the Bat," has just reached me. I have seen the story of which you speak and which attributes the poem to a mythical "Will" Valentine. The statement that it was printed by him in the *Sioux City Tribune* is absolutely false, as an examination of the files of that paper will certainly show. "Casey at the Bat" was first published in the San Francisco *Examiner* in 1888.
>
> I can not give the exact date, of course, but it was some time in the spring or summer of that year. It was the last of many ballads – some better, some worse – that the *Examiner* printed from my pen during my connection with the paper in the capacity of "funny man," so called. These ballads were usually signed "Phin." Casey, I think, was signed with my initials. You ask me what special incentive I had for writing Casey. It was the same incentive that I had for writing a thousand other things. It was my business to write, and I needed the money.
>
> There have been many claimants to the doubtful honor of having written "Casey at the Bat" – among others, I believe, the late "Mike" Kelly of Boston, and it has never seemed to me that it was worth my while to expose their impudence. But "Will" Valentine or his next friend is such a particularly atrocious liar – adducing as he does so many imaginary facts and placarding me by name as a cheap imposter – that I am reluctantly compelled to say something. I am obliged to you for writing to me, and hope you will give publicity to any part of this letter or to all of it, as you may think fit
>
> Yours truly,
> Ernest L. Thayer

He had just mailed that letter when he thought of a good test for finding the true Casey bard, so he wrote another letter to the *News*:

Rome, Grand Hotel Du Quirinal, February 4, 1905.

To the Sporting Editor of the *News*:–

Since writing to you the other day other facts about "Casey" have occurred to me which perhaps will be of interest to you. Except as originally published in the *Examiner*, "Casey" has never been correctly printed–barring one or two cases in which I have furnished the copy. The reason for this I will explain. When the poem was first copied into an Eastern paper–I think by the *New York Sun*–the clipping editor cut off the opening stanzas and began where Casey advances to bat. Later on DeWolf Hopper began to recite the complete poem as it was given to him by Mr. Archibald Gunther, who saw it in the *Examiner*. Some one who heard Hopper's recitation wrote out the first five stanzas from memory–and a very bad memory he must have had–tacked them to the mutilated version as it was printed in the *Sun* and many of its exchanges and then published a combination which has been printed up and down the land as "Casey at the Bat." I think that if the matter were of any importance the easiest way to establish the authorship would be to get the different claimants to furnish a copy which might be compared with the poem as it was first printed in the *Examiner*.

I may say, in conclusion, that though some of the mutilated reprints of Casey have my name on the title page, I have never authorized them. I have left the poem to its fate–except that once I had a few copies printed for circulation among my friends, and only recently, when I am charged with falsely claiming the poem, has it seemed to me my duty to say something of my connection with it. Finally, while a certain "Will" Valentine may have written a base ball poem in a Sioux City paper before 1888, it could not have been "Casey at the Bat" and if anyone is anxious enough to search the files of that paper this fact will become patent. With apologies for troubling you,

Very truly yours,
Ernest L. Thayer

After receipt of the letters, *The Sporting News* did some investigating into the bogus claims of Valentine and others, and used Thayer's letters as a basis for an article written for the January 20, 1906, number, which claimed the authorship issue was finally resolved:

Casey at the Bat

Who wrote "Casey at the Bat" has threatened of late years to become as mysterious a conundrum as "Who Hit 'Billy' Patterson?" But it won't. The mystery has been finally solved and the *News* prints herewith an autograph letter of acknowledgment from its author, Mr. Ernest L. Thayer, who is now traveling abroad. Incidentally, Mr. Thayer's claims have been verified, and the matter may now rest for all time. The author of "Casey at the Bat" is Mr. Ernest L. Thayer, whose home is in Worcester, Mass., but who now spends a good deal of his time on the other side of the Atlantic. He wrote the poem in 1888, while the "Funny Man" of the San Francisco *Examiner*, and it appeared in his column on June 3 of that year over his nom de plume, "Phin."

No contribution to base ball literature, whether prose or verse, ever took the popular fancy like "Casey." Wherever it was heard it made a "hit," and that was reason enough for De Wolf Hopper to recite it, it is believed, first in "Wang." So great has been and is still the popularity of the poem that many impostors have arisen, hoping to filch the fame of its authorship from the man whose brain produced it. One of the compilations of humorous verse credits "Casey" to a Joseph Quinlan Murphy, while a new claimant has recently arisen by proxy in the late "Will" Valentine, who, a theatrical man says, was on the *Sioux City Tribune*.

Humorist of His Class.—Early in the present year the News learned from Mr. Eben Sutton, who has recently removed to this city, that he knew positively that Mr. Thayer was the "only original writer" of "Casey." Mr. Sutton knew Mr. Thayer intimately; in fact, they were classmates and "chums" at Harvard, class of 1885, and are members of the same Greek letter fraternity. Mr. Sutton said that Mr. Thayer was editor-in-chief of the Harvard Lampoon while at the University, was the humorous orator at the class-day exercises, and was an acknowledged wit. After Mr. Thayer's graduation he went to the Pacific Coast and took a position on the San Francisco *Examiner* as the "Funny Man," signing his articles either with his initials or "Phin," as the humor seized him. He had plenty of money, as he is the son of a wealthy hardware manufacturer of Worcester, Mass., and when he tired of the Coast he came back East. Since then he has been dividing his time between his home and abroad, as has already been mentioned.

In the *Secretary's Report* for 1905, class of 1885 secretary Henry Williams gleaned from Thayer's sparse communication that he had spent considerable time abroad, was not now actively engaged in business, but had kept Worcester as his legal residence. In addition, Williams wrote:

The following, clipped from one of the Boston papers relating to our '85 epic "Casey at the Bat," made doubly famous by De Wolf Hopper, is amusing and interesting:

Probably as long as De Wolf Hopper's name is before the public it will be connected with that familiar "epic," "Casey at the Bat." No matter what role Hopper is playing or in what part of the country he is, his audience always insists upon "Casey." Mr. Hopper was asked how he secured the poem.

"Now, thereby hangs a story," he answered. "It was long before 'Wang' ever saw the light. It was in 1887 that Archibald Clavering Gunter sent 'Casey' to me. He never said where he got it but merely requested that I should read it over and recite it the next day when the

Chicago and New York baseball clubs would be in the house. I looked at it and I nearly fainted. We were playing at Wallack's then, and I was in no mood to get anything in shape. My son was ill with diphtheritic sore throat and I believed he was going to die. I told McCaull I couldn't do it, and that was all there was to it. The next day at 1 o'clock I got a wire that the boy would pull through all right and I sat down with 'Casey' at 3 o'clock in the afternoon.

"If 'Casey' is anything it is a mile long. I had it, however, within an hour, and kept in going in my mind. We were playing 'Castles in the Air,' then. Well, the night performance came around and in the boxes sat the two ball teams. There was old Anson, Ewing, and other famous ball players. To make a long story short I pulled 'Casey' on them, and it made an enormous hit.

"After the show I hunted up Gunter and asked him the name of the man who wrote 'Casey.' He said he didn't know and told me he had cut it out of a San Francisco paper some time before, because it had made an impression on him. Will you believe me, I tried for four years to find the man who wrote that thing!

"One night I was playing 'Wang' in Worcester, nearly five years afterward, and I got a note at the theatre which asked me if I would come around to a club I knew after the show and meet the author of 'Casey.' I went and was introduced to Ernest L. Thayer, a manufacturer of Worcester, a charming fellow; every one knew him and liked him. There you are."

It is needless to say that no Eighty-five dinner is complete without a recitation of our classic, the '85 epic, "Casey at the Bat." In the absence of the author, E.L. Thayer, it was recited most acceptably by Roland Boyden, himself a ball tosser of no mean fame. In introducing himself he took occasion to pleasantly satirize the captain of the victorious nine of the morning and the other players [*HUC*, 6 (1905)].

Edward D. Thayer, Jr. Dies

Albert gave up his New York law practice and moved his family to Europe in June 1907. He and Ernest were both across the Atlantic when their brother Ed suffered an appendicitis attack in early July 1907, a couple of weeks after he turned 51. After a week's decline he died at the Scofield mansion at 973 Main Street, Worcester, on July 16. Ed was called the most prominent woolen manufacturer in the East "and probably the largest individual woolen manufacturer in the United States" at the time of his death, in his obituary in the *Worcester Spy*. So Ernest came back to Worcester to settle his brother's extensive estate. When trust companies learned of his effectiveness in this pursuit several of them wanted him to direct their firms, but he turned them all down. (*Harvard University, Class of 1875, Secretary's Report* 10 [1925]; *SPY*, 7/17/1907; and *SBN-P*, 8/22/1940.)

CHAPTER 31

The Authorship Question

In 1908, the twentieth anniversary year of the first publication of "Casey at the Bat," several pretenders to its authorship surfaced around the country. Thayer was frequently asked to provide a history for the poem as proof that he was the rightful author. *Baseball Magazine* published two articles on the authorship question that year; they both contained commentary by Thayer. The first article, written by John W. Glenister in the June issue, was "Who Wrote 'Casey at the Bat'?" He alluded to the great success Hopper had enjoyed in reciting the poem, and asked Thayer's opinion of the authorship controversy surrounding the poem:

> Mr. Thayer says that he had no inkling up to that time of the immense success that had been achieved by Mr. Hopper. Mr. Thayer goes on to say: "The claimants to the authorship of 'Casey' multiply through the years, and I am getting a little tired of the subject. I have heard of as many as three in as many weeks. Some years ago the supporters of a man named Valentine had a long and very circumstantial account about when and where he wrote the verses, in a Los Angeles paper. Valentine was dead at the time, but the story of his career interested me so much that I employed a Pinkerton detective to look into the matter. It is simply impossible to stop this kind of thievery, but I would cheerfully give up a little money for the pleasure of scorching one of the thieves. I started on the trail of two other claimants, only to find that they had found refuge in the grave. If I can get hold of a live one, who is a person of any consideration, I should like to make the beggar ashamed of himself."

In the magazine's October issue Homer Croy got Thayer to say more on the conditions that led up to his creation of the famous baseball lyric:

> I am becoming just a little touchy on the subject, since my friends are alarmingly versatile in throwing it up to me, but here it is without sauce or seasoning:
>
> It was through William R. Hearst that I came to write the now famous poem, "Casey at the Bat." I came to know Mr. Hearst through association with him on the *Lampoon*, Harvard's humorous publication. For a term Mr. Hearst was business manager of that organ, while I did

creative work. During the years 1883, 1884, and 1885 I wrote jokes, composed editorials, and designed drawings, putting in much faithful time. During my junior year I was president of the *Lampoon.*

At the time the *Lampoon* had a splendid corps of men, numbering in the list F.H. Briggs of Springfield, Mass., one of the best men that ever graced the staff; Eugene Lent of San Francisco, now a prominent lawyer; Conway Felton of Philadelphia, a great-nephew of the President of Harvard, Cornelius Conway Felton; W.W. Baldwin of Baltimore, who was Assistant Secretary of State under Cleveland; Tommy Sanborn of Concord, son of Frank Sanborn, poet; Samuel E. Winslow of Worcester, the well-known skate manufacturer; and Adams Crocker of Fitchburg, Mass.

After graduation I went abroad for a year, and on returning had nothing special to do. Meanwhile Hearst had gone back to San Francisco and taken charge of the *Examiner,* and was making things pretty lively, for he was just beginning to display his marvelous ability. At his request I went to that city and became a member of the staff. There I found Briggs drawing pictures and comics, and Lent writing special articles. To me was assigned the task of doing editorials, specials, and reporting. I fear that my work was more varied than I was versatile.

But still I did not have any intention of taking up newspaper work seriously. I had gone to the coast with a view of seeing the country, and for a change rather than learning the newspaper business.

In the fall of 1887 I began to read W.S. Gilbert's "Bab Ballads," and decided that I could do something in that line. I wrote a poem for each Sunday issue of the *Examiner* for three months. Not being particularly robust, however, my health failed and in February, 1888, I went to my brother's mill in Worcester, Mass., for lack of anything else to occupy my attention. I think that "Casey at the Bat" was the last of these attempts of mine.

For a year and six months I wrote voluminously for the *San Francisco Examiner,* turning out everything from editorials to obituaries. The demand was heavy, and the competition *nil.* What impression I may have had on the Pacific Slope I have never been able to gauge. The great, luminous and unforgettable fact in connection with it was that it paid me $5 a column. However, at the end of a year and six months my health broke and I had to return East.

I was never a baseball fan, and never was even interested in any degree in the game and it was only on account of my friend, classmate and associate on the *Lampoon,* Sam Winslow, that I became interested. Naturally, as Sam was captain of the nine – one of the best nines that Harvard ever had – one that went through a season without a defeat – that I felt stirred. I scribbled "Casey" during May, 1888, and it was printed in the *Examiner* on June 3, 1888.

Now prior to the publication of "Casey" in the *Examiner* no one ever heard of "Casey" and those that claim the authorship have been singularly unable to produce a paper containing that bit of verse. The *Examiner* was not then read much in the East, so the verse did not appear at first to get much of a circulation. The *New York Sun* reprinted a portion of the poem – the last eight stanzas, not using the rest owing to lack of space.

There have been made attempts to fill in the first five stanzas that did not appear in the *Sun,* but most of them have been manifestly inferior to the remainder of the verses. A reading of the poem in its entirety cannot but convince one, I am prone to believe, but that they form one continuous whole, and that the man who wrote the first five is also the author of the remaining eight.

I evolved "Casey" from the situation I had seen so often in baseball – a crack batsman coming to the bat with the bases filled, and then fallen down. Every one well knows what immense excitement there is when that situation occurs in baseball, especially when one of the best batsmen of the team comes up. The enthusiasm is at fever heat and if the batsman makes good the crowd goes wild; while, if the batsman strikes out as "Casey" did, the reverse is the case and the silence that prevails is almost appalling – and very often the army of the disappointed cannot refrain from giving vent to their feelings. In '85 Winslow's great Harvard team pulled out game after game in grand style when the issue seemed lost; Winslow, who was a born leader, never letting up but urging his men on to renewed effort and with splendid results.

It was a long time before the "Casey" verses became known. When they appeared in the San Francisco *Examiner* they were signed "E.L.T." They were claimed by one John Quinlan Murphy, of St. Louis. We looked this party up and found he had died. Then there was a Valentine of Sioux City, Nebraska. Another writer has appeared in the East as a claimant. It is asserted that the verses were printed in a New York sporting weekly in 1886. Were that so it is strange indeed they did not attract public attention, that they were not copied as were those printed in the *Examiner.* According to this claimant almost two years intervened from the appearance of his verses and my own. I never knew of the existence of the New York sporting paper.

The publicity of the poem, made through its recitation by Hopper and the declaration of the author, caused me to receive many requests for the original and correct text. For years I never went anywhere that I was not requested to recite "Casey." This was continued to such an extent that it seemed very much like taking a rise out of me. All my classmates were aware of the fact that I wrote "Casey" and they scouted the idea that any one else should claim the authorship.

"Casey at the Bat" has been printed in book, in many editions, and with varying illustrations, and I have generally been given the credit of the authorship. DeWolf Hopper and I became quite good friends through my accredited authorship of the poem that he was reciting to cheering houses.

"But, Mr. Thayer," I cross-questioned, "when you dashed off the immortal 'Casey' did you know that the Muse was hovering low?"

"No," he laughed, "I really didn't, but now – "

"And thus 'Casey of the Mudville Nine,' now dear to millions of hearts, was given to the world."

Henry M. Williams, Harvard class of 1885 secretary, was at least as annoyed as Thayer was about the spurious claims to the authorship of "Casey at the Bat." He took it upon himself, with the help of some Harvard lawyers, to run down the facts behind each claim. They were all exposed as fraudulent, although D'Vys claimed to his death in 1941 that he was the true creator of the poem, anyway ("Casey," 2/17/1933).

George Whitefield D'Vys

George Whitefield D'Vys was born in East Boston, Massachusetts, March 16, 1860. His father was a seafaring man, Captain George Cox D'Vys. His mother was Elizabeth Lucinda (Currie) D'Vys, a musician and writer. His father was also an artist; at one time he was an illustrator for Frank Leslie's, and was the illustrator for Jules Verne's *Arctic Tales.* With this pedigree George W. D'Vys might have been a noted writer himself. He claimed to have written "Casey at the Bat," but the ditties he wrote for the *Somerville Journal* in the early 1900s have none of the style or language of that ballad. Here is a representative poem, which was published on February 27, 1903:

Hurroo Fellers!

Men may talk an' write of their swelldom clubs,
Of the joys of the boys with their ancient tubs.
But there's nothing can equal the keen delight
Of a jolly ol' roaring fo'c'stle night.

In a good snug harbor, in ship staunch an' true,
With no watch to keep, an' with nothing to do
But to smoke an' to listen while mates recite
The wild, stirring yarns of a fo'c'stle night.

There's gallons of coffee, an' plenty of pie,
An' the best of good feeling as hours whirl by.
An' no song ever written equals in might
The songs that are sung on a fo'c'stle night.

Then here's to the ships that at anchor do lay!
They'll stand out to sea at the break of the day.
An' here's to the Jackies who sing an' recite,
An' add to the joys of a fo'c'stle night.

George Whitefield D'Vys
[*WWIA*, 7:613; and SJ, 4/28/1899, 9/28/1900]

It is no wonder that poetry experts rejected the claim of D'Vys. His style may have had its following, but it is hard to imagine that the author of these and other similar verses could have written the cleverly poignant "Casey at the Bat." D'Vys, who lived in Somerville most of his life, had the *Somerville Journal* in his corner. On May 15, 1908, the *Journal* declared, vaguely:

> Authorship Settled
>
> Referring to the controversy now agitating so many editorial pens, as to who wrote "Casey at the Bat," we feel sure that George Whitefield D'Vys, who was for many years a well-known and highly-respected resident of Somerville, knows well his ground when he claims the authorship of the famous ballad, and withal is too wise to foolishly jeopardize a great reputation sought for and earned under the most trying physical conditions.
>
> Realizing his twofold affliction, his friends well understand how eleven years could elapse without his having knowledge of the fact that his verses had won favor, and with the awakening ten years ago, when the Boston Sunday *Globe* printed them under the name of another, no doubt, as Mr. D'Vys states, he received the greatest surprise of his eventful life. At this time he was helplessly crippled at his home here in Somerville, so that to another was given the matter of making a protest, and this unfortunately led to the going astray of the proofs then presented the *Globe* as to his authorship.
>
> All this, however, now bids fair to appear at an opportune moment, and the great question will be forever settled while the tablet called for by the Boston *Journal* must be erected before the house, 25 Houghton street, this city, for years the home of Mr. D'Vys.

Because Thayer would not provide any specific details as to the background of the poem, D'Vys devised a scenario that is plausible on the surface but does not stand up to scrutiny. He claimed that Mudville was a section of Somerville, and the theme of the ballad was taken from a parallel situation in the Chicago-Boston series in 1886. King Kelly struck out with the bases full, and D'Vys, inspired by the mournful scene around him, scribbled the poem in a flash. Since his rugged seafaring father abhorred his literary efforts, D'Vys said, he had to submit the poem anonymously to a New York sports journal (*Sporting Times*). Someone later tacked on the first five stanzas, thus corrupting his gem (*WG*, 6/1/1941).

Since D'Vys claimed authorship of just the last eight stanzas, his Mudville would not need to have the topography described in the fifth stanza—the mountain, the valley, the delta, and the flat. He says the game in question was played in 1886 between the Chicagos and the Bostons in Boston. All the Mudville fans were devastated when King Kelly struck out. Why would they be? Kelly was still with Chicago in 1886. Boston fans, no matter where they lived, would have been overjoyed if Kelly struck out; that would have meant victory for Boston. An artistic man with a literary and musical wife would probably encourage a son's creative urges, not attempt to stifle them. It was Thayer who had the "stern parent," who wanted him to stick to business and forget journalistic endeavors (*BENC*, 1090).

De Wolf Hopper said that D'Vys was just one of "some ten thousand imposters." He said that Thayer was the only one who gave him any other examples of his writing, and he was convinced beyond a doubt that Thayer was the author. "Thayer had an art of using words, giving a lilt to the lines. His sense of the ridiculous was rare. Rare" (*NYT*, 6/1/1941; and *SEP*, 11/14/1925, 9).

Have It Notarized

To Dr. Harry Thurston Peck fell the task of sifting through all the evidence and declaring once and for all who wrote "Casey at the Bat," which in question form was the title of his article in *The Scrap Book* in December 1908. An editor's note gave the background for the probe:

> For twenty years there has been carried on a sharp discussion as to who wrote the popular baseball lyric, "Casey at the Bat." The conclusions hitherto reached have been so unsatisfactory that the editor of *The Scrap Book* decided to have the controversy thoroughly sifted out and a definite result obtained. To this end the subject was turned over to Dr. Harry Thurston Peck, with the request that he follow up every possible clue and go to first-hand sources. As he is not acquainted with any of the claimants to the authorship of the poem, and as he has had long experience in literary investigation, it was felt that he would succeed in solving this much-vexed question with authority, and thereby lay it forever at rest. What follows is his report, made after the most painstaking and accurate research.

The poem appeared at the beginning of the article "so that all readers can have it before them while they consider what I have to report." Moreover, "'Casey at the Bat' deserves to appear at frequent intervals because of its own very genuine merits," wrote Peck. The poem printed was a seriously corrupted version. Where *The Scrap Book* got it is anyone's guess. Since the first known printing of the poem was in the *San Francisco Daily Examiner*, Peck's first inquiry was to persons who had worked on that paper in 1888. Eugene Lent sent the following letter:

> You ask me what I know about the authorship of "Casey at the Bat." In reply I can only say that the poem was written by Mr. Ernest Lawrence Thayer of Worcester, Massachusetts. I am under the impression that Mr. Thayer wrote "Casey at the Bat" at Worcester, and forwarded it by mail to the *Examiner* in this city, where it was first published, because I was at Worcester with Thayer about the time he received a remittance from the *Examiner*, which was in payment of the poem.
>
> Mr. Thayer is a graduate of Harvard of the class of '85, and during the last three years at Cambridge he was president of the *Harvard Lampoon*. A reference to the files of the *Lampoon* for the years '83, '84, and '85 will give one an idea of Thayer's versatility in literature.

> After graduation, Thayer spent a year or more in Paris, and from that city contributed a series of letters to the San Francisco *Examiner*. He then came to San Francisco and did routine journalistic work on the *Examiner*, as well as being part of its editorial staff, for a year or more.
>
> The Sunday Supplement in those days, for the greater part, was written by the regular employees of the paper, and Thayer had a regular column to fill every Sunday, which he did under the name of "Phin."
>
> Thayer also contributed a series of ballads every other Sunday for a period of time, and many humorous poems, none of which, however, ever attained the popularity of "Casey at the Bat."

The next testimony supporting Thayer's claim was Mr. Lewis J. Stellmann, a San Francisco journalist: "There is no reasonable doubt in the minds of old-time newspaper men here that E.L. Thayer is the only and original author of "Casey at the Bat." The circumstances are well remembered, and I have been so fortunate as to find a man who rounds out the whole chain of evidence by saying that he remembers Thayer's being paid for the poem and helping him spend the money."

Theodore F. Bonnet, editor of *Town Talk,* published in San Francisco, wrote:

> I was doing baseball for the *Examiner* when young Hearst came out from Harvard to manage the paper. He brought with him E.L. Thayer, better known as "Phinney" Thayer, Eugene Lent (now a lawyer in San Francisco) and an artist, whose name I do not recall. All were classmates of Hearst at Harvard. While there, I understand Thayer was editor of the *Harvard Lampoon,* and Hearst was the business manager. Thayer was a baseball enthusiast and attended nearly every game played at the old Haight-street grounds. I remember the boys around the office talking about his forthcoming poem on baseball, and we were all much interested when it appeared in print. We never thought, though, that it would become a classic; and it probably never would have, had not De Wolf Hopper recited it all over the country. This was some years after its appearance in 1888, and I never heard of its authorship being disputed until a good while after Hopper took it up. Thayer used to write verse and jokes for the *Examiner*'s editorial page and usually signed them "Phin," as "Casey at the Bat" is signed. There can be no doubt of his authorship, and it is only because Thayer is such a modest, easy-going chap that a prompt and emphatic denial did not dispose of the question, once and for all, years ago.

There was no corroborating evidence to support the people who credited the poem to either Will Valentine or Joseph Quinlan Murphy, so those claims were dismissed. The last claimant dealt with was George Whitefield D'Vys. Peck asked D'Vys to write his version of the poem's composition, since Peck knew of no other person who could support his claim. D'Vys wrote a rambling letter, which Peck included in abridged form. Here is a further abridgement, limited to the events of the Sunday in August 1886, when he claims to have written the last eight stanzas of "Casey at the Bat" in the company of his friend Ed Cleveland:

> I tossed myself upon a knoll overlooking a ball-field. While reclining there and musing, I suddenly observed the diamond. It was all evolution. From there I wafted to the dear old South End ball-grounds – Boston – and there flashed to memory a day I should never forget, when at a crisis a noted player *fanned* and dashed all hope. Then came thoughts of the "king," Mike Kelly; and quickly I was *all* baseball, and then like a flash the incident I have referred to went into a rime. I was fairly wild as it mapped out itself – yes, wild. I wasn't a newspaper correspondent in those days, so had neither note-book nor pencil to jot down what was in my head; but I said it over and over again to "keep it."
>
> Ed came back and had a pencil, but no paper. Over the field came flying a portion of some one's Sunday *Globe*. I secured it, and then in the margin wrote the first and last words of each line and put the memoranda in my pocket. Ed was as wild over that rime as myself, and when I got home I wrote it – "There was ease in Casey's manner, etc., and the thirty-two lines I sent to Mr. O.P. Caylor of the New York *Sporting Times*, of which I held his red card credentials as correspondent.
>
> Yes, sir, I wrote "Casey" as then printed. Who tacked on the front end, I cannot say.

Peck noted that D'Vys claimed to have written the last eight stanzas only. He wrote to Ed Cleveland in Shelby, Montana, for verification of this story. Cleveland replied:

> Your favor under date of June 21 came to hand at last. My reason for not replying to your communication upon receipt of it, was because I wanted to get that poem as you have it, and compare it with what I *know* to be the original, written by George W. D'Vys one Sunday p.m. the last of September, 1889, in Franklin Park, now a part of Boston, known as Dorchester district. I remember it very distinctly, for the circumstances connected therewith made me, in a way, instrumental in leading him to write it.

The three-year discrepancy between D'Vys's and Cleveland's stories makes all the difference in the world. No copy of the *New York Sporting Times* could be found. It had suspended publication by 1908 and O.P. Caylor was dead. A blatant contradiction in the letter from D'Vys was that at first he said he was not a newspaper correspondent in 1886, then in a later paragraph he said he carried red card credentials as correspondent for the *Sporting Times*.

"Having gathered all of this material, and having spent much time upon a careful verification of dates, and having considered the different variants of the poem as it has appeared in many publications, it became evident that the right of authorship belongs either to Mr. Thayer or to Mr. D'Vys," Peck concluded. He then asked each of them to state his case as briefly as possible and to make an affidavit before a notary public or a justice of the peace. Thayer answered immediately, "almost by return mail":

Commonwealth of Massachusetts,
Worcester, ss.

August 19, 1908.

Ernest L. Thayer, of the city and county of Worcester and Commonwealth aforesaid, being duly sworn on oath deposes and says:

All of the thirteen stanzas composing the ballad entitled "Casey at the Bat" were written by me for the San Francisco *Examiner* in the spring of 1888, and were published, I think, on the 3d of June in that year. The exact date of publication can be determined by consulting the file of the *Examiner*. I went to San Francisco in the summer of 1886 at the request of W.R. Hearst for the purpose of joining the staff of the *Examiner*. Mr. Hearst had just received the paper as a gift from his father, who had employed it as a political organ in his campaign for the Senatorship from California. Young Hearst had associated with me at Harvard College in the publication of the *Lampoon*, and when, immediately after leaving college, the *Examiner* fell into his hands, he asked me and two other friends, Eugene Lent and F.H. Briggs, to come out and lend him a hand. I was in San Francisco until the winter of 1887–1888, when my health gave out and I was obliged to return East. When connected with the *Examiner* I wrote a good deal for all departments of the paper, but my most successful contributions were a series of ballads which were begun in the fall of 1887, and continued on Sundays for the rest of the year. After I returned home I still occasionally sent something to the *Examiner*, and "Casey at the Bat" was, I think, the last thing which I sent. In 1896, Hearst asked me to resume the series of ballads in the columns of the New York *Journal*. I wrote four ballads for the *Journal*, now the *American*, in the fall and winter of 1896-1897.

[Seal] Ernest L. Thayer

Personally appeared the above named Ernest L. Thayer to me well known, and signed and made oath to the foregoing affidavit before me.

[Seal] Charles F. Aldrich
Notary Public

I wish to add to my official certificate the statement that I have known Ernest L. Thayer intimately for more than thirty years in this city, where we were both brought up and have lived most of our lives, and where his character for veracity and integrity are unimpeachable, and can be attested by a very large number of its best known citizens. I have known for at least fifteen years that he was the author of "Casey at the Bat," and have heard him recite it certainly as long as that.

Dr. Peck had a lot more trouble getting an answer from D'Vys:

> In answer to my request for an affidavit from Mr. D'Vys, I first received from him a letter stating that he was, at the time, confined to the house by illness, but that he would send a sworn statement at an early date. In the course of a fortnight he wrote again to the effect that he had gone to Boston in search of a particular justice of the peace who was acquainted with his family and before whom he wished to make his affidavit; but that this justice of the peace was temporarily absent. He did not choose to avail himself of the services of the hundreds of notaries public and justices of the peace who were not absent from their offices, but waited another fortnight, and then sent me, without any comment or explanation, a document in all essential particulars identical with his letter which I have already given above. This declaration he did not choose to put into the form of an affidavit. In the first sentence he had originally written: "I, the under signed, George Whitefield D'Vys, . . . do hereby *swear* to the truth of the following statements made by me on this, the thirty-first day of August in the year of our Lord 1908." Before signing the document, however (or, at least, before sending it to me), he erased with his pen the word "swear" and substituted for it the word "declare."

Dr. Peck printed the rambling letter that followed the declaration "since it throws a good deal of light on Mr. D'Vys's literary gifts and mental processes." Fearing that his first story was a fizzle, this time D'Vys went back to 1885, to a fine Sunday afternoon in May, this time with his mother on Cambridge Common. He supposedly wrote what became the last stanza of "Casey" in a small booklet he had while mama read the *Boston Globe*. Their leisure was interrupted by a runaway horse, and the two of them romped after it. When they regained their original location, both the booklet and the *Globe* were gone. D'Vys is sure that whoever grabbed his booklet included that stanza in a poem rightfully belonging to him. Did he give up trying to claim eight stanzas and now wants credit for just one? No, once again he contradicts himself. He says the last stanza "ever stayed by me," and that he later wrote the rest of the poem. After writing D'Vys yet another letter repeating his original request, and "after some further delay and several letters of explanation," Dr. Peck received the following from a notary public in Boston:

> Boston, Mass.
> October 14, 1908
>
> Suffolk, ss.
> Personally appeared before me, a Notary Public for and within the Commonwealth of Massachusetts, George D'Vys, of Cambridge, Massachusetts, and made oath that the statement recently made by him to Professor Harry Thurston Peck, New York City, to be published in *The Scrap Book,* in relation to that portion of the baseball ballad known as "Casey at the Bat," is a true statement of the facts.
>
> [Seal] (Signed) Thomas W. Spencer,
> Notary Public

Professor Peck thought a letter Thayer had written to *Baseball Magazine* on June 29, 1908, contained the answer to the question of why D'Vys claimed just the last eight stanzas as his own:

> D'Vys asserts that he wrote the verses in August, 1886, and that they were printed, at a date unmentioned, in the New York *Sporting Times.* A representative of my lawyer has called on Mr. D'Vys and has asked him when and where he first printed the poem. He replied that it was first printed on August 14, 1886, but refused to say where.
>
> Mr. D'Vys's case, therefore, rests on a simple assertion supported only by a letter which has absolutely no value as evidence, inasmuch as it does not speak of the thing most essential to be known, namely, the date.
>
> There is one other fact which I will ask you to verify, and which throws a certain light on Mr. D'Vys's claim. Shortly after the *Examiner* printed "Casey," it was copied by the New York *Sun* with this significant alteration – the first five stanzas were cut off. This was done, probably, because the clipping editor had an equivalent amount of space to fill up. The *Sun*'s mutilated version was widely copied. In fact, the complete poem was known for some years only through Mr. Hopper's rendering of it and from the efforts of various people who had heard Mr. Hopper supply the missing stanzas. Mr. Hopper has assured me that he obtained his copy directly from the *Examiner* through the late Mr. Archibald Clavering Gunter. The "Casey" which Mr. D'Vys wrote on the grass, as he says, in 1886 was, therefore, this mutilated version which appeared in the *Sun* after June 3, 1888, and which most certainly never appeared anywhere else before that date.

At the conclusion of his investigation, Dr. Peck was sure of the following facts:

> 1. The full thirteen stanzas of "Casey at the Bat" appeared in the San Francisco *Examiner* of June 3, 1888, and were contributed to that paper by Mr. Ernest L. Thayer, of Worcester, Massachusetts, at that time a contributor to the *Examiner,* over the pseudonym of "Phin."
>
> 2. The poem cannot be shown to have appeared in any authentic publication before that date; while afterward it was not only published in many newspapers, but was recited by Mr. De Wolf Hopper on the stage.
>
> 3. No claimant for the authorship can produce a copy of the poem in the files of any magazine or newspaper prior to its appearance in the *Examiner*.
>
> 4. Mr. George W. D'Vys asserts that he wrote eight stanzas of it in August, 1886, and summons Mr. Edward L. Cleveland as a witness to the fact. Mr. Cleveland, however, gives a different date, and says that he positively knows Mr. D'Vys to have first shown him the poem in September, 1889, more than three years later.
>
> 5. Mr. Thayer makes a definite affidavit to the truth of his story before a notary public. Mr. D'Vys, after a long delay, sends an unsworn

> declaration, and then after a second delay sends an attestation in which his declaration is not incorporated; nor is the form of attestation a usual one, in that it is not signed by Mr. D'Vys.
>
> 6. With regard to the internal evidence, it seems obvious to me that the author of the first five stanzas must be the same person as the one who wrote the last eight stanzas. The whole poem, in fact, constitutes what a modern critic of French literature has aptly styled "a seamless unity." Furthermore, the writings of Mr. Thayer, both in the *Harvard Lampoon* and the San Francisco *Examiner,* show humor, facility of expression, and literary skill, such as one might expect from the author of "Casey at the Bat." On the other hand, whatever Mr. D'Vys has written and published falls below this literary standard, and affords no evidence that he could have written so popular and spirited a ballad.
>
> In my judgment, therefore, the evidence seems to be convincing and to prove beyond all question that Mr. Ernest L. Thayer is the author of "Casey at the Bat." As to the sincerity of Mr. D'Vys I do not feel justified in expressing an opinion. But the concrete facts have now been set forth fully.

It is hard to figure out what D'Vys's motivation was for claiming authorship of the poem. Was he a pathetic wanna-be or a clever jokester? He stalled around whenever he was asked for specific proof, had no proof, and yet persisted in his claim of authorship. In the years following this investigation he quoted Professor Peck's findings as support for *his* claim! So many of the things he said seem to be lifted out of statements written by or about Hopper or Thayer; it was as though he incorporated them into his routines as he came across them.

D'Vys claimed that when he composed "Casey" in his mind he had no paper or pencil, but "I said it over and over again to 'keep it'." De Wolf Hopper had been interviewed in a Boston paper in 1905 about his first recital of "Casey," and he said he memorized it in one hour and "kept it going in my mind."

When pinned down to the exact date the poem was published in *Sporting Times,* D'Vys chose August 14, 1886. August 14 was not only Thayer's birthday, it was also the date in 1888 when Hopper first recited "Casey."

D'Vys cleverly contradicted Thayer when he said that he and his energetic mother chased a runaway horse in Cambridge that Sunday afternoon in May 1885. Thayer gave his Ivy Oration on Class Day in June 1885, and in it he remarked: "It will be inferred from what I have said that the climate of Cambridge is peculiarly conducive to uneventful lives. This is the fact. Lightning never strikes there, horses never run away, dogs never fight. Burglars, pickpockets and circuses shun the town. There is no chance in Cambridge for the young man of heroic intentions." His Ivy Oration was published and available to the public (Ivy Oration, Class Day, 6/19/1885).

D'Vys says he lost the little book in which he wrote his poems on

Cambridge Common, and that the thief obviously took the poem as his own. This was in May 1885. He doesn't come straight out and name the man he suspects, but he hopes his audience knows that Ernest Thayer was right there in Cambridge at that time, finishing his final year at Harvard (*WG*, 6/1/1941).

Thayer's Official Modified "Casey"

By the end of 1908 there were many corrupted versions of "Casey at the Bat" being printed and recited across the country. Thayer agreed to send an official version to the *Bookman*; it appeared in the January 28, 1909, number:

"Casey at the Bat"
(The Authorised Version)

[This poem is a classic in the baseball world, and is known by heart to almost every enthusiastic frequenter of the diamond. It was originally published in the *San Francisco Examiner,* and was written by Mr. Ernest L. Thayer, at that time a member of the *Examiner*'s staff, but now a well-known resident of Worcester, Massachusetts. It appeared in 1888, and was immediately copied by the newspapers all over the country, and publicly recited, most conspicuously by Mr. De Wolf Hopper. In the course of time, various inaccuracies crept into the different versions, some of them marring the admirable ballad-metre. We give here by permission of Mr. Thayer the authorised text.—Editors of the *Bookman.*]

The outlook wasn't brilliant for the Mudville nine that day;
The score stood four to two with but one inning more to play;
And then when Cooney died at first, and Barrows did the same,
A pall-like silence fell upon the patrons of the game.

A straggling few got up to go in grim despair. The rest
Clung to that hope which springs eternal in the human breast;
They thought "If only Casey could but get a whack at that—
We'd put up even money now with Casey at the bat."

But Flynn preceded Casey as did also Jimmy Blake,
And the former was a hoodoo, while the latter was a cake;
So upon that stricken multitude grim melancholy sat,
For there seemed but little chance of Casey getting to the bat.

But Flynn let drive a single, to the wonderment of all,
And Blake, the much despis-ed, tore the cover off the ball;
And when the dust had lifted, and men saw what had occurred,
There was Jimmy safe at second and Flynn a-hugging third.

Then from five thousand throats and more there rose a lusty yell;
It rumbled through the valley, it rattled in the dell;

It pounded on the mountain and recoiled upon the flat,
For Casey, might Casey, was advancing to the bat.

There was ease in Casey's manner as he stepped into his place;
There was pride in Casey's bearing and a smile lit Casey's face.
And when, responding to the cheers, he lightly doffed his hat,
No stranger in the crowd could doubt 'twas Casey at the bat.

Ten thousand eyes were on him as he rubbed his hands with dirt;
Five thousand tongues applauded when he wiped them on his shirt.
Then while the writhing pitcher ground the ball into his hip,
Defiance flashed in Casey's eye, a sneer curled Casey's lip.

And now the leather-covered sphere came hurtling through the air,
And Casey stood a-watching it in haughty grandeur there.
Close by the sturdy batsman the ball unheeded sped–
"That ain't my style," said Casey; "Strike one!" the umpire said.

From the benches, black with people, there went up a muffled roar,
Like the beating of the storm-waves on a stern and distant shore;
"Kill him! Kill the umpire!!" shouted some one on the stand;
And it's likely they'd have killed him had not Casey raised his hand.

With a smile of Christian charity great Casey's visage shone;
He stilled the rising tumult; he bade the game go on;
He signalled to the pitcher, and once more the dun sphere flew;
But Casey still ignored it, and the umpire said, "Strike two!"

"Fraud!" cried the maddened thousands and echo answered "Fraud!"
But one scornful look from Casey and the audience was awed.
They saw his face grow stern and cold, they saw his muscles strain,
And they knew that Casey wouldn't let that ball go by again.

The sneer has fled from Casey's lip, his teeth are clinched in hate;
He pounds with cruel violence his bat upon the plate.
And now the pitcher holds the ball, and now he lets it go,
And now the air is shattered by the force of Casey's blow.

Oh, somewhere in this favoured land the sun is shining bright;
The band is playing somewhere, and somewhere hearts are light,
And somewhere men are laughing, and little children shout;
But there is no joy in Mudville–great Casey has struck out.

Ernest L. Thayer.

Each 1885 graduate was allowed 200 words to bring his classmates up to date on his activities in the *Secretary's Report*. Ordinarily, Thayer used a small percentage of the 200 words, but in 1910 he reviewed his life since leaving Harvard:

> Immediately after leaving college I spent a year abroad, then went to San Francisco to join the staff of Hearst's *Examiner*. I wrote for this

paper in various capacities till the winter of 1888, when, my health failing, I returned to Worcester, my home. For the following eight years I remained in Worcester, engaging in a desultory way in the woollen business. In 1892 my health broke down completely, and since then my main concern has been to get it back again. By virtue of an unshakable optimism I have pretty well succeeded in doing so. In 1902 I began to take enough interest in life to find pleasure in foreign travel, and since then I have lived a good deal abroad. The prospect now seems excellent for a serene, if useless, old age.

Williams added: "As the author of 'Casey at the Bat,' Thayer made a contribution of permanent value to English literature. The unwarranted claims by various individuals to its authorship were completely disposed of as the result of investigations conducted by Boyden a year or two ago" (*HUC*, 7 [1910]). The *Secretary's Report* also included an article about "Casey at the Bat":

Eighty-five takes a family pride in Ernest L. Thayer's authorship of the classic, "Casey at the Bat." It has been recited either by its author or by his baseball understudy, Boyden, at every formal dinner of the Class since it became known to the world. No dinner would be complete without it. It has been reprinted in Report V, page 88, and the story of how DeWolf Hopper came to use it for stage recitals was told in Report VI, page 91.

During the past five years a whole crop of aspirants to the authorship of these popular lines has sprung up. The claims of some of them have been urged persistently in newspaper and periodical by the column and page. Finally Thayer determined to establish by legal proof not only the exact facts of its composition by him and first publication, but the falsity of all other claims. Among them was that of a man named D'Vys, who declared he had written and published eight of the verses nearly two years in advance of Thayer. The simple fact is that it was written by Thayer in May and published June 3, 1888, in the *San Francisco Examiner*.

It has also been proved that the paper to which D'Vys claimed he sent it, the New York *Sporting Times*, had not come into existence at the date he sets for its publication; and the copy of that paper of July 29, 1888, actually contains the last eight verses in substantially correct form, except "Casey" is changed to "Kelly," and it is acknowledged as *adapted from the San Francisco Examiner* [*ibid.*].

At this time Albert Spalding was collecting data for his book, *America's National Game*. He wrote to Thayer asking him for the history of the poem. Thayer wrote to Spalding at his Point Loma, California, home from Rome on April 9, 1909: "'Casey at the Bat' was correctly printed in the *Bookman* for January last from copy furnished by me. The poem has no history; it was written in the regular course of business when I was a journalist on the staff of the S.F. *Examiner* (Albert Spalding, 448).

Spalding's book came out in 1911, and he did not hesitate to call "Casey at the Bat" a classic. "Love has its sonnets galore; War its epics in heroic verse; Tragedy its sombre story in measured lines, and Base Ball has 'Casey at the Bat'." By that Time "Base Ball" also had its celebratory song; "Take Me Out to the Ball Game" was written in 1908 by Albert Von Tilzer (music) and Jack Norworth (words); it has been sung in ballparks ever since, especially during the seventh-inning stretch. Anyone who knows the verses knows that the young lady requesting her beau to take her out to the ball game is Miss Katie Casey (*ibid.*, 449; and York Music Co., 1908).

PART V

California — Back to Stay

CHAPTER 32

At Long Last Love

In 1912 Thayer abandoned Worcester as his home for the last time. He went to the Santa Barbara suburb of Montecito in October with the idea of spending the winter at the Miramar resort on the shores of the Pacific Ocean. It was during his stay at the Miramar that he met Rosalind Buel Hammett, widow of Benjamin Forrest Hammett. She was vacationing with her son Buell, who had been given the family name Buel, but changed the spelling. Mrs. Hammett was the daughter of James William Buel, a noted historical author. The twenty books he had written, including *Russian Nihilism and Exile Life in Siberia, The World's Wonders, Sea and Land, Heroes of the Dark Continent, America's Wonderlands,* and *Beautiful Paris,* had aggregate sales of more than 6 million copies. He retired to San Diego, California, after being based in St. Louis during his years of traveling and writing (*HUC*, 8 [1915]; JBB to authors, 12/30/1987, 1/16/1988; and *NCAB*, 75–76).

At the age of 49 Ernest felt the "divine fire and nothing shorter" he had written about so many years before, and on September 9, 1913, just after he turned 50, he and Rosalind were married at the home of her father and stepmother (JBB to authors, 1/16/1988).

On September 10 the *San Diego Union*'s "In Society" by Petronius described the wedding:

> Unpretentious and quiet but charming in its appointments was the wedding of Mrs. Rosalind Buel Hammett of San Diego and Ernest Lawrence Thayer of Santa Barbara, which took place at high noon yesterday in the home of the bride's parents, Mr. and Mrs. J.W. Buel, 3526 Seventh street. The Episcopal ring ceremony was used. Rev. Charles L. Barnes, rector of St. Paul's Episcopal church, performing the ceremony. . . .
>
> In deference to the wishes of the bride and bridegroom the guests were confined to the immediate relatives and intimate friends of the family. . . .
>
> In addition to the bride's parents those present at the ceremony and wedding breakfast were Richard Hall Buel, brother of the bride; Mr. and Mrs. N.H. Crawford of the San Dieguito ranch; Buell Hammett, son of the bride; Miss Eleanor Bissell and Miss Harper of Pasadena, and Rev. Charles L. Barnes.

Family gathering in 1914—James W. Buel, Anne Hill Buel, Dick Buel, Ernest Thayer and Jane Bradley (niece) (courtesy of Jane Bradley).

When they returned from their three-month honeymoon in Japan the Thayers took up residence at La Casita, their seaside bungalow at 2 Hixon Road in Montecito (*SBN-P*, 8/22/1940; and JBB to authors, 2/23/1988).

Mrs. Thayer's niece, Jane Buel Bradley, met her new uncle in 1914. She came to visit Montecito from St. Louis with her father and her mother, Rosalind's sister Marie. "I was six years old and I loved Uncle Ernest on first sight," she wrote. "He had a wonderful way of accepting people as they were, and our whole family, very different individuals, who sometimes clashed, felt the warmest affection for him. . . . We took walks together and he encouraged me to jump over his cane, which he held higher and higher with each jump. Uncle Ernest was deaf and sometimes wore a hearing aid but he preferred not to, since it made a constant noise in his ear that distressed him. He was around fifty then and his hair was shiny silver, quite thick, brushed over one side. His eyes were grey, full of sparkles and humor. His voice was very soft and he spoke with his native Massachusetts accent, always very expressively" (JBB to authors, 12/30/1987).

In the *Secretary's Report* of 1915 Thayer talked in his usual understated way about the past five years of his life: "My life has been quite uneventful. Until the fall of 1912 I passed a good deal of my time abroad. Italy especially attracted me, and above all places in Italy, Florence. In October, 1912, I came out to California, expecting only to pass the winter here; but I met the lady who has become my wife, and we have decided to make California our home. It is a singular fact that this year (1914-1915) there are wintering in this quiet little place four members of the class of 1885."

Secretary Williams told about the new illustrated edition of "Casey at the Bat" that was published by McClurg of Chicago in 1912. Then, as always, he gave an update of "Casey at the Bat": "The public interest in this classic of Thayer's still continues. A new illustrated edition has been printed. More vain attempts have been made to claim the authorship, and new parodies or verses concerning it have been written. It has even been used, illustrated, to advertise Anheuser-Busch" (*HUC*, 8[1915]).

Albert returned from Europe with his family in 1915. They moved back into their home in Flushing, New York. Ellen was now a teacher (*Harvard University, Class of 1875, Secretary's Report,* 10 [1925]).

Back in Binghamton, July 28 was Dan Casey Day. The city honored its favorite son with a five-mile parade through town and a ceremony at Johnson Field, the minor-league ballpark in Johnson City. He was presented the Dan Casey cup by Binghamton's citizens (Henderson, Dave, 34; and *TSN*, 5/23/1935).

Albert Goodwill Spalding

Albert G. Spalding turned 65 on September 2, 1915, and died on September 9. His first wife had died in 1899, and in 1900 he remarried. His second wife – a widow with two children whom Spalding adopted – was a member of the Theosophical Society and wanted to live at the society's picturesque seaside colony at Point Loma, in San Diego. He became an enthusiastic horseman and motorist and was a member of the San Diego Road Commission. In 1910 Spalding won the primary for U.S. senator, but lost the election. It was just as well, for he soon suffered one stroke and later another, which led to his death. His sporting goods company is still going strong. Spalding was elected to the Baseball Hall of Fame in 1939 (Appel and Goldblatt, 351).

CHAPTER 33

Hopper and "Casey" Go Hollywood

De Wolf Hopper, though well into his fifties in 1915, found support for his plan to play the leading role in a silent movie based on "Casey at the Bat." He needed Thayer's permission for the project and further wanted his friend to appear in an introductory scene with him. He flagged the Thayers down on the highway one night after he learned they were on their way to Ojai. Thinking he was a policeman, Mrs. Thayer, who always drove, pulled over. Hopper pleaded his case and Thayer responded yes and no. Yes, he gave permission for the project; no, he wanted no royalties and would not appear on film in an introduction with Hopper (*SBN-P*, 8/22/1940).

During the filming Hopper, who had always fancied himself quite a ballplayer, discovered he was too good to be true. He wrote a verse about his misfortune; it was printed in the *New York Times* under the headline, "The Second Tragedy of the Mighty Casey."

> De Wolf Hopper is eating his heart out today away out in California because the Lambs are gamboling in New York and he cannot gambol with them. The gloom of Mr. Hopper's friend Casey was as a California May day as compared with that of the comedian. In a telegram to Sam Wallack he thus expressed his anguish. Read Mr. Hopper's vers libre and register deep sympathy, not so much for the free verse as for Mr. Hopper:
>
> Hear my tragic story. A shadow has crossed my screen. My heart
> Is filled with static. I am all out of focus.
> Hear the tale; last week it was we were filming "Casey."
> And he and I were at the bat. Picture my pride,
> The bleachers of the little ballpark were
> Filled with native fans; we had real teams; it was
> Real ball; the time had come for me to make
> Casey's home run. No, it is not in the poem,
> But it is in the play. He strikes out later.
> "Can you hit the ball, Hopper?" they asked me.
> "I can," said I, and gripped the good stick.

My blood was up. So was the camera. On came the ball, and I swung
Exultantly. On the nose I hit it, and it drove
To the far outer field, rising not thirty feet from
The Ground. A true home-run hit. Picture my pride;
But now the tragedy. The film was made and shown us.
It immortalized me striking empty air. I had done too well.
No camera could register the swift flight of that hit.
And none will know that I really did this magnificent,
This incredible, this epochal thing.

De Wolf Hopper.

The *Times* Dramatic Department would like an option on the picture rights to this scenario [*NYT*, 6/24/1915].

There was no mention of Hopper's family in the article. He was involved in the fifth of his six marriages in 1915, and in January of that year his second son was born. His fifth wife, Ella Curry, would become one of the most powerful women in Hollywood as gossip columnist Hedda Hopper. Their son, William De Wolf, Jr., who inherited the rich voice of his father, would become a household name, too, as investigator Paul Drake in the long running television series "Perry Mason" (*Jupiter*, 6/5/1988, 8).

The picture was released June 22, 1916. What seemed like a good idea turned out to be a dud. "Fred," in *Variety,* wrote this review on June 23:

> Here is another De Wolf Hopper feature. To the exhibitor who has played Hopper features in the past a word to the wise is sufficient – to those who have not played any of them one needs but to say that this Triangle-Fine Arts feature is just another example of a good idea gone wrong. "Casey at the Bat" has been a standby of Mr. Hopper's in recitative form for many years. It should have made a corking subject for a comedy picture, but William Everett Wing, who adapted the scenario, saw fit to make a cheap mushy heart thriller of the story and the result was that the tale, coupled with Mr. Hopper, who failed utterly to look the part, and who acted it extremely badly, did not turn out at all in the manner that one assumed it would from the title. As a feature film "Casey at the Bat" will fall short of expectations, although the title will attract money.
>
> Fred [*Variety*, 6/23/1916].

CHAPTER 34

World War I

The Thayers' plans to travel to Italy were confounded by World War I. Rosalind organized and managed the Red Cross canteen in Santa Barbara with great success. Ernest wrote to Secretary Williams, "my wife from the beginning of the war threw herself into Red Cross work with an ardor which told on her health." For his part, Ernest put his writing and financial talents to work by serving as local chairman of publicity for the second, third and fourth Liberty Loans, chairman of the second Red Cross War Fund, chairman of the United War Work Fund and cashier in the Salvage Shop. The *Santa Barbara News–Press,* in Thayer's obituary, noted that "he headed the Santa Barbara finance committee, which raised several millions of dollars for war work, the highest per capita percentage in the country." "Casey" was not forgotten during the war; a parody, "Wilhelm at the Bat," made the rounds and helped keep morale up (*SBN-P*, 8/22/1940; and *HUC*, 9 [1925]).

Influenza was the scourge of World War I; it was an epidemic on both sides of the Atlantic and killed an estimated 20 million people worldwide–548,000 in the United States. A little poem, showing how very contagious the disease was, made the rounds:

> Had a little bird, it's name was Enza.
> Opened up the window, in flew Enza.

Phoebe Hearst had contracted a serious case of influenza in Washington, DC. On recovering she returned to the Hacienda, her home in Pleasanton, California. She suffered a relapse, and on April 13, 1919, after suffering for two weeks, Phoebe Hearst, "California's greatest lady," died. She was buried next to her husband, the late senator. At her death she had donated over $21 million to kindergartens and other educational projects, especially those involving the education of women and the underprivileged. "Her benefactions in lectureships, fellowships, scholarships and book funds were innumerable. Mrs. Hearst was a woman of unusual energy, great tenacity of purpose and remarkable aptitude for philanthropy. She was small of stature, erect and graceful, with much tact and wit. She had a gift for the discovery of talent, encouraged ambition wherever she found it" (*DAB*, 489). Will Hearst, who inherited the bulk of her $11 million estate, had been traveling back and forth between his mother's bedside and his architect's office to check on plans for San Simeon. His five sons inherited the Hacienda and the *Examiner* building in San Francisco (WORLD, 521; and Swanberg, 321).

In July 1920 Ernest's dear sister-in-law, Josie, Albert's wife, died at Flushing. Later that year Rosalind lost her father; he died on November 16 in San Diego (*Harvard University, Class of 1875, Secretary's Report,* [1925]; and *NCAB*, 76).

CHAPTER 35

Still Not Sure About "Casey"

Ernest and Rosalind visited Albert and Nellie in April 1921, and on April 27 Ernest was honored at a luncheon at the Harvard Club in Cambridge. There was no scheduled Class of 1885 dinner that year, but the 1885ers couldn't let a rare visit by their Ivy Orator go uncelebrated. Fourteen classmen were present. Roland Boyden recited a sequel to Thayer's ballad written by sportswriter Grantland Rice, which Williams regarded as "a valuable addition to the bibliography on that subject and a fine tribute to its author." While they lunched, a bouquet of crimson roses was sent to Rosalind at the Thayers' hotel (*HUC*, 9 [1925], 284).

Arthur Irwin's Death

Arthur Irwin – star player of the 1880–82 Worcester National League team, first major-league shortstop to wear a fielding glove, captain of Harry Wright's Philadelphia Phillies, manager of several major- and minor-league teams – took his own life in the Atlantic Ocean. He jumped into the inky water around midnight as July 16 became July 17, 1921, from the steamer *Calvin Austin* en route from New York City to Boston. He was under treatment for an abdominal disorder that had bothered him quite a while. He had been told that only a risky, expensive operation would prolong his life beyond two months. The investigation into the suicide, begun by his son Herbert, exposed the double life Irwin had been leading for the last 30 years of his life. While he had a legal wife in Boston – Herbert's mother – he was head of a second household in New York City with a common-law wife, a son named Harold, and two daughters. Neither family was aware of the other. "Harold Irwin of New York visited his father while the latter was a patient at the local hospital, and several days ago when the Boston son, Arthur Herbert Irwin, came here the New Yorker was amazed when people spoke to him concerning the brother of whom he had never heard." Irwin, 63, spent most of his time with his New York family, and on his infrequent visits to Boston would invariably call Herbert by his New York son's name and had to be corrected. The mystery was solved for Herbert when he found out there really was a

Harold. When told of the New York family, legal wife Lizzie Irwin assessed no blame to her husband and said that any missteps he made were entirely the fault of the woman in New York City. A postscript added onto the last note he wrote to Lizzie hinted at Irwin's concealed matrimonial enthusiasm: "The bills were terribly heavy" (*NYT*, 7/17, 7/21/1921).

Twenty-two years after his death, John Patrick Parnell Cahill still had some people convinced that he was the one and only "Casey." *The Sporting News* printed an article titled "An Added Bit of 'Casey' History," written by Winfield Scott, "veteran fan and former player, and now and then contributor to baseball literature, with ideas always worthwhile." Scott asserted, "If there is anything that is settled in the literature of the game, it is that Ernest Thayer wrote 'Casey at the Bat,' and that the 'Casey' concerned was John Patrick Parnell Cahill." He wondered why some New York reporters were still trying to figure out who Casey was. "Whoever made the attempt must be still wet behind the ears and using a nursing bottle. . . . That Cahill was the original 'Casey' is settled beyond doubt–why raise the question now?" (*TSN*, 11/29/1923.)

Burton Stevenson included a letter from Thayer in his *Home Book of Verse* showing his opinion of "Casey" in 1923: "In general quality 'Casey' (at least in my judgment), is neither better nor worse than much of the other stuff. Its persistent vogue is simply unaccountable, and it would be hard to say, all things considered, if it has given me more pleasure than annoyance. The constant wrangling about the authorship, from which I have tried to keep aloof, has certainly filled me with disgust." Considering that all Thayer wanted was to spend his retirement quietly in the company of friends and family and travel when he wanted to, his testiness over the whole "Casey" question is understandable. Had he known in advance what a never-ending source of irritation his ballad was going to be, he probably would have passed up the $5 he got for it (Burton Egbert Stevenson, 126).

Albert Thayer left Flushing in September 1923 and went to Maryland to live with his daughter Ellen, who was teaching in Baltimore. His health was failing by then, and after months of very poor health he died of pneumonia at Ruxton, Maryland, on January 26, 1925. He had just turned 81 (*Harvard University, Class of 1875, Secretary's Report,* 10 [1925]).

After the hard work they both did on the war effort, Ernest and Rosalind adjusted back into a quiet life of travel and leisure. In 1925 Ernest wrote to Secretary Williams, "I have spent the past five years very pleasantly between my home in California and various European places of resort. My business continues to be that of an enthusiastic rooter on the sidelines" (*HUC*, 9 [1925]).

CHAPTER 36

Class of 1885's Pride and Joy

"Casey" was mentioned prominently in the 1925 *Secretary's Report*; if Thayer was ambivalent about having written the thing, his classmates were certainly proud of it and him:

> The classic still interests the public. Grantland Rice wrote a clever metrical appreciation of it entitled "Casey Comes Back," which Boyden has recited to the class. This has recently been reprinted. Rice has also written the "Man Who Never Heard of Casey." During the war "Casey" was parodied in "Wilhelm at the Bat." DeWolf Hopper still recites it upon the stage. Unwarranted claims to its authorship have been renewed. In the November 14, 1925, issue of the *Saturday Evening Post* an article by DeWolf Hopper and W.W. Stout tells much about "Casey at the Bat" and of E.L. Thayer the author, giving the poem in full. "Casey" is frequently reprinted, as called for, in Answers columns and in poetry corners. It is also to be found in Burton Stevenson's "Home Book of Verse" [*HUC*, 9 (1925), 284].

Rice's second poem mentioned above was prompted by a letter from a reader of his column in the New York *Herald Tribune,* "The Sportlight," who said that he had enjoyed Rice's sequel, "Casey's Revenge," but had never heard of the original "Casey at the Bat," and asked where he could get a copy. When Rice recovered, he dedicated his entire column of June 1, 1926, to "The Man Who Never Heard of Casey!" which read in part:

> The million never heard of Keats, or Shelley, Burns, or Poe;
> But they know "the air was shattered by the force of Casey's blow;"
> They never heard of Shakespeare, nor of Dickens, like as not
> But they know the somber drama from old Mudville's haunted lot.

On January 11, 1930, Thayer responded to an inquiry by the *Syracuse Post-Standard* as to the history of the poem. The paper was specifically interested in who "Casey" was, because all of Syracuse wanted to believe that local hero O. Robinson Casey was Thayer's inspiration. Thayer let them down easy, and – significantly – now called "Casey at the Bat" very much the best of the ballads he wrote for the *Examiner*:

> To the Editor of the *Post-Standard*:
>
> About "Casey at the Bat," I am sorry to say there is no story connected with the writing of those stanzas. The verses themselves owe their existence to my enthusiasm for college baseball, not as a player, but as a fan, and to my association while in college with Will Hearst, who engaged me to come to the *Examiner* in San Francisco after I graduated.
>
> I wrote voluminously for the *Examiner* during a period of a year and a half, beginning in the summer of 1886, and had most success with a series of so-called ballads. Some of these were written after I had resigned from the *Examiner* staff. "Casey" was the last and very much the best of the lot. It was written in Worcester, Mass., in the late spring of 1888. I called it "A Ballad of the Republic," as a sub-heading.
>
> The poem had no basis in fact. The only Casey actually involved, and I am not sure about him, was not a ball player. He was a big, dour Irish lad of my high school days. While in the high school I composed, and printed myself, a very tiny sheet, less than two inches by three. In one issue I ventured to gag, as we used to say, this Casey boy.
>
> He didn't like it, and he told me so, and while he discoursed his big, clenched red hands were white at the knuckles. This Casey's name never again appeared in *The Monohippic Gazette,* but I suspect the incident many years later suggested the title for the poem. It was a taunt thrown to the winds. God grant he never catches me.
>
> Ernest L. Thayer
> Santa Barbara, California [*SP-S*, 9/3/1935].

Sometime later in that same year the Thayers went to the Ford dealer in Santa Barbara to purchase a new car. Patrick Mahony, then a 19-year-old salesman and later a writer, recalled the impression Rosalind and Ernest made on him that day:

> I knew Mrs. Thayer slightly through my mother, Mrs. Frances Bliss. Mr. and Mrs. Thayer often came into the garage to have their old car serviced, but Mrs. Thayer always did the driving, as her husband was plagued with deafness at that time and wore a hearing aid. She always did the talking and her husband usually stood shyly by. I must say that Mrs. Thayer was one of the loveliest of Montecito matrons, who owned much dignity and charm. She was the type of woman who brings to one's mind the difference between being pretty and being beautiful. She was indeed striking in the latter sense.
>
> While selling the Thayers a car, I was able to observe Mr. Thayer more closely. The year was 1930 and he was then sixty-seven. In some respects, for me, he gave the impression of being older. His hair was white, but his eyes were young, kindly and alive. His face reflected New England, also London and Paris, which he knew well. There seemed to be humor in his entire countenance. When he talked, he was more whimsical than factual or argumentative, a distinct contrast to his charming wife, who was precise and definitive in her wishes. Both

> behaved with a courtesy which, even in those "modern" days, might have been described as "old world."
>
> I was then nineteen years old, and I recall I was smoking a cigar, doubtless to make myself look older. At once Mr. Thayer made a gesture, adding: "If you want to sell my wife a car, put out that cigar!" This was character-revealing in that Mr. Thayer seemed to be indifferent to everyone except his wife. I could see then that he was the type of man who lives entirely in a world of his own. For the first time I took a good look at him, alerted by this challenging order. The nose was long and mobile, the mouth wide and set, the chin like a wedge of rock....
>
> Actually, there was not much selling to be done, as Mrs. Thayer was a woman who obviously knew what she wanted, and the deal was closed in short order. Afterwards I took the signed contract to Mr. Fillmore, a civic-minded Santa Barbaran, and very popular, and he smilingly said, "That Mr. Thayer is the author of one of the most famous American poems, 'Casey at the Bat'." And to my amazement he proceeded to recite it word for word:
>
> The outlook wasn't brilliant for the Mudville nine that day;
> The score stood four to two, with but one inning left to play –
>
> Since I had come from England only a few years previously, where baseball was despised, I had never heard the verses before, and I soon forgot the incident. Mr. and Mrs. Thayer were often in and out of the Fillmore Ford Agency and we usually exchanged a few words. On one occasion I mentioned the poem, and I saw a flash of youth illuminate his face as he quickly changed the subject [Mahony, 71–75].

Nellie had been in poor health for quite a while, and on February 15, 1932, at the age of 70, she died in Worcester. She and Sam had lived in the same house at 36 Sever Street since they got married in 1886. Sam was still at that address when he died four years later. Ernest, the youngest member of his family, was the only one left now. His sister-in-law Florence Thayer, his nieces, and nephews were still in the East. Ernest had his own family in the West, one that he was proud to be a part of: Rosalind's son, Buell Hammett; a brother, Richard Buel; a sister, Marie Bradley; and a niece, Jane Buel Bradley. Rosalind's son Buell married and, lo and behold, Ernest soon had two grandsons – Benjamin Cowles and Lawrence Thayer Hammett. "Uncle Ernest loved them dearly," said Jane Bradley, "and often spoke of how lucky he was to have married into a ready-made family" (Grove St. [Rural] Cemetery, Thayer sarcophagus; 1887–1937; *WCD*; and JBB to authors, 12/30/1987).

Ernest was still recovering from Nellie's death when the pesky D'Vys resumed his claim to the authorship of "Casey at the Bat." The notice appeared from Cambridge in the *New York Times* on February 21. Thayer responded in the *Times* on March 13:

> I note in *The Times* of Feb. 21 a dispatch from Cambridge, Mass., in which G.W. D'Vys is reported as claiming authorship of "Casey at the Bat." He says he sent the poem in 1886 to the New York *Sporting Times*, where it was published anonymously.
>
> The first number of the New York *Sporting Times* appeared in 1888, and first, or a little later, number printed "Casey at the Bat" as a clipping and duly credited to the San Francisco *Examiner*, where it originally appeared over my initials in June, 1888.
>
> In the Christmas, 1908 issue of *The Scrap Book* an exhaustive examination, "Who Wrote 'Casey at the Bat'?" appeared over the signature of Harry Thurston Peck, at that time Professor of Latin at Columbia University. In the light of all the evidence Professor Peck reached the conclusion that for this, perhaps the greatest of my sins, I was exclusively to blame [*NYT*, 2/21, 3/13/1932].

The *Harvard Alumni Bulletin,* February 17, 1933, reviewed "Casey's" popularity as he approached the age of 45:

> "Casey at the Bat" has been called the great American epic, and if popularity is the test that description of it may be accepted. Someone has ventured the statement that for every person who has read or heard the poems of Edwin Arlington Robinson, for example, a thousand are familiar with "Casey at the Bat," and that similar comparisons could be made of the latter with the works of other American poets, living or dead. It sounds like treason to say so, but possibly even the familiar poems of Longfellow, for many years the favorite American writer of verse, have been eclipsed by this baseball lyric, to give it another definition. Harvard men are interested in it because it was written by a graduate of the College, Ernest L. Thayer, '85, now living in California.

Thayer had admitted in January 1930 that he now considered "Casey at the Bat" to be far and away the best thing he wrote for the *Examiner,* a real switch from his earlier attitude. Then William Lyon Phelps, noted Yale professor, included "Casey" in his anthology *What I Like in Poetry,* and wrote an introduction to the poem that might have reinforced Thayer's new admiration for the ballad:

> This graduate of Harvard University wrote a masterpiece which millions of ambitious men wish they had written. For *Casey* is absolute perfection. The psychology of the hero and the psychology of the crowd leave nothing to be desired. There is more knowledge of human nature displayed in this poem than in many of the works of the psychiatrists. Furthermore, it is a tragedy of Destiny. There is nothing so stupid as Destiny. It is a centrifugal tragedy, by which our minds are turned from the fate of Casey to the universal. For this is the curse that hangs over humanity – our ability to accomplish any feat is in inverse relation to the intensity of our desire. The declamatory art of DeWolf Hopper gave to this tragedy supreme unction.
>
> Dan Casey Again [*SBN-P*, 8/22/1940].

Ernest Thayer and grandson, Ben (Benjamin C. Hammett) in 1935 (courtesy of Jane Bradley).

Every time someone brought "Casey at the Bat" back into public discussion all the would-be authors and "Caseys" came back into view. Dan Casey retired from the Binghamton Railway Company around 1930 and, with his wife Minnie, moved down to Washington, D.C. to be near their daughter Mabel Griswold and her family. The *New York Times* sent a reporter to their home at 603 Quintana Place, NW, to interview Casey, who reminisced once again about the fateful day that fame was thrust upon him. This time he couldn't remember the name of the pitcher who fanned him, whereas in other interviews he used Tim Keefe's name as proof that the poem was about that game in 1887. Some corrupted and unauthorized versions of the poem depict

"Casey" signaling to "Sir Timothy" to throw another pitch. Casey still claimed he was friends with the author. "Thayer meant the poem only as a joke. None of us dreamed it would become as famous as it has," he said in the April 30, 1935, article. Two weeks later the *New York Times* magazine did a follow-up article on Casey with a reprinting of the entire poem, very similar to but not exactly the one that Thayer authorized in 1896. And two weeks after that, on May 23, *The Sporting News* published a picture of the 72-year-old Casey holding a bat, and printed three paragraphs about him in "What They Are Doing Now." In this version Thayer, a Philadelphia sportswriter, "scribbled the poem, which he showed to Casey and then gave to Hopper" (NYT, 4/30/1935; NYT magazine, 5/12/1935; and TSN, 5/23/1935).

CHAPTER 37

Fiftieth Anniversary Reunion of the Class of 1885

Ernest and Rosalind together attended the class of 1885's fiftieth anniversary reunion in June 1935. Events were planned for Class Day, June 19, and Commencement Day, June 20. Headquarters were maintained for three days at the Hotel Somerset in Boston for registration, friendly greetings, and the starting point for buses to the various functions. Judge Robert Grant, 1873, poet and novelist as well as judge, was a hero of Thayer's. He had been an editor on the *Lampoon* in his Harvard days, and inspired Thayer, then still a schoolboy, to try his hand at humorous writing. Albert and Ed, Jr., both students at Harvard when Ernest was growing up, brought the *Lampoon* home for Ernest to read. He wrote this about the judge: "Judge Robert Grant has always stood to me for what was purest and finest in the Harvard tradition. When I was a young student I used to enjoy reading with feelings of hopeless emulation Judge Grant's contributions to the first series of *The Lampoon*. Always since then, and as far as my knowledge goes, he has had the gift of saying and doing the right thing in the right way and with God-given grace and competence." Thayer and Grant met for the first time and talked together just before the Harvard-Yale baseball game on Wednesday, June 19. Afterward the judge sent the following correspondence through the class secretary:

> I was full of pleasure at meeting the author of "Casey at the Bat," from which I have derived unfailing pleasure ever since it was written, and which I have heard recited by my second son at various family gatherings because of the grip which it held upon the younger generation.
>
> Modesty becomes any man, but I think he has a right to feel proud that he has written something dear to the American heart which is found in all the anthologies and is likely to be remembered long after the Class of '85 has joined the long procession of "has beens" [HUC, 10 (1935): 357, 358, 374–75].

Cars were made available for early arrivals on June 18 so that they could tour the newly expanded Harvard campus. On Wednesday the men gathered

Ernest Thayer, 71, at his fiftiethth class reunion. Harvard, 1935 (courtesy of Jane Bradley).

for lunch at Mellon Hall of the Harvard Business School across from Soldier's Field. After lunch a procession formed from all the celebrating graduated classes, with the class of 1885 in front. They paraded by twos to the baseball field for the Harvard-Yale game. Two banners were carried among the paraders. The first was in honor of Captain Sam Winslow's Eighty-five varsity nine. It read:

The Eighty-Five Varsity,
Captain Sam Winslow's champion nine
Won "ten games straight" and cracked the crown
of Yale, Princeton, Dartmouth,
Amherst and Brown.

The second banner was in honor of Ernest L. Thayer, "the creator of mighty Casey at the Bat." This banner read:

An *Eighty-Five* man wrote
"Casey at the Bat"
The Epic of Baseball.

Friends noticed that Thayer was visibly moved by the banner. The 1885 alumni marched over to the Harvard players' bench, displayed the banners, and gave the nine a rousing cheer, but it had the apparent effect of making the team feel inadequate, and Harvard went down to defeat, 9–2. The wives and widows of 1885 arrived at the ballfield late in the game from a luncheon at Secretary Williams's house in Cambridge. From the ballfield the entourage traveled to 17 Quincy Street for a special tea hosted by President and Mrs. Conant. Everyone had a chance to socialize in comfort in the Conant home (*ibid.*, 358; and McGinty [1980], 22).

That evening the men gathered at the Algonquin Club for their class dinner. The room was decorated with "Harvard" and "'85" flags, the two baseball banners carried in the afternoon parade, pen and ink drawings of the 1885 class gate, and a photo of the late William H. Baldwin, who had been chairman of the class committee. Henry Williams, class secretary, had brought along the silver bowl that the class presented to him in 1910; it was filled with crimson roses. At each seating was a reprint of "Casey at the Bat," the sheet music and words of the class song, a song book, and a menu card. Music was furnished by piano, violin, and cello. A summary of the last 50 years, from the point of view of the class of 1885, was displayed prominently:

The World Chronology

As '85 has lived it.
1885–1935

1885 – 85 graduates. An expectant world! Great enthusiasm! Boat race and baseball series won by '85. Greater enthusiasm!
1888 – "Casey at the Bat." By Ernest L. Thayer, '85. Greatest enthusiasm! Homer outdone, but no homer by Casey!
1898 – Spanish War. '85 lays siege to Cuba.
1909 – President Lowell succeeds President Eliot. A great ending and a great beginning!
1910 – The Twenty-fifth! Gift of $105,097.01 (100 cents to the dollar – notice the one cent).
Silver Bowl presented to the Secretary. "The man on the job!"
1914 – The World War. '85 to the rescue!
1916 – Income Taxes. '85 inquires anxiously "Where is the income?"
1918 – The Eighteenth Amendment. '85 despondent but still brave under distress. Loving cup packed away.
1929 – The Depression. '85 depressed with the rest. All in the same boat but not like the boat of '85. No income but no income taxes.

1933 – President Conant succeeds President Lowell. "Great Expectations."
1934 – Eighteenth Amendment abolished. '85 triumphant! Loving cup furbished up. What of the depression anyway!
1935 – June, the Fiftieth! Bank accounts still low, but '85 hopeful! The world is still its oyster! [*ibid.*, 360–68]

After the recitation of several original verses, the following telegram was read by the toastmaster:

> Telegram to Class of Eighty-Five
> Algonquin Club
> Boston, Massachusetts.
> Regret I cannot be with you tonight. Present my deepest regards to Ernest Thayer, my creator. Remember also Roland Boyden, my reciter. Understand that a world-renowned headmaster will recite me tonight. Best wishes to him.
>
> Love and Kisses.
> Casey at the bat [*ibid.*, 368]

Sam Winslow was introduced by the following poem:

> Let others talk of Baby Ruth
>   Baseball for us has one "I am,"
> For fifty years have not, forsooth,
>   Produced another like our Sam.

Winslow in turn introduced Daniel Lothman, who had become the class of 1885's official reciter of "Casey at the Bat" after the death of Roland Boyden. He recited the poem after dinner, and did a great job, "to the wonderment of all." He later wrote this in regard to Thayer's preparation for writing the classic:

> It may not be amiss to recall some of the circumstances that led up to Thayer's writing the kind of poem he did. With an innate poetic instinct Thayer fortunately had a training in English at Harvard that was conducive for developing that instinct as well as his literary ability. Besides, in spending four years at a college that stressed baseball, a sport in which he took a deep interest, he acquired both a technical knowledge of the game and a great enthusiasm for it.
>
> So, you see, at college Thayer had lived in an environment that was ideal for developing the qualifications of a writer of baseball. When the opportunity presented itself, this training bore fruit in the writing of "Casey at the Bat."
>
> "Casey at the Bat" is a contribution to a great sport.
>
> One of the strong points of the poem, it seems to me, aside from its poetic merit, is the fact that the interest which is created in the first line, rises steadily, step by step, without an instant's flagging, until it reaches an unusually strong climax [*ibid.*, 374].

The above missive was included in Williams's section on "Casey at the Bat" in his *Secretary's Report* for 1935. Besides a copy of the updated poem – with the minor changes which Thayer preferred to the original (for some unknown reason) – Williams included an update on "Casey's" career:

> "The Casey Corner" as Whitney, a contributor to it calls it, has been very crowded in the last two years. The Casey Ballad, Casey Epic, Folk Ballad, call it which you will, is now age forty-seven, still popular in even higher esteem and better company than when young. DeWolf Hopper still keeps it on the stage, Broadway knows it in the movies through Wallace Beery, and the Radio has given it the widest range that anything can attain. Albert G. Spalding, the great ball player and manager, has given a thorough-going account of it in his book, "America's National Game"; *The Scrap Book* as early as December, 1908, and the *New York Sunday Times* as late as last May deal with it at length. The *Harvard Alumni Bulletin* of February 17, 1933, has a good four-page story with a photostatic reproduction of the original printing in the *San Francisco Examiner* June 3, 1888, subscribed "Phin," Thayer's intimate nickname with his *Lampoon* friends.
>
> That *Bulletin* article brings another 1885 man into the Casey picture, Hays Gardiner, who was editor of the *Bulletin.* It says that the many amusing features in the history of Casey at the Bat raised Gardiner's interest so that he set out to prepare a variorum edition of it, but his death in 1913 ended his plan. The first few pages of his manuscript and many of his notes are still on the files. How much more there is to be said today! All this well might be a challenge for someone to complete the story and perhaps the variorum.
>
> The ballad continues to be printed and reprinted in daily papers and magazines, and in answer columns. In the latter the question of authorship is inquired for. That question, never really in doubt, was settled finally in 1909 in legal proceeding in Masssachusetts Courts disposing of claims of the impostor George W. D'Vys, who, nevertheless, has continued to get himself in the papers and entertained and feted as its author, although he admitted in print in 1888 that a mangled reprint by him was only an adaptation from the *San Francisco Examiner.*
>
> In recent years two men named Casey, former professional ball players, have each sought notoriety as the actual player who had struck out and so led Thayer to write the poem [*ibid.,* 372–73].

On Commencement Day, the 1885 luncheon spread, hosted by the class of 1885 for all alumni from 1860 through 1888, drew a crowd of 275. (Mr. Morse of 1860 was abroad, but the next oldest, Henry M. Rogers, 1862, came.) After a sumptuous lunch, "washed down, when required, with glasses of Chablis," the group marched to the Alumni Exercises in the quadrangle between Sever Hall and the 1885 gate. There were speeches by witty Alumni Association President Burlingame, President Conant, and the governor of Massachusetts. Cabinet Secretary Wallace and President Neilsen of Smith College received honorary degrees. The "large and distinguished" audience then sang the Seventy-Eighth Psalm, a traditional song for the occasion. "Fair Harvard" was the final number and by 4:00 P.M. the fiftieth anniversary reunion was over. Many members of the class of 1885 were already looking forward to attending Harvard's three hundredth anniversary celebration in August or September 1936. "The Class Committee has its eyes open to see that Eighty-Five is taken care of at that world-famous-to-be ceremonial," assured Secretary Williams (*ibid.*, 368–70).

Ernest and Rosalind had a wonderful time at the reunion; Ernest got to see many old faces, especially his old cronies Eugene Lent and Sam Winslow. Rosalind must have been impressed by the great enthusiasm shown by everyone for her husband's baseball poem.

CHAPTER 38

Conclusion

"Casey" Loses His Voice

De Wolf Hopper was working on a one-year contract as narrator of radio broadcasts of the Kansas City Rhythm Symphony in Kansas City, Missouri, in the summer of 1935. He became noticeably weak toward the end of the summer, when he was about two weeks from completing the radio series. Hopper was 77 years old, and his doctors insisted he take a long rest, but he would not do it. In true theater tradition he insisted "the show must go on." Newton Cross, announcer for the radio show, said Hopper showed signs of weakness during the rehearsal on September 22 just before that evening's program aired, but "He took the microphone with not a blur or quaver. He went through the program like a red-ball freight. He was at his best."

Dr. H.P. Boughnou, who was called in to attend Hopper at his hotel a few hours after the performance, ordered the actor to the hospital immediately. "His heart was gone," the physician said. "He was a sick body, with a mind and spirit that would not admit it." In the hospital Hopper still refused to believe his health was bad. "Tell 'em I'm resting, not sick," he requested in his deep rumbling voice that theatergoers had come to know so well for almost 60 years. His doctors tried to convince Hopper to sleep, as he sat up in bed smoking his pipe. It was only 11:00 P.M., though, and he responded with a wave of his hand, "See you tomorrow, Doc. I never sleep until 3:00 A.M. anyway. Run along while I see what the Cards [the St. Louis National League team] did." He suffered a heart attack at 6:30 the next morning and died, or, as he preferred to think, was "summoned to that theatre above on a run-of-the-play contract." The *New York Times* remarked about Hopper's last words: "A strange rounding out of fate appeared in the actor's last words, which referred to his interest in baseball, the subject of his most famous recitation, 'Casey at the Bat'." "He must also have chuckled to himself in satisfaction at his transformation of an obscure bit of baseball rhyme into the fantastically popular favorite."

Among veterans of the stage, "where any performer's eminence might be disputed endlessly, with logic on all sides, there was grave agreement that, as entertainer and story-teller, as raconteur in a class of his own and as a vital link between generations in the theatre, he was topmost and unique," the *New York Times* stated in his obituary (*NYT*, 9/24/1935).

Cooperstown

After years of work, the National Baseball Hall of Fame was established in 1936. A committee selected five all-time great players as the first inductees; the five were Ty Cobb, Walter Johnson, Christy Mathewson, Babe Ruth, and Honus Wagner. Plans went ahead to build a Hall of Fame and Museum at Cooperstown, New York, to be completed and dedicated in 1939, the acknowledged centennial of the first baseball game played on a diamond (Appel and Goldblatt, vii).

Eugene V. Lent

Ernest lost another classmate, fellow member of the *Lampoon* group and of the *Examiner*'s Harvard Brigade, when Eugene Lent passed away on June 11, 1937, in La Jolla, California. Lent had become an attorney after his stint on the staff of the *Examiner*. He and William F. Humphrey had established a law partnership in San Francisco, Lent's home town. In 1905 they participated in the investigation into the bogus claims to "Casey" authorship. Except for eight months in 1918, which he spent with the Red Cross in France, Lent practiced law continuously until 1924. He then traveled a lot and for years lived in France. Sam Winslow wrote the notice of Lent's death for the *Secretary's Report* (*HUC*, 11 [1939]).

The Kingpin of Ballplayers Dies at 90

George Wright, the last surviving member of the 1869 Cincinnati Red Stockings, died of pneumonia in Dorchester, Massachusetts, on August 21, 1937, after suffering for some time with chronic myocarditis; he was 90 years old. He had become a millionaire in sporting-goods retailing and manufacturing after being forced from baseball in 1880 as the first victim of the reserve rule. He brought ice hockey to this country, stocked the first lawn tennis equipment in the United States (and later manufactured it), and was called "the father of American golf" for designing and laying out the first public golf course in this country, a nine-hole course in Franklin Park, Boston. His sons were outstanding tennis players, and he was a catalyst in the decision of their friend Dwight Davis to offer the Davis Cup in tennis competition. *The Sporting News* said about George Wright a few months after he was presented with National League lifetime pass #1 by league president Ford Frick in

1935: "What a useful life this vigorous character has led; he helped to teach a nation to play." Wright played cricket for ten years after his baseball career ended, and, after playing in the first golf game in New England and probably the country, he played that sport the rest of his life (Appel and Goldblatt, 396–97; NBL, G. Wright; TSN, 8/29/1935; and *BPOST*, 8/22/1937).

Baseball did not forget him, though; besides receiving the #1 lifetime pass, when the commission of 1905 was organized to weigh all the evidence and determine the true origin of baseball, one of its seven members was George Wright. He also was a member of the centennial commission to set up the Baseball Hall of Fame. Within months of his death in 1937 he was elected to the Hall of Fame. Despite being the prototype, the "beau ideal" of the professional shortstop and leadoff hitter, he was not selected as a player but for his overall contribution to baseball. He is still the only person to win a league championship in his only year of managing. (But then, he had a great shortstop!) (*SL*, 5/17/1890; *NYC*, 10/1879; *BPST* 8/22/1937; *NBL*, George Wright; Okrent and Lewine 14; and *National*, 23.)

"Casey" Turns Fifty

"Casey" turned 50 in 1938, and coupled with the impending baseball centennial, Daniel Maurice Casey came into the spotlight as the poem's namesake. Thayer was not feeling well, so he probably didn't care what was going on. Dan Casey acquired a guest spot on Gabriel Heatter's radio program, "We, the People" over the WABC-Columbia network on the evening of March 3. He relived his rendition of the 1887 game as he remembered it, erroneously as always. But Dan Casey was 75, and there were probably very few who could correct him, or would even want to (WABC-Columbia, 3/3/1938).

On April 20 Casey attended a baseball game at Griffith Stadium in Washington, D.C. He used the silver-plated lifetime pass he had just received in a joint presentation by the presidents of the National and American leagues. The *Washington Post* wrote up Casey's night at the ballpark and his reunion after 50 years with one of the few contemporaries of his who was still alive – Connie Mack. Casey told his story yet again; by this time he had remembered once again that Tim Keefe was the pitcher he faced. Why was Casey being humored this way? Baseball was nearing its centennial and was looking high and low for living heroes of the game. Those in authority wanted the public to believe that Casey was the inspiration for the popular poem "Casey at the Bat." Whether his story held water or not was beside the point; it was in baseball's interest to promote the legend. The Hall of Fame was a bit more discerning, though. It refused to take his claim seriously (*Time,* 5/30/1938; and Vlasich 60).

Time reported on "Casey Night," which took place in mid–May. The minor-league Baltimore Orioles invited Casey to relive his strikeout in a prelude to their night game against the Jersey City Giants. They eased Rogers Hornsby, Orioles coach, onto the mound to burn a few in. Though it was a rainy night, "from 2,000 throats and more there rose a lusty yell" as Casey found the first two pitches "not his style." With an 0 to 2 count, his blue eyes blazing, Casey swung but he didn't miss. Fifty-one years later he *still* didn't strike out. He smacked the ball into the infield. He failed to fail. His apology was, "Hornsby didn't have as much on the ball as Tim Keefe did that time" (*Time,* 5/30/1938).

Collier's for May 21, 1938, gave Dan Casey a big spread. In this article Casey dismissed the heretics who claimed that Kelly was the inspiration for the poem. He sniffed, "I'm the man, and not Kelly. I can give you a dozen reasons why. In the first place, King Kelly could hit and he wouldn't have struck out. [Kelly struck out 417 times in his career; probably a few of these occurred in clutch situations.] Secondly, the poem says there was a smile on Casey's face and that he lightly doffed his hat when the fans cheered. Kelly never smiled, he always scowled. And he never doffed his cap to anybody, fans or otherwise. If they cheered King, he'd probably make a face at 'em. As a matter of fact, the fans used to boo the King. He was so good he made 'em mad" (*Collier's*, May 21, 1938, 72).

However, on November 24, 1887, the *San Francisco Daily Examiner* noted, "Kelly was generously cheered when he stepped into the batter's box. He gracefully removed his snow-white cap in response." Thayer not only saw that, he probably wrote the article it came from.

On May 14, 1939, the *Examiner* commissioned an article written by "Daniel Maurice Casey (The Original 'Casey at the Bat')." There were photographs and musings. In this one Casey thought he and McGuire had been traded from the Detroits for "The Big Four"–Brouthers, Richardson, Rowe, and White of Buffalo. But Casey and McGuire went to Philadelphia, not Buffalo. And the Big Four were sold, not traded (Appel and Goldblatt, 47).

Last Years

In 1939 Thayer confirmed to Secretary Williams that his health had not been good since returning from the fiftieth reunion: "I have been ill for much of those five years with periods of great discouragement. I am now getting better. Warmest regards!" Williams added:

> . . . his *Lampoon* is not dead for his letters and comments on current events still sparkle. His immortal "Casey" lives both in print and on the radio. . . .
>
> The greatest compliment to Ernest L. Thayer, after the DeWolf Hopper recitals, is the attention given Casey by the ever popular

> Professor Emeritus William Lyon Phelps of Yale. With data furnished from our '85 files, the professor had Casey printed in two succeeding articles for his syndicated stories in forty papers. One is of "Casey at the Bat" in full, and the other tells of its success and the many attempts at plagiarism. He gives great praise to Thayer's ballad and its imperishable place in balldom.–Casey forever! [HUC, 11 (1939).]

For years friends from around the world who knew Thayer's keen mind and background of study and travel urged him to write, but in his modest way he would reply that he had nothing to say. In later years, through his own deep insight and through reading his favorite masters–Montaigne, Voltaire, Dante, and the Bible–he had developed an individual philosophy and was ready to share it; however, due to his poor health, he didn't have the stamina to write much. "Now I have something to say and I am too weak to say it," he said with appropriate irony. He started a journal of "Notes on Philosophy" on Friday, March 4, 1939; he wrote a paragraph at a time as he had strength (*HUC*, 11 [1939]; 8/22/1940). The following are sample entries:

> Page 5. June 16. Am I perhaps happier than Buddha in possessing an eternal sense of humor? Or does that subtle smile which is always represented on Buddha's countenance, indicate a kindred spirit?
>
> Page 33. July 23, 1940. Philosophy and history can be compared to a coach and four. History is the horses, guided no one knows how, and philosophy is the coach drawn no one knows whither. But whithersoever history goes, philosophy must follow [*SBHS*, Thayer papers].

Lifelong Friend Dies

Samuel Ellsworth Winslow, Ernest's friend since their paths first crossed in childhood, died at the age of 78 after a full life in business, politics, and public service. The hurricane of September 1938, with a death toll of 600, forced Sam and his wife, Bertha, to leave their home in Leicester. He described the destruction to the class secretary: "It wrecked many of our old cherished trees, shrubs and parts of buildings. Enough damage came to us to take away the joy of living in our home–a home for over fifty years." The house and some land were sold to the Leicester Academy, and became part of that campus. The Winslows moved to the Hotel Bancroft in Worcester, and Sam died there, in room 324, on July 11, 1940 (*HUC*, 11 [1939]: 38, 92; and *NCAB*, 452).

Final Days

When Phoebus gilds the sycamores
And through the screen his cold light pours
Then Morpheus quickly takes alarm
And lets my head slip from his arm.

E.L.T.

Ernest grew weaker during the summer of 1940. One week after his seventy-seventh birthday, August 21, he suffered a cerebral hemorrhage and died at La Casita. He had come to terms with his famous poem, and was finally very proud of it. The simple ballad he dashed off to amuse Bay Area readers in the spring of 1888 had become a national treasure. He came to realize what the verses meant to his family, his Harvard classmates and the American public, and acknowledged that there must be something to it, if so many people wanted to be linked to "Casey at the Bat" in one way or another (*SBN-P*, 8/22/1940; *SP-S*, 9/3/1935; and *NYT*, 8/22/1940).

End of the Controversy

George Whitefield D'Vys outlived Ernest Thayer by about nine months. D'Vys died in Northampton, Massachusetts, on May 30, 1941, after a long illness. He was 81 years old. He insisted he was the real author of "Casey at the Bat" till the very last. The *New York Times* printed an obituary for D'Vys on June 1. In it the *Times* acknowledged that D'Vys tried to convince people for 50 years that he was the poem's author. The rest of the article, however, was about Thayer, "the accepted author of the poem." "In *Bartlett's Familiar Quotations,* 1937 edition, the authorship is unequivocally credited to Thayer, with the added footnote that the verse appeared first in the *San Francisco Daily Examiner* on June 3, 1888.

Daniel Maurice Casey

Daniel Maurice Casey was the last survivor of all the principal characters in the "Casey at the Bat" controversy. Michael Joseph (King) Kelly died in 1894; John Patrick Francis Parnell Cahill in 1901; Daniel Henry Casey died in 1915; Roger Connor in 1931; and Orrin Robinson Casey in 1936. Both Samuel Ellsworth Winslow and Ernest Lawrence Thayer died in 1940 and George Whitefield D'Vys died in 1941 (*BENC*, 730, 783, 1090; Casey, 181; and *SP-S*, 11/29/1936).

Daniel Maurice Casey became ill in September 1942 and was taken to a hospital in Washington, D.C. He never recovered, and on February 8, 1943, he died at the age of 80 (*NYT*, 9/5/1942, 2/8/1943; and *TSN*, 2/18/1943). His wife, Minnie, survived him by many years; she was still going strong in 1957. The *Washington Daily News* interviewed her on August 19 of that year, the eve of her ninety-fifth birthday. "She remembers distinctly that day her husband made history. It was in Philadelphia in 1887. She remembers their good friend, poet Ernest Lawrence Thayer, talking to her husband. Dan later told her Mr. Thayer was going to write a poem about him.

You have to admire her loyalty and persistence; she told the same story her husband always told. The funny thing about her story, besides the inaccuracies mentioned earlier, is that – according to the biographical information in Dan Casey's file at the National Baseball Library in Cooperstown – she and Dan did not get married until December 3, 1889 (NBL, Casey folder). Casey acknowledged that date in a 1939 article when he stated that he and Minnie were looking forward to their fiftieth wedding anniversary that December. Ironically, her maiden name was Cahill, the same name as one of her husband's rivals for the "Casey" mantle. Dan was married once before, to Mary Ann McGowan from East Maine, New York, but the date they were married and how and when the marriage ended were not given. Whether they were still married in 1887 is therefore a mystery. We know that Thayer was not in Philadelphia that day, and it is doubtful that Minnie Cahill was there either. Even if she had been married to Dan then – which she wasn't – Dan said in that same 1939 article which he wrote: "My wife, Marie, I call her Minnie, never came to see me pitch" (*WDN*, 8/19/1957; and *EX*, 5/14/1939).

Postscript

Thayer's life fits neatly into three phases: in his youth he wrote voluminously, first for his own high-school newspapers in Worcester, then for the *Harvard Lampoon* and the *San Francisco Daily Examiner*. Baseball fans and students of American culture might find that a number of things he wrote more than 100 years ago are still worth reading today. Besides being fun to read, they give us a better understanding of the young man who wrote "Casey," and they also afford us with a new perspective for viewing the baseball, the humor, and the ideals of an age when the game was first expanding from the Atlantic to the Pacific, and winning universal recognition as our national pastime. For his masterpiece, the immortal "Casey at the Bat," Thayer received a grand total of $5, and soon thereafter entered the second phase of his life, concentrating his attention on the family business of manufacturing wool. Though not as satisfying, perhaps, as writing, it was a much more profitable profession; and this occupied him during the second period of his life. He had a knack for finance, and saved enough money to retire before he was fifty. The last phase of his life, the golden years, began auspiciously enough with his marriage to Rosalind, the love of his life, whom he had met on one of his trips to California. The story might have ended with the proverbial "and they lived happily ever after" – except for the controversies surrounding the baseball classic Thayer had written when he was only 24 years old. But there was a positive side to all the squabbling and wrangling, since in the long run it was another proof of Thayer's ability to write a truly popular ballad. In their own way, the controversies have become as much a part of Casey's story as the poem itself.

Thayer's family thought highly of the baseball ballad. As Jane Bradley,

Thayer's niece, remembers, Rosalind "admired 'Casey at the Bat' and was always very proud of her witty and gifted husband." Richard Buel, Thayer's brother-in-law and a San Diego sportsman, also loved the ballad and made a point of reciting it at private parties. When young Benjamin Hammett, Thayer's grandson, heard that his grandfather's nephew, Ernest Thayer Clary, had learned the poem by heart and was reciting it constantly in Worcester, he took it upon himself to memorize "Casey" too, and recited it for his grandmother, who enjoyed these performances in her old age. Bradley also remembers that "when I had grown up I once asked Uncle Ernest to recite 'Casey' for me. He did so, in his fine, quiet voice. It was not DeWolf Hopper's interpretation, but it was full of feeling, and I was very much moved" (JBB to authors, 12/30/1987, 1/2/88; and conversation with Viola Buel, 10/1988).

"Casey" has also meant a great deal to the baseball community. The fine tributes from Albert G. Spalding, the game's leading authority, and William Lyon Phelps, a Yale professor of all people, appeared in print during Thayer's lifetime and must have been particularly gratifying. On August 31, 1940, just ten days after Thayer's death, Clark Griffith, president of the Washington Senators and a vice president of the American League, suggested that organized baseball erect a memorial to Thayer. This memorial, he proposed, "should be large enough to include every stanza of the poem that has meant as much to baseball as anything I can think of." Griffith said he would present his suggestion at the next meeting of the American League, and also planned to take up the matter with other executives of organized baseball. He had no ideas about where the memorial should be erected and would welcome suggestions from fans as well as baseball men. "Casey at the Bat," he concluded, "has been a fine wholesome factor in promoting our national pastime and I think we should do something to perpetuate the poem and the man who wrote it" (NYT, 8/31/1940).

The Stockton Ports were the first to agree, and the California League club had some pretty definite ideas about how and where Thayer's poem could be best perpetuated. Beginning in the early 1950s, Stockton has staked its claim to fame as "the original Mudville Nine" by staging a "Casey Night," or a "Mudville night," and making it one of the highlights of the season. Players, fans and park attendants get all dressed up in uniforms and costumes of the 1880s, and Casey's tragic strikeout is faithfully reenacted on the field. One Stockton team donned Mudville uniforms for an entire season, and the current club has a Casey mascot who entertains the fans at every home game. In 1954 Darrell Berrigan wrote a lively article for the *Saturday Evening Post* popularizing Stockton's claim to "Mudville" status. More recent writers, notably Martin Gardner and Eugene Murdock, have downplayed the California connection, preferring to concentrate on Casey's rise to prominence in the East, and on the countless sequels and parodies generated by the ballad (Murdock, 31–36).

"Casey at the Bat" has inspired movies, songs, paintings, and even a full-length opera complete with orchestra and chorus. But perhaps the most impressive tribute to the legendary Mudville slugger is Mark Lundeen's seven-foot, six-hundred pound bronze statue of Casey standing in the National Baseball Library today. Lundeen, a Colorado sculptor, created this extraordinary work of art in time for Casey's centennial in 1988. There is ease in Casey's manner, and a smile on Casey's face for the men, women and children who stop to gaze at the sturdy batsman, wondering, perhaps, how he ever got to Cooperstown. Fanning in the bottom of the ninth with two on, two out, and the home team down by two is not exactly the recommended way. If Thayer were still around he would probably find something funny about this. But he would hardly be too surprised. As he wrote one spring, at the beginning of another baseball season: "To-day the bud, to-morrow the leaf. The man who strikes out to-day will make a base hit to-morrow" (*Harvard Lampoon,* May 2, 1884).

Abbreviations Used in the References and Bibliography

Books

BENC *Baseball Encyclopedia*. New York: Macmillan, 1993

DAB *Dictionary of American Biography*. New York: Charles Scribner's Sons, 1928–36

DLB *Dictionary of Literary Biography*. Detroit: Gale Research, 1978–

HUC *Harvard University, Class of 1885, Secretary's Report,* 1–11 (1886–1939)

NCAB *National Cyclopaedia of American Biography*. New York: James T. White, 1892–

SFCD *San Francisco City Directory*

WCD *Worcester City Directory*

WWIA *Who's Who in America*

Newspapers and Magazines

BG *Boston Globe*

BH *Boston Herald*

BPOST *Boston Sunday Post*

BT *Boston Transcript*

CALL *San Francisco Daily Morning Call*

CDE *Cincinnati Daily Enquirer*

CHRON *San Francisco Daily Chronicle*

CR-H *Chicago Record-Herald*

EX *San Francisco Daily Examiner*

HEWP *Hoboken Evening World and Press*

LAH *Los Angeles Herald*

NYC *New York Clipper*

NYS *New York Sun*

NYT *New York Times*

NYTRB *New York Daily Tribune*

OTRIB *Oakland Tribune*

PP *Philadelphia Press*

PST *Porter's Spirit of the Times*

SBN-P *Santa Barbara News-Press*

SEP *Saturday Evening Post*

SJ *Somerville Journal*

SL *Sporting Life*

SP-S *Syracuse Post-Standard*

SPY *Worcester Spy*

STEM *Stockton Evening Mail*

STIN *Stockton Daily Independent*

TRIB *Chicago Tribune*

TSN *The Sporting News*

WDN *Washington (DC) Daily News*

WG *Worcester Gazette*

Correspondence

AST Ernest's brother, Albert Smith Thayer
EDT, Jr. Ernest's brother, Edward Davis Thayer, Jr.
EDT, Sr. Ernest's father, Edward Davis Thayer, Sr.
ELT Ernest Lawrence Thayer
EMT Ernest's mother, Ellen Maria Thayer
ETC Ernest's sister Nellie, Ellen Thayer Clary
JBB Ernest's niece by marriage, Jane Buel Bradley
JET Ernest's sister-in-law, Josephine Ely Thayer
SHC Ernest's brother-in-law, Samuel Heald Clary

Libraries

NBL National Baseball Library
SBHS Santa Barbara Historical Society
WHM Worcester Historical Museum
WHR Worcester History Room, Worcester Public Library

Bibliography

Books

Adams, John. *The Diary and Autobiography of John Adams.* Ed. L.H. Butterfield, Leonard C. Faber, and Wendell D. Garrett. Cambridge, MA: Harvard University Press, 1961.

________. *The Works of John Adams.* Ed. Charles Francis Adams. Boston: Little and Brown, 1851.

Adelman, Melvin. *A Sporting Time: New York City and the Rise of Modern Sport, 1820–1870.* Urbana: University of Illinois Press, 1986.

Anson, Adrian C. *A Ball Player's Career.* Chicago: Era, 1900.

Appel, Martin, and Burt Goldblatt. *Baseball's Best: The Hall of Fame Gallery.* New York: McGraw-Hill, 1980.

Baldwin, Christopher Columbus. *Diary of Christopher Columbus Baldwin, Librarian of the American Antiquarian Society, 1829–1835. Transactions and Collections of the American Antiquarian Society,* 8 (1901).

Bancroft, George. *Literary and Historical Miscellanies.* New York: Harper, 1855.

Bancroft, George, and Joseph Cogswell. *Prospectus of a School to Be Established at Round Hill, Northampton, Massachusetts.* Cambridge, MA: Hilliard and Metcalf, 1823; reprinted *Hampshire Gazette,* July 2, 1823.

________, and ________. *Some Account of the School for the Liberal Education of Boys.* Northampton, MA: Shepard, 1826; reprinted *American Journal of Education* 2 (August 1827): 458–66.

Baragwanath, Albert K. *Currier and Ives.* New York: Abbeville, 1980.

Barber, John Warner. *Historical Collections, Being a General Collection of Interesting Facts, Traditions, Biographical Sketches, Anecdotes, & c.* Worcester, MA: Warren Lazell, 1844.

Bentley, William. *The Diary of William Bentley, D.D.* Salem, MA: Essex Institute, 1905.

Berlage, Gai Ingham. *Women in Baseball: The Forgotten History.* Westport, CT: Praeger, 1994.

Bernard, Duke of Saxe-Weimar-Eisenach. *Travels Through North America, During the Years 1825 and 1826.* Philadelphia: Carey, Lea & Carey, 1828.

Betts, John Rickards. *America's Sporting Heritage, 1850–1950.* Reading, MA: Addison-Wesley, 1974.

Blanchard, John A. *The H Book of Harvard Athletics, 1852–1922.* Cambridge, MA: Harvard University Press, 1923.

Blouin, Francis X. *The Boston Region 1810–1850: A Study of Urbanization.* Ann Arbor: UMI Research Press, 1980.

Bowen, Catherine Drinker. *John Adams and the American Revolution.* Boston: Little, Brown, 1950.

The Boy's and Girl's Book of Sports. Providence, RI: Cory and Daniels, 1835; Geo. P. Daniels, 1836.

The Boy's Book of Sports: Or, Exercises and Pastimes of Youth. New Haven, CT: S. Babcock, 1835.

Brewster, Edwin Tenney. *Life and Letters of Josiah Dwight Whitney.* Boston: Houghton Mifflin, 1909.

Bronson, Walter C. *History of Brown University, 1764–1914.* Providence, RI: Brown University, 1914.

Brooke, John L. *The Heart of the Commonwealth: Society and Political Culture in Worcester County, Massachusetts, 1713–1861.* New York: Cambridge University Press, 1989.

Brown, Richard D. *Massachusetts: A Bicentennial History.* New York: W.W. Norton, 1978.

Canary, Robert H. *George Bancroft.* New York: Twayne, 1974.

Carleton, William. *Traits and Stories of the Irish Peasantry.* 1842. Reprinted, Savage, MD: Barnes and Noble, 1990.

Carruth, Gorton, and Eugene Ehrlich. *American Quotations.* New York: Wings, 1992.

Carver, Robin. *The Book of Sports.* Boston: Lilly, Wait, Colman, and Holden, 1834.

Chadwick, Henry. *Beadle's Dime Base-Ball Player.* New York: Irwin P. Beadle, 1860.

Chasan, Joshua S. *Civilizing Worcester: The Creation of Institutional and Cultural Order, Worcester, Massachusetts, 1848–1876.* Ph.D. dissertation, University of Pittsburgh, 1974.

Children's Amusements. New York: Samuel Wood and Sons, 1820; reprinted, Oxford, NY: Samuel Wood, 1830.

Cleaver, John D. *Heritage of a National Game: Social Baseball, 1845–1875.* M.A. thesis. State University of New York at Oneonta, Cooperstown Graduate Program, 1965.

Crane, Ellery Bicknell. *Historic Homes and Institutions and Genealogical and Personal Memoirs of Worcester County, Massachusetts, with a History of Worcester Society of Antiquity.* New York: Lewis Historical Publishing, 1907.

Crosbie, Laurence M. *The Phillips Exeter Academy: A History.* Exeter, N.H.: Printed for the Academy, 1923.

Cuningham, Charles E. *Timothy Dwight, 1752–1817.* New York: Macmillan, 1942.

Cunningham, Frank H. *Familiar Sketches of the Phillips Exeter Academy and Surroundings.* Boston: James R. Osgood, 1883.

Dana, Richard Henry. *The Journal of Richard Henry Dana.* Ed. Robert F. Lucid. Cambridge: Harvard University Press, 1968.

Deming, Clarence. *Yale Yesterdays.* New Haven, CT: Yale University Press, 1915.

Dickens, Charles. *American Notes for General Circulation.* 1842. reprinted, New York: St. Martin's, 1985.

Diner, Hasia R. *Erin's Daughters in America: Irish Immigrant Women in the Nineteenth Century.* Baltimore: Johns Hopkins University Press, 1983.

Dulles, Foster Rhea. *America Learns to Play: A History of Popular Recreation, 1607–1940.* New York: D. Appleton-Century, 1940.

Durant, John. *Pictorial History of American Sports.* New York: Barnes, 1952.

Dwight, Timothy. *Greenfield Hill.* New York: Childs and Swaine, 1794.

________. *Travels in New England and New York. 1821.* Ed. Barbara Miller Solomon. Cambridge: Belknap Press of Harvard University Press, 1969.

Ellard, Harry. *Base Ball in Cincinnati.* Cincinnati: Press of Johnson and Hardin, 1907.

Elwyn, Alfred L. *Glossary of Supposed Americanisms.* Philadelphia: J.B. Lippincott, 1859.

Emerson, Marion Winslow. *"The Rose Is Red," or Esther Howland's Valentines.* Newburyport, MA: Newburyport, 1953.

Emerson, Ralph Waldo. *Lectures and Biographical Sketches.* Boston: Houghton, Mifflin, 1883.

Erskine, Margaret A. *Heart of the Commonwealth: Worcester.* Woodland Hills, CA: Windsor, 1981.

________. *Mechanics Hall.* Worcester, MA: Commonwealth, 1977.

Gardner, Martin. *The Annotated Casey at the Bat: A Collection of Ballads About the Mighty Casey.* New York: C.N. Potter, 1967; second edition, Chicago: University of Chicago Press, 1984.

Gerber, Helen. *Innovators and Institutions in Physical Education.* Philadelphia: Lea and Febiger, 1971.

Gipe, George. *The Great American Sports Book.* Garden City, NY: Doubleday, 1978.

Goldstein, Warren. *Playing for Keeps.* Ithaca, NY: Cornell University Press, 1989.

Hale, Edward Everett. *Letters on Irish Immigration.* Boston: Phillips, Sampson, 1852.

________. *Public Amusement for Poor and Rich.* Boston: Phillips, Sampson, 1857.

Handlin, Lilian. *George Bancroft: The Intellectual as Democrat.* New York: Harper and Row, 1984.

Hardy, Stephen. *How Boston Played: Sport, Recreation, and Community, 1865–1915.* Boston: Northeastern University Press, 1982.

Harris, Thomas. *An Oration Delivered Before the Philadelphia Medical Society, February 19, 1831.* Philadelphia: James Kay, 1831.

Hartwell, Edward Mussey. *Physical Training in American Colleges and Universities. Circulars of Information of the Bureau of Education, no. 5, 1885.* Washington, DC: U.S. Government Printing Office, 1886.

Hatch, Louis C. *The History of Bowdoin College.* Portland, ME: Loring, Short and Harmon, 1927.

The Heart of the Commonwealth. Worcester: Henry J. Howland, 1856.

Henderson, Robert. *Ball, Bat, and Bishop: The Origins of Ball Games.* New York: Rockport, 1947.

Hoar, George F. *Autobiography of Seventy Years.* New York: Charles Scribner's Sons, 1906.

Holliman, Jennie. *American Sports (1785–1835).* Durham, NC: Seeman, 1931.

Hoover, Mildred Brooke, Hero Eugene Rensch, and Ethel Grace Rensch. *Historic Spots in California.* Stanford: Stanford University Press, 1948.

Hopper, De Wolf and Wesley Winans Stout. *Once a Clown Always a Clown.* Boston: Little, Brown, 1927.

Howe, Mark A. De Wolfe. *The Life and Letters of George Bancroft.* New York: Charles Scribner's Sons, 1908.

Howland, Henry J. *The Worcester Directory for 1866.* Worcester, MA: Henry J. Howland, 1866.

Hughes, Sarah Forbes. *John Murray Forbes: Letters and Recollections.* Boston: Houghton Mifflin, 1899.

Hurd, Richard. *A History of Yale Athletics.* New Haven, CT: R.M. Hurd, 1888.

Hyde, William J. *The Round Hill School 1823 to 1834; An Early Experiment in American Physical Education.* M.A. thesis, University of Massachusetts at Amherst, 1970.

An Illustrated History of San Joaquin County, California. Chicago: Lewis, 1890.

James, Henry. *Charles W. Eliot: President of Harvard University 1869–1909.* Boston: Houghton Mifflin, 1930.

Kaese, Harold. *The Boston Braves.* New York: G.P. Putnam's Sons, 1948.

Kaplan, Martin. The Harvard Lampoon *Centennial Celebration, 1876–1973.* Boston: Little, Brown, 1973.

Kaufman, Martin, John W. Ifkovic, and Joseph Carvalho III. *A Guide to the History of Massachusetts.* New York: Greenwood, 1988.

Kelly, Michael J. *"Play Ball!" Stories of the Diamond Field.* Boston: Emery and Hughes, 1888.

Kirsch, George B. *The Creation of American Team Sports: Baseball and Cricket, 1838–1872.* Urbana: University of Illinois Press, 1989.

Kirsch, Robert, and William S. Murphy. *West of the West.* New York: E.P. Dutton, 1967.

Langley, Henry G. *The San Francisco Directory.* San Francisco: Valentine, 1871–1888.

Lee, Mabel. *A History of Physical Education and Sports in the U.S.A.* New York: John Wiley and Sons, 1983.

Lee, Ruth Webb. *A History of Valentines.* New York: Studio Publications, in association with Thomas Y. Crowell, 1952.

Leonard, Fred Eugene. *A Guide to the History of Physical Education.* Philadelphia: Lea and Febiger, 1923.

Lewis, Oscar. *San Francisco: Mission to Metropolis.* Berkeley, CA: Howell-North Books, 1966.

Longfellow, Henry Wadsworth. *The Letters of Henry Wadsworth Longfellow.* Ed. Andrew Hilen. Cambridge, MA: Belknap Press of Harvard University Press, 1966.

Lucas, John A., and Ronald A. Smith. *The Saga of American Sports.* Philadelphia: Lea and Febiger, 1972.

MacDougall, Hugh Cooke. *Cooper's Otsego County.* Cooperstown: New York State Historical Association, 1989.

Marr, Harriet Webster. *The Old New England Academies.* New York: Comet, 1959.

Messenger, Christian K. *Sport and the Spirit of Play in American Fiction.* New York: Columbia University Press, 1981.

Meynell, Alice. *Essays.* London: Burns, Oates and Washbourne, 1937.

Mooney, James E. *Antislavery in Worcester County, Massachusetts: A Case Study.* Ph.D. dissertation, Clark University, 1971.

Morison, Samuel Eliot. *The Development of Harvard University Since the Inauguration of President Eliot, 1869–1929.* Cambridge, MA: Harvard University Press, 1930.

________. *Three Centuries of Harvard, 1636–1936.* Cambridge, MA: Harvard University Press, 1936.

Mott, Frank Luther. *A History of American Magazines.* Cambridge, MA: Belknap Press of Harvard University Press, 1957–68.

Mount Diablo State Park. Sacramento: Department of Parks and Recreation, State of California, 1985.

Murdock, Eugene. *Mighty Casey, All-American.* Westport, CT: Greenwood, 1984.

National Baseball Hall of Fame and Museum Yearbook (1991). Ed. Bill Guilfoile and

Pat LaFond. Cooperstown, N.Y.: National Baseball Hall of Fame and Museum, Inc., 1991.

Nevins, Allan. *The Emergence of Modern America.* New York: Macmillan, 1927.

Newbery, John. *A Little Pretty Pocket Book.* Worcester, MA: Isaiah Thomas, 1787.

________. *A Little Pretty Pocket Book.* Facsimile of the 1767 London edition, with an introductory essay and bibliography by M.F. Thwaite. New York: Harcourt, Brace and World, 1967.

Nichols, Thomas Low. *Forty Years of American Life.* 1864. Reprinted with a new introduction by Scott Donaldson. New York: Johnson Reprint, 1969.

Noverr, Douglas A. and Lawrence E. Ziewacz. *The Games They Played: Sports in American History, 1865–1980.* Chicago: Nelson-Hall, 1983.

Nutt, Charles. *A History of Worcester and Its People.* New York: Lewis Historical, 1919.

Nye, Russell B. *George Bancroft: Brahmin Rebel.* New York: Alfred A. Knopf, 1945.

Okrent, Daniel, and Harris Lewine, editors. *The Ultimate Baseball Book.* Boston: Houghton Mifflin, 1979.

Old Family Letters, Copied from the Originals for Alexander Biddle. Series A. Philadelphia: J.B. Lippincott, 1892.

Ordinances of the City of Worcester. Worcester, MA: Chas. Hamilton, 1854.

Oriard, Michael. *Sporting with the Gods: The Rhetoric of Play and Games in American Culture.* Cambridge: Cambridge University Press, 1992.

Phelps, William Lyon. *What I Like in Poetry.* New York: Charles Scribner's Sons, 1934.

Powers, Vincent Edward. *"Invisible Immigrants": The Pre-Famine Irish Community in Worcester, Massachusetts, from 1826 to 1860.* New York: Garland, 1989.

Presbrey, Frank Spenser. *Athletics at Princeton: A History.* New York: Frank Presbrey, 1901.

Quennell, Peter, and Hamish Johnson. *Who's Who in Shakespeare.* New York: William Morrow, 1973.

Rice, Franklin P., editor. *Worcester Town Records, 1816. Collections of the Worcester Society of Antiquity* (Worcester, 1891), 10.

________. *Worcester Town Records, 1838–1848. Collections of the Worcester Society of Antiquity* (Worcester, 1895), 15.

Rosenbach, Abraham S.W. *Early American Children's Books.* Portland, ME: Southworth, 1933.

Rosenzweig, Roy. *Eight Hours for What We Will: Work and Leisure in an Industrial City, 1870–1920.* New York: Cambridge University Press, 1983.

Rudolph, Frederick. *Mark Hopkins and the Log: Williams College, 1836–1872.* New Haven, CT: Yale University Press, 1972.

Santayana, George. *Persons and Places.* New York: Charles Scribner's Sons, 1944.

Schlesinger, Arthur M., Jr. *The Age of Jackson.* Boston: Little, Brown, 1953.

Seymour, Harold. *Baseball: The Early Years.* New York: Oxford University Press, 1960.

________. *Baseball: The People's Game.* New York: Oxford University Press, 1990.

________. *The Rise of Major League Baseball to 1891.* Ph.D. dissertation, Cornell University, 1956.

Smith, Myron J., Jr. *Baseball: A Comprehensive Bibliography.* Jefferson, NC: McFarland, 1986.

Smith, Ronald A. *Sports and Freedom: The Rise of Big-Time College Athletics.* New York: Oxford University Press, 1988.

Southwick, Albert B. *Once-Told Tales of Worcester County.* Worcester, MA: Worcester Telegram and Gazette, 1985.

Spalding, Albert G. *America's National Game.* New York: American Sports Publishing, 1911; reprinted, Lincoln: University of Nebraska Press, 1992.

Spalding, John E. *Always on Sunday: The California Baseball League, 1886 to 1915.* Manhattan, KS: Ag, 1992.

Stevenson, Burton Egbert. *Famous Single Poems.* New York: Harcourt, Brace, 1923; revised edition, New York: Dodd, Mead, 1935.

Swanberg, W.A. *Citizen Hearst—A Biography of William Randolph Hearst.* New York: Charles Scribner's Sons, 1961.

Taylor, Anthony R. *Worcester's Architectural Neighborhoods.* Worcester, MA: Worcester Historical Museum, 1984.

Tinkham, George H. *History of Stockton: A Sketch of San Joaquin County.* San Francisco: W.M. Hinton, 1880.

Tuohey, George V. *A History of the Boston Base Ball Club,* Boston: M.F. Quinn, 1897.

Tymeson, Mildred McClary. *Rural Retrospect: A Parallel History of Worcester and Its Rural Cemetery.* Worcester, MA: Albert W. Rice, 1956.

Vlasich, James A. *A Legend for the Legendary: The Origin of the Baseball Hall of Fame.* Bowling Green, Ohio: Bowling Green State University Popular Press, 1990.

Voigt, David Quentin. *American Baseball: From the Gentleman's Sport to the Commissioner System.* Norman: Oklahoma State University Press, 1966; University Park: Pennsylvania State University Press, 1983.

Ward, John Montgomery. *Base-Ball: How to Become a Player, with the Origin, History, and Explanation of the Game.* Philadelphia: Athletic, 1888.

Warren, Edward. *The Life of John Collins Warren.* Boston: Ticknor and Fields, 1860.

Warren, John Collins. *Physical Education and the Preservation of Health.* Boston: William D. Ticknor, 1846.

Webster, Daniel. *The Private Correspondence of Daniel Webster.* Ed. Fletcher Webster. Boston: Little, Brown, 1857.

Weed, Thurlow. *Autobiography of Thurlow Weed.* Ed. Harriet A. Weed. Boston: Houghton Mifflin, 1883.

Wells, Evelyn Kendrick. *The Ballad Tree.* New York: Ronald, 1950.

Williams, Arthur Robert. *The Irishman in American Humor: From 1647 to the Present.* Ph.D. dissertation, Cornell University, 1949.

Wittke, Carl. *The Irish in America.* Baton Rouge: Louisiana State University Press, 1956.

World Almanac and Book of Facts. Ed. Mark S. Hoffman. New York: World Almanac, 1993.

Articles and Essays

Abrams, Robert E. "Charles Farrar Browne (Artemus Ward)." *DLB,* 11 (1982): 60–68.

Adams, Daniel L. "Dr. D.L. Adams: Memoirs of the Father of Base Ball." TSN, 2/29/96.

Austin, Anthony. "75 Years Ago." *New York Times Magazine* (June 9, 1963), 51, 54.

Barney, Robert Knight. "Of Rails and Red Stockings: Episodes in the Expansion of the 'National Pastime' in the American West." *Journal of the West* 17 (1978): 61–69.

Barry, Jay. "He Pitched Baseball's First 'Perfect Game'." *Brown Alumni Monthly* (October 1964), 26–29.

Berczuk, Robert J. "The Casey Controversy." *Broome County Historical Society Newsletter* (Summer 1991), 84–85.

Berrigan, Darrell. "The Truth About Casey." *Saturday Evening Post,* July 3, 1954.

Betts, John Rickard. "Mind and Body in Early American Thought." *Journal of American History* 54 (March 1968): 787–805.

Bishofberger, Thomas E. "Early Flood Control in the California Central Valley." *Journal of the West* 14 (1975): 85–92.

Bishop, William Henry. "San Francisco." *Harper's New Monthly Magazine* 66 (May 1883): 813–32.

Bradlee, Caleb Davis. "George Cheyne Shattuck, M.D." *New England Historical and Genealogical Register* 48 (July 1894): 276–80.

Camp, Walter. "The American National Game of Base Ball." *Century* 79 (1910): 936–48.

________. "College Athletics." *New Englander and Yale Review 44* (January 1885): 138–40.

Carruth, Louise. "Chatham Street, No. 67." Typescript in Worcester Room, Worcester Public Library.

Casey, Frances Goggin. "Casey Never Struck Out." *Yankee* 38 (May 1974): 178–81, 190–91.

"Casey at the Bat." *Harvard Alumni Bulletin* 35 (1933), 532–35.

Chadwick Henry. "Michael J. Kelly." *Spalding's Official Base Ball Guide (1887),* 6–7.

Child, Francis J. "Ballad Poetry." *Johnson's Universal Cyclopaedia* (1894), 1:464–68.

"The City of the Golden Gate." *Scribner's Monthly* 10 (July 1875): 266–82.

"College Life in New England." *Harper's Weekly* 1 (8/1/57): 488–90.

Crackenthorpe, Hiram. "To the Editor of the Knickerbocker." *Knickerbocker* 13 (1839): 445–46.

Croy, Homer. "Casey at the Bat." *Baseball Magazine* 1 (October 1908): 10–12.

Dasher, Thomas E. "William Trotter Porter." *DLB*, 3 (1979): 298–300.

Davis, Andrew M.F. "College Athletics." *Atlantic Monthly* 51 (May 1883): 677–84.

"The Days of the Regattas at Worcester." *New York Tribune* 7/27/1860.

Deane, Bill. "Rickey the Great." *Innings* (July 21, 1986), 18.

Dickens, Charles. "The Irish in America." *All the Year Round* 1 (1869): 510–14.

Dunlop, Richard. "Was This the Real Casey?" *Baseball Digest* 18, no. 6 (July 1959): 41–42.

Dwight, B.W. "Intercollegiate Regattas, Hurdle-Races, and Prize-Contests." *New Englander* 35 (April 1876): 251–79.

Eliot, Charles W. "Annual Report of the President of Harvard College, 1873–74." Harvard University Archives.

________. "Annual Report of the President of Harvard College, 1881–82." Harvard University Archives.

________. "Annual Report of the President of Harvard College, 1882–83." Harvard University Archives.

________. "Inaugural Address, October 19, 1869." Harvard University Archives.

Felton, Cornelius C. "Annual Report of the President of Harvard College, 1859–60." Harvard University Archives.

Ferris, George T. "Mark Twain." *Appleton's Journal of Literature, Science and Art* 12 (1874): 15–18.

Franks, Joel. "Organizing California Baseball, 1859–1893." *Baseball History 4* (1991), 1–23.

Gelber, Steven M. "'Their Hands Are All out Playing.' Business and Amateur Baseball, 1845–1912." *Journal of Sport History* 11 (Spring 1984): 5–27.

Genzmer, George Harvey. "Francis James Child." DAB, 4 (1930): 66–67.

Glenister, John W., "Who Wrote 'Casey at the Bat'?" *Baseball Magazine* 1 (June 1908): 59–60.

Goslow, Charles Brian. "Fairground Days: When Worcester Was a National League City (1880–82)." *Historical Journal of Massachusetts* 19 (1991): 133–54.

"Gymnastic Exercises in Harvard University." *United States Literary Gazette* (May 1, 1826), 115–16.

Hart, Walter Morris. "Professor Child and the Ballad." PMLA 21 (1906): 755–807.

"Harvard and Yale on Lake Quinsigamond." *Worcester Magazine* 4 (August 1902), 59–68.

Henderson, Dave. "Casey's Missing Link," *Empire Sports* 2, no. 8 (August 1983): 33–35.

Henderson, Robert. "How Baseball Began." *Bulletin of the New York Public Library* 41 (1937): 287–91.

Higginson, Thomas Wentworth. "Gymnastics." *Atlantic Monthly* 7 (March 1861): 283–302.

________. "Intercollegiate Athletics." *Scribner's Monthly* 5 (January 1873): 366–68.

________. "Saints, and Their Bodies." *Atlantic Monthly* 1 (March 1858): 582–95.

Husman, John Richmond. "J. Lee Richmond's Remarkable 1879 Season." *The National Pastime* 4, no. 2 (Winter 1985): 65–70.

Jeffries, John. "Physical Culture the Result of Moral Obligation." *American Quarterly Observer* 1 (1833): 251–70.

Jones, Steven Swann. "Francis James Child." DLB 64 (1988): 23–28.

Jupiter, Harry. "Baseball's Greatest Showstopper." *San Francisco Examiner Image* (June 5, 1988): 2–8.

Lewis, Guy. "The Beginning of Organized Sport." *American Quarterly* 22 (1970): 222–29.

Livermore, Abiel Abbot. "Physical Culture." *North American Review* 81 (July 1855): 51–69.

Lucas, John A. "Thomas Wentworth Higginson, Early Apostle of Health and Fitness." *Journal of Health, Physical Education and Recreation* 42 (1971): 30–33.

McGinty, Brian. "The Old Ball Game." *Pacific Historian* 25 (1981): 13–25.

________. "Thayer Went Casey." *Westways* 72 (June 1980): 18–22.

Mahony, Patrick. "Ernest Lawrence Thayer at the Bat." *Noticias* 24 (Winter 1978): 71–75.

Mason, Julian. "Owen Wister." DLB, 9 (1981): 166–72.

Merwin, Henry C. "The Irish in American Life." *Atlantic Monthly* 77 (March 1896): 289–301.

Miles, Edwin A. "President Adams' Billiard Table." *New England Quarterly* 45 (1972): 31–43.

Miley, Jack. "I Did So Strike Out!" *Collier's* (May 21, 1938), 14–15, 72.

Moore, Charles. "Charles Eliot Norton." DAB, 13 (1934): 569–72.

Moore, Jim. "Baseball, Politics and Humor in Cooper's *Home as Found.*" Paper presented at the Fifth Annual Symposium on Baseball and the American Culture, Cooperstown, 1993.

________. "Mark Twain and the Em Quads: A 'Square' Deal." *The Californians: The Magazine of California History* 9, no. 1 (May/August 1991): 48–54.

"Mudville Man." *Time* (May 30, 1938): 26.

"New Haven Gymnasium." *Boston Medical Intelligencer* 5 (January 22, 1828): 574–76; and *Quarterly Christian Spectator* 2 (January 1828): 467.

"News from Amherst." *University Quarterly* 2 (July 1860): 148.
Oakey, Alex F. "A Word to the Wise." *Overland Monthly,* n.s., 18 (August 1891): 132–43.
O'Hagan, Anne. "The Athletic Girl." *Munsey's Magazine 25* (1901), 729–50.
Overmyer, Jim. "City of Diamond Heroes." In *Troy's Baseball, Heritage.* Ed. Richard A. Puff. Troy: Committee to Preserve Troy's Baseball Heritage, 1992.
Park, Roberta J. "The Man Who Made 'Casey' Famous." *The Hero in Transition.* Ed. Ray B. Browne and Marshall W. Fishwick. Bowling Green, Ohio: Bowling Green University Popular Press, 1983, pp. 241–48.
"The Parks of San Francisco." *Overland Monthly,* n. s., 17 (March 1891): 225–43.
Paxson, Frederick Logan. "Phineas Taylor Barnum." DAB, 1 (1928): 636–39.
Peck, Harry Thurston. "Who Wrote 'Casey at the Bat'?" *The Scrap Book* 6 (December 1908): 947–54.
Peirson, Abel. "Abel Peirson's Address." *Journal of Health* 2 (January 12, 1831): 145.
Perry, Ralph B. "Charles William Eliot." DAB, 6 (1931): 71–78.
________. "William James." DAB 9 (1932): 590–600.
Perry, Roger N. "Memory Bank: WPI Marks the First Century of Alonzo Kimball's Seal." *WPI Journal* (Spring 1988), 47.
Phillips, Walter B. "Baseball in the 80s." *Harvard Alumni Bulletin* 17 (1915): 503–6.
Porter, William T. "To Our Friends." *Spirit of the Times* 1 (December 10, 1831): 11.
"The Restaurants of San Francisco." *Overland Monthly,* n. s., 20 (December 1891): 561–63.
Richards, Eugene. "College Athletics." *Popular Science Monthly* 24 (February 1884): 446–53.
Richardson, Sophia Foster. "Tendencies in Athletics for Women in Colleges and Universities." *Popular Science Monthly* 50 (1897), 517–26.
Ripley, A.L. "Gentlemanliness in College Athletics." *New Englander and Yale Review* 44 (January 1884): 141–42.
Roe, Alfred S. "The City of Worcester." *New England Magazine,* n. s., 23 (January 1901): 543–67.
________. "The Homes and Haunts of George Bancroft." *New England Magazine,* n.s., 23 (October 1900): 161–80.
Roosevelt, Teddy. "Professionalism in Sports." *North American Review* 151 (August 1890): 187–91.
________. "The Value of an Athletic Training." *Harper's Weekly* 37 (December 23, 1893): 1236.
"Round Hill School." *American Journal of Education* 1 (July 1826): 437–39.
Sandrof, Ivan. "Worcester's Seal and Motto." Undated newspaper clipping in Worcester Room, Worcester Public Library.
Sargent, Dudley A. "Physical Education in Colleges." *North American Review* 136 (February 1883): 166–80.
"The School at Northampton." *United States Literary Gazette* (February 15, 1825), 331–32.
Scudder, Horace E. "A Group of Classical Schools." *Harper's New Monthly Magazine* 55 (October 1877): 704–16.
________. "Harvard University." *Scribner's Monthly* 12 (July 1876): 337–59.
Sedgwick, Arthur G. "The Regulation of College Sports." *Nation* 38 (February 28, 1884): 182–83.
________. "Sports in and out of Colleges." *Nation* 36 (March 29, 1983): 268–69.
Shattuck, George Cheever. "Centenary of the Round Hill School." *Proceedings of the Massachusetts Historical Society* 57 (1923): 205–9.

Sloane, William M. "George Bancroft – In Society, in Politics, in Letters." *Century* 33 (January 1887): 473–87.

Spaulding, Henry G. "Mens Sana." *Harvard Magazine* 4 (June 1858): 200–2, Harvard University Archives.

Starr, Harris Elwood. "Michael J. Kelly." *DAB*, 10 (1933): 309–10.

Stevenson, John M. "When Baseball Started at Yale." *Yale Alumni Weekly* (March 28, 1913).

Sullivan, James E. "The Origin of Base Ball." *Spalding's Official Base Ball Guide* (1908), 35–49.

Thoreau, Henry David. "Thomas Carlyle and His Works." *Graham's Magazine* 30 (1847): 147–54.

Tuckerman, Charles K. "An Hour with George Bancroft." *Magazine of American History* 25 (1891): 227–32.

Vail, Robert W.G. "Isaiah Thomas." *DAB*, 18 (1936): 435–36.

Vermilyea, Natalie. "Kranks' Delight: California Baseball 1858–1888." *The Californians: The Magazine of California History* 8, no. 6 (March/April 1991): 32–41.

Vermilyea, Natalie, and Jim Moore. "Casey at the Bat: A Ballad of the Republic." *The Californians* 6, no. 3 (May/June 1988): 42–49.

Walker, Francis A. "College Athletics." *Harvard Graduates' Magazine* 2 (September 1893): 2–4.

Warren, John Collins. "The Importance of Physical Education." In *Introductory Discourse and Lectures Delivered in Boston Before the Convention of Teachers and Other Friends of Education, Assembled to Form the American Institute of Instruction, August 1830*. Boston: Hilliard, Gray, Little and Wilkins, 1831.

Williams, Alfred M. "Native Irish Humor." *Catholic World* 37 (April 1883): 58–68.

Workman, Fanny Bullock. "The City of Worcester – The Heart of the Commonwealth." *Bay State Monthly* 3 (August 1885): 147–64.

Worth, George J. "Thomas Hughes." *DLB*, 18 (1983): 148–53.

Xiques, Donez. "Charles Eliot Norton." *DLB*, 64 (1988): 187–99.

Index